IELTS
Easy Writing

IELTS Easy Writing

발행일	2017년 8월 2일

지은이	전 현 선		
펴낸이	손 형 국		
펴낸곳	(주)북랩		
편집인	선일영	편집	이종무, 권혁신, 송재병, 최예은, 이소현
디자인	이현수, 이정아, 김민하, 한수희	제작	박기성, 황동현, 구성우
마케팅	김회란, 박진관, 김한경		
출판등록	2004. 12. 1(제2012-000051호)		
주소	서울시 금천구 가산디지털 1로 168, 우림라이온스밸리 B동 B113, 114호		
홈페이지	www.book.co.kr		
전화번호	(02)2026-5777	팩스	(02)2026-5747
ISBN	979-11-5987-511-3 13740(종이책)		979-11-5987-512-0 15740(전자책)

잘못된 책은 구입한 곳에서 교환해드립니다.
이 책은 저작권법에 따라 보호받는 저작물이므로 무단 전재와 복제를 금합니다.

이 도서의 국립중앙도서관 출판예정도서목록(CIP)은 서지정보유통지원시스템 홈페이지(http://seoji.nl.go.kr)와
국가자료공동목록시스템(http://www.nl.go.kr/kolisnet)에서 이용하실 수 있습니다.
(CIP제어번호 : CIP2017018487)

(주)북랩 성공출판의 파트너
북랩 홈페이지와 패밀리 사이트에서 다양한 출판 솔루션을 만나 보세요!

홈페이지 book.co.kr • **블로그** blog.naver.com/essaybook • **원고모집** book@book.co.kr

IELTS
Easy Writing

전현선 지음

IELTS Writing
고득점 실전 전략

북랩 book Lab

Preface
IELTS writing

Academy

    Task 1: Graph(at least 150)

    Task 2: Essay(at least 250)

General

    Task 1: Letter(at least 150)

    Task 2: Essay(at least 250)

1. 채점기준

    I. Task Response(요구사항 부합)

    II. Coherence and Cohesion(논리정연함과 언어의 결속성)

    III. Lexical Resource(어휘력)

    IV. Grammatical Range and Accuracy(문법의 다양성과 정확성)

2. 구체적 설명

    I Task Response(요구사항 부합)

      - 질문의 의도 파악

      - 질문내용에 맞게 글쓰기

    II Coherence and Cohesion(논리 정연함과 언어의 결속성)

      - Coherence(논리 정연함)

```
┌─────────────────────────────────────────────────┐
│  Introduction(서론)                              │
└─────────────────────────────────────────────────┘

┌─────────────────────────────────────────────────┐
│  Body 1    - topic sentence(주제문장)            │
│            - supporting sentence(부연설명)       │
│            - ending sentence(생략가능)           │
└─────────────────────────────────────────────────┘

┌─────────────────────────────────────────────────┐
│  Body 2    - topic sentence(주제문장)            │
│            - supporting sentence(부연설명)       │
│            - ending sentence(생략가능)           │
└─────────────────────────────────────────────────┘

┌─────────────────────────────────────────────────┐
│  Conclusion(결론)                                │
└─────────────────────────────────────────────────┘
```

- Cohesion(언어의 결속성)

  문장과 문장의 자연스러운 연결

- 연결어(As a result/however/accordingly…)

  With the advent of the Internet, people around the world have been able to shop online. This method of purchasing products provides people with many advantages. **However,** many consumers believe that offline shopping malls still offer a more enjoyable experience. I am for the former for the following reasons.

III Lexical Resource(어휘력)

 - 상황에 맞고 수준 높은 어휘
 - 반복사용(X)
 - 특히 대명사 사용유의

   Ex) Enjoying sports is one way of releasing stress. It is also good for health.(O)

   　　Enjoying sports is one way of releasing stress. These are also good for health.(x)

   　　→Enjoying이 단수이기 때문에 It를 사용

Ⅳ Grammatical Range & Accuracy(문법의 다양성과 정확성)
- 정확성
- 다양한 문법지식(가정법/관계사절/분사구문/비교법 등)
    Ex) quick and easily(X) → quickly and easily(병렬구조)

TIP (IELTS 공식안내)

1. Writing 시험은 정답을 요하는 시험이 아니라 영어로 주어진 정보를 전달하고 의견을 표현하는 능력을 평가합니다.
2. Task 1은 150 단어, Task 2는 250 단어 이상을 작성하셔야 하며, 이보다 짧게 작성할 경우에는 감점됩니다.
3. Writing 답안지 작성 시 문제의 문장을 그대로 적는다면 그 부분은 단어 수에서 제외됩니다. 응시자 본인의 표현으로 작성해야 합니다.
4. Academic Task 1에서는 주어진 데이터를 임의로 해석하거나 자료 결과를 추측하지 말고 주어진 자료만을 가지고 기술해야 합니다.
5. Academic Task 2에서는 작성자의 논점과 견해를 뒷받침할 수 있는 내용이나 주장을 예를 들면서 작성하고 결론에는 앞 문단에서 작성한 내용을 바탕으로 맺음합니다.
6. Task 1 작성에는 20분을, Task 2 작성에는 40분을 권유합니다. 각 Task에서 처음 5분 동안은 작성할 글을 구성하고, 마지막 5분 동안에는 작성한 글을 읽으며 실수한 부분은 없는지 확인합니다.

/www.ieltskorea.org. 제공

---

3. Essay Type

Type 1	advantages & disadvantages(장단점)
Type 2	A Type(agree or disagree)/B Type(to what extent disagree or agree/discuss/outweigh/opinions)(찬성/반대)
Type 3	causes & effects/problems & solutions(문제/해결책)

Type 1 (advantages and disadvantages)

Tourism is becoming a good source of revenue for many countries. Discuss the **advantages and the disadvantages** of developing this industry.

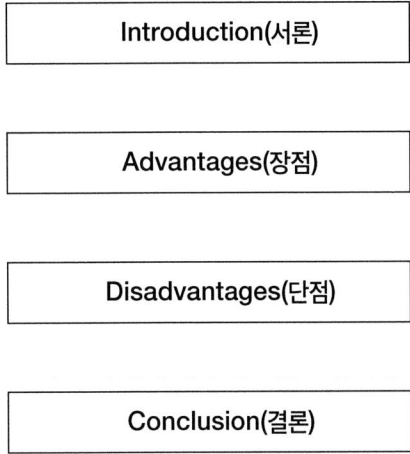

Type 2

(A Type) agree or disagree
In modern society, traditional food is being replaced by fast food. **Do you agree or disagree with this statement?**

(B Type) agree or disagree (to what extent)/discuss/opinion/outweigh
Is it a good idea for teenagers to have jobs while they are still students? **To what extent** do you agree?

	A Type	B Type
Introduction	Trongly Agree(강력하게 동의)	Partially Agree(부분적 동의)
Body 1	Agree(Disagree)	Disagree(Agree)
Body 2	Agree(Disagree)	Agree(Disagree)
Conclusion	Agree(Disagree)	Agree(Disagree) partially

** B type을 A type 구조로 **strongly agree/strongly disagree**로 주장할 수 있음

Type 3 (causes & effects/problems & solutions)

The crime rate has increased dramatically in many countries. Discuss some possible **reasons** for this increase and suggest **solutions** to this problem.

Introduction(서론)

Problems/Causes(문제점)

Solutions/Effects(해결책)

Conclusion(결론)

Essay Template

Type 1(Advantage & Disadvantage)

Introduction

Ⅰ. (Issue에 대한 배경설명)In recent years, there have been a lot of controversies regarding(명사주제)
Ⅱ. (Issue 제기)Some people assume that**(advantages)**,
Ⅲ. (Issue 제기)However, others argue that**(disadvantages)**
Ⅳ. (에세이 할 일)In this essay, I will elaborate on the **positive and negative aspects** of(명사주제)

Body 1

Ⅰ. On the one hand,	there are **several merits** of(명사주제)
Ⅱ. Topic sentence	(우선)First/firstly/To begin with
Ⅲ. 부가적인 문장	(다시 말해서)In order words/That is/To be specific
	예시 (예를 들어)For example/For instance/To illustrate this
Ⅰ. Topic sentence	(두 번째는)Second/In addition
Ⅱ. 부가적인 문장	(다시 말해서)To put it another way/That is to say
	증거 (~에 따르면)According to ~/Studies have indicated that~
Ⅲ.마무리 문장(선택사항)	(그러므로) Therefore/Thus/Hence

Body 2

Ⅰ. On the other hand, (명사주제)has(have) **drawbacks** as well.

나머지는 **Body 1**과 같은 형식

Conclusion

Ⅰ. (결론) To sum up, as mentioned above, (명사주제), although having a few drawbacks, is(are) more likely to have benefits.
Ⅱ. 제안(선택사항) Therefore, It is advisable(바람직한)that S+V

Type 2(A Type) Agree or Disagree(strongly) Opinion/Discuss

Introduction

Ⅰ. (Issue에 대한 배경설명)	The issue of (명사주제) has become a high profile around the world.
Ⅱ. (반대되는 Issue)	Some people argue that ~ **disagree(agree)**
Ⅲ. (에세이 할 일)	However, this essay will spell out the reason why **I agree(disagree)** with this statement.

Body 1

Ⅰ. Topic sentence (분명하고 간결)	(우선)**First**/Most importantly, ~
Ⅱ. 부가적인 문장 (다시 말해서)	In other words/That is/To be specific
	예시 (예를 들어)For example/For instance/To illustrate this
	증거 (~에 따르면)According to ~/Studies have indicated that~
Ⅲ. 마무리 문장(선택)	(그러므로)Therefore/Thus/Hence,

Body 2

Ⅰ. Topic sentence(분명하고 간결)	(두 번째는)**second**
	나머지는 Body1과 같은 형식

Conclusion

Ⅰ. (결론)	To sum up, **I strongly agree(disagree)** that S+V
Ⅱ. Topic sentence(요약/재언급)	As I mentioned above, <u>(first) and (second) are the main reasons for my argument</u>
Ⅲ. 마무리(선택 사항)	Therefore, it is compelling(권장할 만한) for 주어 to 동사

Type 2(B Type) Agree or Disagree (to what extent)/Discuss/Opinion/Outweigh: partly (부분적)⟶ (A type 도 가능)

Introduction

Ⅰ. (issue에 대한 배경설명)	The issue of (명사주제) has become a controversy around the world.
Ⅱ. (반대되는 Issue 제기)	Some people say that ~ **disagree(agree)**
Ⅲ. (에세이 할 일)	Regarding this issue, I **partially agree(disagree)** with the idea of (명사주제). The following are the reasons.

Body 1

Ⅰ.	To begin with, there are several reasons why I am **in favor of** this issue.
Ⅱ. Topic sentence(분명하고 간결)	(첫 번째)First/Most importantly, ~
Ⅲ. 부가적인 문장	(다시 말해서)In other words/That is/To be specific
	예시 (예를 들어)For example/For instance/To illustrate this
	증거 (~에 따르면)According to ~ ,
Ⅳ. 마무리(선택사항)	(그러므로)Therefore/Thus/Hence,

Body 2

Ⅰ.	On the contrary, it is believed that(명사주제) has(have) **a negative side** as well.
Ⅱ. Topic sentence	(첫 번째)Firstly

나머지는 Body 1과 같은 형식

Conclusion

Ⅰ. (결론)	To sum up, I **agree(disagree) to some extent** that ~
Ⅱ. Topic sentence	(요약/재언급)Although having some drawbacks(merits), (주제)is(are) more likely to have a positive effect on ~.
Ⅲ. 마무리(선택사항)	(그러므로)Hence, it is convincing(설득력 있는)for 주어 to 동사

Type 3(causes & effects/problems & solutions)

Introduction

Ⅰ. (배경설명)	In recent years, (명사주제) has(have) become a very serious and pressing issue. However, there are also several ways to address the matter.
Ⅱ. (에세이 할 일)	In this essay, I will analyze **problems** caused by(명사주제) and discuss **ways** to help reduce this concerns.

Body 1

Ⅰ. (원인1)	**The main cause** of this problem is~
Ⅱ. 부가적 문장	(다시 말해서)In other words/That is/To be specific
	예시 (예를 들어)For example/For instance/To illustrate this
Ⅰ. (원인2)	**Another reason** is ~
Ⅱ. 부가적 문장	(다시 말해서)That is to say/To put it another way
	증거 (~따르면)According to~/Studies have indicated that~
Ⅲ. 마무리 문장	(그러므로)Therefore/Thus/Hence,

Body 2

Ⅰ. 해결책	However, there are **a couple of methods** to tackle such concerns. One of them to combat the problem is to …
	나머지는 **Body 1**과 같은 형식

Conclusion

Ⅰ. (결론)	In conclusion, as stated above, there are **a few challenges and solutions**. Although it is not easy to find out the right answer, it is desirable(바람직한)for governments and people involved to cooperate with each other to battle this concern.

IELTS Easy Writing

Contents

Preface
    IELTS writing / **4**

Unit 1 Technology

1. Advanced technology / **16**
2. Mobile phone / **31**
3. Computer / **46**
4. Nuclear technology / **60**

Unit 3 Social issues

1. Overpopulation / **150**
2. Financial support / **165**
3. The crime rate / **181**
4. The death penalty / **197**

Unit 2 Education

1. Co-ed school / **76**
2. Physical punishment / **90**
3. Studying English / **105**
4. Teenager's job / **120**
5. Practical skill in university / **135**

Unit 4 The environment

1. Rainforest / **212**
2. Global warming / **226**
3. Waste problem / **241**
4. Zoo / **255**

Unit 5　Culture

1. Online shopping / **270**
2. Advertisement / **283**
3. Traveling / **296**
4. Traffic taxes / **311**

Unit 6　Health

1. Health and diet / **328**
2. Obesity / **343**
3. Smoking / **358**

Task 1

Introduction　/ **374**

1. Line graph 1 / **377**
2. Line graph 2 / **385**
3. Pie chart 1 / **394**
4. Pie chart 2 / **403**
5. Bar graph 1 / **412**
6. Bar graph 2 / **421**
7. Table 1 / **429**
8. Table 2 / **437**
9. Line+Pie / **447**
10. Bar+Table / **456**
11. Diagram / **465**
12. Flow chart / **473**

Writing Topics / **482**

IELTS Easy Writing

Unit 1

Technology

1. Advanced technology
2. Mobile phone
3. Computer
4. Nuclear technology

1. Advanced technology

You should spend about 40 minutes on this task.

Write about the following topic:

> Advanced technology has been beneficial to human life. However, there are also disadvantages of modern technology. Describe the merits and demerits.

Give reasons for your answer and include any relevant examples from your own knowledge or experience.

Write at least 250 words.

INTRODUCTION

발전된 기술은 사람들의 삶에 긍정적 그리고 부정적 영향을 준다.

현대기술의 장점과 단점을 알아본다.

BODY 1 (advantages)

1. 삶을 편리하고 편안하게 해준다.
    - → 작업장의 복잡하고 위험한 일을 기계가 대신
    - → 집안일을 가전기기가 대신

BODY 2 (disadvantages)

1. 기술에 너무 많이 의지한다.
    - → 컴퓨터 고장 시 문제 발생
2. 실업-사회적 문제

CONCLUSION

단점들도 있지만 적절히 사용한다면 현대기술은 사람들의 삶에 유용하다.

발전된 기술은 인간 생활에 도움이 되고 있다. 그러나 현대기술의 단점들 또한 있다. 장단점들을 설명해라.

INTRODUCTION

최근에, 현대기술은 엄청난 변화를 가져오고 있고 그것은 대부분은 사람들의 삶에 긍정적이다. 그러나, 일반적인 믿음과 달리, 어떤 사람들은 기술이 인간에게 부정적인 영향을 준다고 여전히 주장한다. 이 에세이는 현대기술의 장점들과 단점들을 고려할 것이다.

BODY 1

한편으로는, 현대기술이 사람들의 삶을 더욱더 편리하고 편안하게 한다. 산업 로봇들과 같은 발전된 기술혁신 덕택으로, 노동자들은 작업장에서 복잡하고 위험한 공정에서 손으로 일을 할 필요가 없다. 이것은 노사를 안전하고 생산적이게 만든다. 집안일의 경우에, 주부들은 과거에는 집안일을 가전기기 도움 없이 했고, 그것은 지루하고 피곤한 것이었다. 다행히, 세탁기 그리고 로봇청소기와 같은 다양한 종류의 가전제품의 발전은 그들에게 집안일을 최소한으로 노력으로 가능하게 하고 그들이 더 생산적인 일을 하고 그들의 삶을 즐길 수 있도록 하고 있다. 이처럼, 사람들은 현대기술의 긍정적인 영향을 받고 있다.

BODY 2

이에 반해서, 기술적 발전과 관련해서 소홀히 할 수 없는 단점들이 있다. 첫째로, 사람들은 기술에 너무 의지하는 경향이 있다. 기술적 결함에 직면했을 때, 이것은 사람들을 혼란에 빠트릴 수 있다. 예를 들면, 만약 컴퓨터가 고장 난다면, 대부분의 사람은 더 이상 많은 것을 할 수 없다. 이러한 기계에 대한 의존은 너무 강해서 사람들은 그것의 도움 없이는 일을 수행할 수 없다. 이러한 경우에서 보여진 것처럼, 사람들의 삶은 현대기술에 과도하게 지배될 수 있다. **둘째로, 기술적 발전은 실업을 가속화시킨다.** 그것은 발달된 기계와 정밀한 설비들이 많은 직장에서 노동력을 대체하고 있기 때문이다. 이것은 과실들, 범죄들 그리고 심지어 자살과 같은 사회적 문제를 초래하고 있다. 그러므로 발전된 기술이 현대사회에 악영향을 줄 수 있다.

CONCLUSION

결론은, 현대기술이 부정적 효과를 가지고 있지만, 그것은 긍정적인 측면들을 더 가지고 있는 것 같다. 그러므로, 따라서, 만약 사람들이 발전된 기술을 현명하고 적절하게 잘 이용한다면, 그것은 사람들의 삶과 사회에 전적으로 유용할 수 있다.

문장에 필요한 어휘

> 1. in recent years/in recent times/recently; 최근에
> 2. developed(modern/contemporary/high/cutting edge/state-of-the-art/bleeding-edge/advanced) technology; 현대기술/첨단기술
> 3. a sea of changes/a big change; 엄청난 변화
> 4. predominantly/mainly/mostly; 대부분은/주로

최근에, 현대기술은 엄청난 변화를 가져오고 있고 그것은 대부분의 사람들의 삶에 긍정적이다.
In recent years, developed technology has brought a sea of changes, which is predominantly positive, to people's lives.

> 5. having said that/on the other hand/however; 그러나
> 6. contrary to; ~와는 다르게
> 7. negatively/adversely/in the negative; 부정적으로

그러나, 일반적인 믿음과 달리, 어떤 사람들은 기술은 인간에게 부정적인 영향을 준다고 여전히 주장한다.
Some people, having said that, still argue that, contrary to common belief, technology affects humans negatively.

> 8. merit/advantage/good point; 장점
> 9. demerit/disadvantage/bad point/drawback/downside; 단점

이 에세이는 현대기술의 장점들과 단점들을 고려할 것이다.
This essay will consider the merits and demerits of contemporary technology.

> 10. on the one hand/meanwhile; 한편으로는

한편으로는, 현대기술이 사람들의 삶을 더욱더 편리하고 편안하게 한다.
On the one hand, modern technology makes people's lives much more convenient and comfortable.

> 11. with the help of ~/thanks to; ~의 도움으로
> 12. technological innovation; 기술혁신
> 13. manually; 손으로
> 14. in complicated and dangerous process; 복잡하고 위험한 공정

산업 로봇들과 같은 발전된 기술혁신 덕택으로, 노동자들은 작업장에서 복잡하고 위험한 공정에서 손으로 일을 할 필요가 없다.

With the help of advanced technological innovation like industrial robots, laborers do not need to do their work manually in complicated and dangerous process at workplaces.

> 15. labor and management/labor and business; 노사
> 16. secure/safe; 안전한
> 17. productive; 생산적인

이것은 노사를 안전하고 생산적이게 만든다.

It makes labor and management secure and productive.

> 18. in the past; 과거에
> 19. do housework/do house chores/do household chores; 집안일을 하다
> 20. without the aid of; ~의 도움없이
> 21. home appliances/household equipment; 가전기기
> 22. tiring and tiresome; 지루하고 피곤한

집안일의 경우에, 과거에 주부들은 집안일을 가전기기 도움 없이 했고, 그것은 지루하고 피곤한 것이었다.

In the case of housework, homemakers in the past did housework, without the aid of home appliances, which was tiring and tiresome.

> 23. luckily/fortunately; 다행히
> 24. enable A to B; A가 B하는 것이 가능하다

다행히, 세탁기와 로봇청소기 같은 다양한 종류의 가전제품의 발전은 그들에게 최소한의 노력으로 집안일을 할 수 있게 한다.

Luckily, the development of various kinds of household equipment like washing machines and robot vacuum cleaners enables them to do household chores with minimal effort,

> 25. allow A to B; A가 B하는 것을 허락하다(하게 하다)

그것은 그들이 더 생산적인 일을 하고 현대사회에서 그들의 삶을 즐길 수 있도록 하고 있다.
, which allows them to do more productive work and enjoys their lives in modern society.

> 26. like this; 이처럼
> 27. be influenced by/be affected by/be under the influence of; 영향을 받다

이처럼, 사람들은 현대기술의 영향을 긍정적으로 받고 있다.
Like this, people are influenced positively by current technology.

> 28. on the other hand/on the contrary/In contrast/by contrast; 반면에
> 29. associated with/related to; 관련된

이에 반해서, 기술적 발전과 관련해서 소홀히 할 수 없는 단점들이 있다.
On the other hand, there are drawbacks associated with technological development that should not be ignored.

> 30. have(has) a tendency to/tend to/be inclined to/be prone to/be liable to; ~하는 경향이 있다
> 31. rely on/depend on/resort to; ~에 의지하다
> 32. throw somebody into confusion(chaos/mess); 누군가를 혼란에 빠뜨리다
> 33. technological imperfection(deficiency/flaw/defection/fault); 기술적 결함

첫째로, 사람들은 기술에 너무 의지하는 경향이 있다. 그리고, 이것은 기술적인 결함에 직면했을 때 이것은 사람들을 혼란에 빠트릴 수 있다.
Firstly, people have a tendency to depend on technology too much, and this could throw them into confusion when faced technical imperfection.

> 34. provided(that) S+V/supposing (that)S+V/if S+V; 만약 ~이라면
> 35. break down/go wrong; 고장 나다
> 36. no longer; 더 이상~ 아니다

예를 들면, 만약 컴퓨터가 고장 난다면, 대부분의 사람은 더 이상 많은 일들을 할 수 없다.
For example, when computers break down, most people are no longer able to do many things.

37. dependency on; ~에 대한 의존은
38. so A that 주어 cannot B/too A to B; 너무 A 해서 B 할 수 없다

이러한 기계에 대한 의존은 너무 강해서 사람들은 그것의 도움 없이는 일을 수행할 수 없다.
Their dependency on machines is so high that they cannot perform tasks without its assistance.

39. Tip) when/while/though/if/as if/wherever+(S+be동사 생략)+형용사/분사/명사/부사구
    As (it is) seen in this case; 이러한 경우에서 보여진 것처럼
40. substantially/significantly/greatly/considerably; 상당히

이러한 경우에서 보여진 것처럼, 사람들의 삶은 현대기술에 과도하게 지배될 수 있다.
As seen in this case, people's lives can be substantially controlled by modern technology.

41. accelerate/fuel; 가속화시키다
42. unemployment/joblessness; 실업

둘째로, 기술적 발전은 실업을 가속화시킨다.
Secondly, technological progress accelerates unemployment.

43. precision/delicate; 정밀한/정교한
44. labor force/workforce/labor; 노동력

그것은 발달된 기계와 정밀한 설비들이 많은 직장에서 노동력을 대체하고 있기 때문이다.
It is because advanced machines and precision equipment have replaced the labor force in many workplaces,

45. lead to/result in/give rise to/bring about + N; 초래하다
46. delinquency/fault/mistake; 과실
47. crime/offense/criminal act; 범죄
48. suicide; 자살

그리고 이것은 과실, 범죄 그리고 심지어 자살과 같은 사회적 문제를 초래하고 있다.
, and this has led to social problems such as delinquencies, crimes, and even suicides.

Unit 1 Technology

1. Advanced technology

> 49. thus/in this context/therefore/as a result/consequently/hence; 그러므로/따라서
> 50. have(has) adverse(harmful/pernicious/detrimental) effects(influences/impacts) on+A; A에 악영향을 끼치다.

그러므로, 발전된 기술은 현대사회에 악영향을 줄 수 있다.

Therefore, the developed technology could have adverse effects on modern society.

> 51. in conclusion/to sum up/in short/in summary; 결론적으로
> 52. be more likely to ~; 더 ~ 할 것 같다

결론은, 현대기술이 부정적인 효과를 가지고 있지만, 그것은 더 긍정적인 측면들을 가지고 있는 것 같다.

In conclusion, modern technology has negative impacts, it is more likely to have positive points.

> 53. make good use of/make advantage of; 잘 이용하다
> 54. appropriately/properly/adequately/correctly; 적절하게
> 55. entirely/completely/fully/totally; 전적으로

그러므로, 만약 사람들이 발전된 기술을 현명하고 적절하게 잘 이용한다면, 그것은 사람들의 삶과 사회에 전적으로 유용할 수 있다.

In this context, if people make good use of advanced technology wisely and appropriately, it can be entirely useful to people's lives and societies.

구문연습

1. 최근에/현대기술은/가져오고 있다/엄청난 변화를/그것은 대부분은 긍정적이다/인간의 삶에

_____
_____

2. 그러나/어떤 사람들은 여전히 주장한다/우리의 믿음과 달리/기술은 영향을 준다/인간에게/부정적인

_____
_____

3. 이 에세이는/고려할 것이다/장점들과 단점들을/현대기술의

_____
_____

4. 한편으로는/현대기술이/사람들의 삶을 만든다/더욱 더 편리하고 편안하게

_____
_____

5. 덕택으로/산업 로봇들과 같은 발전된 기술혁신/노동자들은 할 필요가 없다/손으로/복잡하고 위험한 공정을/직장에서

_____
_____

6. 이것은 만든다/노사를/안전하고 생산적이게

_____
_____

1. Advanced technology 23

7. 집안일의 경우에/주부들은/과거에/해야만 했다/집안일들을/가전기기 도움 없이/그것은/지루하고 피곤한 것이었다

_____
_____

8. 다행히/다양한 종류의 가전제품의 발전은/세탁기와 로봇청소기 같은/가능하게 하다/그들이/집안일을 하다/최소한의 노력으로

_____
_____

9. 이것은 허락하다/그들이 더 생산적인 일을 하고/그들의 삶을 즐기다/현대 사회에서

_____
_____

10. 이처럼/사람들은/영향받고 있다/긍정적인/현대기술의

_____
_____

11. 다른 한편으로는/단점들이 있다/기술적 발전과 관련해서/소홀히 할 수 없는

_____
_____

12. 첫째로/사람들은/경향이 있다/기술에 의지한다/너무 많이

_____
_____

13. 그리고/이것은/그들을 혼란에 빠뜨린다/직면했을 때/기술적 결함에

_____
_____

14. 예를 들면/컴퓨터가 고장 났을 때/대부분의 사람들은/더 이상할 수 없다/많은 일들을

_____

_____

15. 그들의 의존은/기계에 대한/너무 강해서/그들은 수행할 수 없다/일을/그것의 도움 없이는

_____

_____

16. 이러한 경우에서 보여진 것처럼/사람들의 삶은/과도하게 지배될 수 있다/현대기술에 의해

_____

_____

17. 둘째로/기술 발전은/가속화시킨다/실업을

_____

_____

18. 그것은 때문이다/발달된 기계와 정밀한 설비들이 대체한다/노동력을/많은 직장에서

_____

_____

19. 그리고 초래하고 있다/사회적 문제들을/과실들/범죄들 그리고 자살들과 같은

_____

_____

20. 그러므로/발전된 기술이/악영향을 줄 수 있다/현대사회에

_____

_____

Unit 1 Technology

1. Advanced technology

21. 결론은/현대기술이/부정적인 효과를 가지고 있다/그러나 그것은/더 가지고 있는 것 같다/긍정적인 측면들을

_____

_____

22. 따라서/만약 사람들이 잘 이용하다/발전된 기술들/현명하고 적절하게/그것은/전적으로/유용할 수 있다/사람들의 삶과 사회에

_____

_____

Answer

Unit 1
Technology

1. In recent years, developed technology has brought a sea of changes, which is predominantly positive, to people's lives.
2. Some people, having said that, still argue that, contrary to common belief, technology affects humans negatively.
3. This essay will consider the merits and demerits of contemporary technology.
4. On the one hand, modern technology makes people's lives much more convenient and comfortable.
5. With the help of advanced technological innovation like industrial robots, laborers do not need to do their work manually in complicated and dangerous process at workplaces.
6. It makes labor and management secure and productive.
7. In the case of housework, homemakers in the past did housework without the aid of home appliances, which was tiring and tiresome.
8. Luckily, the development of various kinds of household equipment like washing machines and robot vacuum cleaners enables them to do household chores with minimal effort,
9. , which allows them to do more productive work and enjoys their lives in modern society.
10. Like this, people are influenced positively by current technology.
11. On the other hand, there are drawbacks associated with technological development that should not be ignored.
12. Firstly, people have a tendency to depend on technology too much,
13. , and this could throw them into confusion when faced technical imperfection.
14. For example, when computers break down, most people are no longer able to do many things.
15. Their dependency on the machine is so high that they cannot perform tasks without its assistance.
16. As seen in this case, people's lives can be substantially controlled by modern technology.
17. Secondly, technological progress accelerates unemployment.
18. It is because advanced machines and precision equipment have replaced the labor force in many workplaces,
19. , and this has led to social problems such as delinquencies, crimes, and even suicides.
20. Therefore, the developed technology could have adverse effects on modern society.
21. In conclusion, modern technology has negative impacts, but it is more likely to have positive points.
22. In this context, if people make good use of advanced technology wisely and appropriately, it can be entirely useful to people's lives and societies.

You should spend about 40 minutes on this task.

Write about the following topic:

> **Advanced technology has been beneficial to human life. However, there are also disadvantages of modern technology. Describe the merits and demerits.**

Give reasons for your answer and include any relevant examples from your own knowledge or experience.

Write at least 250 words.

Answer

In recent years, developed technology has brought a sea of change, which is predominantly positive, to people's lives. Some people, having said that, still argue that, contrary to common belief, technology affects humans negatively. This essay will consider the merits and demerits of contemporary technology.

On the one hand, modern technology makes people's lives much more convenient and comfortable. With the help of advanced technological innovation like industrial robots, laborers do not need to do their work manually in complicated and dangerous process at workplaces. It makes labor and management secure and productive. In the case of housework, homemakers in the past did housework, without the aid of appliances, which was tiring and tiresome. Luckily, the development of various kinds of household equipment like washing machines and robot vacuum cleaners enables them to do household chores with minimal effort, which allows them to do more productive work and enjoys their lives in modern society. Like this, people are influenced positively by current technology.

On the other hand, there are drawbacks associated with technological development that should not be ignored. Firstly, people have a tendency to depend on technology too much, and this could throw them into confusion when faced technical imperfection. For example, when computers break down, most people are no longer able to do many things. Their dependency on the machine is so high that they cannot perform tasks without its assistance. As seen in this case, people's lives can be substantially controlled by modern technology. **Secondly, technological progress accelerates unemployment.** It is because advanced machines and precision equipment have replaced the labor force in many workplaces, and this has led to social problems such as delinquencies, crimes, and even suicides. Therefore, the developed technology could have adverse effects on modern society.

In conclusion, modern technology has negative impacts, but it is more likely to have positive points. In this context, if people make good use of advanced technology wisely and appropriately, it can be entirely useful to people's lives and societies.

2. Mobile phone

You should spend about 40 minutes on this task.

Write about the following topic:

> It is true that the use of mobile phone has been on the rise, and it also has great influences on people's lives. What is your opinion of using a mobile phone?

Give reasons for your answer and include any relevant examples from your own knowledge or experience.

Write at least 250 words.

INTRODUCTION

휴대폰은 삶을 편리하게 해 준다.

그러나 간과할 수 없는 몇 가지 단점들이 있다.

BODY 1 (advantages)

1. 대화를 쉽게 할 수 있음.

2. 어플리케이션을 이용한 편리성

BODY 2 (disadvantages)

1. 무분별한 정보가 가득

2. 범죄에 이용

CONCLUSION

적절하고 현명하게 사용해야 한다.

휴대폰 사용이 증가되고 있고 사람들의 삶에 많은 영향을 주는 것은 사실이다. 휴대폰 사용에 대한 당신의 의견은 어떠한가?

INTRODUCTION

다양한 현대기술의 발전이 있어왔고 이 도움으로 대부분의 사람들은 오늘날 그들의 삶을 더 편리하고 편안하게 하기 위해서 휴대폰을 사용해 오고 있다. 그러나, 일부 사람들은 그들의 휴대폰이 유용한지 아닌지에 대한 의문을 제기한다. 다음 토론은 휴대폰 사용의 장단점에 관한 것이다.

BODY 1

<u>**휴대폰의 가장 큰 이점은 사람들이 그것을 가지고 다니는 한 거리의 제한 없이 효율적으로 대화하는 것이다.**</u> 대부분 사람들에게, 휴대폰은 필수품이 되었다. 그들은 시간과 공간에 상관없이 그들의 가족들이나 친구들과 연락하기를 원하기 때문이다. 더욱이 긴급한 상황에서, 그들은 휴대폰으로 911에 전화함으로써 어려움에 대처할 수 있다. <u>**다른 이점은 사람들은 스마트폰 어플리케이션을 가지고 많은 것을 해결할 수 있다는 것이다.**</u> 다운로드한 어플리케이션들로 그들은 새로운 언어들 그리고 요리법들을 배울 수 있다. 또한 온라인 쇼핑사이트는 지금 모바일 플랫폼을 가지고 있어서 그것은 소비자들이 온라인에서 쇼핑할 때 휴대폰 결제가 가능하게 한다. 요즘 핀 테크(financial+technology)는 고객들이 은행을 대신하여 휴대폰으로 입출금과 같은 은행업무를 수행 가능하게 한다. 이것은 그들이 오고 가는 시간과 비용들을 절약할 수 있게 한다. 이와 같이, 휴대폰의 사용은 사람들의 삶의 방식에 매우 유익하다.

BODY 2

<u>**그와는 반대로, 휴대폰의 사용은 사용자의 삶에 해로운 영향을 줄 수 있다. 첫째, 휴대폰은 다양한 정보를 가지고 있지만, 또한 쓸모 없고 무분별한 정보들로 가득 차 있다.**</u> 특히 어린이들이나 청소년들은 저속하고 선정적인 자료들에 무분별하게 접근할 수 있다. 이러한 것들은 그들의 사회 정서적 발달에 전혀 도움이 되지 않는다. <u>**더욱이, 스마트폰에서의 모바일 어플리케이션은 아마도 범죄에 이용될 수 있다.**</u> 범죄자들은 사진들, 집주소 그리고 심지어 은행계좌들 같은 개인적인 정보들을 얻기 위해 몇 가지 어플리케이션을 해킹하는 것으로 알려져 있다. 사실상, 휴대폰과 관련된 많은 사건들이 있다. 예를 들면, 요즘, SMS(짧은 메시지 서비스)피싱이 종종 발생하고 있다. 그것은 사람들을 유인하고 그들의 정보를 모으기 위해 문자 메세지를 이용한다. 그러므로, 이러한 부정적인 면들이 간과되어서는 안 된다.

CONCLUSION

결론은, 이 모든 것을 고려해 볼 때, 휴대폰의 효율적인 사용은 우리에게 편리함을 제공하고 일상생활에서 생산성을 증가시킨다. 그러나 만약 현명하게 사용하지 않으면, 이것은 또한 사생활을 침해하고 사람들의 안전을 위협할 수 있다. 따라서, 휴대폰을 적절하고 현명하게 사용하는 것이 중요하다.

문장에 필요한 어휘

> 1. modern(developed/contemporary/high/cutting-edge/state-of-art/bleeding-edge/advanced) technology; 현대기술/첨단기술

다양한 현대기술 발전이 있어왔다.
There have been numerous modern technological advances,

> 2. convenient and comfortable; 편리하고 편안한

그리고, 이 도움으로 대부분의 사람들은 오늘날 그들의 삶을 더 편리하고 편안하게 하기 위해서 휴대폰을 사용해 오고 있다.
, and with this help, most people today have used a mobile phone to make their lives more convenient and comfortable.

> 3. having said that/however/yet/though/but; 그러나
> 4. raise the question of(pose the question of/cast doubt on) whether s+v; ~인지 아닌지에 대한 의문을 제기하다

그러나, 일부 사람들은 휴대폰이 유용한지 아닌지에 대한 의문을 제기한다.
Some, having said that, raise the question of whether the mobile phone is beneficial or not.

> 5. pro and con/advantage and disadvantage/merit and demerit; 장단점

다음 토론은 휴대폰 사용의 장단점에 관한 것이다.
The following discussion is the pros and cons of the usage of cell phones.

> 6. communicate/have a word/talk; 대화하다
> 7. barriers/obstacles; 장벽들/장애들
> 8. so long as/while/when; ~하는 한

휴대폰의 가장 큰 이점은 사람들이 그것을 가지고 다니는 한 거리의 제한 없이 효율적으로 대화하는 것이다.
The biggest benefit of mobile phones is for people to communicate efficiently without distance barriers so long as individuals carry them.

9. a must/a necessity/a must-have; 필수품

대부분의 사람들에게, 휴대폰은 필수품이 되고 있다.
For most people, mobile phones have become a must.

10. contact/get in touch with/make contact with; ~와 연락하다
11. regardless of/without reference to; ~에 상관없이

그들은 시간과 장소에 관계없이 그들의 가족들이나 친구들과 연락하기를 원하기 때문이다.
It is because they want to contact their families or friends by phone regardless of time and place.

12. in the case of/in terms of/when it comes to/in light of/with respect to; ~의 경우/~에 대해 말하자면
13. cope with(deal with/handle) difficulties(trouble/hardships); 어려움에 대처하다

더욱이, 긴급한 상황에서 그들은 휴대폰으로 911에 전화함으로써 어려움에 대처할 수 있다.
Moreover, in the case of emergency situations, they can cope with difficulties by dialing 911 with a mobile phone.

14. merit/good point/advantage/benefit; 이점

다른 이점은 사람들은 스마트폰 어플리케이션을 가지고 많은 것들을 해결할 수 있다는 것이다.
Another merit is that people can solve many things with smartphone applications.

15. recipe/cooking method/cooking technique; 요리법

다운로드한 어플리케이션들로 그들은 새로운 언어 그리고 요리법들을 배울 수 있다.
By download applications, they can learn new languages and recipes.

16. mobile payment; 모바일 결제

또한 온라인 쇼핑 사이트는 모바일플랫폼을 가지고 있어서 그것은 소비자들에게 그들이 온라인에서 쇼핑할 때 모바일 결제를 가능하게 한다.
Also, online shopping sites have mobile platforms which make it possible for customers to use mobile payment when they shop online.

> 17. Fintech; 재정과 기술의 합성어
> 18. allow A to B; A가 B 하는 것을 허락하다
> 19. conduct/carry out/perform; 수행하다
> 20. deposit and withdraw transaction; 입출금 거래
> 21. on behalf of/in place of/in lieu of; 대신하여

요즘, 핀테크(재정+기술)는 고객들이 은행을 대신해 휴대폰을 가지고 입출금거래와 같은 은행 업무를 수행하게 한다.

Nowadays, Fintech(financial+technology) allows customers to conduct banking services like deposit and withdraw transactions on behalf of the bank with mobile phones,

> 22. enable A to B; A가 B 하는 것을 가능하게 하다
> 23. cost/expense/spending; 비용
> 24. commuting; 오고 감/출퇴근

이것은 그들이 오고 가는 시간과 비용들을 절약할 수 있게 한다.
, which enables them to save time and cost for commuting.

> 25. like this/in this manner; 이와 같이/이처럼
> 26. be of benefit to N/be of help to+N; 유익하다/도움이 되다

이와 같이, 휴대폰의 사용은 사람들의 삶의 방식에 매우 유익하다.
Like this, using mobile phones is of great benefit to people's way of lives.

> 27. on the contrary/on the other hand/in contrast/by contrast/on the flip side; 그와는 반대로
> 28. have(has) pernicicious(harmful/detrimental/adverse) effects(impacts/influences) on ~; ~에 해로운 영향을 주다

그와는 반대로, 휴대폰의 사용은 사용자의 삶에 해로운 영향을 줄 수 있다.
On the contrary, the use of mobile phones can have a pernicious effect on people's lives.

> 29. a broad(wide/great)range(variety)of information; 다양한 정보
> 30. indiscriminate/thoughtless/indiscreet; 무분별한
> 31. as well/also/likewise; 또한/마찬가지로

첫째, 휴대폰은 다양한 정보를 가지고 있지만, 또한 쓸모 없고 무분별한 정보들로 가득 차 있다.
First, mobile phones have a broad range of information, but they are flooded with useless and indiscriminate data as well.

> 32. in particular/particularly/specially/notably; 특히
> 33. get access to/have(has) access to/gain access to/access; 접근하다
> 34. obscene and sexual(sensational/suggestive) materials; 저속하고 선정적인 자료들
> 35. of no help; 전혀 도움이 안 되는

특히 어린이들이나 청소년들은 외설적이고 선정적인 자료들에 접근할 수 있다. 이러한 것들은 그들의 사회 정서적 발달에 전혀 도움이 되지 않는다.

In particular, children and the youth could get access to a lot of obscene and sexual materials indiscreetly with their mobile phones, which is of no help to their social and emotional development.

> 36. furthermore/moreover/in addition/what is more; 더욱이
> 37. crimes/offenses/delinquencies(청소년); 범죄들

더욱이, 스마트폰에서의 모바일 어플리케이션은 범죄에 사용될 수 있다.

Furthermore, mobile applications in smart phones can be used for crimes.

> 38. it is reported that S+V; 보고되고 있다
> 39. criminal/offender/convict/culprit; 범죄자
> 40. hack; 해킹하다
> 41. acquire/obtain; 얻다
> 42. bank account; 은행계좌

범죄자들은 사진들, 집주소 그리고 심지어 은행계좌들 같은 개인적인 정보들을 얻기 위해 몇 가지 어플리케이션을 해킹하는 것으로 알려져 있다.

It is reported that criminals hack some applications to acquire personal information like photos, home address, and even bank account.

> 43. in fact/as a matter of fact/actually/in reality/virtually; 사실상
> 44. a large number of(great numbers of/plenty of/many) crimes; 많은 범죄들
> 45. related to/associated with/involved with; 관련된

사실상, 휴대폰과 관련된 많은 수의 사건들이 있다.

In fact, there are a large number of crimes related to mobile phones.

> 46. for instance/for example/to illustrate; 예를 들면
> 47. phishing; 개인의 정보를 캐내려는 사기성 행위

예를 들면, 요즘, SMS(짧은 메시지 서비스) 피싱이 종종 발생하고 있다.

For instance, nowadays, SMS(short message service) phishing happens at times.

> 48. induce/allure/entice; 유인하다
> 49. collect/accumulate/gather; 모으다

그것은 사람들을 유인하고 그들의 정보를 모으기 위해 문자 메세지를 이용한다.
It uses text messages to induce people and to collect their information.

> 50. therefore/thus/hence/as a result/in this context; 그러므로

그러므로, 이러한 부정적인 면들이 간과되어서는 안 된다.
Therefore, these downsides should not be overlooked.

> 51. take A into consideration/take A into account/consider A/take account of A; A를 고려하다
> 52. efficient/effective; 효율적인
> 53. provide A with B/provide B to(for) A; A에게 B를 제공하다
> 54. increase(raise/promote) productivity; 생산성을 높이다

결론은, 이 모든 것을 고려해 볼 때, 휴대폰의 효율적인 사용은 우리에게 편리함을 제공하고 일상생활에서 생산성을 증가시킨다.
In conclusion, taking all these into consideration, the efficient use of mobile phones provides us with convenience and increases productivity in everyday lives.

> 55. violate/infringe/invade/intrude; 침해하다/침범하다
> 56. endanger A/threaten A/put A at risk/put A in danger/imperil A; A를 위협하다/위태롭게 하다

그러나, 만약 현명하게 사용하지 않으면, 이것은 또한 사생활을 침해하고 사람들의 안전을 위협할 수 있다.
However, if not wisely used, they can also violate our privacy and endanger people's security.

> 57. imperative/essential/vital/important/of importance/significant/fundamental; 중요한
> 58. appropriately and sensibly/properly and reasonably; 적절하고 현명하게

따라서, 휴대폰을 적절하고 현명하게 사용하는 것이 중요하다.
Thus, it is imperative to use mobile phones appropriately and sensibly.

구문연습

1. 있어왔다/현대 과학기술의 발전이/그리고 이 도움으로/대부분의 사람들은/오늘날/사용해 오고 있다/휴대폰을/그들의 삶을 편리하고 편안하게 하기 위해서

_____
_____

2. 일부 사람들은/그러나/의문을 제기한다/휴대폰이 유용한지 아닌지에 대한

_____
_____

3. 다음 토론은/장점들과 단점들이다/휴대폰의 사용에 대한

_____
_____

4. 가장 큰 이점은/휴대폰의/사람들이/효율적으로 대화하는 것이다/거리의 제한 없이/그것을 가지고 다니는 동안

_____
_____

5. 대부분의 사람들에게/휴대폰은 되고 있다/필수품이

_____
_____

6. 이것은 때문이다/그들은 원한다/연락을/그들의 가족들이나 친구들/전화로/시간과 공간에 상관없이

_____
_____

7. 더욱이/긴급한 상황에서/그들은 어려움에 대처할 수 있다/911에 전화함으로써/휴대폰으로

_____
_____

8. 다른 이점은/사람들은 해결할 수 있다/많은 것들을/스마트폰 어플리케이션으로

_____
_____

9. 다운로드한 어플리케이션들로/그들은 배울 수 있다/새로운 언어/그리고 요리법

_____
_____

10. 또한/온라인 쇼핑 사이트는/모바일 플랫폼을 가지고 있다/이것은 가능하다/소비자들이/이용하는 것을/휴대폰 결재를/그들이 쇼핑할 때/온라인에서

_____
_____

11. 요즘/핀테크(재정+기술)/고객들에게 허락한다/은행업무를 행하도록/입출금거래와 같은/은행을 대신해서/휴대폰으로

_____
_____

12. 이것은 가능하게 하다/그들이/시간과 비용들을 절약하는 것을/오고 가는

_____
_____

13. 이와 같이/휴대폰의 사용은/매우 유익하다/사람들의 삶의 방식에

_____
_____

14. 그와는 반대로/휴대폰의 사용은/줄 수 있다/해로운 영향을/사용자의 삶에

15. 첫째/휴대폰은 가지고 있다/다양한 정보/그러나 그들은 가득 차 있다/쓸모 없고 무분별한 정보들로/또한

16. 특히/어린이들과 청소년들은/접근하다/많은 저속하고 선정적인 자료들에/무분별하게/휴대폰을 가지고/그것은 전혀 도움이 안 된다/그들의 사회 정서적 발달에

17. 더욱이/모바일 어플리케이션은/스마트폰에서/사용될 수도 있다/범죄를 저지르는 데

18. 그것은 알려져 있다/범죄자들은/해킹한다/몇 가지 어플리케이션/그들의 정보를 얻기 위해서/사진들, 집주소 그리고 심지어 은행계좌

19. 사실상/있다/많은 범죄들이/휴대폰과 관련된

20. 예를 들면/요즘 SMS phishing이/발생하고 있다/종종

21. 그것은 이용한다/문자 메세지를/사람들을 유인하고 모으기 위해/그들의 정보를

_____
_____

22. 그러므로/이러한 부정적인 면들이/안 된다/간과해서는

_____
_____

23. 결론은/이 모든 것을 고려해 볼 때/휴대폰의 효율적인 사용은/제공한다/우리에게/편리함을 그리고/증가시킨다/생산성을/일상생활에서

_____
_____

24. 그러나/현명하게 사용하지 않으면/그것은 또한 침해할 수 있다/우리의 사생활을/그리고 위태롭게 한다/사람들의 안전을

_____
_____

25. 따라서/그것은 중요하다/휴대폰을 사용하는 것이/적절하게 그리고 현명하게

_____
_____

Answer

1. There have been numerous modern technological advances, and with this help, most people today have used a mobile phone to make their lives more convenient and comfortable.
2. Some, having said that, raise a question of whether the mobile phone is beneficial or not.
3. The following discussion is the pros and cons of the usage of cell phones.
4. The biggest benefit of mobile phones is for people to communicate efficiently without distance barriers so long as individuals carry them.
5. For most people, mobile phones have become a must.
6. It is because they want to contact their families or friends by phone regardless time and place.
7. Moreover, in the case of emergency situations, they can cope with difficulties by dialing 911 with a mobile phone.
8. Another merit is that people can solve many things with smartphone applications.
9. By download applications, they can learn new languages and recipes.
10. Also, online shopping sites have mobile platforms which make it possible for customers to use mobile payment when they shop online.
11. Nowadays, Fintech(financial+ technology) allows customers to conduct banking services like deposit and withdraw transactions on behalf of the bank with mobile phones,
12. , which enable them to save time and cost for commuting.
13. Like this, using mobile phones is of great benefit to people's way of life.
14. On the contrary, the use of mobile phones can have a pernicious effect on people's lives.
15. First, mobile phones have a broad range of information, but they are flooded with useless and indiscriminate data as well.
16. In particular, children and the youth could get access to a lot of obscene and sexual materials indiscreetly with their mobile phones, which is of no help to their social and emotional development.
17. Furthermore, mobile applications in smart phones can be used for crimes.
18. It is reported that criminals hack some applications to acquire personal information like photos, home address, and bank account.
19. In fact, there are a large number of crimes related to mobile phones.
20. For instance, nowadays, SMS (short message service) phishing happens at times.
21. It uses text messages to induce people and to collect their information.
22. Therefore, these downsides should not be overlooked.
23. In conclusion, taking all these into consideration, the efficient use of mobile phones provides us with convenience and increases our productivity in our everyday lives.
24. However, if not wisely used, they can also violate our privacy and endanger people's security.
25. Thus, it is imperative to use mobile phones appropriately and sensibly.

You should spend about 40 minutes on this task.

Write about the following topic:

> It is true that the use of mobile phone has been on the rise, and it also has great influences on people's lives. What is your opinion of using a mobile phone?

Give reasons for your answer and include any relevant examples from your own knowledge or experience.

Write at least 250 words.

Answer

There have been numerous modern technological advances, and with this help, most people today have used a mobile phone to make their lives more convenient and comfortable. Some, having said that, raise the question of whether the mobile phone is beneficial or not. The following discussion is the pros and cons of the usage of cell phones.

The biggest benefit of mobile phones is for people to communicate efficiently without distance barriers so long as individuals carry them. For most people, mobile phones have become a must. It is because they want to contact their families or friends by phone regardless of time and place. Moreover, in the case of emergency situations, they can cope with difficulties by dialing 911 with a mobile phone. **Another merit is that people can solve many things with smartphone applications**. By download applications, they can learn new languages and recipes. Also, online shopping sites have mobile platforms which make it possible for customers to use mobile payment when they shop online. Nowadays, Fintech(financial+ technology) allows customers to conduct banking services like deposit and withdraw transactions on behalf of the bank with mobile phones, which enable them to save time and cost for commuting. Like this, using a mobile phone is of great benefit to people's way of life.

On the contrary, the use of mobile phones can have a pernicious effect on people's lives. **First, mobile phones have a broad range of information, but they are flooded with useless and indiscriminate data as well.** In particular, children and the youth could get access to a lot of obscene and sexual materials indiscreetly with their mobile phones, which is of no help to their mental development. **Furthermore, mobile applications in smart phones can be used for crimes.** It is reported that criminals hack some applications to acquire personal information like photos, home address, and even bank account. In fact, there are a large number of crimes related to mobile phones. For instance, nowadays, SMS (short message service) phishing happens at times. It uses text messages to induce people and to collect their information. Therefore, these downsides should not be overlooked.

In conclusion, taking all these into consideration, the efficient use of mobile phones provides us with convenience and increases productivity in everyday lives. However, if not wisely used, they can also violate our privacy and endanger people's security. Thus, it is imperative to use mobile phones appropriately and sensibly.

3. Computer

You should spend about 40 minutes on this task.

Write about the following topic:

> Computers have been made use of the way people study. Do the advantages of using computers as a study tool outweigh the disadvantages?

Give reasons for your answer and include any relevant examples from your own knowledge or experience.

Write at least 250 words.

INTRODUCTION

컴퓨터의 출현은 사람의 학습에 많은 변화를 주고 있다.

학습의 도구로써 컴퓨터는 장점과 단점을 가지고 있다.

BODY 1 (advantages)

1. 시간과 노력 절약
2. 다양한 자료/강의제공

BODY 2 (disadvantages)

1. 보관된 자료 삭제/표절
2. 무분별한 정보
3. 오락거리가 많음

CONCLUSION

학습의 도구로써 컴퓨터 사용은 몇 가지 장점들과 단점들이 있지만 현명하고 적절히 사용하면 이롭다.

컴퓨터는 사람들이 공부하는 방법으로 이용되고 있다. 학습의 도구로써 컴퓨터 사용의 장점이 단점을 능가하는가?

INTRODUCTION

컴퓨터의 출현은 사람들이 다양한 지식을 얻는 방법에 상당한 변화를 가져오고 있다. 이 경향은 대부분 이롭지만, 그것에 대한 부정적인 측면이 또한 있다. 이 에세이에서, 학습을 위한 컴퓨터 사용의 장점들과 단점들이 토론될 것이다.

BODY 1

오늘날, 학생들은 컴퓨터와 함께 학습하는 데 드는 시간과 노력을 절약할 수 있다. 컴퓨터는 다양한 정보를 제공하는 것 이외에도 그것은 파일을 저장하고 그리고 빠르고 확실하게 전송을 가능하게 하기 때문이다. 컴퓨터 이용 이전에는, 학생들은 자료들과 노트들을 가지고 다녀야만 했고 그들의 가방이나 학교 사물함의 많은 공간을 차지했다. 뿐만 아니라, 컴퓨터 사용의 이점은 인터넷은 학생들이 쉽게 접근할 수 있는 다양한 강의들과 자료들을 제공한다는 것이다. 요즘은 많은 학교들과 교육기관들이 컴퓨터 지원 학습 프로그램들을 수행하고 있어서, 컴퓨터가 유용한 학습도구로써 필수품이 되고 있다. 예를 들면, 많은 대학들은 컴퓨터를 통한 원격 학습을 시간과 장소에 상관없이 학생들에게 제공하고 학생들은 과제를 컴퓨터로 제출한다. 이처럼, 학습하는 데 유용한 도구가 되는 컴퓨터의 몇 가지 이점들이 있다.

BODY 2

부정적인 면에서, 저장된 정보가 우연히 삭제되고 모방되는 경우가 있다. 다른 상황에서, 인터넷상의 디지털 자료들은 우연히 또는 의도적으로 표절되고 왜곡될 수 있다. 때때로, 이것은 부정직함, 사기 등과 같은 몇 가지 사회문제들을 야기한다. 덧붙여서, 인터넷은 무분별하고 쓸모 없는 자료들로 넘쳐나고 있다. 만약 학생들이 어떤 정보가 신뢰성이 있는지 구별할 능력이 없다면, 그들은 그러한 정보에 의해 악영향을 받을 수 있다. 다른 단점 요인으로 온라인상에서 넘쳐나는 오락들은 학습으로부터의 집중을 분산시키고 학습을 방해할 수 있다. 이러한 관점에서, 컴퓨터는 학습의 도구로써 학생들에게 유용하지 않을 수 있다.

CONCLUSION

요약하자면, 위에서 언급한 것처럼, 학습에 있어서 컴퓨터의 이용은 비록 몇 가지 단점들은 있지만, 더 많은 장점들을 가지고 있다. 핵심은 컴퓨터는 학습을 위해서 현명하고 적절하게 이용되어야 한다는 것이다.

문장에 필요한 어휘

> 1. the advent of ~; ~의 출현
> 2. significant/considerable/comparative; 상당한
> 3. acquire(get/gain/obtain)knowledge; 지식을 얻다
> 4. a broad(wide/great) range(variety)of knowledge; 다양한 지식

컴퓨터의 출현은 사람들이 다양한 지식을 얻는 방법에 상당한 변화를 가져 오고 있다.
The advent of the computer has made significant changes in the way people acquire a broad range of knowledge.

> 5. factor/aspect/part/cause/influence; 요인/원인

이 경향은 주로 이롭지만, 그것에 대한 부정적인 측면이 또한 있다.
Although this trend is most beneficial, there are also some negative factors for it.

> 6. pro and con/advantage and disadvantage/merit and demerit/strength and weakness; 장점과 단점

이 에세이에서, 학습을 위한 컴퓨터 사용의 장점들과 단점들이 토론될 것이다.
In this essay, the pros and cons of using computers for studying will be discussed.

> 7. time and effort/time and trouble; 시간과 노력

오늘날, 학생들은 컴퓨터로 학습하는 데 드는 시간과 노력을 절약할 수 있다.
Today, students could save much time and effort when studying with computers.

> 8. It is because S+V; 그것은 ~이기 때문이다
> 9. besides/other than/aside from; ~외에도
> 10. transfer/send/dispatch; 전송하다
> 11. enable A to B; A가 B 하는 것을 가능하게 하다
> 12. quickly and reliably; 빠르고 확실하게

그것은 컴퓨터들이 다양한 정보를 제공하는 것 이외에도 그것은 파일을 저장하고 그리고 빠르고 확실하게 전송을 가능하게 하기 때문이다.

It is because computers also enable them to transfer and store files quickly and reliably, besides providing various information.

---
13. before/prior to; 이전에
14. carry/bring; 가지고 다니다
15. take up space(room); 공간을 차지하다

컴퓨터 이용 이전에는, 학생들은 자료들과 노트를 가지고 다녀야만 했고 그들의 가방이나 선반의 많은 공간을 차지했다.

Before the use of computers, students had to carry files and notes that took up large spaces in their bags or school lockers.

---
16. not only that/In addition to that/furthermore/moreover; 뿐만 아니라
17. benefits/good points/virtues; 이점들
18. materials/resources/references/data/sources; 자료들
19. access/have access to/get access to+ N~에 접근하다

뿐만 아니라, 컴퓨터 사용의 이점은 인터넷은 학생들이 쉽게 접근할 수 있는 다양한 강의들과 자료들을 제공한다는 것이다.

Not only that, the benefits of using computer are that the Internet provides a wide variety of lectures and materials students can access.

---
20. plenty of/a number of/a slew of; 많은/다수의
21. conduct/carry out/organize/manage/administer; 수행하다/운영하다
22. computer-assisted(based) learning programs; 컴퓨터 지원 학습 프로그램
23. a necessity/a necessary/a must- have item; 필수품
24. a useful(valuable) tool/a helpful device; 유용한 도구

요즘은 많은 학교나 교육기관들이 컴퓨터 지원 학습프로그램을 수행하고 있어서, 컴퓨터가 유용한 학습도구로써 필수품이 되고 있다.

Nowadays, as plenty of schools and educational organizations conduct computer-assisted learning programs, computers have become a necessity as a useful educational tool.

25. to illustrate/for example/for instance/for one thing; 예를 들면
26. distance learning; 원격 학습
27. regardless of; 상관없이
28. assignment/task/project; 과제
29. submit/hand in/turn in/present; 제출하다

예를 들면, 많은 대학들은 컴퓨터를 통한 원격학습을 시간과 장소에 상관없이 학생들에게 제공하고 학생들은 과제를 컴퓨터로 제출한다.

To illustrate, Distance Learning Courses in universities give lectures and references, regardless of time and location, to students who submit assignments on a computer.

30. like this/in this manner; 이처럼

이처럼, 학습하는 데 유용한 도구가 되는 컴퓨터의 몇 가지 이점들이 있다.

Like this, there are a few good points of computers that make them a useful tool for studying.

31. on the downside/on the minus side/on the negative side; 부정적인 측면은
32. occasion/case; 경우
33. delete/get rid of/clear; 제거하다
34. imitate/copy; 모방하다
35. by accident/accidentally; 우연히

부정적인 면에서 저장된 정보가 우연히 삭제되고 모방되는 경우가 있다.

On the downside, there are occasions when the information stored can be deleted and copied by accident.

36. plagiarize/pirate; 표절하다
37. distort/strain; 왜곡하다
38. intentionally/deliberately/on purpose; 의도적으로

다른 상황에서, 인터넷상의 디지털 자료들은 우연히 또는 의도적으로 표절되고 왜곡될 수 있다.

In other situations, digital information on the Internet can be plagiarized and distorted accidentally or intentionally.

> 39. at times/sometimes/occasionally/from time to time/now and then/once in a while; 때때로
> 40. give rise to/lead to/bring about/result in+N; 일으키다/야기하다
> 41. a social problem(concern/issue/matter/trouble); 사회적 문제

때때로, 이것은 부정직함, 사기 등과 같은 몇 가지 사회문제들을 야기한다.
At times, this gives rise to a few social problems such as dishonesty, fraud and so on.

> 42. moreover/furthermore/what's more; 더욱이
> 43. teem with/rich in/be full of; 풍부하다
> 44. unreasonable/thoughtless/senseless; 무분별한
> 45. useless(worthless/unhelpful/valueless) information; 쓸모 없는 정보

덧붙여서, 인터넷은 무분별하고 쓸모 없는 자료들로 넘쳐나고 있다.
Moreover, the Internet is teeming with unreasonable and useless information.

> 46. provided that/providing (that)/S+V; 가령 ~라면
> 47. adversely affect; 악영향을 주다

만약 학생들이 어떤 정보가 신뢰성이 있는지 구별할 능력이 없다면, 그들은 그러한 정보에 의해 악영향을 받을 수 있다.
Provided that students have no ability to tell which information is reliable, they could be adversely affected by such information.

> 48. entertainment/amusement; 오락
> 49. the flood of/overflow; 넘쳐나는
> 50. distract A from B; A가 B하는 데 집중이 안 되게 하다(산만하게 하다)
> 51. get(stand) in the way of; 방해가 되다

다른 단점 요인은 온라인에서 넘쳐나는 오락들은 공부에 집중을 분산시키고 학습을 방해할 수 있다.
Another minus factor is that the flood of entertainment online could distract attention away from studying and get in the way of learning.

52. in this respect/in this sense/in this light/in this regard; 이런 관점에서
53. of little use/useless/valueless; 유용하지 않은

이런 관점에서, 컴퓨터는 학습의 도구로써 학생들에게 유용하지 않을 수 있다.
In this respect, computers can be of little use to students as an educational device.

54. to sum up/in conclusion/to conclude/In short; 요약하자면
55. as stated above/as mentioned above; 위에서 언급한 것처럼
56. drawback/disadvantage/demerit/minus/downside; 단점

요약하자면, 위에서 언급한 것처럼, 학습에 있어서 컴퓨터의 이용은 비록 몇 가지 단점들은 있지만, 더 많은 장점을 가지고 있다.
To sum up, as stated above, the use of computers in studying, although having some drawbacks, has much more strengths.

57. the bottom line is that S+V; 결론은 ~이다
58. appropriately/correctly/adequately/properly; 적절하게

핵심은 컴퓨터는 학습을 위해서 현명하고 적절하게 이용되어야 한다는 것이다.
The bottom line is that computers should be utilized wisely and appropriately for studying.

구문연습

1. 컴퓨터의 출현은/상당한 변화를 가져 오고 있다/사람들이 다양한 지식을 얻는 방법에

_____

_____

2. 이 경향은 대부분 이롭지만,/부정적인 측면이 또한 있다/그것에 대한

_____

_____

3. 이 에세이에서/장점들과 단점들이/컴퓨터 사용의/공부를 위한/토론될 것이다

_____

_____

4. 오늘날/학생들은 절약할 수 있다/시간과 노력을/공부할 때/컴퓨터로

_____

_____

5. 그것은 ~ 때문이다/컴퓨터들은/또한 가능하게 하다/그들이/저장하고 전송하는/파일들을/빠르고 믿을 수 있게/이외에도/제공하는 것/다양한 정보를

_____

_____

6. 컴퓨터 이용 이전에는/학생들은 해야만 했다/물리적으로 가지고 다녀야 했다/파일들과 노트들은/차지했다/많은 공간들을/그들의 가방 또는 학교 사물함의

_____

_____

7. 뿐만 아니라/컴퓨터 사용의 이점은/인터넷은/제공한다는 것이다/다양한 강의들과 자료들을/학생들이 쉽게 접근할 수 있는

_____
_____

8. 요즘/~함에 따라서/많은 학교들과 교육기관들이/수행하다/컴퓨터 지원 학습 프로그램들을

_____
_____

9. 컴퓨터는 필수품이 되고 있다/유용한 학습도구로써

_____
_____

10. 예를 들면/원격 학습과정은/대학에서/제공한다/강의들과 자료들을/시간과 장소에 상관없이/학생들에게/학생들은 제출한다/과제를/컴퓨터를 통해서

_____
_____

11. 이처럼/몇 가지 컴퓨터의 이점들이 있다/그들을 유용한 도구로 만드는/학습을 위해

_____
_____

12. 부정적인 면에서/경우들이 있다/저장된 정보는/제거될 수 있고 복사될 수 있다/우연히

_____
_____

13. 다른 상황에서/디지털 정보들은/인터넷상에서/표절되고 왜곡될 수 있다/우연히 또는 의도적으로

_____
_____

14. 때때로/이것은 일으킨다/몇 가지 사회문제들을/부정직함, 사기 등등과 같은

_____

_____

15. 덧붙여서/인터넷은 넘쳐나고 있다/무분별하고 쓸모 없는 자료들로

_____

_____

16. 만약 학생들이/구별할 능력이 없다면/어떤 정보가 신뢰성이 있는지/그들은 악영향을 받을 수 있다/그러한 정보에 의해

_____

_____

17. 다른 부정적인 요인은/넘쳐나는 오락들은/온라인에서/집중을 분산시킨다/학습으로부터/그리고 방해할 수 있다/공부를

_____

_____

18. 이러한 관점에서/컴퓨터는 유용하지 않을 수 있다/학생들에게/학습의 도구로써

_____

_____

19. 요약하자면/위에서 언급한 것처럼/컴퓨터의 사용이/학습에 있어서/비록 몇 가지 단점들을 가지고 있지만/가지고 있다/더 많은 장점들을

_____

_____

20. 핵심은 ~이다/컴퓨터는 이용되어야 한다/현명하고 적절하게/학습을 위해서

_____

_____

Answer

1. The advent of the computer has made significant changes in the way people acquire a broad range of knowledge.

2. Although this trend is most beneficial, there are also some negative factors for it.

3. In this essay, the pros and cons of using computers for studying will be discussed.

4. Today, students could save much time and effort when studying with computers.

5. It is because computers also enable them to transfer and store files quickly and reliably, besides providing various information.

6. Before the use of computers, students had to carry files and notes that took up large spaces in their bags or school lockers.

7. Not only that, the benefits of using computers are that the internet provides a wide variety of lectures and materials students can access.

8. Nowadays, as plenty of schools and educational organizations conduct computer-assisted learning programs,

9. computers have become a necessity as a useful educational tool.

10. To illustrate, Distance Learning Courses in universities give lectures and references, regardless of time and location, to students who submit assignments on a computer.

11. Like this, there are a few good points of computers that make them a useful tool for studying.

12. On the downside, there are occasions when the information stored can be deleted and copied by accident.

13. In other situations, digital information on the internet can be plagiarized and distorted accidentally or intentionally.

14. At times, this gives rise to a few social problems such as dishonesty, fraud and so on.

15. Moreover, the Internet is teeming with unreasonable and useless information.

16. Provided that students have no ability to tell which information is reliable, they could be adversely affected by such information.

17. Another minus factor is that the flood of entertainment online could distract attention away from studying and get in the way of learning.

18. In this respect, computers can be of little use to students as an educational device.

19. To sum up, as stated above, the use of computers in studying, although having some drawbacks, has much more strengths.

20. The bottom line is that computers should be utilized wisely and appropriately for studying.

You should spend about 40 minutes on this task.

Write about the following topic:

> **Computers have been made use of the way people study. Do the advantages of using computers as a study tool outweigh the disadvantages?**

Give reasons for your answer and include any relevant examples from your own knowledge or experience.

Write at least 250 words.

Answer

    The advent of the computer has made significant changes in the way people acquire a broad range of knowledge. Although this trend is most beneficial, there are also some negative factors for it. In this essay, the pros and cons of using computers for studying will be discussed.

    Today, students could save much time and effort when studying with computers. It is because computers also enable them to transfer and store files quickly and reliably, besides providing various information. Before the use of computers, students had to carry files and notes that took up large spaces in their bags or school lockers. **Not only that, the benefits of using computers are that the Internet provides a wide variety of lectures and materials students can access.** Nowadays, as plenty of schools and educational organizations conduct computer-assisted learning programs, computers have become a necessity as a useful educational tool. To illustrate, Distance Learning Courses in universities give lectures and references, regardless of time and location, to students who submit assignments on a computer. Like this, there are a few good points of computers that make them a useful tool for studying.

    On the downside, there are occasions when the information stored can be deleted and copied by accident. In other situations, digital information on the Internet can be plagiarized and distorted accidentally or intentionally. At times, this gives rise to a few social problems such as dishonesty, fraud and so on. **Moreover, the Internet is teeming with unreasonable and useless information**. Provided that students have no ability to tell which information is reliable; they could be adversely affected by such information. **Another minus factor is that the flood of entertainment online could distract attention away from studying and get in the way of learning**. In this respect, computers can be of little use to students as an educational device.

    To sum up, as stated above, the use of computers in studying, although having some drawbacks, has much more strengths. The bottom line is that computers should be utilized wisely and appropriately for studying.

4. Nuclear technology

You should spend about 40 minutes on this task.

Write about the following topic:

> Nuclear technology provided clean, efficient energy, while it also poses a threat to world peace. What are its advantages and disadvantages?

Give reasons for your answer and include any relevant examples from your own knowledge or experience.

Write at least 250 words.

INTRODUCTION
핵 기술에 대해서 논쟁이 되고 있다. 장점과 단점을 토론하겠다.

BODY 1 (advantages)
1. 질병치료에 도움
2. 저렴하고 깨끗한 에너지

BODY 2 (disadvantages)
1. 핵 발전소의 위험
2. 핵 무기 사용

CONCLUSION
몇 가지 장단점들이 있다.
효율적인 자원으로 사용하면 핵 기술은 유용할 수 있다.

핵 기술은 저렴하고 깨끗한 에너지를 제공한다. 반면에 그것은 또한 세계평화를 위협한다. 장점과 단점은 무엇인가?

INTRODUCTION

최근에 핵 기술은 많은 많은 논쟁들을 일으키고 있다. 핵 기술이 깨끗하고 효율적이기 때문에 대체 에너지 원이 될 수 있다는 것은 잘 알려진 사실이다. 그러나, 핵 기술의 보유는 또한 인류에게 중대한 위협이 되고 있다. 이 에세이는 핵 기술의 장단점을 자세히 설명할 것이다.

BODY 1

한편으로는, 핵 기술은 몇 가지 장점들이 있다. 그중 하나는 질병을 치료하는 데 잘 이용되고 있다는 것이다. 핵 기술의 덕택으로, 환자들은 더 빠르고 효율적으로 의료적 도움을 받을 수 있다. 연구에 따르면, 오늘날 병원들에서 사용되고 있는 모든 치료의 1/3은 방사선과 관련된다. **뿐만 아니라, 핵 에너지는 화석연료들과 같은 전통적인 에너지자원과 비교하여 저렴하고 깨끗한 에너지를 공급할 수 있다.** 따라서, 많은 나라가 에너지 자원과 의학적 치료로써 도움을 받기 때문에 핵 에너지는 필요하다.

BODY 2

다른 한편으로는, 핵 기술은 핵발전소와 핵무기에 의해 발생하는 엄청난 위험을 가져올 수 있다는 것이다. 핵발전소들의 폭발과 같은 재해들이 있어왔다. 이러한 것 때문에 거대한 지역이 황폐화되고 많은 사람들이 다쳤다. 그 결과 영향을 받은 이들은 많은 증상으로 힘겨워하고 있다. 예를 들어, 2010년에, 쓰나미는 일본원자력 발전소 중의 하나를 덮쳤다. 그 재난의 여파로, 원자력 발전소로부터 방사능 유출이 발생했고 이러한 것은 일본뿐만 아니라 주변 국가들에게 큰 타격을 주었다. **더욱이, 핵 기술은 핵 무기들을 제조하는 데 이용되고 있다.** 이러한 것은 인간에게 치명적이다. 한가지 예로, 일본이 1945년 원자 폭탄 폭격을 당했을 때, 사상자수는 상당했다. 최근에는 북한이 핵 실험을 시행하고 있다고 보고된다. 이것은 한반도뿐만 아니라 세계 전역의 평화를 위협한다. 이처럼 핵 기술은 인간에게 치명적인 무기가 될 수 있다.

CONCLUSION

결론은, 위에서 언급한 것처럼, 핵 기술은 몇 가지 이점들을 가지고 있다. 동시에, 그것은 사람들이나 환경에 또한 위험하다. 따라서, 만약 국가들과 관련된 사람들이 실용적인 자원으로써 현명하게 그리고 합리적으로 활용한다면 유용할 수 있다.

문장에 필요한 어휘

---

1. in recent years/recently/lately/of late; 최근에
2. nuclear technology; 핵 기술
3. controversy/debate/argument; 논쟁
4. spark/trigger/provoke/set off; 일으키다/유발하다/야기하다

최근에 핵 기술은 많은 논쟁들을 일으키고 있다.
In recent years, nuclear technology has sparked a lot of controversies.

---

5. it is a well-known fact that/it is common knowledge that S+V: 잘 알려진 사실이다
6. alternative power source; 대체 에너지원

핵 기술이 깨끗하고 효율적이기 때문에 좋은 대체 에너지원일 수 있다는 것은 알려진 사실이다.
It is a well-known fact that nuclear technology can be a good alternative power source since it is clean and efficient.

---

7. pose grave threats to/threaten/pose serious risks to; ~에게 중대한 위협을 가하다

그러나, 핵 기술의 보유는 또한 인류에게 중대한 위협이 되고 있다.
However, the possession of nuclear technology also poses grave threats to humanity.

---

8. spell out/elaborate on/explain in full detail; 자세히 설명하다
9. advantage and disadvantage/pro and con/merit and demerit; 장단점

이 에세이는 핵 기술의 장단점을 자세히 설명할 것이다.
This essay will spell out the advantages and disadvantages of nuclear technology.

---

10. on the one hand/meanwhile; 한편으로는
11. merit/advantage/benefit; 장점

한편으로는, 핵 기술은 몇 가지 장점들이 있다.
On the one hand, nuclear technology has several merits.

> 12. make use of/utilize/ take advantage of/employ/use; 이용하다/활용하다
> 13. treat/cure; 치료하다

그들 중 하나는 질병을 치료하는 데 잘 이용되고 있다는 것이다
One of them is that it has been made good use of treating diseases.

> 14. with the help of/thanks to; 도움으로
> 15. patient/sicker/sufferer; 환자

핵 기술의 덕택으로, 환자들은 더 빠르고 효율적으로 의료적 도움을 받을 수 있다.
With the help of nuclear technology, patients can receive medical help more quickly and efficiently.

> 16. according to; ~에 따르면
> 17. radiation; 방사선

연구에 따르면, 오늘날 병원들에서 사용되고 있는 모든 치료의 1/3은 방사선을 포함한다.
According to research, today a third of all procedures used in hospitals involve radiation.

> 18. in addition to that/on top of that/not only that; 뿐만 아니라/그 외에도
> 19. provide/offer/supply/give; 공급하다
> 20. compared to/in comparison with/as compared with; 비교하여
> 21. conventional/traditional; 전통적인/보통 행해지고 있는
> 22. fossil fuels; 화석연료

뿐만 아니라, 핵 에너지는 화석연료들과 같은 전통적인 에너지 자원과 비교하여 저렴하고 깨끗한 에너지를 공급할 수 있다.
In addition to that, nuclear energy is also able to provide cheap and clean energy compared to the conventional energy sources, including fossil fuels.

4. Nuclear technology

> 23. benefit from; ~로부터 도움을 받다

따라서, 많은 나라가 에너지 자원과 의학적 치료로써 도움을 받기 때문에 핵 에너지는 필요하다.
Thus, nuclear power is necessary because many nations benefit from clean power sources and medical treatments.

> 24. on the other hand/on the contrary/in contrast/by contrast/on the flip side; 다른 한편으로는/그에 반하여
> 25. immense/tremendous/massive; 엄청난
> 26. peril/threat/danger/risk; 위험

다른 한편으로는, 핵 기술은 핵발전소와 핵무기에 의해 발생하는 엄청난 위험을 가져올 수 있다.
On the other hand, nuclear technology can also bring immense perils caused by nuclear power plants and weapons.

> 27. the explosion of nuclear stations(plants); 핵 발전소들의 폭발

핵 발전소들의 폭발과 같은 재해들이 있어왔다.
There have been disasters such as the explosion of nuclear power stations.

> 28. a great number of (plenty of) people; 많은 사람들
> 29. struggle with(suffer from/be sick with) symptoms; 증상으로 고통받다
> 30. as a result; 그 결과로서

이러한 것 때문에 거대한 지역이 황폐화되고 많은 사람들이 다쳤다. 그 결과 영향을 받은 이들은 많은 증상들로 힘겨워하고 있다.
Because of which large regions were devastated, and a great number of people were hurt. As a result, those affected struggle with many symptoms.

> 31. for example/for instance/to illustrate; 예를 들어

예를 들어, 2010년에, 쓰나미가 일본 원자력 발전소 중의 하나를 덮쳤다.
For example, in the year 2010, a tsunami struck one of Japan's power plants.

32. in the wake of the disaster/in the aftermath of the disaster; 그 재난의 여파로
33. leak/spill/leakage; 누출
34. take a toll on; 큰 타격을 주다/큰 피해를 주다
35. A as well as B; B뿐만 아니라 A도

그 재난의 여파로, 원자력 발전소로부터 방사능유출이 발생했고 이러한 것은 일본뿐만 아니라 주변국가들에게 큰 타격을 주었다.

In the wake of the disaster, a radiation leak from a nuclear plant occurred, which took a toll on the neighboring countries as well as Japan.

36. furthermore/in addition/moreover; 더욱이
37. lethal/mortal/fatal/deadly; 치명적인

더욱이, 핵무기를 제조하는 데 이용되고 있다. 이것은 인간에게 치명적이다.

Furthermore, nuclear technology has been utilized in the manufacture of nuclear weapons, which are lethal to human beings.

38. for one thing/to cite one example; 한 예로써
39. be bombed with; ~로 폭격당하다
40. the toll of dead and injured/the toll of casualties; 사상자의 수
41. considerable/high/significant; 상당한

한 가지 예로, 일본이 1945년 원자 폭탄 폭격을 당했을 때, 사상자수는 상당했다.

For one thing, when Japan was bombed with atomic bombs in 1945, the toll of dead and injured was considerable.

42. it is reported that S+V; 보고되다
43. conduct(perform/carry out/do) nuclear tests; 핵실험을 하다

최근에는 북한이 핵 실험을 시행하고 있다고 보고되다.

Recently, it is reported that North Korea has conducted nuclear tests.

44. Korean peninsula; 한반도
45. not only A but(also) B/B as well as A; A뿐만 아니라 B

이것은 한반도뿐만 아니라 세계 전역의 평화를 위협한다.

It threatens not only peace on the Korean peninsula but in the entire world.

> 46. with this; 이로써

이처럼 핵 기술은 인간에게 치명적인 무기가 될 수 있다.
With this, nuclear technology can be deadly weapons to humans.

> 47. as (I) mentioned above/as (I) stated above; 위에서 언급된 것처럼

결론은, 위에서 언급된 것처럼, 핵 기술은 몇 가지 이점들이 있다.
In conclusion, as mentioned above, nuclear technology has several benefits,

> 48. at the same time/at once/simultaneously/at a time; 동시에
> 49. dangerous/perilous/hazardous/risky; 위험한
> 50. as well/too/also/likewise; 또한

동시에, 그것은 사람들이나 환경에 또한 위험하다.
at the same time, it is dangerous to people and the environment as well.

> 51. consequently/as a result/therefore/hence/thus; 따라서/그러므로
> 52. involved/related/associated; 관련된
> 53. beneficial/constructive/valuable/advantageous; 유익한

따라서, 만약 국가들과 관련된 사람들이 실용적인 자원으로써 현명하게 그리고 합리적으로 활용한다면 유용할 수 있다.
Consequently, if nations and individuals involved take advantage of it wisely and reasonably as a practical resource, it can be beneficial.

구문연습

1. 최근에/핵 기술은 일으키고 있다/많은 논쟁들을

2. 그것은 잘 알려진 사실이다/핵 기술이/될 수 있다/좋은 대체 에너지자원/왜냐하면 그것은/깨끗하고 효율적이기 때문이다

3. 그러나/핵 기술의 보유는/또한/중대한 위협이다/인류에게

4. 이 에세이는/자세히 설명할 것이다/장점들과 단점들을/핵 기술의

5. 우선/핵 기술은/몇 가지 장점들이 있다

6. 그들 중 하나는/그것은 잘 이용되고 있다/질병을 치료하는 데

7. 핵 기술의 덕택으로/환자들은/받는다/의료적 도움/더 빠르고 효율적으로

8. 연구에 따르면/오늘날/모든 치료의 3분의 1은/사용되고 있는/병원에서/포함한다/방사선을

9. 뿐만 아니라/핵 에너지는/또한 공급할 수 있다/저렴하고 깨끗한 에너지를/전통적인 에너지자원과 비교해서/화석연료들과 같은

10. 따라서/핵 에너지는 필요하다/많은 나라가 도움을 받다/깨끗한 에너지 자원/그리고/의학적인 치료

11. 다른 한편으로는/핵 기술은/또한 가져올 수 있다/엄청난 위험을/발생하는/핵발전소나 핵무기에 의해

12. 재해들이 있어왔다/폭발과 같은/핵 발전소들의

13. 이러한 것 때문에 거대한 지역이/황폐화되고/많은 사람들이 다쳤으며/그 결과/영향을 받은 사람들은/많은 증상으로 힘겨워하고 있다

14. 예를 들어/2010년에/쓰나미는 덮쳤다/일본 발전소 중 한 곳을

_____
_____

15. 그 재난의 여파로서/방사능유출/원자력 발전소로부터/발생했다/이러한 것은 큰 타격을 주었다/주변국가들에게/일본

_____
_____

16. 더욱이/핵 기술은/이용되고 있다/핵 무기를 제조하는 데/이것은 치명적이다/인간에게

_____
_____

17. 한가지 예로/일본이 폭격당했을 때/원자폭탄에 의해/사상자는/상당했다

_____
_____

18. 최근에/보고되다/북한이/핵실험해오고 있다

_____
_____

19. 그것은 위협한다/뿐만 아니라/한반도의 평화/세계전역까지도

_____
_____

20. 이로써/핵 기술은/일 수 있다/치명적인 무기/인간에게

_____
_____

Unit 1 Technology

4. Nuclear technology   69

21. 결론은/위에서 언급한 것처럼/핵 기술은/가지고 있다/몇 가지 이점들을

_____
_____

22. 동시에/그것은 위험하다/사람들에게 그리고 환경에/또한

_____
_____

23. 결과적으로/만약 국가들과 관련된 사람들이/그것을 활용한다면/현명하게 그리고 합리적으로/실용적인 자원으로써/이것은 유용할 수 있다

_____
_____

Answer

1. In recent years, nuclear technology has sparked a lot of controversies.
2. It is a well-known fact that nuclear technology can be a good alternative power source since it is clean and efficient.
3. However, the possession of nuclear technology also poses grave threats to humanity.
4. This essay will spell out the advantages and disadvantages of nuclear technology.
5. On the one hand, nuclear technology has several merits.
6. One of them is that it has been made good use of treating diseases.
7. With the help of nuclear technology, patients can receive medical help more quickly and efficiently.
8. According to research, today a third of all procedures used in hospitals involve radiation.
9. In addition to that, nuclear energy is also able to provide cheap and clean energy compared to the conventional energy sources, including fossil fuels.
10. Thus, nuclear power is necessary because many nations benefit from clean power sources and medical treatments.
11. On the other hand, nuclear technology can also bring immense perils caused by nuclear power plants and weapons.
12. There have been disasters such as the explosion of nuclear power stations.
13. Because of which large regions were devastated, and a great number of people were hurt. As a result, those affected struggle with many symptoms.
14. For example, in the year 2010, a tsunami struck one of Japan's power plants.
15. In the wake of the disaster, a radiation leak from a nuclear plant occurred, which took a toll on the neighboring countries as well as Japan.
16. Furthermore, nuclear technology has been utilized in the manufacture of nuclear weapons, which are lethal to human beings.
17. For one thing, when Japan was bombed with atomic bombs in 1945, the toll of dead and injured was considerable.
18. Recently, it is reported that North Korea has conducted nuclear tests.
19. It threatens not only peace on the Korean peninsula but in the entire world.
20. With this, nuclear technology can be deadly weapons to humans.
21. In conclusion, as mentioned above, nuclear technology has several benefits,
22. At the same time, it is dangerous to people and the environment as well.
23. Consequently, if nations and individuals involved take advantage of it wisely and reasonably as a practical resource, it can be beneficial.

You should spend about 40 minutes on this task.

Write about the following topic:

> **Nuclear technology provided clean, efficient energy, while it also poses a threat to world peace. What are its advantages and disadvantages?**

Give reasons for your answer and include any relevant examples from your own knowledge or experience.

Write at least 250 words.

Answer

In recent years, nuclear technology has sparked a lot of controversies. It is a well-known fact that nuclear technology can be a good alternative power source since it is clean and efficient. However, the possession of nuclear technology also poses grave threats to humanity. This essay will spell out the advantages and disadvantages of nuclear technology.

On the one hand, nuclear technology has several merits. One of them is that it has been made good use of treating diseases. With the help of nuclear technology, patients can receive medical help more quickly and efficiently. According to research, today a third of all procedures used in hospitals involve radiation. **In addition to that, nuclear energy is also able to provide cheap and clean energy** compared to the conventional energy sources, including fossil fuels. Thus, nuclear power is necessary because many nations benefit from clean power sources and medical treatments.

On the other hand, nuclear technology can also bring immense perils caused by nuclear power plants and weapons. There have been disasters such as the explosion of nuclear power stations. Because of which large regions were devastated, and a great number of people were hurt. As a result, those affected struggle with many symptoms. For example, in the year 2010, a tsunami struck one of Japan's power plants. In the wake of the disaster, a radiation leak from a nuclear plant occurred, which took a toll on the neighboring countries as well as Japan. **Furthermore, nuclear technology has been utilized in the manufacture of nuclear weapons,** which are lethal to human beings. For one thing, when Japan was bombed with atomic bombs in 1945, the toll of dead and injured was considerable. Recently, it is reported that North Korea has conducted nuclear tests. It threatens not only peace on the Korean peninsula but in the entire world. With this, nuclear technology can be deadly weapons to humans.

In conclusion, as mentioned above, nuclear technology has several benefits, at the same time, it is dangerous to people and the environment as well. Consequently, if nations and individuals involved take advantage of it wisely and reasonably as a practical resource, it can be beneficial.

IELTS Easy Writing

Unit 2

Education

1. Co-ed school
2. Physical punishment
3. Studying English
4. Teenager's job
5. Practical skill in University

1. Co-ed school

You should spend about 40 minutes on this task.

Write about the following topic:

> Some people think that it is better to educate boys and girls in separate schools. Others, however, believe that boys and girls benefit more from attending mixed schools. Discuss both views and give your own opinion.

Give reasons for your answer and include any relevant examples from your own knowledge or experience.

Write at least 250 words.

INTRODUCTION
학교교육 유형에 대한 논쟁이 계속되고 있다.
남녀공학과 단일성별학교는 몇 가지의 장점들과 단점들을 가지고 있다.

BODY 1 단일 성별학교 장점(남녀공학 단점)
공부에 집중할 수 있다.

BODY 2 단일 성별학교 단점(남녀공학 장점)
남녀학생 교류기회 없다.

CONCLUSION
몇 가지 단점들이 있지만 남녀공학의 장점이 훨씬 월등하므로 활성화되어야 한다.

어떤 사람들은 단일 성별학교에서 학생들을 교육시키는 것이 더 낫다고 생각한다. 그러나, 다른 이들은 학생들은 남녀공학 학교에 다니는 것이 이익이 된다고 생각한다. 두 가지 의견들과 자신의 의견을 제시하라.

INTRODUCTION

학교교육 유형에 대한 논란이 계속되어 오고 있다. 일부의 부모들과 선생님들은 남녀공학에 다니는 것은 학생들에게 도움이 된다고 믿는다. 그러나, 다른 사람들은 남학생과 여학생을 분리하는 것에 찬성한다. 내 의견으로는, 두 견해는 장단점을 가지고 있다. 이 에세이는 다음과 같이 이 문제에 대해서 논의할 것이다.

BODY 1

남학생과 여학생을 분리하는 데는 몇 가지 이점들이 있다. 우선, 단일성별학교에서의 학생들은 좀더 편안하게 무언가를 배울 수 있다. 사실상 학생들이 청소년기에 서로 관심을 가지는 것은 아주 당연하다. 이러한 상황은 학생들을 공부에서 멀어지게 할 수 있고 학교생활에 지장을 줄 수 있다. 예를 들어, 반 여학생에게 반한 남학생은 그들이 공부 대신에 청소년기의 연애감정에 집중할 수 있다. 연구에 따르면, 단일학교 학생의 성적이 남녀공학에 다니는 학생보다 훨씬 낫다고 한다. 따라서, 남녀학생들을 분리함으로써 학습분위기가 학생들을 위해 만들어질 수 있고 거기에서 그들은 그들의 학업에 훨씬 더 집중할 수 있다.

BODY 2

반면에, 남학생들과 여학생들이 다른 학교에서 공부하는 것은 몇 가지 문제에 또한 마주친다. 단일성별학교는 학생들에게 이성과 교류할 기회를 제공하지 못한다. 그 결과, 졸업생들은 사회 생활에서 서로 의견과 생각을 공유하는 게 어렵다는 것을 발견한다. 사실상, 아이들의 인격형성기는 성별과 관계없이 다른 학생들과 어떻게 어울리고 대화하는지에 대해 배우고 성인의 삶을 준비하는 최상의 시기이다. 이러한 점에서, 남녀공학은 학생들이 다양한 주제에 대한 그들의 관점을 함께 교류하도록 많은 기회를 제공한다. 이것은 가까운 미래에 학생들이 사회생활에 적응하도록 유도한다.

CONCLUSION

요약하자면, 우리는 남녀공학과 단일 성별학교들은 장점들과 단점들을 가지고 있다. 그렇지만, 내 의견으로는 남녀공학의 장점들이 단점들을 훨씬 능가한다고 생각한다. 이러한 상황으로 볼 때, 부모들과 선생님들이 남녀공학의 교육을 활성화시키는 것이 설득력이 있다.

문장에 필요한 어휘

> 1. the controversy over/the debate over/the question of; ~에 대한 논란
> 2. schooling/school education; 학교교육
> 3. ongoing/constant; 계속적인

학교교육의 유형에 대한 논란이 계속되어 오고 있다.
The controversy over the type of schooling has been an ongoing issue.

> 4. a co-ed school/a school for both genders/a coeducational school/a mixed school; 남녀공학

일부의 부모들과 선생님들은 남녀공학에서 공부하는 것은 학생들에게 더 도움이 된다고 믿는다.
Some parents and teachers believe that attending co-ed schools is more beneficial for schoolchildren.

> 5. having said that/however/on the other hand; 그러나/다른 한편으로는
> 6. be for/agree with/prefer/be in favour of; 찬성하다
> 7. separate/divide; 분리하다

그러나, 다른 사람들은 남학생과 여학생을 분리시키고 그들을 다른 학교에서 교육시키는 것을 찬성한다.
Others, having said that, are for separating boys and girls.

> 8. in my opinion/from my point of view; 내 의견으로는
> 9. view/perspective/viewpoint; 견해

내 의견으로는, 두 견해는 장단점을 가지고 있다.
In my opinion, both views have merits and demerits.

> 10. as follows; 다음과 같이

이 에세이는 다음과 같이 이 문제에 대해서 논의할 것이다.
This essay will discuss this issue as follows.

11. separate; 분리하다
12. male and female students; 남학생과 여학생들

남학생과 여학생을 분리하는 데는 몇 가지 이점들이 있다.
There are some benefits to separating male and female students.

13. first of all/to begin with/above all; 우선
14. single-sex schools; 단일성별학교

우선, 단일성별학교에서의 학생들은 좀더 편안하게 무언가를 배울 수 있다.
First of all, students in single-sex schools could have an easier time learning things.

15. in fact/in reality/as a matter of fact/virtually/actually; 사실상
16. it is natural/it stands to reason/it is proper that S+V; 당연하다
17. in adolescence; 청소년기
18. feel attracted to/have an affinity for/feel drawn to/feel an attraction to; ~에 매력을 느끼다

사실상 학생들이 청소년기에 서로 관심을 가지는 것은 아주 당연하다.
In fact, it is quite natural for students in adolescence to feel attracted to each other.

19. lead A to B/cause A to B; A가 B하도록 이끈다
20. distract: 관심이 멀어지다/산만하게 하다
21. interfere with/disturb/interrupt; ~를 방해하다

이러한 상황은 학생들을 공부에서 멀어지게 할 수 있고 학교생활에 지장을 줄 수 있다.
The circumstances could lead students to distract studying and interfere with school life.

22. have(has) a crush on; 반하다
23. instead of/in place of/in place of; ~대신에
24. adolescent romances: 청소년기의 연애감정

예를 들어, 반 여학생에게 반한 남학생은 그들의 공부 대신에 청소년기의 연애감정에 집중할 수 있다.
For example, boys who have a crush on a female classmate could focus on adolescent romances instead of their study.

> 25. according to; ~에 따르면

연구에 따르면, 단일학교학생의 성적이 남녀공학에 다니는 학생보다 훨씬 낮다고 한다.
According to research, school records in single-sex schools are much better than those in co-ed schools.

> 26. therefore/thus/as a result/in this context/consequently/hence; 따라서
> 27. academic atmosphere(environment); 면학분위기
> 28. pay attention to/focus on/concentrate on; 집중하다

따라서, 남녀 학생들을 분리함으로써 면학분위기가 학생들을 위해서 만들어질 수 있고 거기에서 그들은 그들의 학업에 훨씬 더 집중할 수 있다.
Therefore, by separating boys and girls, an academic atmosphere can be created for students in which they could pay far more attention to their learning.

> 29. on the flip side/on the other hand/on the contrary/in contrast/by contrast; 반면에
> 30. encounter/face/confront; 마주치다/직면하다
> 31. as well/also/likewise/too; 또한

반면에, 남학생들과 여학생들이 다른 학교에서 공부하는 것은 몇 가지 문제에 또한 마주친다.
On the flip side, boys and girls studying in different schools encounter some problems as well.

> 32. provide A with B/provide B to(for) A; A에게 B를 제공하다
> 33. interact with; ~와 교류하다

단일성별학교는 학생들이 이성과 교류할 기회를 제공하지 못한다.
Single-sex schools do not provide an opportunity for students to interact with the other gender.

> 34. graduates; 졸업생들
> 35. share ideas and opinions; 의견과 생각을 공유하다

그 결과, 졸업생들은 사회 생활에서 서로 의견과 생각을 나누는 것이 어렵다는 것을 발견한다.
As a result, graduates find it difficult to share ideas and opinions with each other in their social life.

> 36. the formative years/the formative period; 인격 형성기
> 37. mingle and converse; 어울리고 대화하다
> 38. regardless of; ~에 상관없이
> 39. gear up for/prepare for/be ready for/make preparation for; ~을 위한 준비를 하다.
> 40. adult life; 성인기의 삶

사실상, 아이들의 인격형성기는 성별과 관계없이 어떻게 어울리고 대화하는지에 대해 배우고 성인의 삶을 준비하는 최상의 시기이다.

In reality, the formative years of children are the best time to learn more about how to mingle and converse with schoolchildren regardless of gender and to gear up for adult life.

> 41. in this respect; 이러한 점에서
> 42. chance/opportunity/occasion; 기회
> 43. point of view/viewpoint/perspective/standpoint; 관점

이러한 점에서, 남녀공학은 학생들이 다양한 주제에 대한 그들의 관점을 함께 교류하도록 많은 기회를 제공한다.

In this respect, co-ed schools offer many chances for students to exchange their points of views on various subjects together,

> 44. adapt to/adjust to+N; 적응하다
> 45. down the road; 앞으로/언젠가는

이것은 앞으로 학생들이 사회생활에 적응하도록 유도한다.

, which cause children to adapt to their social life down the road.

> 46. to sum up/in conclusion/to conclude; 요약하자면
> 47. merits/good point/benefit/advantage; 장점
> 48. demerit/bad point/disadvantage/drawback; 단점

요약하자면, 남녀공학과 단일 성별학교들은 장점들과 단점들을 가지고 있다.

To sum up, co-ed schools and single-sex schools have their merits and demerits.

> 49. far outweigh; 훨씬 우세하다

나의 의견은, 그렇지만. 남녀공학의 장점들이 단점들을 훨씬 능가한다고 생각한다.

In my opinion, the advantages of co-ed schools far outweigh the disadvantages, though.

> 50. promote/expand/increase; 활성화시키다/증진시키다
> 51. compelling/convincing/persuasive; 설득력 있는

이러한 상황으로 볼 때, 부모들과 선생님들이 남녀공학의 교육을 활성화시키는 것이 설득력이 있다.

Given this situation, it is compelling for parents and teachers to promote mixed school education.

구문연습

1. 논란이/학교 유형에 대한/계속되어 오고 있다

2. 일부의 부모들과 선생님들은 믿는다/남녀공학에 다니는 것은/도움이 된다/학생들에게

3. 다른 이들은/그러나/찬성하다/남학생과 여학생을 분리하는 것을

4. 내 의견으로는/두 가지 견해는/가지고 있다/장점들과 단점들을

5. 이 에세이는/토론할 것이다/이 문제를/다음과 같이

6. 있다/몇 가지 이점들이/분리하는 데/남학생과 여학생을

7. 우선/학생들은/단일성별학교에서의/더 편안한 시간을 가질 수 있다/무언가를 배우는 데에

8. 사실상/그것은/ 아주 당연하다/청소년기 학생들이/매력을 느끼는 것은/서로

9. 이것은 학생들을/멀어지게 할 수 있다/그리고/지장을 줄 수 있다/학교생활을

10. 예를 들어/남학생은/반하다/반 여학생에게/집중할 수 있다/청소년기의 연애감정에/대신에/그들의 공부

11. 연구에 따르면/학생성적은/단일성별학교에서/훨씬 낫다/그것보다/남녀공학보다

12. 따라서/분리시킴으로써/남학생들과 여학생들을/면학분위기는/만들어질 수 있다/학생들을 위해서/거기서/그들은 훨씬 더 집중하다/그들의 학업에

13. 반면에/공부하는 남학생과 여학생은/다른 학교에서/몇 가지 문제들을 마주친다/또한

14. 단일성별학교는/제공하지 않는다/기회를/학생들이/교류하는 것을/이성과

15. 따라서/졸업생들은/발견한다/그것이 어렵다는 것을/생각과 의견을 공유하는 것을/서로/사회생활에서

_____

_____

16. 사실상/아이들의 인격형성기는/최상의 시간이다/배우는데/어떻게 어울리고 대화하는지를/학생들과/성별과 상관없이//그리고 준비하기 위해서/성인생활을

_____

_____

17. 이러한 점에서/남녀공학은/제공한다/많은 기회들을/학생들이/교류하는 데/그들의 관점을/다양한 주제에 대해/함께

_____

_____

18. 이러한 상황은/유도한다/학생들을/사회생활에 적응하도록/가까운 미래에

_____

_____

19. 요약하자면/남녀공학과 단일성별학교들은/가지고 있다/장점들과 단점들을/

_____

_____

20. 내 의견은/장점들이/남녀공학에서/훨씬 능가한다/단점들을/그렇지만

_____

_____

21. 이러한 상황으로 볼 때,/설득력이 있다/부모들과 선생님들이/활성화시키는 것이/남녀공학교육을

_____

_____

1. Co-ed school

Answer

1. The controversy over the type of schooling has been an ongoing issue.

2. Some parents and teachers believe that attending co-ed schools is more beneficial for schoolchildren.

3. Others, having said that, are for separating boys and girls.

4. In my opinion, both views have merits and demerits.

5. This essay will discuss this issue as follows.

6. There are some benefits to separating male and female students.

7. First of all, students in single-sex schools could have an easier time learning things.

8. It is quite natural for students in adolescence to feel attracted to each other.

9. The circumstances could lead students to distract studying and interfere with school life.

10. For example, boys who have a crush on a female classmate could focus on adolescent romances instead of their study.

11. According to research, school records in single-sex schools are much better than those in co-ed schools.

12. Therefore, by separating boys and girls, an academic atmosphere can be created for students in which they could pay far more attention to their learning.

13. On the flip side, boys and girls studying in different schools encounter some problems as well.

14. Single-sex schools do not provide an opportunity for students to interact with the other gender.

15. As a result, graduates find it difficult to share ideas and opinions with each other in their social life.

16. In reality, the formative years of children are the best time to learn more about how to mingle and converse with schoolchildren regardless of gender to gear up for adult life.

17. In this respect, co-ed schools offer many chances for students to exchange their points of views on various subjects together,

18. , which cause children to adapt to their social life down the road.

19. To sum up, co-ed schools and single-sex schools have their merits and demerits.

20. In my opinion, the advantages of co-ed schools far outweigh the disadvantages, though.

21. Given this situation, it is compelling for parents and teachers to promote mixed school education.

You should spend about 40 minutes on this task.

Write about the following topic:

> **Some people think that it is better to educate boys and girls in separate schools. Others, however, believe that boys and girls benefit more from attending mixed schools. Discuss both views and give your own opinion.**

Give reasons for your answer and include any relevant examples from your own knowledge or experience.

Write at least 250 words.

Answer

The controversy over the type of schooling has been an ongoing issue. Some parents and teachers believe that attending co-ed schools is more beneficial for schoolchildren. Others, having said that, are for separating boys and girls. In my opinion, both views have merits and demerits. This essay will discuss this issue as follows.

There are some benefits to separating male and female students. First of all, students in single-sex schools could have an easier time learning things. In fact, it is quite natural for students in adolescence to feel attracted to each other. The circumstances could lead children to distract studying and interfere with school life. For example, boys who have a crush on a female classmate could focus on adolescent romances instead of their study. According to research, school records in single-sex schools are much better than those in co-ed schools. Therefore, by separating boys and girls, an academic atmosphere can be created for students in which they could pay far more attention to their learning.

On the flip side, boys and girls studying in different schools encounter some problems as well. Single-sex schools do not provide an opportunity for students to interact with the other gender. As a result, graduates find it difficult to share ideas and opinions with each other in their social life. In reality, the formative years of children are the best time to learn more about how to mingle and converse with schoolchildren regardless of gender and to gear up for adult life. In this respect, co-ed schools offer many chances for students to exchange their points of views on various subjects together, which could lead children to adapt to their social life down the road.

To sum up, coeducation schools and single-sex schools have their merits and demerits. In my opinion, the advantages of co-ed schools far outweigh the disadvantages, though. Given this situation, it is compelling for parents and teachers to promote mixed school education.

2. Physical punishment

You should spend about 40 minutes on this task.

Write about the following topic:

> Some parents say corporal punishment, at times, necessary to educate children. They state that the benefits of this punishment far outweigh the demerits. What is your opinion?

Give reasons for your answer and include any relevant examples from your own knowledge or experience.

Write at least 250 words.

INTRODUCTION

체벌은 아이들을 교육시키는 데 때때로 사용되고 있다.

그러나 많은 부정적인 측면들이 있다.

BODY 1 (disagree)

1. 체벌은 아이들에게 정서적 그리고 신체적으로 해로운 영향
→ 폭력이 문제해결의 수단으로 정당화
→ 연약한 신체와 정신에 손상

BODY 2 (disagree)

1. 체벌은 교육의 효과가 없음
→ 효과가 지속되지 못하고 역효과 일어남
→ 아이와 부모의 관계가 악화

CONCLUSION

체벌은 많은 단점들을 가지고 있다.

부모들은 아이를 교육시키는 데 체벌이 아닌 합리적 방법을 선택해야 한다.

어떤 부모들은 체벌이 아이들을 교육시키는 데 필요하다고 말한다. 그들은 체벌에 대한 이점이 단점보다 훨씬 크다고 생각한다. 어느 정도 동의하는지?

INTRODUCTION

체벌은 아이들을 훈육하는 데 때때로 사용되고 있다. 왜냐하면 많은 부모들은 아이들의 잘못된 행동을 바로잡는 데 가장 적절하고 쉬운 방법이라고 믿는 경향이 있기 때문이다. 그러나 어떤 부모들은 훈육과 관련해서 체벌에 대한 효과에 의문을 제기한다. 나로서는, 체벌을 가하는 것에 동의하지 않는다. 다음의 의견들은 그 이유들이다.

BODY 1

<u>우선, 체벌은 아이들의 정서적, 신체적 발달에 해로운 영향을 줄 수 있다. 아이들에게 체벌을 가하는 것은 그들에게 그러한 폭력은 받아들여질 수 있는 것이라는 잘못된 개념을 줄지도 모른다.</u> 이것은 체벌이 잘못된 것을 바로 잡는 데 필요하다는 견해를 야기할지도 모른다. 예를 들어, 체벌을 경험한 아이들은 누군가가 실수를 하는 한 체벌하는 것은 이치에 맞는다고 생각할 것이다. 그런 이유로, 그들이 성장한 후에 그들은 똑같은 방법으로 그들의 아이들을 체벌하는 경향이 있다. 더욱이, 아이들의 신체는 아직 완전히 발달하지 못했고 그래서 아직은 정신적, 신체적으로 취약하다. 그러므로 <u>아이들에게 고통을 가하는 것은 연약한 정신과 신체에 손상을 주는 것이다.</u> 그리고 또한 그 상처들이 치유되는 데는 시간이 걸린다. 이처럼, 폭력에 의해 처벌하는 것은 악순환을 야기할 수 있고 아이들의 신체적 그리고 정신적 건강에 해를 줄 수 있다.

BODY 2

<u>그것 외에도, 체벌은 아이들에게 아무 도움이 안 된다. 우선, 체벌에 기대된 이로운 효과는 오래 지속되지 못하고 결국 역효과를 낳는다.</u> 사실상, 아이들을 꾸짖고 다시 잘못 행동하는 것을 막는 초기의 목적은 전혀 성취되지 못할 것이다. 이것에 덧붙여서, 체벌은 아이들이 그들의 잘못을 깨닫도록 허용하지 않는다. 사실상, 이러한 종류의 체벌은 아이들 사이에 두려움을 불러일으키고 체벌을 피하기 위해서 다음에는 거짓말을 하도록 유도한다. <u>더욱이, 아이들을 위한 체벌의 교육적 의도가 그들의 부모에 향하는 분노와 다른 부정적인 감정으로 변할지도 모른다.</u> 따라서, 부모와 아이의 관계는 교육적 도구로써의 체벌 때문에 악화될 수 있다.

CONCLUSION

요약하면, 위에서 언급한 것처럼, 체벌에 몇 가지 단점들이 존재하는 것은 분명하다. 그러한 체벌의 효과는 부모들이 기대하는 것처럼 교육적이지도 생산적이지도 않다. 그러므로, 부모들은 아이들을 체벌이 아닌 합리적인 방법으로 훈육시켜야 한다는 것이 설득력이 있다.

문장에 필요한 어휘

> 1. physical(corporal/bodily) punishment/punish physically; 체벌
> 2. occasionally/at times/once in a while/sometimes; 때때로
> 3. discipline/educate/instruct; 훈육하다/지도하다

체벌은 아이들을 교육시키는 데 때때로 사용되고 있다.
Physical punishment is occasionally used to discipline children

> 4. have a tendency to/tend to/be inclined to/be liable to; 하는 경향이 있다
> 5. appropriate/proper/right; 적절한
> 6. impose(inflict/delivery) punishment; 벌을 가하다
> 7. wrong behavior/wrong-doing/misdeed; 잘못된 행동/비행

왜냐하면 많은 부모들은 아이들의 잘못된 행동을 바로잡는 데 가장 적절하고 쉬운 방법이라고 믿는 경향이 있기 때문이다.
since many parents have a tendency to believe that it is the most appropriate and easiest way to correct the wrong behavior of their children.

> 8. raise the question of; ~에 대한 의문을 제기한다
> 9. concerning/regarding/as regards; 관련해서

그러나 어떤 부모들은 훈육과 관련해서 체벌에 대한 효과에 의문을 제기한다.
However, some raise the question of the effects of physical punishment concerning discipline.

> 10. as for me/in my case/from my point of view; 내 경우에는
> 11. be for the idea/be in favor of the idea/agree with the idea/support the idea; 그 의견에 찬성하다

나로서는, 체벌에 동의하지 않는다.
As for me, I am not for corporal punishment.

> 12. argument/view/idea; 의견/논쟁

다음의 의견들은 그 이유들이다.
The following arguments are the reasons.

> 13. above all/first of all/the first and foremost/to start with/to begin with; 우선
> 14. have(has) detrimental(negative/harmful/pernicious) effects(influences/impacts) on; 해로운 영향을 끼친다
> 15. emotional and physical development; 정서적 그리고 신체적 발달

우선, 체벌은 아이들의 정서적 그리고 신체적 발달에 해로운 영향을 줄 수 있다.
Above all, corporal punishment could have detrimental effects on children's emotional and physical development.

> 16. inflict(impose) corporal punishment on somebody/dole out punishment to somebody; 체벌하다
> 17. the wrong idea(conception); 잘못된 개념
> 18. acceptable/suitable/adequate; (사회적으로) 용납되는/받아들여지는

아이들에게 체벌을 가하는 것은 그들에게 그러한 폭력은 받아들여질 수 있는 것이라는 잘못된 개념을 줄지도 모른다.
Inflicting corporal punishment on children may give them the wrong idea that such violence is acceptable.

> 19. lead to/result in/give rise to/bring about; 야기하다/초래하다/일으키다

이것은 체벌이 잘못된 것을 바로잡는 데 필요하다는 견해를 야기할지도 모른다.
This may lead to the view that corporal punishment is necessary to correct wrongdoings.

> 20. for example/for instance/to illustrate; 예를 들면
> 21. reasonable/justifiable; 정당화할 수 있는/이치에 맞는
> 22. so long as S+V/as long as S+V; ~ 하는 한/~하기만 하면

예를 들어, 체벌을 경험한 아이들은 누군가가 실수를 하는 한 체벌하는 것은 이치에 맞는다고 생각한다.
For example, children who experience physical punishment would think doling out corporal punishment to somebody is reasonable so long as they have made a mistake.

> 23. on that account; 그런 이유로
> 24. grow up/be raised/be brought up; 성장하다

그런 이유로, 그들이 성장한 후에 똑같은 방법으로 그들의 아이들을 체벌하는 경향이 있다.

On that account, after they grow up, they would tend to punish their children in the same way.

> 25. moreover/furthermore/in addition; 더욱이
> 26. vulnerable/sensitive/susceptible; 취약한/영향 받기 쉬운

더욱이, 아이들의 신체는 아직 완전히 발달하지 못했고, 그래서 아직은 정신적, 신체적으로 취약하다.

Moreover, children are not yet fully developed, and hence they are still vulnerable mentally and physically.

> 27. therefore/thus/hence/as a result/consequently/in this context; 그러므로/따라서
> 28. fragile/sick/weak/delicate/feeble; 연약한
> 29. a wound/an injury/a bruise; 상처

그러므로 그들에게 고통을 가하는 것은 연약한 정신과 신체에 손상을 주는 것이다. 그리고 또한 그 상처를 치유하는 데 시간이 걸린다.

Therefore, imposing pain upon them might damage their fragile mind and body, and it also takes a long time for the wounds to heal.

> 30. in this way/like this; 이렇게 하여
> 31. a vicious cycle(circle); 악순환
> 32. physical and mental well-being; 신체적, 정신적 건강

이처럼, 폭력의 사용에 의한 처벌은 악순환을 야기할 수 있고 아이들의 신체적, 정신적 건강에 해를 줄 수 있다.

In this way, punishment by the use of violence could result in a vicious cycle and could harm children's physical and mental well-being.

> 33. on top of that/besides that/In addition to that; 그 외에도/그 밖에도
> 34. lead A nowhere; A에게 아무 도움이 안 된다/효과가 없다

그것 이외에도, 체벌은 아이들에게 아무 도움이 안 된다.

On top of that, physical punishment leads children nowhere.

35. ultimately/in the end/finally/after all; 결국
36. counterproductive; 역효과를 낳는/비생산적인

우선, 그들에게 기대된 이로운 효과는 오래 지속하지 못하고 결국 역효과를 낳는다.
To begin with, the expected beneficial effect on it does not last long and is ultimately counterproductive.

37. initial purpose(intention/aim); 초기의 의도
38. scold/rebuke; 꾸짖다
39. prevent(deter/stop/prohibit/inhibit) A from B; A가 B하는 것을 막다
40. make a mischief; 잘못된 행동하다
41. achieve/accomplish/fulfill; 성취하다

사실상, 체벌의 초기 목적인 아이들을 꾸짖고 다시 잘못 행동하는 것을 막는 것은 전혀 성취되지 못할 것이다.
In fact, the initial purpose of physical punishment, which is to scold children and prevent him or her from remaking mischief, would not be achieved at all.

42. allow A to B/enable A to B; A에게 B하는 것을 허용하다/허락하다

이것에 덧붙여서, 체벌은 아이들이 그들의 잘못을 깨닫도록 허용하지 않는다.
In addition to that, physical punishment does not allow children to realize what they have done wrong.

43. in reality/in fact/virtually/actually; 사실상
44. tell a lie/tell a untruth; 거짓말하다
45. prompt/generate/trigger/cause/provoke/incur/induce; 발생시킨다/초래하다

사실상, 이러한 종류의 체벌은 아이들 사이에 두려움을 불러일으키고 체벌을 피하기 위해서 다음에는 거짓말을 하도록 유도한다.
In reality, this kind of penalty only causes fear among children that may prompt them to tell a lie next time to avoid the punishment.

> 46. turn into; ~로 변하다
> 47. negative (hard)feelings toward(against); ~에 대해 부정적인 감정

더욱이 아이들을 위한 체벌의 교육적 의도는 그들의 부모에 향하는 분노와 다른 부정적인 감정으로 변할지도 모른다.

Moreover, the educational intention of physical punishment for children may turn into resentment and other negative feelings toward their parents.

> 48. due to/because of/on account of/owing to+ N; ~ 때문에
> 49. educational tool(measure/step/means/way); 교육적인 도구/수단

따라서, 부모들과 자식들간의 관계는 교육적 도구로써의 체벌 때문에 악화될 수 있다.

As a result, the relationship between parents and children could become worse, due to physical punishment as an educational tool.

> 50. to sum up/In conclusion/In short/In summary; 요약하면
> 51. as mentioned above/as stated above; 위에서 언급한 것처럼
> 52. apparent/obvious/clear/evident; 분명한/확실한
> 53. drawback/demerit/shortcoming/disadvantage; 단점

요약하면, 위에서 언급한 것처럼, 체벌에 몇 가지 단점들이 존재하는 것은 분명하다.

To sum up, as mentioned above, it is apparent that some drawbacks of corporal punishment exist.

> 54. not as A as B; B만큼 A가 아니다
> 55. productive/effective/efficient; 생산적인/효율적인

그러한 체벌의 효과는 부모들이 기대한 만큼 교육적이지도 생산적이지도 않다.

The effect of such a kind of punishment is not as educational and productive as parents expect.

> 56. convincing/persuasive/compelling/valid; 설득력 있는

그러므로, 부모들이 아이들을 체벌이 아닌 합리적인 방법으로 훈육하는 것이 설득력이 있다.

Therefore, it is convincing for parents to discipline children in sensible ways, but not with physical punishment.

구문연습

1. 체벌은/때때로/사용되고 있다/아이들을 훈육하는 데

2. 왜냐하면/많은 부모들은/믿는 경향이 있기 때문이다/그것은 가장 적절하고 쉬운 방법이다/바로잡는 데/아이들의 잘못된 행동을

3. 그러나, 어떤 부모들은 의문을 제기한다/체벌에 대한 효과/훈육과 관련해서

4. 나의 경우에는/동의하지 않는다/체벌에

5. 다음의 의견은/그 이유들이다

6. 우선/체벌은 해로운 영향을 줄 수 있다/어린이들에게/감정적으로 그리고 신체적 발달에

7. 체벌을 가하는 것은/어린이에게 줄지 모른다/그들에게 잘못된 개념을/그러한 폭력은/용납될 수 있다고

_____

_____

8. 이것은 견해를 야기할지도 모른다/체벌이 필요하다/잘못을 바로잡기 위해서

_____

_____

9. 예를 들어/체벌을 경험한 아이들은/누군가를 체벌하는 것은/이치에 맞다/그들이 실수를 하는 한

_____

_____

10. 그런 이유로/그들이 성장한 후에/그들은 체벌하는 경향이 있을 것이다/그들의 자녀들을/똑같은 방법으로

_____

_____

11. 더욱이/아이들은/아직 완전히 성장하지 않았고/그러므로 아직은 취약하다/정신적, 신체적으로

_____

_____

12. 그러므로/그들에게 체벌을 가하는 것은/손상시킬지도 모른다/그들의 연약한 정신과 신체에/그것은 시간이 걸릴 것이다/치유하는 데/그 상처를

_____

_____

13. 이처럼/처벌하는 것은/폭력에 의해/초래할 수 있다/악순환을/그리고 해를 끼칠 수 있다/아이들의 신체적 그리고 정신적 건강에

_____

_____

14. 그것 이외에도/체벌은 결코 아이들에게/도움이 안 된다

15. 우선, 체벌에 기대된 이로운 효과는/오래 지속되지 않고/결국 역효과를 낳는다

16. 사실상, 체벌의 초기의 목적은/그것은 아이를 꾸짖는 것이다/그리고 다시 못하게 하는 것이다/그와 그녀가/잘못된 행동을/다시는/전혀 성취되지 않을 것이다

17. 덧붙여서/체벌은 허용하지 않는다/어린이가/깨닫게 하는 것을/그들이 잘못한 것

18. 사실상/이런 종류의 체벌은/단지 일으킨다/아이들 사이에 공포를/그것은 그들에게 초래할지도 모른다/다음에 거짓말하게/체벌을 피하기 위해서

19. 더욱이/교육적 의미는/체벌에 대한/변할지도 모른다/분노와 다른 부정적인 감정/그들의 부모들을 향한

20. 따라서/부모들과 자식들과의 관계는/악화될 수 있다/체벌 때문에/교육적인 도구로써의

21. 요약하면/위에서 언급한 것처럼/그것은 분명하다/몇몇의 단점/체벌에 대한/존재한다

_____

_____

22. 그러한 체벌의 효과는/교육적이지도 생산적이지도 않다/부모들이 기대하는 것처럼

_____

_____

23. 그러므로/그것은 설득력이 있다/부모들이/아이들을 교육시킨다/합리적인 방법으로/체벌이 아닌

_____

_____

Answer

1. Physical punishment is occasionally used to discipline children
2. since many parents have a tendency to believe it is the most appropriate and easiest way to correct the wrong behavior of their children.
3. However, some raise the question of the effects of physical punishment concerning discipline.
4. As for me, I am not for corporal punishment.
5. The following arguments are the reasons.
6. Above all, corporal punishment could have detrimental effects on children's emotional and physical development.
7. Inflicting corporal punishment on children may give them the wrong idea that such violence is acceptable.
8. This may lead to the view that corporal punishment is necessary to correct wrongdoings.
9. For example, children who experience physical punishment would think doling out corporal punishment to somebody is reasonable so long as they have made a mistake.
10. On that account, after they grow up, they would tend to punish their children in the same way.
11. Moreover, children are not yet fully developed, and hence they are still vulnerable mentally and physically.
12. Therefore, imposing pain upon them might damage their fragile mind and body, and it also takes a long time for the wounds to heal.
13. In this way, punishment by the use of violence could result in a vicious cycle and could harm children's physical well-being.
14. On top of that, physical punishment leads children nowhere.
15. To begin with, the expected beneficial effect on it does not last long and is ultimately counterproductive.
16. In fact, the initial purpose of physical punishment, which is to scold children and prevent him or her from remaking mischief, would not be achieved at all.
17. In addition to that, physical punishment does not allow children to realize what they have done wrong.
18. In reality, this kind of penalty only causes fear among children that may prompt them to tell a lie next time to avoid the punishment.
19. Moreover, the education intention of physical punishment for education may turn into resentment and other negative feelings toward their patents.
20. As a result, the relationship between parents and children could become worse due to physical punishment as an educational tool.
21. To sum up, as mentioned above, it is apparent that some drawbacks of corporal punishment exist.
22. The effect of such a kind of punishment is not as educational and productive as parents expect.
23. Therefore, it is convincing for parents to discipline children in sensible ways, but not with physical punishment.

You should spend about 40 minutes on this task.

Write about the following topic:

> **Some parents say corporal punishment is at times necessary to educate children. They state that the benefits of this punishment far outweigh the demerits. What is your opinion?**

Give reasons for your answer and include any relevant examples from your own knowledge or experience.

Write at least 250 words.

Answer

Physical punishment is occasionally used to discipline children since many parents have a tendency to believe that it is the most appropriate and easiest way to correct the wrong behaviour of their children. However, some raise the question of the effects of physical punishment concerning discipline. As for me, I am not for corporal punishment. The following arguments are the reasons.

Above all, corporal punishment could have detrimental effects on children's emotional and physical development. Inflicting corporal punishment on children may give them the wrong idea that such violence is acceptable, and this may lead to the view that corporal punishment is necessary to correct wrongdoings. For example, children who experience physical punishment would think doling out corporal punishment to somebody is reasonable so long as they have made a mistake. On that account, after they grow up, they would tend to punish their children in the same way. Moreover, children are not yet fully developed, and hence they are still vulnerable mentally and physically. Therefore, **imposing pain upon them might damage their fragile mind and body,** and it also takes a long time for the wounds to heal. In this way, punishment through the use of violence could result in a vicious cycle and could harm children's physical and mental well-being.

On top of that, physical punishment leads children nowhere. To begin with, the expected beneficial effect on it does not last long and is ultimately counterproductive. In fact, the initial purpose of physical punishment, which is to scold children and prevent him or her from remaking mischief, would not be achieved at all. In addition to that, physical punishment does not allow children to realize what they have done wrong. In reality, this kind of penalty only causes fear among children that may prompt them to tell a lie next time to avoid the punishment. **Moreover, the educational intention of physical punishment for children may turn into resentment and other negative feelings toward their parents.** As a result, the relationship between parents and children could become worse, due to physical punishment as an educational tool.

To sum up, as mentioned above, it is apparent that some drawbacks of corporal punishment exist. The effect of such a kind of punishment is not as educational and productive as parents expect. Therefore, it is convincing for parents to discipline children in sensible ways, but not with physical punishment.

3. Studying English

You should spend about 40 minutes on this task.

Write about the following topic:

> Some people believe that studying English in an English-speaking country is the best way to learn the language. What is your opinion?

Give reasons for your answer and include any relevant examples from your own knowledge or experience.

Write at least 250 words.

INTRODOCTION

영어는 보편적 언어이고 일부는 영어를 영어권에서 배우는 것이 가장 효율적이라고 주장한다. 이것에 대한 두 가지 측면의 의견을 제시하겠다.

BODY 1

1. 영어권에서 영어를 배우는 것은 효율적인 방법
   → 영어환경에 노출-언어를 사용하는 기회 많음
   → 영어권 문화나 생활양식에 친숙-언어이해 도움

BODY 2

1. 영어권에서 영어를 배우는 것은 학생들에게 부정적인 영향
   → 그들 자신의 나라에 많은 언어자료와 학원들이 존재
   → 외국에서 공부하는 것은 비용이 많이 든다.
   → 언어/문화적 장벽

CONCLUSION

영어권 나라에서 영어를 공부하는 것에 대한 몇 가지 단점도 있지만 언어를 습득하는 데 있어서 더 효율적인 방법인 것 같다.

영어권 나라에서 영어를 배우는 것은 언어를 배우는 최상의 방법이다. 이 의견에 대한 당신의 생각은?

INTRODUCTION

영어가 최근에 보편적인 언어가 되고 있다는 것은 잘 알려진 사실이다. 따라서, 세계각국의 사람들은 다른 언어들보다 영어를 배우고 싶어한다. 이것과 관련해서, 어떤 사람들은 언어를 배우는 가장 효과적인 방법은 영어권에서 공부하는 것이라고 주장한다. 그러나, 다른 이들은 이 의견에 반대한다. 이 에세이에서, 나는 두 가지 의견을 자세히 설명하겠다.

BODY 1

한편으로는, 영어권 나라에서 영어를 배우는 것이 언어를 습득하는 효율적인 방법이라는 것은 분명하다. 그러한 나라에 머무름으로써, 국제 학생들은 영어를 말하고 듣는 많은 기회를 가질 수 있는 영어환경에 더 깊숙이 노출될 수 있고, 이러한 것은 언어기술의 빠른 발전을 가져온다. 덧붙여서, 외국 학생들은 영어권 나라들에서 사람들의 생활양식과 같은 문화에 친숙해질 수 있다. 이러한 것은 더 나은 문화의 이해와 언어발달을 야기한다. 예를 들어, 외국에서 홈스테이 프로그램은 생활양식을 이해하고 대화기술을 발전시키는 데 좋은 경험이 된다. 이것을 통해서, 학생들은 홈스테이 가족과 공동체 그리고 등등과 같은 다른 상황에서 현지인들과 어울리기 때문이다. 그러므로 영어권 문화에 대한 노출은 언어구사능력을 매우 발전시킬 수 있다.

BODY 2

다른 한편으로는, 영어권 나라에서 영어를 배우는 것은 학생들에게 또한 부정적인 영향을 끼칠 수 있다고 믿는다. 실제로는, 사람들이 그들 자신의 나라에서 공부할 수 있는 다양한 자료들과 학원들이 있다. 그러므로 학생들이 해외에 갈 필요가 없다는 것이 주장되고 있다. 더욱이, 외국에 머무르는 비용은 모국에서 머무르는 것과 비교하여 상당히 높다. 그것뿐만 아니라, 외국학생들은 거대한 언어적 그리고 문화적인 장벽들에 직면할 수 있고 그러한 것들 때문에 그들이 외국환경에 적응하는 데 힘들다. 어떤 경우에는, 그들은 공부하기 위해서 외국에 머물 때 우울증과 향수병을 경험할 수도 있다. 따라서, 외국에서 영어를 배우는 것은 어렵고 힘든 도전일 수 있다.

CONCLUSION

요약하자면, 영어권 나라에서 영어를 배우는 것은 장점들과 단점들이 있다. 내 의견으로는, 비록 부정적인 영향이 있지만 그곳에서 영어를 배우는 것은 사람들의 배움에 훨씬 더 유익한 영향을 끼칠 수 있는 것 같다. 왜냐하면 그들은 영어문화에 직접적으로 접근할 기회를 가질 것이고 이런 상황에서 더 자주 영어를 사용할 것이기 때문이다.

문장에 필요한 어휘

> 1. it is a well-known fact that S+V; 잘 알려진 사실이다
> 2. universal (common) language; 보편적인 언어
> 3. in recent years/in recent times/lately/of late/recently; 최근에

영어가 최근에 보편적인 언어가 되고 있다는 것은 잘 알려진 사실이다.
It is a well-known fact that English has become a universal language in recent years.

> 4. accordingly/for this(that) reason/on that account; 그래서/그런 이유 때문에
> 5. be keen to/be anxious to/be dying to/ be eager to; ~하기를 원하다
> 6. more than; ~보다

따라서, 세계 각국의 사람들은 다른 언어들보다 영어를 배우고 싶어한다.
Accordingly, people around the world are keen to learn English more than other languages.

> 7. in this regard; 이것과 관련해서
> 8. argue/maintain/state/stress/believe; 주장하다
> 9. the most efficient(successful/useful/helpful) way; 가장 효과적인 방법
> 10. the English-speaking world/an English–speaking country(nation); 영어권 나라

이것과 관련해서, 어떤 사람들은 언어를 배우는 가장 효과적인 방법은 영어권에서 공부하는 것이라고 주장한다.
In this regard, some people argue that the most efficient way to learn English is to study in the English-speaking world.

> 11. however/but/on the contrary/in contrast/by contrast; 그러나/그와는 반대로
> 12. be against/disagree with/be not in favor of; ~에 반대한다

그러나, 다른 이들은 이 의견에 반대한다.
Others, however, are against this idea.

> 13. spell out/elaborate on/explain in full detail; 상세히 설명하다

이 에세이에서 나는 두 가지 의견을 자세히 설명하겠다.
In this essay, I will spell out both ideas.

> 14. clear-cut/clear/apparent; 분명한
> 15. acquire/learn/study; 습득하다

한편으로는, 영어권 나라에서 영어를 배우는 것이 언어를 습득하는 효율적인 방법이라는 것은 분명하다.
On the one hand, it is clear-cut that learning English in an English-speaking country is an effective way of acquiring the language.

> 16. be exposed to+N; 노출되다
> 17. English environment(surroundings); 영어환경
> 18. gain(get/have) opportunities; 기회를 갖다

그러한 나라에서 머무름으로써, 국제학생들은 영어를 말하고 듣는 많은 기회를 가질 수 있는 환경에 더 깊숙이 노출될 수 있다.
By being in such countries, international students could be more deeply exposed to English environment where they could gain a lot of opportunities to speak and listen to English,

> 19. result in/give rise to/lead to/bring about+ N; 초래하다/야기하다
> 20. rapid development/fast advancement; 빠른 발전

이러한 것은 그들의 언어기술의 빠른 발전을 야기할 수 있다.
, which could result in the rapid development of their language skills.

> 21. in addition to that/furthermore/what's more/moreover/not only that; 덧붙여서
> 22. be familiar with/be acquainted with; 친근하다

덧붙여서, 외국학생들은 영어권 나라들에서 사람들의 생활양식을 포함한 문화에 친숙해질 수 있다.
In addition to that, international students could be familiar with the culture, including people's lifestyles in English-speaking countries,

> 23. a better understanding of culture; 더 나은 문화 이해

이러한 것은 더 나은 문화의 이해와 언어발달을 초래한다.
, which could give rise to a better understanding of culture and the development of language.

> 24. to give an illustration/for instance/for example; 예를 들어
> 25. develop/improve/better/promote; 발전시키다/향상시키다

예를 들어, 외국에서 홈스테이 프로그램은 생활양식을 이해하고, 대화기술을 발전시키는 데 좋은 경험이다.
To give an illustration, a homestay program in a foreign country is a great experience to understand the lifestyle and develop their communication skill

> 26. locals/natives; 현지인
> 27. mingle(mix) with/get along with; ~와 어우러지다

이것을 통해서, 학생들은 홈 스테이 가족과 공동체 그리고 등등과 같은 다른 상황에서 지역민들과 어울릴 수 있다.
From this, learners mingle with the locals in different situations such as homestay families, communities and so on.

> 28. therefore/thus/hence/consequently; 그러므로/따라서
> 29. the exposure to; ~에 대한 노출
> 30. immensely/highly/greatly/extremely/terribly; 매우/대단히/과하게
> 31. a command of the language; 언어구사능력

그러므로, 영어권 문화에 대한 노출은 언어구사능력을 매우 발전시킬 수 있다.
Therefore, the exposure to English culture can improve immensely a command of the language. .

> 32. on the other hand/on the flip side/meanwhile/on the contrary/in contrast; 다른 한편으로는
> 33. it is believed that S+V; ~를 믿는다
> 34. have(has) a negative(detrimental/harmful/pernicious) influence(effect/impact) on; 부정적인 영향을 주다
> 35. as well/also/likewise; 또한

다른 한편으로는, 영어권 나라에서 영어를 배우는 것은 학생들에게 또한 부정적인 영향을 끼칠 수 있다.
On the other hand, it is believed that learning English in English-speaking countries can have an adverse influence on the students as well.

> 36. in reality/in fact/as a matter of fact/actually/virtually; 실제로는/사실상
> 37. a wide(whole/broad/great) range(variety) of; 다양한
> 38. allow A to B/enable A to B; A가 B하는 것을 가능하게 하다

실제로는, 사람들이 그들의 나라에서 영어를 배울 수 있게 하는 다양한 자료들과 학원들이 있다.
In reality, there are various materials and academics, which allow people to learn English in their country.

> 39. necessary/essential/indispensable; 필요한/중요한
> 40. go abroad(overseas); 외국에 가다

그러므로, 학생들이 해외에 갈 필요 없다는 것이 주장되고 있다.
Thus, it is argued that it is not necessary for students to go abroad.

> 41. the cost of ~; ~에 대한 비용
> 42. compared to/as compared with/in comparison with; ~와 비교하여

더욱이, 해외에 머무르는 비용은 모국에서 머무르는 것과 비교하여 과도하게 높다.
Moreover, the cost of staying overseas is extremely high compared to being in one's native country.

> 43. face/confront; 직면하다
> 44. immense linguistic and cultural barriers; 엄청난 언어적이고 문화적 장벽들

그것뿐만 아니라, 외국학생들은 엄청난 언어적이고 문화적인 장벽들에 직면할 수 있다.
Not only that, international students can face immense linguistic and cultural barriers.

> 45. adjust to/adapt to +N/acclimate; 적응하다
> 46. exotic surroundings/foreign environment; 외국환경

이러한 것들 때문에, 그들이 외국환경에 적응하는 게 힘들다.
Due to which it can be hard for them to adjust to exotic surroundings

> 47. in some cases; 어떤 경우에는/때로는
> 48. depression/melancholia; 우울증
> 49. homesickness/nostalgia; 향수병

어떤 경우에는, 그들은 공부하기 위해서 외국에 머물 때 우울증과 향수병을 경험한다.
In some cases, they experience depression and homesickness when they stay abroad to study.

> 50. daunting/challenging/demanding/harsh; 어려운/두려운/위협적인

따라서, 외국에서 영어를 배우는 것은 어렵고 힘든 도전일 수 있다.
Hence, learning English overseas could be a harsh and daunting challenge.

> 51. to sum up/In conclusion/In short; 요약하자면
> 52. benefit/advantage/merit; 이점

요약하자면, 영어권 나라에서 영어를 배우는 것은 장점들과 단점들을 가지고 있다.
To sum up, learning English in the English-Speaking world has both benefits and drawbacks.

> 53. be far(much) more likely to+v; 더 ~일 거 같다
> 54. beneficial/useful/helpful; 유익한

내 의견으로는, 비록 부정적인 영향들이 있지만 그곳에서 영어를 배우는 것은 사람들의 배움에 훨씬 더 많은 유익한 영향을 줄 거 같다.
In my view, studying English there, although having adverse effects, is far more likely to have beneficial impacts on people's learning

> 55. have(get/gain) access to+N/access; ~에 접근하다
> 56. under these circumstances; 이러한 상황에서

왜냐하면 그들은 영어문화에 직접적으로 접근할 기회들을 가질 것이고 이런 상황에서 더 자주 영어를 사용할 것이기 때문이다.
since they would have great opportunities to have direct access to English culture and use English more frequently under these circumstances.

구문연습

1. 그것은/잘 알려진 사실이다/영어가 되고 있다/보편적인 언어가/최근에

_____
_____

2. 따라서, 세계 각국의 사람들은/영어를 배우고 싶어한다/다른 언어들보다

_____
_____

3. 이것과 관련해서/어떤 사람들은 주장한다/가장 효과적인 방법은/언어를 배우는/머무르는 것이다/영어권 나라에

_____
_____

4. 그러나/다른 이들은/반대한다/이 의견에

_____
_____

5. 이 에세이에서/나는 자세히 설명할 것이다/두 가지 의견을

_____
_____

6. 한편으로는/그것은 분명하다/영어를 배우는 것은/영어권 나라에서/효율적인 방법이다/언어를 습득하는

_____
_____

7. 머무름으로써/그러한 나라들에/외국 학생들은/더 노출될 수 있다/영어 환경에

_____

_____

8. 거기에서/그들은 얻을 수 있다/많은 기회를/영어를 말하고 듣는

_____

_____

9. 이러한 것은/야기할 수 있다/빠른 발달/그들은 언어기술들의

_____

_____

10. 덧붙여서/외국 학생들은/친숙해질 수 있다/문화에/사람들의 생활방식과 같은/영어권 나라들에서

_____

_____

11. 그것은 초래한다/더 나은 문화 이해/그리고/언어의 발달을

_____

_____

12. 예를 들어/홈스테이 프로그램은/외국에서/좋은 경험이다/생활양식을 이해하는 데/그리고 발전시키는 데/그들의 대화기술을

_____

_____

13. 이것을 통해/학생들은/현지인들과 어울릴 수 있다/홈스테이 가족과 공동체 그리고 등등과 같은/다른 장소들에서

_____

_____

14. 그러므로/외국문화에 대한 노출은/매우 발전시킬 수 있다/언어구사능력을

_____
_____

15. 다른 한편으로는/믿어진다/영어를 배우는 것은/영어권에서/부정적인 영향을 끼칠 수 있다/학생들에게/또한

_____
_____

16. 사실상/다양한 자료들과 학원들이 있다/그것들은/허용한다/사람들이/영어를 배우는 것을/그들 자신의 나라에서

_____
_____

17. 그러므로/주장되고 있다/그것은 반드시 필요한 것은 아니다/학생들이/해외에 가는 것은

_____
_____

18. 더욱이/외국에 머무르는 비용은/매우 높다/비교하면/모국에 머무르는 것과

_____
_____

19. 그것뿐만 아니라/외국학생들은 직면할 수 있다/거대한 언어적이고 문화적인 장벽들

_____
_____

20. 이러한 것들 때문에/그것은 어려울 수 있다/그들이/외국의 환경에 적응하는 데/

_____
_____

21. 어떤 경우에는/그들은/경험한다/우울증과 향수병을/외국에 머물 때/공부하기 위해서

_____
_____

22. 따라서/영어를 공부하는 것은/외국에서/어렵고 힘든 도전일 수 있다

_____
_____

23. 요약하면/언어를 배우는 것은/영어권 나라에서/가지고 있다/장점과 단점들을

_____
_____

24. 내 의견으로는/영어를 공부하는 것은/거기에서/비록 부정적인 영향을 가지고 있지만/훨씬 더일 거 같다/좋은 영향을 끼치다/사람들의 배움에

_____
_____

25. 왜냐하면/그들은 기회를 갖다/영어 문화에/직접적으로 접근할 수 있는/사용할 것이다/영어를/더 자주/이런 상황에서

_____
_____

Answer

1. It is a well-known fact that English has become a universal language in recent years.
2. Accordingly, people around the world are keen to learn English more than other languages.
3. In this regard, some people argue that the most efficient way to learn English is to study in the English-speaking world.
4. Others, however, are against this idea.
5. In this essay, I will spell out both ideas.
6. On the one hand, it is clear-cut that learning English in an English-speaking country is an effective way of acquiring the language.
7. By being in such countries, international students could be more deeply exposed to English environment.
8. where they could gain a lot of opportunities to speak and listen to English,
9. , which could result in the rapid development of their language skills.
10. In addition to that, international students could be familiar with the culture, including people's lifestyles in English-speaking countries,
11. , which could give rise to a better understanding of culture and the development of language.
12. To give an illustration, a homestay program in a foreign country is a great experience to understand the lifestyle and develop their communication skill.
13. From this, learners mingle with the locals in different situations such as homestay families, communities and so on.
14. Therefore, the exposure to an English culture can improve immensely a command of the language.
15. On the other hand, it is believed that learning English in English-speaking countries can have an adverse influence on the students as well.
16. In reality, there are various materials and academics, which allow people to learn English in their country.
17. Thus, it is argued that it is not necessary for students to go abroad.
18. Moreover, the cost of staying overseas is extremely high compared to being in one's native country.
19. Not only that, international students can face immense linguistic and cultural barriers.
20. Due to which it can be hard for them to adjust to exotic surroundings.
21. In some cases, they experience depression and homesickness when they stay abroad to study.
22. Hence, learning English overseas could be a harsh and daunting challenge.
23. To sum up, learning English in the English-speaking world has both benefits and drawbacks.
24. In my view, studying English there, although having adverse effects, is far more likely to have beneficial impacts on people's learning
25. since they would have great opportunities to have direct access to English culture and use English more frequently under these circumstances.

You should spend about 40 minutes on this task.

Write about the following topic:

> **Some people believe that studying English in an English-speaking country is the best way to learn the language. What is your opinion?**

Give reasons for your answer and include any relevant examples from your own knowledge or experience.

Write at least 250 words.

Answer

It is a well-known fact that English has become a universal language in recent years. Accordingly, people around the world are keen to learn English more than other languages. In this regard, some people argue that the most efficient way to learn English is to study in the English-speaking world. Others, however, are against this idea. In this essay, I will spell out both ideas.

On the one hand, it is clear-cut that learning English in an English-speaking country is an effective way of acquiring the language. By being in such countries, international students could be more deeply exposed to English environment where they could gain a lot of opportunities to speak and listen to English, which could result in the rapid development of their language skills. In addition to that, international students could be familiar with the culture, including people's lifestyles in English-speaking countries, which could give rise to a better understanding of culture and the development of language. To give an illustration, a homestay program in a foreign country is a great experience to understand the lifestyle and develop their communication skill. From this, learners mingle with the locals in different situations such as homestay families, communities and so on. Therefore, the exposure to an English culture can improve immensely a command of the language.

On the other hand, it is believed that learning English in English-speaking countries can have an adverse influence on the students as well. In reality, there are various materials and academics, which allow people to learn English in their country. Thus, it is argued that it is not necessary for students to go abroad. Moreover, the cost of staying overseas is extremely high compared to being in one's native country. Not only that, international students can face immense linguistic and cultural barriers, due to which it can be hard for them to adjust to exotic surroundings. In some cases, they experience depression and homesickness when they stay abroad to study. Hence, learning English overseas could be a harsh and daunting challenge.

To sum up, learning English in the English-speaking world has both benefits and drawbacks. In my view, studying English there, although having adverse effects, is far more likely to have beneficial impacts on people's learning since they would have great opportunities to have direct access to English culture and use English more frequently under these circumstances.

4. Teenager's job

You should spend about 40 minutes on this task.

Write about the following topic:

> Recently, teenagers have tended to work while they are still students. Do the advantages of this trend outweigh the disadvantages?

Give reasons for your answer and include any relevant examples from your own knowledge or experience.

Write at least 250 words.

INTRODUCTION
요즘 십대들이 학교에 다니는 동안 직업을 갖는다.
긍정적이고 부정적인 측면이 있다.

BODY 1 (disadvantages)
1. 공부에 집중해야 함
2. 학교 활동에 집중해야 함

BODY 2 (advantages)
1. 일 경험은 미래를 설계하는 좋은 기회
2. 경제적인 부담을 덜 수 있음

CONCLUSION
일하는 것은 단점보다는 장점이 많으므로 일할 수 있는 기회를 제공해야 한다.

최근에 십대들은 그들이 학생일 때 직업을 갖는다. 이 경향에 대한 장점이 단점보다 크다고 생각하는가?

INTRODUCTION

요즘 일부회사에서 학교에 다니는 십대들을 고용하고 있는 것은 잘 알려진 사실이다. 이것과 관련해서, 어떤 사람들은 직업을 갖는 것은 십대들이 그들의 성인기를 대비하기 위해서 중요한 단계라고 주장한다. 나는 이 의견에 대해 부분적으로 동의한다. 다음이 몇 가지 이유이다.

BODY 1

일반적으로, 십대들은 학교에서 성적을 향상시키기 위해서 공부에 집중해야만 한다. 만약에 십대들이 직업을 갖는다면 피곤하거나 학업을 게을리하는 것은 당연하다. 그들이 매일 피로에 지쳐서 집에 돌아올 경우 과제나 시험을 위한 복습을 더 이상 할 시간이 없을지도 모른다. **이것에 덧붙여서, 십대들은 학교 활동에 참여하는 많은 기회를 가지고 있고 이것은 학교 밖에서 일하는 것보다 그들의 전반적인 성장을 발전시킬 수 있다.** 예를 들어 그들이 캠핑 그리고 대회 같은 과외활동에 참가할 수 있고, 그러한 것은 그들이 우정이나 협동심을 발전시키는 데 도움을 줄 수 있다. 이러한 이유들을 감안하면, 십대들이 학창시절 동안 직업을 갖는 게 아니라, 그들의 학교생활에 집중하는 것이 바람직하다.

BODY 2

그러나, 일하는 경험은 그들의 미래를 설계하는 데 훌륭한 기회이다. 사실상, 일하는 학생들은 다양한 지식과 정보를 풍부한 경험으로부터 얻을 수 있고 심지어 직업적인 기술까지 연마할 수 있다. 그들은 그들의 돈을 어떻게 관리하고 다양한 배경의 사람들과 어떻게 대화하는지를 배울 수 있다. 그것은 대학에서 전공을 결정하는 데 있어서 그리고 교육 후에 어떤 종류의 직업을 그들이 추구하고자 하는 것을 결정할 때 그들에게 매우 도움이 될 수 있다. 예를 들어, 몇몇의 학생들은 고등학교 때 레스토랑에서 보조로서 파트타임 일을 했다. 그 이후에 그들은 요리사가 되었다. 이처럼, 일 경험은 미래의 일을 결정하는 데 긍정적인 영향을 준다. **덧붙여서, 학생들은 그들의 대학 수업료와 필요한 경비들을 위해 돈을 저축할 수 있다.** 이것은 어느 정도 그들의 부모님의 재정적인 부담을 줄여준다. 이러한 이유들 때문에 학교에 다닐 때 직업을 갖는 것은 학생들의 미래를 위해 보람 있는 경험이다.

CONCLUSION

요약하면, 비록 몇 가지 단점들을 가지고 있지만, 학교 다니는 동안 일을 하는 것은 십대들에게 상당한 도움이 된다. 직업을 갖는 것은 학생들이 스스로 미래를 설계할 수 있고 그들의 대학교육을 재정적으로 지원하는 것을 가능하게 만들기 때문이다. 그러므로, 부모들과 선생님들은 그들이 일을 못하도록 하는 게 아니라 지지해야 한다.

문장에 필요한 어휘

> 1. It is a well-known fact that S+V; 잘 알려진 사실이다
> 2. a number of/numbers of/numerous/plenty of/a large number of/a good many; 많은 수
> 3. employ/hire/take on; 고용하다

요즘 일부회사에서 학교에 다니는 십대들을 고용하고 있는 것은 잘 알려진 사실이다.
It is a well-known fact that nowadays some workplaces employ teenagers who are still in school.

> 4. in this regard/in this respect/in this relation; 이것과 관련해서/이런 점에서
> 5. argue/believe/maintain/assert; 주장하다
> 6. significant/essential/important/critical/crucial/vital; 중요한
> 7. step/process/phrase/stage; 단계/과정
> 8. gear up for/prepare for/be ready for/make preparation for; ~에 대비하다/준비하다
> 9. adulthood/adult period; 성인기

이것과 관련해서, 어떤 사람들은 직업을 갖는 것은 십대들이 그들의 성인기를 대비하기 위해서 중요한 단계라고 주장한다.
In this regard, some people argue that taking a job is a significant step for teens to gear up for their adulthood.

> 10. agree with/be in favor of/be for/approve of/consent to; ~에 동의하다

나는 이 의견에 대해 부분적으로 동의한다. 다음이 그 몇 가지 이유이다.
I partially agree with this comment. The following are some of the reasons.

> 11. in general/generally/commonly; 일반적으로
> 12. should/had better/ought to/be supposed to; 해야 한다
> 13. focus on/concentrate on/pay more attention to +N; ~에 집중하다.
> 14. grades/results/marks; 성적
> 15. improve/better/advance/progress; 향상시키다

일반적으로, 십대들은 학교에서 그들의 성적을 향상시키기 위해서 그들의 공부에 집중해야만 한다.
In general, teens should focus on their studies to improve their grades in school.

16. It is natural(proper/rightful) that S+V; 당연하다
17. neglect their studies/make little efforts to do their schoolwork; 공부를 게을리하다
18. hold(have/get) a job/be in wor k; 직업을 갖다

만약에 그들이 직업을 갖는다면 그들이 피곤하거나 공부를 게을리하는 것은 당연하다.
It is natural for students to be tired and thus neglect their studies if they hold a job.

19. no longer; 더 이상 ~ 않다
20. assignments/home assignments; 과제
21. with exhaustion; 피로에 지쳐서

그들이 매일 피로에 지쳐서 집에 돌아올 경우 과제나 시험을 위한 복습을 더 이상 할 시간이 없을지도 모른다.
They may no longer have time to do their assignments or review for a test if they come home with exhaustion every day.

22. in addition to that/on top of that/not only that/additionally; 이것에 덧붙여서
23. have opportunities(chances/occasions) to; 기회를 갖다
24. attend(participate in/take part in) school activities; 학교 활동에 참가하다

이것에 덧붙여서, 십대들은 학교 활동에 참여하는 많은 기회를 가지고 있고,
In addition to that, teenagers have many opportunities to attend school activities,

25. boost/develop/stimulate/encourage/enhance/improve/raise; 촉진시키다/강화시키다
26. overall(general/whole) growth; 전반적인 성장

이것은 학교 밖에서 일하는 것보다 그들의 전반적인 성장을 더 발전시킬 수 있다.
, which could boost their overall growth rather than work outside of school.

27. for instance/for example/to illustrate/to give an illustration; 예를 들어
28. get involved in/take part in/participate in; 참가하다
29. extracurricular (after-school) activities; 과외활동

예를 들어, 그들이 캠핑 그리고 대회 같은 과외활동에 참가할 수 있고,
They could, for instance, get involved in extracurricular activities, including camping or competitions,

> 30. friendship and cooperation; 우정과 협동심

그러한 것은 그들이 우정이나 협동심을 발전시키는 데 도움을 줄 수 있다.
, which could help them develop friendship and cooperation.

> 31. given that; 감안할 때/고려하면
> 32. make sense/be logical/stands to reason; 이치에 맞다

이러한 이유들을 감안하면, 십대들이 그들의 학창시절 동안 직업을 구하는 게 아니고 그들의 학교생활에 집중하는 것이 바람직하다.
Given that these reasons, it makes sense for teenagers to concentrate on their school lives and not to find a job during their school years.

> 33. work experience; 직업 경험/일 경험

그러나, 일하는 경험은 그들의 미래를 설계하는 데 훌륭한 기회이다.
However, work experience is an excellent way for teenage students to plan their future.

> 34. in fact/as a matter of fact/virtually/actually; 사실상
> 35. acquire/get/catch/take/find; 얻다
> 36. a far-reaching (wide/broad) range (variety) of/various/diverse/varied; 다양한
> 37. a wealth of(a great deal of /rich) experience; 풍부한 경험
> 38. hone(work out/develop/advance) professional skill; 직업적인 기술을 연마하다/발전시키다

사실상, 일하는 학생들은 다양한 지식과 정보를 풍부한 경험으로부터 얻을 수 있고 심지어 직업적인 기술까지 연마할 수 있다.
In fact, students working can acquire a far-reaching range of knowledge and information from a wealth of experience, even honing their professional skills.

> 39. manage/handle/cope with/deal with; 다루다
> 40. backgrounds/circumstances/surroundings; 배경

그들은 돈을 어떻게 관리하고 다양한 배경의 사람들과 어떻게 대화하는지를 배울 수 있다.
They could learn how to manage money and communicate with people from various backgrounds.

41. a great help/a good help; 대단한 도움
42. make a decision about; ~에 대해 결정하다
43. major/specialty; 전공
44. pursue/seek/look for; 추구하다/찾다

그것은 또한 대학에서 전공을 결정하는 데 있어서 그리고 교육을 마친 이후에 그들이 추구하고자 하는 어떤 종류의 직업을 결정할 때 그들에게 매우 도움이 될 수 있다.

It could also be a great help to them in making decisions about their majors in college and what kinds of job they would like to pursue after education.

45. assistant; 보조

예를 들어, 몇몇의 학생들은 고등학교 때 레스토랑에서 보조로서 파트타임 일을 했다.

Some students, for example, worked part-time at a restaurant as assistants when they were in high school.

46. following that/after that; 그 후에
47. have positive(affirmative/great/significant) influences(effects/impacts) on; 긍정적인/상당한 영향을 주다

그 후에, 그들은 요리사가 되었다. 이처럼, 일 경험은 미래의 일을 결정하는 데 긍정적인 영향을 준다.

Following that, they became chefs. Like this, work experience could have positive influences on the determination of a future job.

48. can afford to+동사/be capable of+N/have power(energy) to +동사; 여력이 있다
49. tuition fees/school fees/tuition; 수업료
50. necessary expenses(costs); 필요경비

덧붙여서, 학생들은 그들의 대학 수업료와 필요한 경비들을 위해 돈을 저축할 여력이 있다.

Additionally, students could afford to save money for their tuition fees and necessary expenses in college,

51. somewhat/to some extent(degree)/more or less; 어느 정도
52. financial burden on the parents; 부모님의 재정적 부담
53. curtail/ease/lessen/lighten/reduce; 줄이다

이것은 어느 정도 그들의 부모님의 재정적인 부담이 줄어든다.

, which somewhat curtails the financial burden on the parents.

> 54. while (students are) in school; 학교에 다니는 동안
>   **Tip:** when/while/though/if/as if/wherever+ (S+V)+형용사/명사/분사/부사구
> 55. a rewarding experience; 보람 있는 경험

이러한 이유들 때문에 학교에 다니는 동안 직업을 갖는 것은 학생들의 미래를 위해 보람 있는 경험이다.
For all these reasons, having a job while in school is a rewarding experience for the students' future.

> 56. to sum up/in conclusion/in short; 요약하면
> 57. during the academic year/during the school year; 학기 중에
> 58. drawback/demerit/disadvantage; 단점
> 59. of benefit(of+추상명사=형용사); 이익이 되는/혜택이 되는
>   **Tip:** of importance =important/of value =valuable/of use =useful/of help=helpful

요약하면, 비록 몇 가지 단점들을 가지고 있지만, 학기 중에 일하는 것은, 십대들에게 상당히 도움이 된다.
To sum up, working during the academic year, although having a couple of drawbacks, is of great benefit to teenagers,

> 60. design/plan/project; 설계하다
> 61. on one's own/for oneself/without assistance; 스스로
> 62. financially/economically; 재정적으로
> 63. support/back/uphold; 지지하다

그것은 직업을 갖는다는 것은 학생들이 스스로 미래를 설계할 수 있고 그들의 대학교육을 재정적으로 지원하는 것을 가능하게 만들기 때문이다.
, which is why having a job makes it possible for students to design the future on their own and support their university education financially.

> 64. thus/therefore/consequently/as a result/in this context; 따라서/그러므로
> 65. deter(prevent/prohibit/stop/inhibit) A from B; A가 B하는 것을 막다

그러므로 부모들과 선생님들은 그들의 일을 못하게 하는 게 아니라, 그들을 지지해야 한다.
Thus, parents and teachers should not deter them from working but support them.

구문연습

1. 그것은 잘 알려진 사실이다/요즘/일부직장에서/십대들을 고용한다/학교에 다니는

_____
_____

2. 이것과 관련해서/어떤 사람들은 주장한다/직업을 갖는 것은/중요한 단계이다/십대들이/준비를 하기 위해서/그들의 성인기를

_____
_____

3. 나는 이 의견에 대해 부분적으로 동의한다/다음이 그 몇 가지 이유이다

_____
_____

4. 일반적으로/십대들은 집중해야만 한다/그들의 공부에/향상시키기 위해서/그들의 성적을/학교에서

_____
_____

5. 그것은 당연하다/학생들이/피곤해하고/그리고 게을리한다/그들의 교육을/만약 그들이 갖는다면/직업을

_____
_____

6. 그들은 더 이상 시간이 없을지도 모른다/과제를 할/또는 시험을 위한 복습을/만약 그들이 집에 온다면/피로에 지쳐서/매일

_____
_____

7. 이것에 덧붙여서/십대들은/많은 기회들을 가지고 있다/학교 활동들을 참여할

_____

_____

8. 그것은 발전시킨다/그들의 전반적인 성장을/학교 밖에서 일하는 것보다

_____

_____

9 그들은 할 수 있다/예를 들어/참가하다/과외 활동들에/캠핑이나 대회들을 포함해서

_____

_____

10. 이러한 것은 도울 수 있다/그들이 발전시키는 데/우정과 협동심을

_____

_____

11. 이러한 이유들을 감안하면/바람직하다/십대들이/집중하는 것은/그들의 학교 생활에/직업을 구하는 것이 아니라/학교생활 동안

_____

_____

12. 그러나/직업경험은/훌륭한 기회이다/십대 학생들이/미래를 계획하는 데

_____

_____

13. 사실상/일하는 학생들은/얻을 수 있다/다양한 지식과 정보들을/풍부한 경험으로부터/심지어 연마하다/직업적인 기술을

_____

_____

14. 그들은 배울 수 있다/어떻게 돈을 관리하고/사람과 대화하는 방법을/다양한 배경으로부터

_____
_____

15. 그것은 또한 매우 도움이 될 수 있다/그들이 결정하는 데 있어서/그들의 전공에 대해/대학에서/그리고 어떤 종류의 직업을/그들이 추구하고 싶은/교육 후

_____
_____

16. 몇몇의 학생들은/예를 들어/레스토랑에서 파트타임 일을 했다/보조로서/그들이 고등학교 때

_____
_____

17. 그 후에/그들은 요리사가 되었다/이처럼/일 경험은/긍정적인 영향을 준다/결정하는 데/미래의 직업을

_____
_____

18. 덧붙여서/학생들은 돈을 저축할 여력이 있다./그들의 수업료와 필요한 경비를 위해서/대학에서

_____
_____

19. 이것은/어느 정도/줄어든다./부모님들의 재정적 부담이

_____
_____

20. 이러한 이유들 때문에/직업을 갖는 것은/학교 다닐 동안/보람 있는 경험이다/학생들의 미래를 위해

_____
_____

4. Teenager's job

21. 요약하면/일을 한다는 것은/학교 시절 동안/비록 몇 가지 단점들을 가지고 있지만/상당한 도움이 된다/십대들에게

_____
_____

22. 그것은 이유이다/직업을 가지는 것은/가능하게 만든다/학생들이/미래를 계획하는 데/스스로/그리고 지원하다/그들의 대학교육을/재정적으로

_____
_____

23. 그러므로/부모님들과 선생님들은/그들이 일하는 것을 저지하는 것이 아니라/그들을 지원해야 한다

_____
_____

Answer

1. It is a well-known fact that nowadays some workplaces employ teenagers who are still in school.
2. In this regard, some people argue that taking a job is a significant step for teens to gear up for their adulthood.
3. I partially agree with this comment. The following are some of the reasons.
4. In general, teens should focus on their studies to improve their grades in school.
5. It is natural for students to be tired and thus neglect their studies if they hold a job.
6. They may no longer have time to do their assignments or review for a test if they come home with exhaustion every day.
7. In addition to that, teenagers have many opportunities to attend school activities,
8. , which could boost their overall growth rather than work outside of school.
9. They could, for instance, get involved in extracurricular activities, including camping or competitions,
10. , which could help them develop friendship and cooperation.
11. Given these reasons, it makes sense for teenagers to concentrate on their school lives and not to find a job during their school years.
12. However, work experience is an excellent chance for teenage students to plan their future.
13. In fact, students working can acquire a far-reaching range of knowledge and information from a wealth of experience, even honing their professional skills.
14. They could learn how to manage money and communicate with people from various backgrounds.
15. It could also be a great help to them in making decisions about their majors in college and what kinds of job they would like to pursue after education.
16. Some students, for example, worked part-time at a restaurant as assistants when they were in high school.
17. Following that, they become chefs. Like this, work experience could have positive influences on the determination of a future job.
18. Additionally, students could afford to save money for their tuition fees and necessary expenses in college,
19. , which somewhat curtails the financial burden on the parents.
20. For all these reasons, having a job while in school is a rewarding experience for the students' future.
21. To sum up, working during the academic year, although having a couple of drawbacks, is of great benefit to teenagers,
22. , which is why having a job makes it possible for students to design the future on their own and support their university education financially.
23. Thus, parents and teachers should not deter them from working but support them.

You should spend about 40 minutes on this task.

Write about the following topic:

> **Recently, teenagers have tended to work while they are still students. Do the advantages of this trend outweigh the disadvantages?**

Give reasons for your answer and include any relevant examples from your own knowledge or experience.

Write at least 250 words.

Answer

It is a well-known fact that nowadays some workplaces employ teenagers who are still in school. In this regard, some people argue that taking a job is a significant step for teens to gear up for their adulthood. I partially agree with this comment. The following are some of the reasons.

In general, teens should focus on their studies to improve their grades in school. It is natural for students to be tired and thus neglect their studies if they hold a job. They may no longer have time to do their assignments or review for a test if they come home with exhaustion every day. **In addition to that, teenagers have many opportunities to attend school activities**, which could boost their overall growth rather than work outside of school. They could, for instance, get involved in extracurricular activities, including camping or even competitions, which could help them develop friendship and cooperation. Given that these reasons, it makes sense for teenagers to concentrate on their school lives and not to find a job during their school years.

However, work experience is an excellent chance for teenage students to plan their future. In fact, students working can acquire a far-reaching range of knowledge and information from a wealth of experience, even honing their professional skills. They could learn how to manage money and communicate with people from various backgrounds. It could also be a great help to them in making decisions about their majors in college and what kinds of job they would like to pursue after education. Some students, for example, worked part-time at a restaurant as assistants when they were in high school. Following that, they became chefs. Like this, work experience could have positive influences on the determination of a future job. **Additionally, students could afford to save money for their tuition fees and necessary expenses in college**, which somewhat curtails the financial burden on the parents. For all these reasons, having a job while in school is a rewarding experience for the students' future.

To sum up, working during the academic year, although having a couple of drawbacks, is of great benefit to teenagers, which is why having a job makes it possible for students to design the future on their own and support their university education financially. Thus, parents and teachers should not deter them from working but support them.

5. Practical skill in University

You should spend about 40 minutes on this task.

Write about the following topic:

> Many people believe that universities should offer theoretical knowledge rather than give vocational training to students. Do you agree or disagree?

Give reasons for your answer and include any relevant examples from your own knowledge or experience.

Write at least 250 words.

INTRODUCTION

대학에서의 이론교육과 기술교육에 대한 논쟁이 있다.

개인적으로 기술교육이 더 필요하다고 생각한다. 다음은 이유들이다.

BODY 1 (disagree)

1. 학생 측면에서
   → 직업을 얻을 기회가 많다.

BODY 2 (disagree)

1. 회사 측면에서
   → 시간과 비용을 절약(신입사원교육)

CONCLUSION

대학이 이론교육보다는 직업교육에 집중해야 한다.

많은 사람들은 대학들은 실습보다는 이론적인 지식을 제공해야만 한다고 생각한다. 동의하는지 또는 동의하지 않은지?

INTRODUCTION

사회가 발전함에 따라, 회사들은 전보다는 실용적인 기술을 가진 전문적이고 수준 높은 근로자들이 필요하다. 이러한 점에서 어떤 사람들은 대학들은 학생들에게 완전히 이론적인 지식을 교육시키는 대신에 실질적인 기술을 가르쳐야 한다고 주장한다. 나는 동일한 생각을 가지고 있고 이유는 다음과 같다.

BODY 1

학생들과 관련해서는, 직업 교육을 받은 대학 졸업생들은 더 많은 직업 기회를 갖는 경향이 있다. 다시 말해서, 그들은 다양한 기술을 요구하는 회사에서 특별한 일을 어떻게 다루는지를 알기 때문에 경쟁력에서 이점을 갖는다. 많은 고용주들이 실용적인 기술들을 가진 지원자의 고용을 선호하는 것은 사실이다. 이런 이유 때문에, 많은 학생들은 더 빨리 직업을 구하기 위해서 기술대학으로 바꾸고 있다. 인문대학은 주로 학문적 수업에 주력하기 때문에 인문대학을 졸업한 졸업생들이 이공계대학의 졸업생들보다 보수가 좋은 직업에 대한 낮은 가능성을 가지고 있다는 연구가 있다. 발전하는 기술과 함께, 이러한 상황은 더욱더 심화될 것이다. 그러므로, 대학이 학생들에게 실기교육을 제공하는 것은 더 나은 선택이다.

BODY 2

회사들 측면에서 말하자면, 그들은 신입사원 교육으로부터 발생되는 시간과 경비를 절약할 수 있다. 사실상, 회사는 신규 채용 후 직업훈련을 제공하고 있고, 이러한 것은 신입사원이나 고용주들에게 도움이 되지만 개인적 그리고 사회적 낭비일 수 있다. 만약 대학들이 직업훈련을 제공한다면 회사의 비용이 줄어들 것이고, 근로자들은 학교에서 배운 기술을 가지고 그들의 일에서 능력을 활용하고 발전시킬 것이다. 또한 이러한 것들은 회사들이 힘든 상황에서 생존할 수 있게 하고 사업분야에서 변화하는 요구에 따라갈 수 있게 할 것이다.

CONCLUSION

결론은, 이러한 모든 것을 고려할 때, 직업교육은 대학 졸업생들과 회사에게 몇 가지 이점을 가지고 있다. 왜냐하면, 그것은 학생들에게 미래에 가치 있는 직업을 갖게 하고 회사들은 비용을 절감할 수 있기 때문이다. 그러므로, 대학들과 관련된 사람들이 대학에서의 직업교육에 더 많은 관심을 갖는 것이 설득력이 있다.

문장에 필요한 어휘

> 1. specialized and sophisticated/professional and high-quality; 전문적이고 수준 높은
> 2. employee/worker/laborer; 근로자
> 3. practical/real/professional/useful/vocational/occupational; 실용적인
> 4. than ever before/than before/than in the past; 전보다/과거보다

사회가 발전함에 따라, 회사들은 전보다는 실용적인 기술을 가진 전문적이고 수준 높은 근로자들이 필요하다.

As society develops, companies need specialized and sophisticated employees with practical skills more than ever before.

> 5. in this respect/in this light/in this regard; 이런 점에서
> 6. argue/state/stress/believe/suggest; 주장한다

이러한 점에서, 어떤 사람들은 대학들은 학생들에게 완전히 이론적인 지식을 교육시키는 대신에 실질적인 기술을 가르쳐야 한다고 주장한다.

In this respect, some people argue that universities should teach real skills to students instead of educating them with throughly theoretical knowledge.

> 7. reasons/causes/factors/culprits; 이유들
> 8. as follows; 다음과 같다

나는 동일한 생각을 가지고 있고 이유는 다음과 같다.

I have the same idea, and the reasons are as follows.

> 9. concerning/regarding/as regards/with respect to; ~에 관련해서
> 10. graduates; 졸업생들
> 11. tend to/have a tendency to/be liable to/be inclined to; ~하는 경향이 있다
> 12. obtain(gain/have) opportunities(chances/occasions); 기회를 얻다

학생들과 관련해서, 직업교육을 받은 대학 졸업생들은 더 많은 직업기회를 갖는 경향이 있다.

Concerning students, university college graduates who have received vocational training tend to obtain more job opportunities.

> 13. in other words/to put it another way/that is/that is to say; 다시 말해서
> 14. have an edge in/have an advantage in; 이점을 갖는다.
> 15. handle/manage/deal with/cope with; 다루다
> 16. require/claim/demand; 요구하다
> 17. various skills/a variety of techniques; 다양한 기술

다시 말해서, 그들은 다양한 기술을 요구하는 회사에서 특별한 일을 어떻게 다루는지를 알기 때문에 경쟁력에서 이점을 갖는다.

In other words, they have an edge in competitiveness because they know how to handle specific tasks in companies that require various skills.

> 18. it is true that/it is clear that/it is certain that S+V; 사실이다
> 19. prefer to; 선호하다
> 20. employer/hirer; 고용주
> 21. applicant/job seeker; 지원자/구직자

많은 고용주들이 실용적인 기술들을 가진 지원자의 고용을 선호하는 것은 사실이다.

It is true that many employers prefer to hire applicants with practical skills.

> 22. for/due to/on account of/owing to/because of+N 구; 때문에
> 23. shift/transmit/move; 옮기다
> 24. land(obtain/have/gain) a job/look for (seek) employment; 직장을 구하다

이런 이유 때문에, 많은 학생들은 더 빨리 직업을 구하기 위해서 기술대학으로 바꾸고 있다.

For this reason, many students are shifting to technical colleges to land a job more quickly.

> 25. a liberal art college/a college of liberal arts; 문과대학
> 26. a college of science; 이과대학

인문대학을 졸업한 졸업생들이 이공계대학의 졸업생들보다 보수가 좋은 직업에 대한 낮은 가능성을 가지고 있다는 연구가 있다.

There is research that graduates from liberal arts colleges have a lower likelihood of a well-paid job than those from a college of science

> 27. focus on/concentrate on/pay attention to; 주력하다/집중하다

인문대학은 주로 학문적 수업에 주력하기 때문에.

since liberal arts colleges mainly focus on academic lectures.

> 28. intensify/strengthen/enhance/solidify; 심화하다/강화하다

발전하는 기술과 함께, 이러한 상황은 더욱더 심화될 것이다.
With developing technologies, this situation will be much more intensified.

> 29. therefore/thus/as a result/consequently/hence/in this context; 그러므로/따라서
> 30. offer/provide/give; 제공하다

그러므로, 대학이 학생들에게 실기교육을 제공하는 것은 더 나은 선택이다.
Therefore, it is a better option for universities to offer practical training to students.

> 31. when it comes to/in terms of/in the case of/in light of; ~에 대해 말하자면

회사들 측면에서 말하자면, 그들은 신입사원 교육으로부터 발생되는 시간과 경비를 절약할 수 있다
When it comes to companies, they can save time and cost resulting from training recruits.

> 32. vocational(professional/occupational) training; 직업훈련
> 33. be of benefit to; ~에 유익하다

사실상, 회사는 신규 채용 후 직업훈련을 제공하고 있고, 이러한 것은 신입사원이나 고용주들에게 도움이 된다.
In fact, they have provided vocational training after hiring new workers, which is of benefit to both new employees and employers.

> 34. personal/individual/private; 개인적인
> 35. waste/loss/damage; 낭비/손실

그러나, 개인적이고 사회적인 낭비일 수 있다.
However, it can be a personal and social waste.

> 36. provided (that)/on condition that/providing S+V; 만약 ~이라면/~하는 조건이라면
> 37. exploit(harness/tap into/utilize/display/use) abilities; 능력을 이용하다
> 38. develop/better/improve/advance; 발전시키다

만약 대학들이 직업훈련을 제공한다면, 회사의 비용이 줄어들 것이고, 근로자들은 학교에서 배운 기술을 가지고 그들의 일에서 능력을 활용하고 발전시킬 것이다.

Provided that universities offer professional training, companies' expenses will be reduced, and employees will exploit and develop their abilities in their businesses with skills gained in schools,

> 39. enable A to B; A가 B하는 것을 가능하게 하다
> 40. harsh(terrible/desperate) circumstances(conditions/situations); 힘든 상황
> 41. keep up with/catch up with/keep pace with; 보조를 맞추다

또한 이러한 것은 회사들이 힘든 상황에서 생존할 수 있게 하고 사업분야에서 변화하는 요구에 따라갈 수 있게 할 것이다.

, which would also enable companies to survive in harsh circumstances and keep up with the changing demands of the business area.

> 42. in conclusion/to sum up/to conclude; 결론은
> 43. all things considered; 모든 상황을 고려할 때

결론은, 모든 상황을 고려할 때, 직업교육은 대학 졸업생들과 회사들에게 몇 가지 이점을 가지고 있다.

To conclude, all things considered, vocational education has several benefits for university graduates and companies,

> 44. decent job(occupation); 가치 있는 직업
> 45. in the future/someday/down the road; 앞으로/언젠가는
> 46. curtail/cut back on/cut down on/reduce/lessen; 줄이다

왜냐하면, 그것은 학생들에게 미래에 가치 있는 직업을 갖게 하고 회사들은 비용을 절감할 수 있기 때문이다

, since it allows students to have decent jobs in the future, and companies can curtail costs.

> 47. compelling/persuasive/convincing; 설득력이 있는
> 48. pay attention to/take an interest in/get interested in; 관심을 갖다

그러므로, 대학들과 관련된 사람들이 대학에서의 직업교육에 더 많은 관심을 갖는 것이 설득력이 있다.

Hence, it is compelling for universities and people involved to pay more attention to professional education in universities.

구문연습

1. 사회가 발전함에 따라서/회사들은/필요하다/전문적이고 수준 높은 근로자들을/실용적인 기술을 가진/전보다는

_____
_____

2. 어떤 사람들은/주장한다/대학들은/가르쳐야 한다고/실용적인 기술들을/학생들에게/그들을 교육하는 것 대신에/완전하게 이론적인 지식을 가지고

_____
_____

3. 나는 동일한 생각을 가지고 있다/그리고 그 이유는/다음과 같다.

_____
_____

4. 학생들과 관련해서/대학 졸업생들은/직업교육을 받아온/경향이 있다/더 많은 직업기회를 갖는

_____
_____

5. 다시 말해서/그들은 이점을 갖는다/경쟁력에서/왜냐하면/그들은 알기 때문이다/어떻게 다루는지를/특별한 일을/회사에서

_____
_____

6. 회사는 요구한다/다양한 기술들을

_____
_____

7. 그것은 사실이다/많은 고용주들이/고용하는 것을 선호한다/지원자들을/다양한 기술을 가진

_____

_____

8. 이런 이유 때문에/많은 학생들은/바꾸고 있다/기술대학으로/직업을 얻기 위해서/더 빨리

_____

_____

9. 연구가 있다/문과 대학 졸업생들은/낮은 가능성을 가지고 있다/보수가 좋은 직업에 대한/이공계대학 졸업생들보다

_____

_____

10. 왜냐하면/인문대학은/주로/집중하기 때문이다/학문적인 수업들에

_____

_____

11. 발전하는 기술과 함께/이러한 상황은/더욱 더 심화될 것이다

_____

_____

12. 그러므로/이것은 나은 선택이다/대학들이/실기 교육을 제공하는 것/학생들에게

_____

_____

13. 회사에 대해 말하자면/그들은 절약할 수 있다/시간과 비용/~부터 발생된/신입사원 훈련

_____

_____

14. 사실상/제공해오고 있다/직업교육을/고용한 후에/신입사원들을

15. 이러한 것은/도움이 된다/둘 다/신입사원들과 고용주들

16. 그러나/이것은 일 수 있다/개인적 그리고 사회적 낭비

17. 만약 대학들이/제공한다/직업 훈련을/그 회사의 비용이/줄어들 것이고/근로자들은 활용하고 발전시킬 것이다/그들의 능력을/그들의 일에서/학교에서 배운 기술을 가지고

18. 이것은 또한 가능하게 할 것이다/회사들이/살아남을 수 있게 하고/힘든 상황에서/그리고 뒤쳐지지 않게 한다/변화하는 요구에/사업분야에서의

19. 결론은/모든 상황을 고려할 때/직업 교육은/몇 가지 이점들을 가지고 있다/졸업생들과 회사들에게/왜냐하면 그것은 허락한다/그들이 남부럽지 않은 직장을 갖는 것을/앞으로/회사들은 절약할 수 있다/비용을

20. 그러므로/설득력이 있다/대학들과 관련된 사람들이/관심을 갖는 것이/기술 교육에/대학에서

Answer

1. As society develops, companies need specialized and sophisticated employees with practical skills more than ever before.
2. In this respect, some people argue that universities should teach real skills to students instead of educating them with throughly theoretical knowledge.
3. I have the same idea, and the reasons are as follows.
4. Concerning students, university/college graduates who have received vocational training tend to obtain more job opportunities.
5. In other words, they have an edge in competitiveness because they know how to handle specific tasks in companies.
6. Companies require various skills.
7. It is true that many employers prefer to hire applicants with practical skills.
8. For this reason, many students are shifting to technical colleges to land a job more quickly.
9. There is research that graduates from liberal arts colleges have a lower likelihood of a well-paid job than those from a college of science
10. since liberal arts colleges mainly focus on academic lectures.
11. With developing technologies, this situation will be much more intensified.
12. Therefore, it is a better option for universities to offer practical training to students.
13. When it comes to companies, they can save time and cost resulting from training recruits.
14. In fact, they have provided vocational training after hiring new workers,
15. , which is of benefit to both new employees and employers.
16. However, it can be a personal and social waste.
17. Provided that universities offer professional training, companies' expenses will be reduced, and employees exploit and develop their abilities in their businesses with skills gained in schools,
18. , which also would enable companies to survive in harsh circumstances and keep up with the changing demands of the business area.
19. In conclusion, all things considered, vocational education has several benefits for university graduates and companies,
20. , since it allows students to have decent jobs in the future and companies can curtail costs.
21. Hence, it is compelling for universities and people involved to pay more attention to professional training in universities.

You should spend about 40 minutes on this task.

Write about the following topic:

> **Many people believe that universities should offer theoretical knowledge rather than give vocational training to students. Do you agree or disagree?**

Give reasons for your answer and include any relevant examples from your own knowledge or experience.

Write at least 250 words.

Answer

As society develops, companies need specialized and sophisticated employees with practical skills more than ever before. In this respect, some people argue that universities should teach real skills to students instead of educating them with throughly theoretical knowledge. I have the same idea, and the reasons are as follows.

Concerning students, university/college graduates who have received vocational training tend to have more job opportunities. In other words, they have an edge in competitiveness because they know how to handle specific tasks in companies that require various skills. It is true that many employers prefer to hire applicants with practical skills. For this reason, many students are shifting to technical colleges to land a job more quickly. There is research that graduates from liberal arts colleges have a lower likelihood of a well-paid job than those from a college of science since liberal arts colleges mainly focus on academic lectures. With developing technologies, this situation will be much more intensified. Therefore, it is a better option for universities to offer practical training to students.

When it comes to companies, they can save time and cost resulting from training recruits. In fact, they have provided vocational training after hiring new workers, which is of benefit to both new employees and employers. However, it can be a personal and social waste. Provided that universities offer professional training, companies' expenses will be reduced, and employees will exploit and develop their abilities in their businesses with skills gained in schools, which would also enable companies to survive in harsh circumstances and keep up with the changing demands of the business area.

In conclusion, all things considered, vocational education has several benefits for university graduates and companies, since it allows students to have decent jobs in the future, and companies can curtail costs. Hence, it is compelling for universities and people involved to pay more attention to professional training in universities.

IELTS *Easy Writing*

Unit 3

Social issues

1. Overpopulation
2. Financial support
3. The crime rate
4. The death penalty

1. Overpopulation

You should spend about 40 minutes on this task.

Write about the following topic:

> Overpopulation of urban areas has led to numerous problems. Identify serious ones and suggest ways that governments and individuals can tackle these problems.

Give reasons for your answer and include any relevant examples from your own knowledge or experience.

Write at least 250 words.

INTRODUCTION

대도시에서의 과잉 인구는 중대한 문제이다.

이 에세이는 그 이유들과 해법들을 제시할 것이다.

BODY 1 (problems)

1. 삶의 질 저하
2. 실업의 증가
3. 환경적 피해

BODY 2 (solutions)

1. 주택문제 해결
2. 지역산업 발전
3. 교통시스템 정비(환경문제)

CONCLUSION

큰 도시에서 인구과잉에 의한 문제는 심각하다. 정부와 사람들이 책임을 공유하면 문제를 해결할 것이다.

도시의 과잉인구는 많은 문제들을 야기하고 있다. 몇 가지 중대한 문제점들과 정부와 개인들이 이 문제들을 해결할 수 있는 방법들을 밝히라.

INTRODUCTION

세계의 대부분 지역에서, 인구는 놀랍도록 증가하고 있고 주로 주요도시에 널리 퍼져 있다. 그리고 그것은 세계의 가장 큰 걱정 중의 하나가 되고 있다. 국민과 정부는 이 문제를 심각하게 고려해야만 한다. 이 에세이는 과잉 인구에 대한 해법들과 함께 문제들을 제시할 것이다.

BODY 1

몇 가지 문제들이 인구과잉 때문에 발생한다. 우선, 인구과잉은 많은 도시에서 삶의 질을 악화시킨다. 한 가지 예로써, 비위생적인 상태에서의 인구과밀과 주거는 중대한 건강문제들을 만들어 내고 질병들을 일으킨다. **계속되는 인구증가의 다른 심각한 결과는 실업의 증가이다.** 이것은 범죄율 증가를 초래한다. 왜냐하면, 일부 사람들은 실업에 의해 발생된 가난으로부터 벗어나기 위해서 범죄를 택하기 때문이다. **마지막으로, 과잉 인구에 의해서 일어난 환경적인 피해가 심각하다.** 그것은 큰 도시들에서의 급격한 차량의 증가는 교통문제뿐만 아니라 이산화탄소 배출로 인한 공기 오염을 발생시키기 때문이다. 이와 같이, 도시 인구의 과도한 증가는 몇 가지 부정적인 측면을 가지고 있다.

BODY 2

해법에 대해 말하자면, 시민들과 정부는 큰 도시에서의 인구과잉을 해결하기 위한 실행 가능한 조치를 해야 한다. 정부는 **주택 문제를 해결**해야 한다. 특히 도시 인구의 분산을 위해서 주요도시 외곽에 거주지역을 확장해서 주택 문제를 해결해야 한다. **실업 문제에 대해서는**, 정부는 인구를 분산하기 위해서 지역사회에 산업을 촉진하고 고용을 증진시켜야 한다. 이러한 것은 주요한 도시에서의 실업과 범죄율 또한 낮춰준다. 마지막으로, 인구과잉에 따른 **환경문제를 해결하기 위해서**, 시민들은 그들의 차보다 버스나 지하철 같은 대중교통을 이용해야만 한다. 이를 위해서, 시민들이 그들을 편리하게 이용할 수 있도록 잘 정비된 대중교통시스템을 만들어야 한다 서울을 예로 들면, 교통혼잡과 서울에서의 인구집중을 완화시키기 위해서 지하철 시스템이 잘 정비되어오고 있다. 그 결과, 교통문제 뿐만 아니라 대기오염문제도 어느 정도 해결하는 데 도움이 되고 있다.

CONCLUSION

결론적으로, 도시에서의 인구과잉에 의해 야기된 문제들이 매우 광범위한 것은 분명하다. 만약 사람들과 정부가 위에서 언급한 방법으로 책임을 공유한다면, 그들은 인구 과잉으로부터 문제들을 해결할 것이다.

문장에 필요한 어휘

---

1. be on the rise/be on the increase; 증가하고 있다
2. alarmingly/amazingly/surprisingly/startlingly; 놀랍도록
3. prevalent/general; 널리 퍼진/일반적인
4. mainly/predominantly/mostly; 주로

세계의 대부분 지역에서, 인구는 놀랍도록 증가하고 있고 주로 주요도시에 널려 퍼져 있다.

In most parts of the world, the population has been alarmingly on the rise and mainly prevalent in major cities,

---

5. concern/problem/difficulty/worry; 걱정

그리고 그것은 세계의 가장 큰 걱정 중의 하나가 되고 있다.

, and it has become one of the world's biggest concerns.

---

6. take A into account/take A into consideration/consider A/think over A; A를 고려하다

국민들과 정부들은 심각하게 이 문제를 고려해야만 한다.

Individuals and governments have to take this issue into account seriously.

---

7. present/represent/show/introduce; 제시하다
8. problem/cause/reason/ground; 이유/문제
9. along with/in company with/coupled with; ~와 함께/결부된
10. solution/approach/answer/alternative/option; 해법

이 에세이는 과잉 인구에 대한 해법들과 함께 문제들을 제시할 것이다.

This essay will present the problems of overpopulation along with solutions.

---

11. a couple of/several/a few; 몇 가지
12. come about/take place/break out/occur/generate; 발생하다/일어나다
13. because of/due to/owing to/on account of; ~때문에

몇 가지 문제들이 인구과잉 때문에 발생한다.

A couple of main problems come about because of overpopulation.

14. first of all/first and foremost/to begin with; 우선
15. deteriorate/become worse/aggravate/compromise; 악화시키다/악화되다

우선, 인구과잉은 많은 도시에서 삶의 질을 악화시킨다.
First of all, overpopulation deteriorates the quality of living in many cities.

16. for one thing/for instance/for example/to illustrate; 예를 들어
17. overcrowding; 과밀/혼잡
18. poor sanitation(hygiene); 열악한 위생
19. significant/serious/heavy/grave; 중대한
20. illness/disease/sickness; 질병

한 예로써, 인구 과밀과 열악한 위생시설을 갖춘 주거는 중대한 건강문제들을 만들어 내고 질병들을 일으킬 수 있다.
For one thing, overcrowding and housing with poor sanitation cause significant health problems, bringing about illnesses.

21. serious result/grave consequence; 심각한 결과
22. ever- growing population/ever-increasing population; 계속 증가하는 인구
23. the rise of unemployment; 실업증가

계속되는 인구증가의 다른 심각한 결과는 실업의 증가이다.
Another serious result of an ever-growing population is the rise of unemployment,

24. lead to/give rise to/result in/bring about+ N; 야기하다/초래하다
25. an increasing crime rate; 증가하는 범죄율
26. escape from; ~으로부터 벗어나다
27. caused by/generated by/originated by resulting from; ~에 의해 야기된
28. unemployment/joblessness; 실업

이것은 범죄율 증가를 초래한다. 왜냐하면, 일부 사람들은 실업에 의해 발생된 가난으로부터 벗어나기 위해서 범죄를 택하기 때문이다.
, which could lead to an increasing crime rate because some choose crimes to escape from poverty caused by unemployment.

> 29. environmental damage(impact); 환경적 피해
> 30. considerable/high/significant; 상당한

마지막으로, 과잉 인구에 의해서 일어난 환경적인 피해가 심각하다.
Lastly, the environmental damage generated by overpopulation is considerable.

> 31. carbon dioxide emission 이산화탄소 배출

그것은 큰 도시들에서의 급격한 차량의 증가는 교통문제뿐만 아니라 이산화탄소로 인한 공기 오염을 발생시키기 때문이다.
It is because the rapid increase in vehicles in large cities gives rise to air pollution resulting from carbon dioxide emission as well as traffic problem.

> 32. like this/in this way; 이와 같이/이렇게 하여
> 33. adverse/negative/minus; 부정적인

이와 같이, 도시인구의 과도한 증가는 몇 가지 부정적인 측면을 가지고 있다.
Like this, the excessive growth of urban population has some adverse aspects.

> 34. when it comes to/in light of/with respect to/as regards+N; ~에 대해 말하자면
> 35. feasible/workable/viable/practicable; 실행 가능한
> 36. take steps(measures/actions); 조치를 취하다
> 37. settle/tackle/address/solve/resolve/sort out; 해결하다

해법에 대해 말하자면, 사람들과 정부들은 대도시에서의 인구과잉을 해결하기 위한 실행 가능한 조치를 해야 한다.
When it comes to solutions, individuals and governments should take feasible steps to settle excess population in big cities.

> 38. housing problem; 주택문제

정부는 대도시에서 주택문제를 해결해야 한다.
Governments should sort out the housing problem.

> 39. in particular/particularly/specially/especially; 특별히
> 40. expand/enlarge/widen; 확장하다
> 41. residential districts(areas); 거주 지역들
> 42. population decentralization; 인구의 분산
> 43. in the outskirts of ~/in the suburbs of; ~의 근교에

특히 도시 인구의 분산을 위해서 주요도시 외곽에 거주지역을 확장해서 주택 문제를 해결해야 한다.

In particular, they ought to expand the residential districts for population decentralization on the outskirts of the main urban cities.

> 44. employment/hiring; 고용
> 45. disperse/decentralize; 분산시키다

실업문제에 대해서는, 정부는 인구를 분산하기 위해서 특히 지역 사회에 산업을 촉진하고 고용을 증진시켜야 한다.

In light of the unemployment problem, governments should boost industries and promote employment, especially in local areas to disperse population,

> 46. unemployment; 실업
> 47. as well/too/also/likewise; 또한

이러한 것은 실업과 대도시에서의 범죄율을 또한 낮출 수 있다.

, which can lower unemployment and the crime rate in the major cities as well.

> 48. citizens/the public/individuals/the general public; 시민/대중
> 49. had better/should/ought to/be supposed to; 해야만 한다
> 50. public transportation/public transport; 대중교통
> 51. rather than; 보다 오히려

마지막으로, 인구과잉에 의한 환경문제와 관련해서, 시민들은 그들의 차보다 버스나 지하철 같은 대중교통을 이용해야만 한다.

Finally, as regards environmental concerns from overpopulation, citizens had better use public transport like buses and underground rather than their cars.

> 52. to this end/to that end; 이것을 위해서
> 53. well-organized/well-maintained; 잘 정비된

이를 위해서, 시민들이 그들을 편리하게 이용할 수 있도록 잘 정비된 대중교통시스템을 만들어야 한다.

To this end, governments are supposed to build a well-organized transportation system for citizens to use them conveniently.

> 54. ease/reduce/relieve/alleviate; 완화시키다
> 55. the concentration of population; 인구집중
> 56. traffic congestion/traffic jam; 교통혼잡

서울을 예로 들면, 교통혼잡과 서울에서의 인구집중을 완화시키기 위해서 교통 시스템이 잘 정비되어오고 있다.

Take Seoul, for example, where the traffic system has been well-maintained to lessen the concentration of population and the traffic congestion.

> 57. as a result/in consequence; 그 결과
> 58. of help/helpful; 도움이 되는
> 59. to some extent/to some degree/somewhat/more or less; 어느 정도

그 결과, 어느 정도 교통 문제뿐만 아니라 대기오염 문제도 해결하는 데 도움이 되고 있다.

As a result, its policy is of help to solve not only air pollution but also traffic problems to some extent.

> 60. in conclusion; 결론적으로
> 61. it is clear-cut that/it is certain that/there is no doubt that S+V; 분명하다
> 62. urban areas/city areas/metro regions; 도시 지역들
> 63. far-reaching/far-flung/extensive; 광범위한

결론적으로, 도시에서의 인구과잉에 의해 야기된 문제들이 광범위한 것은 분명하다.

In conclusion, it is clear-cut that the problems caused by overpopulation in urban areas are far-reaching.

> 64. share responsibility; 책임을 공유한다

만약 사람들과 정부가 위에서 언급한 방법으로 책임을 공유한다면, 그들은 인구과잉으로부터 문제들을 해결할 것이다.

If individuals and governments share responsibility in the way mentioned above, they will resolve the difficulties of overpopulation.

구문연습

1. 세계의 대부분 지역에서/인구는/놀랍도록/증가해 오고 있다/그리고 주로/널리 퍼져 있다/주요도시에

2. 그것은 되고 있다/가장 큰 걱정 중에 하나/세계에서

3. 정부와 국민들은/고려해야만 한다/이 문제를/심각하게

4. 이 에세이는/제시할 것이다/문제들을/인구과잉의/해법과 함께

5. 몇 가지 문제들이/발생한다/인구과잉 때문에

6. 우선/인구과잉은/악화시키다/삶의 질을/많은 도시에서

7. 한 예로써/인구과밀과 주거/열악한 위생시설을 갖춘/야기한다/중대한 건강문제/질병들을 일으킨다

8. 다른 심각한 결과는/계속 증가하는 인구의/실업의 증가이다

9. 그것은/초래한다/범죄율 증가를/왜냐하면/일부 사람들은 택하기 때문이다/범죄를/벗어나기 위해서/가난으로부터/실업에 의해 발생된

10. 마지막으로/환경적인 피해가/인구과잉에 의해 야기된/상당하다

11. 그것은 때문이다/급격한 차량의 증가는/큰 도시에서/발생시킨다/공기 오염/이산화탄소 배출로 인한/뿐만 아니라/교통문제들

12. 이와 같이/도시에서의 과도한 인구증가는/가지고 있다/몇 가지의 부정적인 측면들을

13. 해법에 대해 말하자면/정부들과 사람들은/실행 가능한 조치를 해야 한다/해결하기 위해서/인구 과잉을/큰 도시에서의

14. 정부는 해결해야 한다/주택문제를

15. 특히/그들은 확장시켜야 한다/거주지역을/인구분산을 위해서/주요도시의 외곽에

16. 실업문제에 대해 말하자면/정부들은/산업을 발전시키고/고용을 촉진해야 한다/특히/지방에/인구를 분산시키기 위해서

17. 이것은 낮출 수 있다/실업을/그리고 범죄율/큰 도시들에서/또한

18. 마지막으로/환경문제와 관련해서/인구과잉으로 야기된/시민들은 이용해야만 한다/대중교통을/버스나 지하철과 같은/그들의 차보다

19. 이를 위해서/정부는 만들어야만 한다/잘 정비된 교통 시스템을/시민들이 그것을 이용하도록/그들을/편리하게

20. 서울을 예로 들면/거기에 지하철 시스템이/잘 정비되어 있어왔다/줄이기 위해서/인구집중 그리고 교통 혼잡

21. 그 결과/이러한 정책은/도움이 된다/대기오염을 해결하는 데/뿐만 아니라 교통문제/어느 정도

_____

_____

22. 결론은/그것은 분명하다/과잉 인구에 의해 발생된 문제들은/도시들에서/광범위하다

_____

_____

23. 만약/사람들과 정부가/책임을 공유한다면/위에서 언급한 방법으로/그들은 해결할 것이다/문제들을/과잉 인구로부터

_____

_____

Answer

1. In most parts of the world, the population has been alarmingly on the rise and mainly prevalent in major cities,

2. , and it has become one of the world's biggest concerns.

3. Governments and individuals have to take this issue into account seriously.

4. This essay will present the problems of overpopulation along with solutions.

5. A couple of main problems come about because of overpopulation.

6. First of all, overpopulation deteriorates the quality of living in many cities.

7. For one thing, overcrowding and housing with poor sanitation cause significant health problems, bringing about illnesses.

8. Another serious result of an ever-growing population is the rise of unemployment,

9. , which could lead to an increasing crime rate because some choose crimes to escape from poverty caused by unemployment.

10. Lastly, the environmental damage generated by overpopulation is considerable.

11. It is because the rapid increase in vehicles in large cities gives rise to air pollution resulting from carbon dioxide emission as well as traffic problems,

12. Like this, the excessive growth of urban population has some adverse aspects.

13. When it comes to solutions, individuals and governments should take feasible steps to settle excess population in big cities.

14. Governments should sort out the housing problem.

15. In particular, they ought to expand the residential districts for population decentralization on the outskirts of major urban cities.

16. In light of the unemployment problem, governments should boost industries and promote employment, especially in local areas to disperse population,

17. , which can lower unemployment and the crime rate in major cities as well.

18. Finally, as regards environmental concerns from overpopulation, citizens had better use public transport like buses and underground rather than their cars.

19. To this end, governments are supposed to build a well-organized transportation system for citizens to use them conveniently.

20. Take Seoul, for example, where the traffic system has been well-maintained to lessen the concentration of population and the traffic congestion.

21. As a result, its policy is of help to solve not only air pollution but also traffic problems to some extent.

22. In conclusion, it is clear-cut that the problems caused by overpopulation in urban areas are far-reaching.

23. If individuals and governments share responsibility in the way mentioned above, they will resolve the difficulties of overpopulation.

You should spend about 40 minutes on this task.

Write about the following topic:

> **Overpopulation of urban areas has led to numerous problems. Identify serious ones and suggest ways that governments and individuals can tackle these problems.**

Give reasons for your answer and include any relevant examples from your own knowledge or experience.

Write at least 250 words.

Answer

In most parts of the world, the population has been alarmingly on the rise and mainly prevalent in major cities, and it has become one of the world's biggest concerns. Individuals and governments have to take this issue into account seriously. This essay will present the problems of overpopulation along with solutions.

A couple of main problems have come about because of overpopulation. First of all, overpopulation deteriorates the quality of living in many cities. For one thing, overcrowding and housing with poor sanitation cause significant health problems, bringing about illnesses. **Another serious result of an ever-growing population is the rise of unemployment,** which could lead to an increasing crime rate because some choose crimes to escape from poverty caused by unemployment. **Lastly, the environmental damage generated by overpopulation is considerable.** It is because the rapid increase in vehicles in large cities gives rise to air pollution resulting from carbon dioxide emission as well as traffic problems. Like this, the excessive growth of urban population has some adverse aspects.

When it comes to solutions, individuals and governments should take feasible steps to settle excess population in big cities. Governments should sort out the housing problem. In particular, they ought to expand the residential districts for population decentralization on the outskirts of the main urban cities. **In light of the unemployment problem, governments should boost industries and promote employment, especially in local areas to disperse population,** which can lower unemployment and the crime rate in the major cities as well. **Finally, as regards environmental concerns from overpopulation,** citizens had better use public transport like buses and underground rather than their cars. To this end, governments are supposed to build a well-organized transportation system for citizens to use them conveniently. Take Seoul, for example, where the underground system has been well-maintained to lessen the concentration of population and the traffic congestion. As a result, its policy is of help to solve not only air pollution but also traffic problems to some extent.

In conclusion, it is clear-cut that the problems caused by overpopulation in urban areas are far-reaching. If individuals and governments share responsibility in the way mentioned above, they will resolve the difficulties of overpopulation.

2. Financial support

You should spend about 40 minutes on this task.

Write about the following topic:

> Many advanced countries are giving financial aid to underdeveloped countries. However, this has not solved the problem of poverty in these nations, and so other types of help should be provided. To what extent do you agree or disagree with this statement?

Give reasons for your answer and include any relevant examples from your own knowledge or experience.

Write at least 250 words.

INTRODUCTION
선진국들이 가난한 나라에 경제적 원조를 하는 것에 대한 논쟁이 있다.

재정적 원조는 상황을 개선시키지 않는다. 다른 접근법이 시행되어야 한다.

BODY 1 (재정적 지원 효과없음)
1. 부패가 원인
2. 교육의 부족

BODY 2 (다른 방법으로 지원필요)
1. 교육적 지원
   → 교육시스템/시설/자료

CONCLUSION
단지 경제적 지원에 반대하고 고기를 주는 것보다 고기 잡는 법을 가르쳐줘야 한다.

많은 선진국들은 저 개발국들에게 재정적 지원을 하고 있다. 그러나 이것은 빈곤의 문제를 해결하지 못하고 있다. 어느 정도 이 문제에 대해 동의 또는 비동의하는지?

INTRODUCTION

선진국들이 저개발국들에게 경제적 원조를 해야만 하는지에 대한 주제는 논쟁의 문제가 되고 있다. 어떤 사람들은 재정적인 지원은 후진국들의 빈곤해결에 도움이 된다고 주장한다. 그러나, 내 의견으로는, 재정적 도움은 그들 나라의 상황을 개선시키지 않고 다른 접근법이 실행되어야 한다.

BODY 1

나는 경제적 지원은 후진국의 열악한 경제상황을 개선시키지 않는다고 확실하게 믿는다. 첫 번째 이유는 사회 전반에 걸친 부패가 가난한 나라가 직면한 고질적임 문제들 중 하나이기 때문이다. 비록 선진국이 재정적인 도움을 준다 해도, 그것은 절실하게 도움이 필요한 일반사람에게는 도달하지 않는다. 이것은 정치가들과 영향력 있는 사업가들과 같은 기득권층이 대부분의 금전상의 원조를 가져가기 때문이다. 이것은 부자들과 가난한 사람들의 격차를 더 크게 만들고 사회 문제들을 또한 일으킨다. **다른 문제는 가난한 나라에서의 교육의 부족이다.** 교육의 부족은 국민들이 그들의 권리를 알지 못하는 경향이 있고 가난을 있는 그대로 받아들인다. 이것은 개개인 그리고 국가가 발전할 기회를 잃어버리는 것이다. 이러한 이유 때문에, 그들은 부자나라들로부터 받은 경제적 도움에도 불구하고 가난에서 벗어날 수가 없다.

BODY 2

한편으로는, 경제적인 지원 대신에 가난한 나라들을 돕기 위한 다른 조치가 있어야만 한다. 가장 중요한 것은, 후진국들이 질 좋은 교육체계, 시설들 그리고 자료들과 같은 교육적 지원을 경제적 정치적 개선을 위해 받는 것이 필요하다. 교육은 가난한 나라의 시민들이 그들의 권리뿐만 아니라 기술과 재능을 가진 인간으로써의 자기의 잠재력을 알게 할 수 있다. 이것은 더 나아가 경제적인 발전과 부패 억제와 같은 정치적인 개혁에 상당히 기여할 수 있다. 사실상, 요즘 많은 선진국들이나 WORLD VISION과 같은 관련된 국제기구들은 경제적 곤경에 처해 있는 국가들을 위해 교육적인 지원을 하고 있다. 예를 들어, 그들은 실질적인 농업기술을 가르치고 학교를 건립하고 다양한 교육자료들을 제공한다. 조사에 따르면, 이 정책은 빈곤국가에서의 사람들의 삶에 실질적인 영향을 주고 있다. 이러한 맥락에서, 교육적인 접근은 빈곤에서 벗어나기 위한 긴 안목에서 보면 부정부패에 맞서기 위한 최상의 해법이다.

CONCLUSION

결론은, 나는 경제적 지원이 후진국의 가난을 해결하지 못해오고 있다는 의견에 전적으로 동의한다. 비록 이 복잡한 문제를 해결하는 것은 힘든 일이지만, 자금 지원 대신에, 교육적인 지원이 빈곤국가들에게 실질적인 도움이 될 수 있다. 전통적인 속담을 사용하자면, 후진국들이, 단지 고기를 받는 것보다, 고기를 잡는 방법을 배우는 것이 더 낫기 때문이다.

문장에 필요한 어휘

> 1. developed(advanced) countries(nations); 선진국들
> 2. undeveloped(underdeveloped) nations(countries)/backward countries; 후진국들
> 3. financial(economic/monetary) assistance(support/aid/help/fund); 재정적 지원
> 4. a controversial issue/a matter of argument(debate); 논쟁의 문제

선진국들이 저개발국들에게 경제적 원조를 해야만 하는지에 대한 주제는 논쟁의 문제가 되고 있다.

The topic of whether developed countries should give financial assistance to undeveloped nations has become a controversial issue.

> 5. argue/claim/assert/believe/maintain; 주장하다
> 6. of help/of benefit/helpful/beneficial; 도움이 되는
> 7. address/tackle/sort out/solve/resolve; 해결하다

어떤 사람들은 재정적인 지원은 후진국의 빈곤해결에 도움이 된다고 주장한다.

Some people argue that financial support to underdeveloped countries is of great help to address the problem of poverty.

> 8. in my opinion/from my point of view/in my judgment; 내 의견으로는
> 9. improve/better/make better; 개선하다
> 10. approach/procedure/way/method/manner/measure; 접근/방법

내 의견으로는, 그러나, 재정적 도움은 그들 나라의 상황을 개선시키지 않고 다른 접근법이 실행되어야 한다.

In my opinion, though, funding does not improve the situations in those countries, and another approach should be carried out.

> 11. certainly/strongly/firmly/definitely/obviously/greatly; 확실히
> 12. the poor(atrocious/deteriorating) economic situation(circumstances/surroundings); 열악한 경제상황

나는 경제적 지원은 후진국의 열악한 경제상황을 개선시키지 않는다고 확실히 믿는다.

I certainly believe that financial help does not improve the poor economic situation in underdeveloped countries.

> 13. corruption/decay; 부패
> 14. face/confront; 직면하다
> 15. low-developed(underdeveloped/undeveloped) countries; 가난한 나라들
> 16. chronic problems(issues/troubles); 고질적인 문제들

첫 번째 이유는 사회전반에 걸친 부패가 가난한 나라가 직면한 고질적인 문제들 중 하나이기 때문이다.

The first reason is that corruption across all society is one of the chronic problems low-developed countries face.

> 17. even though/although S+V; 비록~이지만
> 18. give/provide/offer; 주다
> 19. desperately/urgently/seriously/really; 절실하게

비록 선진국이 재정적인 도움을 준다 해도, 그것은 절실하게 도움이 필요한 일반사람에게는 도달하지 않는다.

Even though wealthy nations give financial help, it does not reach the people who desperately need assistance.

> 20. the establishment; 기득권층
> 21. politician/statesman; 정치가
> 22. financial grants(aid/support/assistance)/funding assistance; 금전적 지원

이것은 정치가들과 영향력 있는 사업가들과 같은 기득권층이 대부분의 금전상의 원조를 가져가기 때문이다.

It is because the establishment such as politicians and influential people in business take most of the financial grants.

> 23. lead to/result in/bring about/give rise to; 초래하다/야기하다
> 24. the haves/the affluent/the rich/the wealthy/the privileged/the advantaged; 부자들
> 25. the have-nots/the poor/the unprivileged/the needy/the disadvantaged; 가난한 사람들
> 26. as well/also/likewise; 또한

그것은 부자와 가난한 사람들의 격차를 더 크게 만들고 또한 사회적 문제들을 일으킨다.

It leads to an even greater gulf between the haves and the have-nots, giving rise to social problems as well.

> 27. the lack of education/deficient in education; 교육의 부족
> 28. poverty-stricken nations/impoverished countries/poverty nations; 가난에 시달리는 나라들

다른 문제는 가난한 나라에서의 교육의 부족이다.
Another issue is the lack of education in poverty-stricken countries.

> 29. have no tendency to/do not tend to; ~하지 않는 경향이 있다
> 30. be aware of/know/find out; 알다
> 31. as it is/as it comes; 있는 그대로

교육의 부족은 국민들이 그들의 권리를 알지 못하는 경향이 있고 가난을 있는 그대로 받아들인다.
They have no tendency to be aware of their rights and accept their poverty as it is,

> 32. advance/develop/improve/better; 발전하다/성장하다

이것은 개개인 그리고 국가가 발전할 기회를 잃어버리는 것이다.
, which loses their opportunities for individuals and nations to advance.

> 33. get out of/come out of/depart from/escape from; 벗어나다
> 34. despite/albeit/in spite of; ~에도 불구하고

이러한 이유 때문에, 그들은 부자나라들로부터 받은 경제적 도움에도 불구하고 가난에서 벗어날 수가 없다.
For these reasons, they could not get out of poverty despite the economic aid they receive from wealthier nations.

> 35. in place of/in lieu of/instead of; 대신에
> 36. measure/step/action/way; 조치

한편으로는, 경제적인 지원 대신에 가난한 나라들을 돕기 위한 다른 조치가 있어야만 한다.
Meanwhile, in place of financial support, there should be other measures to help undeveloped countries.

> 37. most importantly/first and most importantly; 가장 중요한 것은
> 38. facility/equipment; 시설
> 39. material/reference/source; 자료

가장 중요한 것은, 후진국들은 질 좋은 교육체계, 시설들 그리고 자료들과 같은 교육적 지원을 경제적 정치적 개선을 위해 받는 것이 필요하다.

Most importantly, it is necessary for underdeveloped countries to receive educational support, for economic and political improvement, including a good quality school system, facilities, and materials.

> 40. enable A to B; A가 B하는 것을 가능하게 하다
> 41. potential/potential power; 잠재력
> 42. not just(only) A but also B/B as well as A; A뿐만 아니라 B도

교육은 가난한 나라의 시민들이 그들의 권리뿐만 아니라 기술과 재능을 가진 인간으로서의 자기의 잠재력을 알게 할 수 있다.

Education enables citizens in undeveloped countries to be aware, not just of their rights, but also of their potential as human beings with skills and talents,

> 43. contribute to/make a contribution to+N; 기여하다
> 44. significantly/considerably/greatly/a great deal; 상당히
> 45. curb/restrict/deter/stop; 억제하다/줄이다

이러한 것은 더 나아가 경제적인 발전과 그리고 부패 단절과 같은 정치적 개혁에 상당히 기여한다.

, which can further contribute significantly to the economic development and political reform like curbing corruption.

> 46. in fact/as a matter of fact/in reality/actually/virtually; 사실은
> 47. organization/institution/agency; 기관/단체
> 48. provide A for(to) B/provide B with A; B에게 A를 제공하다
> 49. be in economic trouble; 경제적 어려움에 처해 있다

사실상, 요즘 많은 선진국들이나 WORLD VISION과 같은 관련된 국제기구들은 경제적 어려움에 처해 있는 국가들을 위해 교육적인 지원을 하고 있다.

In fact, nowadays many advanced countries and organizations involved like World Vision provide educational support for countries that are in economic trouble.

> 50. to illustrate/for instance/for example; 예를 들어
> 51. practical/practicable/useful/viable; 실용적인/실질적인
> 52. a (broad/far-reaching/wide) range (variety) of; 다양한

예를 들어, 그들은 실질적인 농업기술을 가르치고 학교를 건립하고 다양한 교육자료들을 제공한다.

To illustrate, they teach practical agricultural skills, build schools, and offer a broad range of teaching materials.

> 53. according to; ~에 따르면
> 54. have(has) substantial(practical/actual/real) influences(effects/impacts) on; 실질적인 영향을 끼치다

조사에 따르면, 이 정책은 빈곤국가에서의 사람들의 삶에 실질적인 영향을 주고 있다.

According to research, this policy has substantial influences on people's lives in impoverished countries.

> 55. in this context/therefore/thus/as a result/consequently/hence; 이러한 맥락에서/따라서/그러므로
> 56. educational access(approach/method/way); 교육적인 접근
> 57. far and away(by far) the best; 가장 최상의
> 58. lift(emerge/pull/get) out of poverty; 가난에서 벗어나다
> 59. fight against; ~에 맞서다
> 60. in the long run/after all/in the end; 긴 안목으로 보면/결국에는

이러한 맥락에서, 교육적인 접근은 빈곤에서 벗어나기 위한 긴 안목으로 보면 정치적 부정부패에 맞서기 위한 최상의 해법이다.

In this context, the educational access could be far and away the best solution to lift out of poverty and fight against corruption in the long run.

> 61. to conclude/in conclusion/to sum up; 결론은
> 62. agree with/be in favor of/be for; ~에 찬성한다

결론은, 나는 경제적 지원이 후진국의 가난을 해결하지 못해오고 있다는 의견에 전적으로 동의한다.

To conclude, I completely agree with the view that financial support has not solved the poverty of underdeveloped nations.

> 63. put an end to+N; 마무리 짓다
> 64. demanding/tough/difficult/hard; 힘든/큰 노력을 요구하는

비록 이 복잡한 문제를 마무리 짓는 것은 힘든 일이지만, 자금 지원 대신에, 교육적인 지원이 빈곤국가들에게 실질적인 도움을 줄 수 있다.

Though putting an end to this complicated problem is demanding, instead of funding assistance, an educational fund could be of real help to poverty nations,

> 65. to use a traditional proverb; 전통적인 속담을 사용하자면,

전통적인 속담을 사용하자면, 경제적으로 후진국들은, 단지 고기를 받는 것보다 고기 잡는 방법을 배우는 것이 더 낫기 때문이다.

, since it is better for backward countries financially, to use a traditional proverb, to learn how to fish rather than only receive fish.

구문연습

1. 주제는/선진국들이 제공해야 하는지에 대한/경제적 원조를/저개발국가들에게/되어왔다/논쟁의 문제가

---

2. 어떤 사람들은 주장한다/재정적 지원이/후진국들에게/도움이 된다/빈곤을 해결하는 데

---

3. 내 의견으로는/그러나/재정적 도움은/상황을 개선시키지 않는다/이러한 국가들에서/그리고 다른 접근법이/실행되어야 한다

---

4. 나는 확실히 믿는다/경제적인 지원은/개선시키지 않는다/열악한 경제 상황을/후진국들에서

---

5. 첫 번째 이유는 이다/사회전반에 걸친 부패가/고질적인 문제들 중 하나/가난한 나라가 직면한

---

6. 비록 선진국이/재정적 지원을 준다 해도/그것은 도달하지 않는다/도움이 필요한 사람들에게/절실히

---

2. Financial support

7. 이것은 이유이다/기득권층이/정치가들과 영향력 있는 사업가들이/가져간다/대부분의 금전적 도움을

_____

_____

8. 그것은 만든다/더 큰 격차를/가난한 사람과 부자 사이의/이러한 것은/일으킨다/사회적 문제를/또한

_____

_____

9. 다른 문제는/교육의 부재이다/가난한 나라에서의

_____

_____

10. 교육의 부재는/알지 못하는 경향이 있다/그들의 권리를/그리고 받아들인다/그들의 가난을/있는 그대로

_____

_____

11. 그것은/잃어버린다/그들의 기회를/개개인과 국가가/발전하는

_____

_____

12. 이러한 이유 때문에/그들은/가난으로부터 벗어날 수 없다/경제적 도움에도 불구하고/그들이 받는/부자나라들로부터

_____

_____

13. 한편으로는/대신에/경제적 도움/있어야 한다/다른 조치들이/가난한 나라를 돕기 위한

_____

_____

14. 가장 중요한 것은/필요하다/후진국들이/교육적 지원을 받는 것이/경제적 정치적 개선을 위해/같은/질 좋은 교육적 체계/시설들 그리고 자료들

_____

_____

15. 교육은 가능하게 한다/가난한 나라 사람들에게/알게 한다/그들의 권리뿐만 아니라/그들의 잠재력을/기술과 재능을 가진 인간으로서

_____

_____

16. 이러한 것들은/더 나아가/상당히/기여할 수 있다/경제적 발전과/정치적인 개혁/부패 억제와 같은

_____

_____

17. 사실상/요즘/많은 선진국들과 기관들은/관련된/월드비전과 같은/제공한다/교육적인 지원을/경제적 곤경에 처한 나라들에

_____

_____

18. 예를 들어/그들은 가르친다/실질적인 농업 기술들을/학교를 설립하고/그리고 제공한다/다양한 교육적 자료들을

_____

_____

19. 조사에 따르면/이 정책은/실질적인 영향을 준다/사람들의 삶에/빈곤 국가에서의

_____

_____

20. 이러한 맥락에서/교육적 접근은/가장 최상의 해결책일 수 있다/빈곤에서 벗어나기 위한/그리고 부정부패를 척결하기 위한/긴 안목에서

_____
_____

21. 결론은/나는 동의한다/확실하게/그 의견에/재정적 지원이/빈곤을 해결하지 못하고 있다/가난한 나라들의

_____
_____

22. 비록/마무리 짓는 것은/이 복잡한 문제를/힘든 일이지만

_____
_____

23. 자금 지원 대신에/교육적 지원이 줄 수 있다/실질적인 도움을/빈곤국가들에게

_____
_____

24. 왜냐하면/더 낫기 때문이다/후진국들이/전통적인 속담을 사용하자면/배운다/고기를 잡는 방법을/단지 고기를 받는 것보다는

_____
_____

Answer

1. The topic of whether developed countries should give financial assistance to undeveloped nations has become a controversial issue.
2. Some people argue that financial support to underdeveloped countries is of great help to address the problem of poverty.
3. In my opinion, though, funding does not improve the situations in those countries, and another approach should be carried out.
4. I certainly believe that financial help does not improve the poor economic situation in underdeveloped countries.
5. The first reason is that corruption across all society is one of the chronic problems low-developed countries face.
6. Even though wealthy nations give financial help, it does not reach the people who desperately need assistance.
7. It is because the establishment such as politicians and influential people in business take most of the financial grants.
8. It leads to an even greater gulf between the haves and the have-nots, giving rise to social problems as well.
9. Another issue is the lack of education in poverty-stricken countries.
10. They have no tendency to be aware of their rights and accept their poverty as it is,
11. , which loses their opportunities for individuals and nations to advance.
12. For these reasons, they could not get out of poverty despite the economic aid they receive from wealthier nations.
13. Meanwhile, in place of financial support, there should be other measures to help undeveloped countries.
14. Most importantly, it is necessary for underdeveloped countries to receive educational support, for economic and political improvement, including a good quality school system, facilities, and materials.
15. Education enables citizens in underdeveloped countries to be aware, not just of their rights, but also of their potential as human beings with skills and talents,
16. , which can further contribute significantly to the economic development and political reform like curbing corruption.
17. In fact, nowadays many advanced countries and organizations involved like World Vision provide educational support for countries that are in economic trouble.
18. To illustrate, they teach practical agricultural skills, build schools, and offer a broad range of teaching materials.
19. According to research, this policy has substantial influences on people's lives in impoverished countries.
20. In this context, the educational access could be far and away the best solution to lift out of poverty and fight against corruption in the long run.
21. To conclude, I completely agree with the view that financial support has not solved the poverty of underdeveloped nations.
22. Though putting an end to this complicated problem is demanding,
23. , instead of funding assistance, an educational fund could be of real help to poverty nations,
24. , since it is better for backward countries financially, to use a traditional proverb, to learn how to fish rather than only receive fish.

Unit 3 Social issues

You should spend about 40 minutes on this task.

Write about the following topic:

> **Many advanced countries are giving financial aid to underdeveloped countries. However, this has not solved the problem of poverty in these nations, and so other types of help are provided. To what extent do you agree or disagree with this statement?**

Give reasons for your answer and include any relevant examples from your own knowledge or experience.

Write at least 250 words.

Answer

The topic of whether developed countries should give financial assistance to undeveloped nations has become a controversial issue. Some people argue that financial support to underdeveloped countries is of great help to address the problem of poverty. In my opinion, though, funding does not improve the situations in those countries, and another approach should be carried out.

I certainly believe that financial help does not improve the poor economic situation in underdeveloped countries. The first reason is that corruption across all society is one of the chronic problems low-developed countries face. Even though wealthy nations give financial help, it does not reach the people who desperately need assistance. It is because the establishment such as politicians and influential people in business take most of the financial grants. It leads to an even greater gulf between the haves and the have-nots, giving rise to social problems as well. **Another issue is the lack of education in poverty-stricken countries.** They have no tendency to be aware of their rights and accept their poverty as it is, which loses their opportunities for individuals and nations to advance. For these reasons, they could not get out of poverty despite the economic aid they receive from wealthier nations.

Meanwhile, in place of financial support, **there should be other measures to help undeveloped countries. Most importantly, it is necessary for underdeveloped countries to receive educational support**, for economic and political improvement, including a good quality school system, facilities, and materials. Education enables citizens in undeveloped countries to be aware, not just of their rights, but also of their potential as human beings with skills and talents, which can further contribute significantly to the economic development and political reform like curbing corruption. In fact, nowadays many advanced countries and organizations involved like World Vision provide educational support for countries that are in economic trouble. To illustrate, they teach practical agricultural skills, build schools, and offer a broad range of teaching materials. According to research, this policy has substantial influences on people's lives in impoverished countries. In this context, the educational access could be far and away the best solution to lift out of poverty and fight against corruption in the long run.

To conclude, I completely agree with the view that financial support has not solved the poverty of underdeveloped nations. Though putting an end to this complicated problem is demanding, instead of funding assistance, an educational fund could be of real help to poverty nations, since it is better for backward countries financially, to use a traditional proverb, to learn how to fish rather than only receive fish.

3. The crime rate

You should spend about 40 minutes on this task.

Write about the following topic:

> **The crime rate has increased rapidly around the world. Discuss some causes for this rise and suggest workable solutions to this problem.**

Give reasons for your answer and include any relevant examples from your own knowledge or experience.

Write at least 250 words.

INTRODUCTION

    범죄율이 증가하고 있다.

    원인과 해결책을 설명하겠다.

BODY 1 (reasons)

    1. 빈부격차

    2. 도덕성 결여

BODY 2 (solutions)

    1. 빈부격차 해소

    2. 사법제도 강화

CONCLUSION

    이유를 철저히 분석하여 문제를 해결한다.

범죄율은 많은 나라에서 급격하게 증가하고 있다. 이 증가에 대한 가능성 있는 이유들과 문제에 대한 해결책을 제시하라.

INTRODUCTION

범죄율이 전 세계적으로 상당히 증가해 오고 있다는 것은 사실이다. 비록 정부와 관련 기관들은 적극적으로 이 문제를 해결하려 적극적으로 노력해 오고 있지만 범죄율을 감소시키는 것은 쉽지 않다. 이 에세이에서, 나는 증가하는 범죄율의 몇 가지 원인들과 실행 가능한 해결책을 자세히 설명하겠다.

BODY 1

<u>우선, 범죄가 증가하고 있는 데는 몇 가지 이유가 있다. 첫 번째, 부자들과 가난한 사람들의 빈부격차는 상당히 심화되고 있다.</u> 일반적으로 경제적인 어려움을 겪는 일부의 빈곤층은 삶의 어려움에 대한 해결책으로써 범죄를 저지르는 경향이 있다. 더욱이, 그들은 당국으로부터 적절한 대우를 받지 못한다고 믿고 사회로부터 소외된다고 느끼는 경향이 있다. 이런 상황에서, 소외 계층이 그들 자신의 필요를 충족하기 위해서 위법행위에 의지한다. 예를 들면, 그들은 생존을 위한 현금이나 물건을 얻기 위해 강도를 저지른다. <u>두 번째, 도덕성이 최근에 현저히 약해지고 있고 물질주의는 오늘날 과거보다 더욱 강해지고 있다.</u> 다시 말해서, 사람에 대한 가치를 그들의 인격과 도덕성보다 물질적인 부에 두고 있다. 이러한 가치관에 대한 변화는 사람들에게 범죄를 저지르도록 유도한다.

BODY 2

<u>결과적으로, 정부는 이 문제를 해결하기 위해서 노력하는 것이 중요하다. 우선, 그들은 부자들과 가난한 사람들의 빈부격차를 줄여야 한다.</u> 그들이 이것을 성취하기 위해서 사회적 복지와 교육 시스템이 효율적으로 계획되어야 하고 이러한 것들이 낮은 사회적 위치에 있는 사람들에게 나은 미래를 찾을 수 있도록 동등하게 기회들을 제공해야 한다. 그것에 덧붙여서 범죄율이 더욱더 증가하는 것을 막기 위해 사법제도가 강화되어야 한다. 다시 말해서, <u>강력한 법 집행과 형사처벌이 필요하다.</u> 그것을 위해서 정부는 경찰들에게 최신 장비와 발전된 수사기술을 제공해야 한다. 이뿐만 아니라, 범죄자들이 출소 후 사회에 적응할 수 있도록 적절한 갱생프로그램이 시행되어야 한다.

CONCLUSION

결론은, 위에서 언급한 것처럼, 범죄증가의 몇 가지 이유들이 있고, 그것을 해결하는 접근법들 또한 제시되었다. 범죄들에 대한 이유들을 철저하게 분석함으로써 문제를 해결하기 위해 적절한 해결책들이 적용되어야 한다. 이러한 방법으로, 사회는 범죄 없는 사회가 될 수 있다.

문장에 필요한 어휘

> 1. it is a fact that+S+V; ~라는 것은 사실이다.
> 2. the crime rate; 범죄율
> 3. be on the rise/be on the increase/climb up/go up; 증가하고 있다
> 4. significantly/considerably/dramatically/rapidly/fairly; 상당히

범죄율이 전 세계적으로 상당히 증가해 오고 있다는 것은 사실이다.
It is a fact that the crime rate has been on the rise significantly in various parts of the world.

> 5. governments/authorities; 정부
> 6. relevant/related/associated; 관련된
> 7. actively/aggressively/affirmatively; 적극적으로
> 8. address/deal with/cope with/sort out/tackle/resolve/solve/settle; 해결하다/다루다

비록 정부와 관련기관들은 적극적으로 이 문제를 해결하려고 적극적으로 노력해 오고 있지만,
Even though governments and relevant organizations have been actively trying to address the issue,

> 9. cut down on/cut back on/reduce/lessen/weaken/decrease/decline; 줄이다

범죄율을 줄이는 것은 쉽지 않다.
It is not easy to cut down on the crime rate.

> 10. spell out/elaborate on/describe in full detail; 자세히 설명하다
> 11. culprit/reason/cause/ground; 이유
> 12. feasible/possible/workable/viable/practicable; 실행 가능성 있는
> 13. solution/approach/answer/key; 해법/접근법

이 에세이에서, 나는 증가하는 범죄율의 몇 가지 원인들과 실행 가능한 해결책을 자세히 설명하겠다.
In this essay, I will spell out several culprits and feasible solutions to the increasing crime rate.

> 14. to begin with/first of all/first and foremost; 우선
> 15. a couple of/a few/several; 몇 가지

우선, 범죄가 증가하고 있는 데는 몇 가지 이유가 있다.
To begin with, there are a couple of issues that causes the crime rate to rise.

> 16. the gap(gulf) between the haves and the have-nots; 부자들과 가난한 사람들의 격차
>   ⇨ the haves/the rich/the wealthy/the affluent/the privileged; 부자들
>   ⇨ the have-nots/the poor/those in need/the needy/the unprivileged/the impoverished; 가난한 사람들
> 17. widen/broaden; 넓다

첫 번째, 부자들과 가난한 사람들의 빈부격차는 상당히 심화되고 있다.
First, the gap between the haves and the have-nots has considerably widened.

> 18. undergo/go through/suffer; 겪다
> 19. financial(economic) difficulty(concern/problem/trouble); 재정적 어려움
> 20. tend to/have a tendency to/be inclined to/be liable to; 하는 경향이 있다
> 21. commit a crime; 범죄를 저지르다
> 22. as a solution to ~; ~에 대한 해결책으로써
> 23. hardship/difficulty/distress/adversity; 어려움

일반적으로, 어려움을 겪는 일부의 빈곤한 사람들은 삶의 어려움에 대한 해결책으로써 범죄를 저지르는 경향이 있다.
In general, some impoverished people who have undergone financial difficulties tend to commit crimes as a solution to life's hardship.

> 24. moreover/furthermore/in addition/what is more; 더욱이
> 25. due to/because of/owing to/on account of+N/구; ~ 때문에
> 26. social status(position/standing); 사회적 지위
> 27. be isolated from/be removed from/be separated from/be far from/be excluded from; ~로부터 소외되다/~로부터 배제되다

더욱이, 그들은 그들이 당국으로부터 적절한 대우를 받지 못한다고 믿고 사회로부터 소외된다고 느끼는 경향이 있다.
Moreover, they usually believe they do not obtain proper treatment from the authorities and have a tendency to feel isolated from society.

> 28. circumstances/situations/conditions; 현상/상황
> 29. the disadvantaged/the underprivileged/a neglected class of people; 소외계층
> 30. resort to +N/have resort to +N; ~에 의지하다

이런 상황에서, 소외 계층이 그들 자신의 필요를 충족하기 위해서 위법행위에 의지한다.
In these circumstances, the disadvantaged resort to misconduct to meet their own needs.

> 31. for instance/for example/to illustrate/for one thing; 예를 들면
> 32. commit a robbery/carry out a robbery; 강도를 저지르다
> 33. acquire/obtain/have/get/gain; 얻다

예를 들면, 그들은 생존을 위한 현금이나 물건을 얻기 위해 강도를 저지른다.
For instance, they commit a robbery to acquire just money or other items for survival.

> 34. second/In the next place/In the second place; 두 번째로
> 35. morality/ethicality; 도덕성/윤리성
> 36. weaken/abate/diminish/let up; 약해지다
> 37. in recent years/lately/recently/of late/in recent times; 최근에
> 38. materialism; 물질주의
> 39. noticeably/remarkably/exceptionally/prominently/strikingly; 현저하게/두드러지게
> 40. become much stronger/be much stronger/grow strong/grow powerful; 강해지다
> 41. in the past; 과거

두 번째는, 도덕성이 최근에 현저히 약해지고 있고 물질주의는 오늘날 과거보다 더욱 강해지고 있다.
Second, morality has noticeably weakened in recent years, and materialism has become much stronger today than it was in the past.

> 42. that is to say/that is/in other words/to put it another way; 다시 말해서
> 43. wealth/fortune/property; 부/재산
> 44. character/personality; 인격
> 45. mortality/ethics; 도덕성

다시 말해서, 사람에 대한 가치를 그들의 인격과 도덕성보다 물질적인 부에 두고 있다.
That is to say, a person's worth puts in his/her material wealth rather than in their character and morality.

> 46. changes in values; 가치관에 있어 변화들
> 47. lead A to B/cause A to B; A가 B하도록 야기하다

이러한 가치관에 대한 변화는 사람들에게 범죄를 저지르도록 유도한다
These changes in values have led people to commit a crime.

> 48. consequently/therefore/thus/hence/as a result; 결과적으로
> 49. vital/important/crucial/significant/essential/imperative; 중요한
> 50. make considerable(great) efforts to; 대단히 노력하다

결과적으로, 정부는 이 문제를 해결하기 위해서 노력하는 것이 중요하다.
Consequently, it is vital for governments to make considerable efforts to tackle the issue.

> 51. bridge the gap(gulf) between A and B; (A와 B 사이의) 공백을 메우다

우선, 그들은 부자들과 가난한 사람들의 빈부격차를 줄여야 한다.
Firstly, they should bridge the gulf between the affluent and the needy.

> 52. achieve/accomplish/win/gain; 성취하다
> 53. social welfare; 사회 복지

그들이 이것을 성취하기 위해 사회적 복지와 교육 시스템이 효율적으로 계획되어야 한다.
For them to achieve it, social welfare and education systems should be planned efficiently,

> 54. provide A with B/provide B to(for) A; A에게 B를 제공하다
> 55. opportunity/chance/occasion; 기회
> 56. social status(position/standing); 사회적 지위

이러한 것들이, 낮은 사회적 위치에 있는 사람들에게 나은 미래를 찾을 수 있도록 동등하게 기회들을 제공해야 한다.
, which should provide opportunities equally for people in low social statuses to find a better future.

> 57. in addition to that/on top of that/not only that; 이것에 덧붙여서
> 58. justice system; 사법제도
> 59. reinforce/strengthen/beef up/intensify; 강화하다
> 60. deter(prevent/stop/prohibit/ban) A from B; A가 B하지 못하게 하다

그것에 덧붙여서, 범죄율이 더 증가하는 것을 막기 위해 사법제도가 강화되어야 한다.
In addition to that, justice systems should be reinforced to deter the crime rate from a further increase.

> 61. implementation/enforcement; 시행
> 62. criminal(punishment/prosecution); 형사 처벌
> 63. necessary/required; 필요한

다시 말해서, 강력한 법 집행과 형사처벌이 필요하다.
In other words, the strict implementation of laws and criminal punishments are necessary.

> 64. to that end; 그것을 위해서
> 65. furnish A with B/provide A with B; A에게 B를 제공하다
> 66. investigation techniques; 수사 기술

그것을 위해서 정부는 경찰들에게 최신 장비와 발전된 수사기술을 제공해야 한다
To that end, governments should furnish police officers with the latest equipment and advanced investigation techniques.

> 67. rehabilitation system; 재발/갱생 시스템
> 68. practice/enforce/put in force/implement/put in practice; 실행하다
> 69. adjust to/adapt to+N; 적응하다
> 70. after release/after discharge from prison; 출소 후

이뿐만 아니라, 범죄자들이 출소 후 사회에 적응할 수 있도록 적절한 갱생프로그램이 시행되어야 한다.
Not only that, a proper rehabilitation system should be practiced for offenders to adjust to society after release.

> 71. as stated above/as mentioned above; 위에서 언급한 것처럼
> 72. as well/also/too/likewise; 또한/마찬가지로

결론은 위에서 언급한 것처럼, 범죄증가의 몇 가지 이유들이 있고, 그것을 해결하는 접근법들 또한 제시되었다.

In conclusion, as stated above, there are a few reasons for the increasing crime rate, and several approaches to unravel it are suggested as well.

---

73. analyze/research/examine; 분석하다
74. appropriate/proper/right; 적절한
75. apply to; 적용하다

범죄들에 대한 이유들을 철저하게 분석함으로써, 문제를 해결하기 위해 적절한 해결책들이 적용되야만 한다.

By analyzing the reasons for crimes thoroughly, appropriate solutions should be applied to sort out the problem.

---

76. in this way; 이러한 방법으로
77. a crime-free society; 범죄 없는 사회

이러한 방법으로, 사회는 범죄 없는 사회가 될 수 있다.

In this way, the society can become a crime-free society.

구문연습

1. 사실이다/범죄율이 상당히 증가해오고 있다/전 세계적으로

_____
_____

2. 비록 정부와 관련 기관들은/적극적으로/노력해 오고 있다/해결하려고/그 문제를

_____
_____

3. 그것은 쉽지 않다/줄이는 것은/범죄율을

_____
_____

4. 이 에세이에서/나는 자세히 설명하겠다/몇 가지 원인들과/실행 가능한 해결책을/증가하는 범죄율에 대한

_____
_____

5. 우선/여러 가지 이유들이 있다/범죄율이 증가하고 있는데

_____
_____

6. 첫 번째는/부자들과 가난한 사람들의 빈부격차가/상당히 심화되고 있다

_____
_____

7. 일반적으로/일부의 가난한 사람들은/겪어오고 있는/재정적 어려움을/경향이 있다/범죄를 저지르는/해결책으로써/삶의 어려움에 대한

_____
_____

8. 더욱이/그들은 항상 믿는다/그들이 적절한 대우를 받지 못한다고/정부당국으로부터/그리고 소외감을 느끼는 경향이 있다/사회로부터

_____
_____

9. 이런 상황에서/소외계층이/의지한다/위법행위에/하기 위해서/충족하기 위해서/그들 자신의 필요를

_____
_____

10. 예를 들어/그들은 강도를 저지른다/얻기 위해/현금이나 다른 물품을/생존을 위한

_____
_____

11. 두 번째는/도덕성이 현저하게 약해지고 있다/최근에

_____
_____

12. 물질주의가 더 강해지고 있다/오늘날/과거보다

_____
_____

13. 다시 말해서/사람에 대한 가치를/두고 있다/그의 그리고 그녀의 물질적인 부에/그들의 인격과 도덕성보다

_____
_____

14. 이러한 변화들은/가치에 있어서/사람들을 유도한다/범죄들을 저지르라고

___

___

15. 결과적으로/이것은 중요하다/정부가/노력하는 것이/문제를 해결하기 위해서

___

___

16. 첫 번째로/그들은 격차를 줄여야 한다/부자들과 가난한 사람들의

___

___

17. 그들이 이것을 성취하기 위해서/사회적 복지와 교육체계들이/계획되어야 한다/효율적으로

___

___

18. 이것은 제공해야만 한다/기회들을/균등하게/사람들에게/낮은 사회적 위치에 있는/찾기 위해서/더 좋은 미래를

___

___

19. 이것에 덧붙여서/사법제도들은 강화되어야만 한다/범죄율을 막기 위해서/더 증가로부터

___

___

20. 다시 말해서/강력한 법의 시행과 범죄자들의 처벌이/필요하다

___

___

21. 그것을 위해서/정부는 제공해야 한다/경찰들에게/최신 장비와 발전된 수사기술을

22. 이것뿐만 아니라/적절한 갱생프로그램이/시행되어야 한다/범죄자들이/적응할 수 있도록/사회에/출소 후에

23. 결론은/위에서 언급한 것처럼/몇 가지 이유들이 있다/범죄증가에 대한/그리고 몇 가지 접근법들은/그것을 해결하기 위해/제시되었다/또한

24. 분석함에 의하여/범죄들에 대한 이유들을/철저하게/적절한 해결책들이/적용되어야 한다/해결하기 위해서/그 문제를

25. 이러한 방법으로/사회는 될 수 있다/범죄 없는 사회가

Answer

1. It is a fact that the crime rate has been on the rise significantly in various parts of the world.
2. Even though governments and relevant organizations have been actively trying to address the issue.
3. It is not easy to cut down on the crime rate.
4. In this essay, I will spell out several culprits and feasible solutions to the increasing crime rate.
5. To begin with, there are a couple of issues that cause the crime rate to rise.
6. First, the gap between the haves and the have-nots has considerably widened.
7. In general, some impoverished people who have undergone financial difficulties tend to commit crimes as a solution to life's hardship.
8. Moreover, they usually believe they do not obtain proper treatment from the authorities and have a tendency to feel isolated from society.
9. In these circumstances, the disadvantaged resort to misconduct to meet their own needs.
10. For instance, they commit a robbery to acquire money or other items for survival.
11. Second, morality has noticeably weakened in recent years.
12. Materialism has become much stronger today than it was in the past.
13. That is to say, a person's worth puts in his/her material wealth rather than in their character and mortality.
14. These changes in values have led people to commit a crime.
15. Consequently, it is vital for governments to make considerable efforts to tackle the issue.
16. Firstly, they should bridge the gulf between the affluent and the needy.
17. For them to achieve it. social welfare and education systems should be planned efficiently,
18. , which should provide opportunities equally for people in low social statuses to find a better future.
19. In addition to that, justice systems should be reinforced to deter the crime rate from a further increase.
20. In other words, the strict implementation of laws and criminal punishments are necessary.
21. To that end, governments should furnish police officers with the latest equipment and advanced investigation techniques.
22. Not only that, a proper rehabilitation system should be practiced for offenders to adjust to society after release.
23. In conclusion, as stated above, there are a few reasons for the increasing crime rate, and several approaches to unravel it are suggested as well.
24. By analyzing the reasons for crimes thoroughly, appropriate solutions should be applied to sort out the problem.
25. In this way, the society can become a crime-free society.

You should spend about 40 minutes on this task.

Write about the following topic:

> **The crime rate has increased rapidly around the world. Discuss some causes for this rise and suggest workable solutions to this problem.**

Give reasons for your answer and include any relevant examples from your own knowledge or experience.

Write at least 250 words.

Answer

It is a fact that the crime rate has been on the rise significantly in various parts of the world. Even though governments and relevant organizations have been actively trying to address the issue, it is not easy to cut down on the crime rate. In this essay, I will spell out several culprits and feasible solutions to the increasing crime rate.

To begin with, there are a couple of issues that cause the crime rate to rise. First, the gap between the haves and the have-nots has considerably widened. In general, some impoverished people who have undergone financial difficulties tend to commit crimes as a solution to life's hardship. Moreover, they usually believe they do not obtain proper treatment from the authorities and have a tendency to feel isolated from society. In these circumstances, the disadvantaged resort to misconduct to meet their own needs. For instance, they commit a robbery to acquire money or other items for survival. **Second, morality has noticeably weakened in recent years, and materialism has become much stronger today than it was in the past.** That is to say, a person's worth puts in his/her material wealth rather than in their character and morality. These changes in values have led people to commit a crime.

Consequently, it is vital for governments to make considerable efforts to tackle the issue. Firstly, they should bridge the gulf between the affluent and the needy. For them to achieve it, social welfare and education systems should be planned efficiently, which should provide opportunities equally for people in low social statuses to find a better future. **In addition to that, justice systems should be reinforced to deter the crime rate from a further increase.** In other words, the strict implementation of laws and criminal punishments are necessary. To that end, governments should furnish police officers with the latest equipment and advanced investigation techniques. Not only that, a proper rehabilitation system should be practiced for offenders to adjust to society after release.

In conclusion, as stated above, there are a few reasons for the increasing crime rate, and several approaches to unravel it are suggested as well. By analysing the reasons for crimes thoroughly, appropriate solutions should be applied to sort out the problem. In this way, the society can become a crime-free society.

4. The death penalty

You should spend about 40 minutes on this task.

Write about the following topic:

> A few countries punish the criminal with the death penalty. However, others think life imprisonment is a better punishment for crimes. What is your view?

Give reasons for your answer and include any relevant examples from your own knowledge or experience.

Write at least 250 words.

INTRODUCTION

사형제도에 대한 논쟁이 계속되고 있다.

비윤리적이고 아무도 삶을 앗아갈 권리가 없다. 사형반대에 대한 이유를 설명하겠다.

BODY1(사형반대)

1. 사형이 범죄를 막지 못한다.
2. 무죄인 사람이 사형을 당할 가능성이 있다.

BODY2(종신형선호)

1. 사형 대신 종신형의 판결을 해야 한다.
   → 감옥에서 남은 삶 동안 반성과 피해자에 대한 사죄

CONCLUSION

사형이 범죄 예방에 대한 해결책이 아니다.

대신에 긴 형량과 종신형이 실행되어야 한다.

몇몇 나라들은 사형으로써 범죄자를 처벌한다. 그러나, 다른 사람들은 종신형이 범죄에 대한 더 나은 처벌이라고 생각한다. 어느 정도 동의하는가?

INTRODUCTION

사형이나 종신형 집행에 대한 계속적인 논쟁이 있어왔다. 많은 사람들은 심각한 중죄에 대한 처벌로써 사형에 찬성한다. 그러나, 나는 그것이 비윤리적이고 아무도 삶을 빼앗을 권리가 없기 때문에 사형에 반대한다. 다음의 문단에서, 나는 그 이유를 자세히 설명하겠다.

BODY 1

우선, 사형이 사람들이 범죄를 저지르는 것을 막을 수 있다는 분명한 증거가 없다. 다시 말해서, 사형이 범죄에 대한 억제책으로써 적절한 처벌이 아니다. 사실상, 사형제도가 있는 나라들의 범죄율이 그것을 시행하지 않는 다른 나라보다 훨씬 높다. 그것은 일부의 범죄자들은 그들이 범행을 하기 전 그들이 받을지도 모르는 처벌에 대해서 거의 생각하지 않기 때문이다. 계획적인 범죄에 있어서는, 범죄자들은 잡히지 않기 위해서 주의를 한다. **덧붙여서, 무엇보다도, 무죄인 사람들이 부당하게 유죄를 선고 받고 사형을 당할 가능성이 있다.** 실제로 사형집행 후에 무죄가 증명되는 실제 사례들이 있다. 이것은 사형 반대자들이 계속 주장해 온 것이다. 이러한 맥락에서 나는 사형은 시행되면 안 된다고 믿는다.

BODY 2

사형 대신에, 당국은 범죄자들에게 종신형 선고를 해야 한다. 다시 말해서, 남은 삶 동안 고통스러울 수 있도록 수감되어야 하고, 그 감옥에서 그들은 잘못된 행동 그리고 피해자와 사회의 정신적 충격을 반성해야 한다. 이러한 점에서, 종신형이 강하고 긴 고통이고 그것은 사형보다 범죄자들에게 더 심한 처벌일 수 있다. 그러므로, 당국이 사형보다 종신형을 집행하는 것이 설득력이 있다.

CONCLUSION

결론은, 사형은 그의 비효율성과 부정적인 결과들 때문에 흉악범죄 처벌을 위한 최상의 해법은 아니다. 모든 것을 고려할 때, 종신형이 최고 형량으로서 고려되어야 하는 것이 이치에 맞다.

문장에 필요한 어휘

> 1. ongoing/constant/continuous; 계속되는
> 2. enforcement/execution; 집행
> 3. capital punishment/the death penalty/the punishment of death/execution; 사형
> 4. life imprisonment/life in prison/life sentence/life in jail/imprisonment in life; 종신형

사형이나 종신형 집행에 대한 계속적인 논쟁이 있어 왔다.
There has been an ongoing debate over the enforcement of either capital punishment or life imprisonment.

> 5. approve of/agree with/be in favor of; ~에 찬성하다
> 6. a felony/a grave offense; 중죄

많은 사람들은 심각한 중죄에 대한 처벌로써 사형에 찬성한다.
Many approve of the death penalty as an appropriate punishment for a serious felony.

> 7. be against/be not in favor of/disagree with; 반대한다
> 8. immoral; 비도덕적인
> 9. have(has) the right to; ~할 권리가 있다
> 10. take a life; 삶을 앗아가다

그러나, 나는 그것이 비윤리적이고 아무도 삶을 빼앗을 권리가 없기 때문에 사형에 반대한다.
However, I am against capital punishment since it is immoral and no one has the right to take a life.

> 11. elaborate on/spell out/explain in full detail; 자세히 설명하다

다음의 문단에서, 나는 그 이유들을 자세히 설명하겠다.
In the following paragraphs, I will elaborate on the reasons.

> 12. above all/to begin with/first of all/for a start/first and foremost; 우선/먼저
> 13. clear-cut(undeniable) evidence/hard proof/smoking gun; 명백한 증거
> 14. evidence/proof; 증거
> 15. deter(stop/prohibit/prevent) A from B; A가 B하는 것을 막다
> 16. commit a crime/commit a criminal act; 범죄를 저지르다

우선, 사형이 사람들이 범죄를 저지르는 것을 막을 수 있다는 분명한 증거가 없다.

Above all, there is no clear-cut evidence that capital punishment can deter people from committing crimes.

> 17. in other words/to put it another way/that is/that is to say; 다시 말해서
> 18. proper/appropriate/suitable; 적절한
> 19. as a deterrent; 억제수단으로

다시 말해서, 사형이 범죄에 대한 억제책으로써 적절한 처벌이 아니다.

In other words, execution is not a proper punishment as a deterrent against crimes.

> 20. in fact/in reality/as a matter of fact/actually/virtually; 사실상
> 21. the crime rate; 범죄율
> 22. still(far/much/even) higher; 훨씬 높다
> 23. implement/carry out/conduct; 시행하다

사실상 사형제도가 있는 나라들의 범죄율이 그것을 시행하지 않는 다른 나라보다 훨씬 높다.

In fact, the crime rate in countries that impose the death penalty is still higher than that of the countries which do not implement it.

> 24. that is because S+V; 이러한 것은 ~ 때문이다
> 25. criminal/offender/culprit/prisoner; 범죄자
> 26. rarely/barely/seldom/hardly; 거의 ~하지 않는다

그것은 일부의 범죄자들은 죄를 범하기 전에 그들이 받을지도 모르는 처벌에 대해 거의 생각하지 않기 때문이다.

That is because some criminals rarely think about the punishment they would receive before they commit a crime.

> 27. concerning/regarding/with respect to/as regards/respecting; ~에 대해서
> 28. a premeditated crime/a calculated crime; 계획적인 범죄
> 29. take precaution/be careful/be discreet/mind; 주의하다/조심하다
> 30. get caught/be taken/be arrested; 잡히다

계획적인 범죄에 있어서는, 범죄자들은 잡히지 않기 위해서 주의를 한다.
Concerning a premeditated crime, the criminals take all precautions not to get caught.

> 31. in addition to that/on top of that/furthermore/moreover; 덧붙여서
> 32. most of all/above all/first of all; 무엇보다도/가장 중요한 것은
> 33. possibility/likelihood/probability; 가능성
> 34. innocent people/the innocent; 무죄인 사람
> 35. be convicted/receive a verdict of guilty/be sentenced to+N; 유죄판결을 받다
>   → be sentenced to jail(금고형에 처해지다)
>   → be sentenced to death(사형이 선고되다)
>   → be sentenced to life imprisonment(종신형을 받다)
> 36. execute/carry out execution/put somebody to death; 사형하다/처형하다

덧붙여서, 무엇보다도, 무죄인 사람들이 부당하게 유죄를 선고 받고 사형을 당할 가능성이 있다.
In addition to that, most of all, there is the possibility that innocent people could be wrongly convicted and executed.

> 37. real(actual) examples(cases/instances); 실제 사례들
> 38. innocence/not guilty/acquitted; 무죄

실제로, 사형 집행 후에 무죄가 증명되는 실제 사례들이 있다.
In reality, there are real examples where innocence was proved after execution.

> 39. opponent/dissenter/objector; 반대자
> 40. consistently/continuously/constantly; 계속적으로

이것은 사형 반대자들이 계속 주장해 온 것이다.
It is what capital punishment opponents have constantly claimed.

> 41. in this context/therefore/thus/hence/as a result; 이러한 맥락에서

이러한 맥락에서 나는 사형은 시행되면 안 된다고 믿는다.
In this context, I believe that the death penalty should not be enforced.

42. instead of/in place of/In lieu of; ~ 대신에
43. the authorities; 당국
44. sentence A to B; A에게 B 판결을 내리다

사형 대신에 당국은 범죄자에게 종신형 선고를 해야 한다.
Instead of the death penalty, the authorities should sentence offenders to life in prison.

45. undergo/go through/suffer from/experience; 겪다
46. overwhelming/extreme/severe; 극심한/과도한/견디기 어려운
47. distress/suffering/pain; 고통
48. be imprisoned; 갇히다
    → be imprisoned for life; 무기 징역을 받다
49. for the rest of one's life; 남은 삶 동안

다시 말해서, 범죄자들이 극심한 고통을 겪도록 그들은 남은 삶 동안 수감되어야 한다.
To put it another way, for criminals to undergo overwhelming distress, they should be imprisoned for the rest of their life,

50. reflect on wrongdoing; 죄를 반성하다
51. trauma/psychological trauma; 정신적 충격
52. the victims; 피해자들

그리고, 감옥에서, 그들의 잘못된 행동 피해자나 사회의 정신적 충격을 반성해야 한다.
, and in prison, they must reflect on their wrongdoing and the trauma of the victims and society.

53. in this respect; 이 점에 있어서
54. intense and prolonged pain; 강하고 긴 고통
55. a severe(heavy/intensive/serious) punishment; 중한 벌

이 점에 있어서, 종신형이 강하고 긴 고통이고 그것은 사형보다 범죄자들에게 심한 처벌일 수 있다.
In this respect, life imprisonment is the intense and prolonged pain, and it can be a more severe punishment to criminals than the death penalty.

> 56. compelling/reasonable/advisable/desirable/persuasive; 설득력 있는/타당한
> 57. rather than; ~보다는

그러므로, 당국이 사형보다 종신형을 집행하는 것이 설득력이 있다.

It is, therefore, compelling for the authorities to implement a life sentence rather than capital punishment.

> 58. in conclusion/to sum up/In short; 결론은
> 59. the solution to/the answer to/the key to: ~에 대한 해법
> 60. atrocious/fierce/cruel/brutal; 흉악한
> 61. on account of/due to/because of/owing to; ~ 때문에
> 62. ineffectiveness and unfavorable consequences; 비효율성과 부정적인 결과들

결론은, 사형은 그의 비효율성과 부정적인 결과 때문에 흉악범죄 처벌을 위한 최상의 해법은 아니다.

In conclusion, the death penalty is not the best solution to punishment for atrocious crimes on account of its ineffectiveness and unfavourable consequences.

> 63. all things considered; 모든 것을 고려할 때
> 64. make sense/stand to reason/be logical; 이치에 맞다
> 65. deem/consider/regard; 고려하다/생각하다
> 66. a maximum punishment/a maximum penalty; 최고 형량

모든 것을 고려할 때, 종신형이 최고 형량으로서 고려되어야 하는 것이 이치에 맞다.

All things considered, it makes sense that life imprisonment should be deemed as maximum punishment.

구문연습

1. 계속적인 논쟁이 있어왔다/집행에 대한/사형 또는 종신형

_____
_____

2. 많은 사람들은/사형에 찬성한다/심각한 중죄에 대한 적절한 처벌로써

_____
_____

3. 그러나/나는 반대한다/사형을/왜냐하면 이것은 비윤리적이고/아무도 권리가 없다/삶을 앗아갈

_____
_____

4. 다음의 문단에서/나는 자세히 설명할 것이다/그 이유들을

_____
_____

5. 우선/분명한 증거는 없다/사형이/막을 수 있다/사람이 범죄를 저지르는 것을

_____
_____

6. 다시 말해서/사형은 적절한 처벌이 아니다/범죄에 대한 억제로써

_____
_____

7. 사실상/범죄율은/사형제도가 있는 나라들에서/훨씬 높다/다른 나라보다/그것을 시행하지 않는

8. 이것은/때문이다/일부의 범죄자들은/거의 생각하지 않는다/그들이 받을 처벌을/그들이 범죄를 저지르기 전에

9. 계획적인 범죄에 있어서/범죄자들은/모든 주의를 한다/잡히지 않기 위해서

10. 덧붙여서/무엇보다도/가능성이 있다/무죄인 사람들이/부당하게 유죄를 선고 받고/사형을 당한다/판단 착오로

11. 실제로/실제의 사례들이 있다/무죄가 증명된/사형집행 후에

12. 이것은 ~ 것이다/사형반대론자들이/계속 주장해온

13. 이러한 맥락에서/나는 믿는다/사형은 시행되지 말아야 한다

14. 사형 대신에/당국은/선고를 해야만 한다/범죄자들에게/종신형을

15. 다시 말해서/범죄자가/극심한 고통을 겪도록/그들은 수감되어야 한다/남은 인생 동안

16. 그리고/감옥에서/그들은 반성해야 한다/그리고/정신적 충격을/희생자들이나 사회의

17. 이러한 면에서/종신형은 강하고 긴 고통이고/더 심한 처벌일 수 있다/범죄자들에게/사형보다

18. 그것은/그러므로/설득력이 있다/당국이/실행하는 것이/종신형을/사형보다는

19. 결론은/사형은 아니다/최상의 해결책이/흉악범죄를 처벌하는 데/비효율성과 부정적인 결과 때문에

20. 모든 것을 고려할 때/이것은 이치에 맞다/종신형이 고려되어야 한다/최고형량으로써

Answer

1. There has been an ongoing debate over the enforcement of either capital punishment or life imprisonment.

2. Many approve of the death penalty as an appropriate punishment for a serious felony.

3. However, I am against capital punishment since it is immoral and no one has the right to take a life.

4. In the following paragraphs, I will elaborate on the reasons.

5. Above all, there is no clear-cut evidence that capital punishment can deter people from committing crimes.

6. In other words, execution is not a proper punishment as a deterrent against crimes.

7. In fact, the crime rate in countries that impose the death penalty is still higher than that of the countries which do not implement it.

8. That is because some criminals rarely think about the punishment they would receive before they commit a crime.

9. Concerning a premeditated crime, the criminals take all precautions not to get caught.

10. In addition to that, most of all, there is the possibility that innocent people could be wrongly convicted and executed.

11. In reality, there are real examples where innocence was proved after execution.

12. It is what capital punishment opponents have constantly claimed.

13. In this context, I believe that the death penalty should not be enforced.

14. Instead of the death penalty, the authorities should sentence offenders to life in prison.

15. To put it another way, for criminals to undergo overwhelming distress, they should be imprisoned for the rest of their life,

16. , and in prison, they must reflect on their wrongdoing and the trauma of the victims and society.

17. In this respect, life imprisonment is the intense and prolonged pain, and it can be a more severe punishment to criminals than the death penalty.

18. It is, therefore, compelling for the authorities to carry out a life sentence rather than capital punishment.

19. In conclusion, the death penalty is not the best solution to punishment for atrocious crimes on account of its ineffectiveness and unfavourable consequences.

20. All things considered, it makes sense that life imprisonment should be deemed as maximum punishment.

You should spend about 40 minutes on this task.

Write about the following topic:

> A few countries punish the murderer with the death penalty. However, others think life imprisonment is a better punishment for murderers. What is your opinion?

Give reasons for your answer and include any relevant examples from your own knowledge or experience.

Write at least 250 words.

Answer

There has been an ongoing debate over the enforcement of either capital punishment or life imprisonment. Many approve of the death penalty as an appropriate punishment for a serious felony. However, I am against capital punishment since it is immoral and no one has the right to take a life. In the following paragraphs, I will elaborate on the reasons.

Above all, there is no clear-cut evidence that capital punishment can deter people from committing crimes. In other words, execution is not a proper punishment as a deterrent against crimes. In fact, the crime rate in countries that impose the death penalty is still higher than that of the countries which do not implement it. That is because some criminals rarely think about the punishment they would receive before they commit a crime. Concerning a premeditated crime, the criminals take all precautions not to get caught. In addition to that, most of all, there is the possibility that innocent people could be wrongly convicted and executed. In reality, there are real examples where innocence was proved after execution. It is what capital punishment opponents have consistently claimed. In this context, I believe that the death penalty should not be enforced.

Instead of the death penalty, the authorities should sentence offenders to life in prison. To put it another way, for criminals to undergo overwhelming distress, they should be imprisoned for the rest of their life, and in prison, they must reflect on their wrongdoing, the trauma of the victims and society. In this respect, life imprisonment is the intense and prolonged pain, and it can be a more severe punishment to criminals than the death penalty. It is, therefore, compelling for the authorities to carry out a life sentence rather than capital punishment.

In conclusion, the death penalty is not the best solution to punishment for atrocious crimes on account of its ineffectiveness and unfavourable consequences. All things considered, it makes sense that life imprisonment should be deemed as maximum punishment.

IELTS Easy Writing

Unit 4

The environment

1. Rainforest
2. Global warming
3. Waste problem
4. Zoo

1. Rainforest

You should spend about 40 minutes on this task.

Write about the following topic:

> It is true that rainforests are threatened by human activities. Some people say that rainforests can be destroyed for human development. However, others are against this opinion. What is your view?

Give reasons for your answer and include any relevant examples from your own knowledge or experience.

Write at least 250 words.

INTRODUCTION
열대 우림이 여러 가지 요인들에 의해 파괴되고 있는 것은 사실이다.
보호와 개발에 대한 두 가지 의견을 제시하겠다.

BODY1(보호)
1. 생태계를 위해 보호
2. 지구온난화 방지를 위해 보호

BODY2 (개발)
1. 열대 우림을 희생해서라도 개발은 인간을 위해 필요

CONCLUSION
발전과 열대 우림의 보존에 대한 균형이 필요하다.

열대 우림이 인간의 활동들에 의해서 위협을 받고 있는 것은 사실이다. 어떤 사람들은 열대 우림은 인간의 발전을 위해 파괴될 수 있다고 주장한다. 그러나, 다른 이들은 이 의견에 반대한다. 당신의 견해는 무엇인가?

INTRODUCTION

열대 우림의 많은 부분이 인구의 팽창과 발전을 위한 공간을 만들기 위해 파괴되고 있다는 것은 일반적인 사실이다. 일부의 사람들은 열대 우림을 보존하는 것은 인간뿐만 아니라 동식물들에게 중요하다고 믿는다. 반면에, 다른 사람들은 발전을 위해서 열대 우림을 어느 정도 손상시키는 것은 불가피하다고 주장한다. 이 에세이는 다음과 같은 두 가지 의견을 고려할 것이다.

BODY 1

우선, 열대 우림은 생태계를 위해서 보호되어야만 한다. 왜냐하면 그것은 현존하는 동식물뿐만 아니라 아직 발견되지 않은 종에도 서식지를 제공하기 때문이다. 만약 열대 우림의 파괴가 일어나면, 사람들은 불치병을 치료하는 데 해답을 가질 수 있는 새로운 식물과 동물 종들을 발견하는 기회를 잃을 것이다. 이것에 덧붙여서, **무분별한 열대 우림의 파괴는 지구 온난화를 초래한다.** 열대 우림의 엄청난 손실을 가져오는 감소는 환경에 돌이킬 수 없는 손상을 주고 기온변화와 녹는 빙하로 인한 해수면의 상승과 같은 심각한 문제들을 발생시킨다. 이러한 이유들 때문에, 지구온난화를 막기 위해서 열대 우림을 보호하는 것이 아주 바람직하다.

BODY 2

다른 한편으로는, 인간의 발전을 위해 열대 우림의 손실은 피할 수 없다. 세계적으로 계속되는 인구 증가로 인해 인간을 위한 많은 식량뿐만 아니라 더 많은 공간이 필요하다는 것은 분명하다. 이러한 것을 위해, 세계에서 가장 큰 열대 우림인 아마존은 사람들의 삶을 위해 작물을 재배하고 공간을 만들기 위해 개발되고 있다. 따라서, 만약 그것이 열대 우림의 무분별한 파괴가 아니라면, 인간의 복지와 이익을 위해 그들은 이용될 수 있다.

CONCLUSION

요약하자면, 열대 우림이 보호되어야 하지만 그들은 개발의 대가로 어느 정도 손상되고 있다. 그러므로, 만약 열대 우림이 규제 없이 개발된다면, 동물과 식물에게 위협이 될 것이고 결국에는 멸종될 수 있다. 따라서, 개발자들과 정부들은 발전과 보존 사이에서 현명하고 적절하게 균형을 유지해야 한다.

문장에 필요한 어휘

---

1. it is a common fact that S+V; 그것은 일반적인 사실이다.
2. rainforests/tropical rainforests; 열대 우림
3. flatten/knock down/pull down/ruin/destroy/demolish/ravage; 파괴하다/무너뜨리다
4. development/growth/advancement/progress/exploitation; 발전

열대 우림의 많은 부분은 인구의 팽창과 발전을 위한 공간을 만들기 위해 파괴되고 있다는 것은 일반적인 사실이다.

It is a common fact that large parts of rainforests are being flattened to make space for human population expansion and development.

---

5. conserving/protecting/keeping/preserving; 보존하는 것
6. essential/important/crucial/vital/significant; 중요한
7. fauna and flora; 동식물
8. B as well as A/not only A but also B; A뿐만 아니라 B

일부는 열대 우림을 보존하는 것은 인간뿐만 아니라 동식물들에게 중요하다고 믿는다.

Some believe that conserving rainforest is essential for fauna and flora as well as human beings.

---

9. in contrast/by contrast/on the contrary/on the other hand; 반면에/다른 한편으로는
10. argue/maintain/state/assert; 주장하다
11. for the sake of/for/in behalf of/for the good of; ~을 위해서
12. to some degree/to some extent/to a certain degree/somewhat/more or less; 어느 정도
13. inevitable/unavoidable/necessary/unpreventable; 불가피한/피할 수 없는

반면에, 다른 사람들은 발전을 위해서 열대 우림을 어느 정도 손상시키는 것은 불가피하다고 주장한다.

In contrast, others argue that for the sake of advancement, the damage of rainforests to some extent is inevitable.

---

14. as follows/in the following manner; 다음과 같이

이 에세이는 다음과 같이 두 가지 의견을 고려할 것이다.

This essay will consider both opinions as follows.

15. first of all/to begin with/above all/first and foremost; 우선
16. ecosystem/ecological system; 생태계
17. provide A to(for) B/provide A with B/supply A with B; A에게 B를 제공하다; A에게 B를 제공하다
18. habitat/home; 서식지
19. fauna and flora/animals and plants; 동식물

우선, 열대 우림은 생태계를 위해서 보존되어야 한다, 왜냐하면 그것은 현존하는 동식물뿐만 아니라 아직 발견되지 않는 종에도 서식지를 제공하기 때문이다.

First of all, rainforests should be preserved for the ecosystem since it provides habitats for undiscovered species as well as existing fauna and flora.

20. lose(miss) opportunities/forfeit the occasions; 기회들을 잃다
21. find/get/seek; 찾다
22. species; 종

만약 열대 우림의 파괴가 일어나면, 사람들은 새로운 식물과 동물 종들을 발견하는 기회를 잃어버릴 것이다.

If the destruction of rainforest occurs, people will lose opportunities to find new plants and animal species

23. hold(get) the answer/reach(find) a solution/find a solution; 해답을 얻다
24. incurable(permanent/terminal) diseases(illness); 불치병

그것은 불치병을 치료하는 데 해답을 가질 수 있다.

that could hold the answer to the treatment of incurable diseases.

25. in addition to that/furthermore/moreover/what is more; 덧붙여서
26. reckless/ruthless/heedless/careless/inconsiderate/thoughtless; 무모한
27. A contribute to B/A make a contribution to B/B be attributed to A; A가 B에 기여하다
28. global warming; 지구온난화

이것에 덧붙여서, 무분별한 열대 우림의 파괴는 지구 온난화를 초래한다.

In addition to that, the reckless destruction of rainforests contributes to global warming.

1. Rainforest

29. devastating/shocking/tremendous; 엄청난 손실을 가하는/충격적인
30. inflict damage on; ~에 손상을 주다/~에 손해를 입히다
31. irreparable/irretrievable/irrecoverable; 돌이킬 수 없는
32. critical(serious/severe) problem; 심각한 문제
33. give rise to/lead to/result in/bring about; 일으키다/초래하다
34. climate change and sea level rise; 기후변화와 해수면 상승
35. generated by/caused by originated by/resulting from; ~ 로 일어난
36. melting glaciers; 녹는 빙하들

그것은 열대 우림의 엄청난 손실을 가져오는 감소는 환경에 돌이킬 수 없는 손상을 주고 기후변화와 녹는 빙하로 인한 해수면 상승과 같은 심각한 문제들을 발생시킨다.

It is because the devastating decline of rainforests inflicts irreparable damage on the environment, giving rise to critical problems, including climate changes and rising sea levels generated by melting glaciers.

37. for these reasons; 이러한 이유들 때문에
38. highly/greatly/deeply/strongly; 매우/아주
39. desirable/advisable/worthwhile/valuable; 바람직한/가치가 있는
40. curb/deter/prevent/stop/fight against; 막다

이러한 이유들 때문에, 지구온난화를 막기 위해서 열대 우림을 보호하는 것이 아주 바람직하다.

For these reasons, it is highly desirable to protect rainforests to curb global warming.

41. the loss of; ~의 손실

다른 한편으로는, 인간의 발전을 위해 열대 우림의 손실은 피할 수 없다.

On the other hand, the loss of tropical rainforests is unavoidable for human progress.

42. it is clear-cut(apparent/clear/obvious/undeniable) that S+V; 분명하다
43. on account of/because of/due to/owing to; ~때문에
44. the ever-increasing(ever-rising) population; 계속 증가하는 인구
45. worldwide/globally/around the globe; 세계적으로

세계적으로 계속되는 인구 증가로 인해 인간을 위한 식량뿐만 아니라 더 많은 공간이 필요한 것은 분명하다.

It is clear-cut that not only more space but also food is needed for human beings, on account of the ever- increasing population worldwide.

> 46. cultivate/farm; 경작하다

이러한 것을 위해, 세계에서 가장 큰 열대 우림인 아마존은 사람들의 삶을 위해 작물을 재배하고 공간을 만들기 위해 개발되고 있다.

For which the Amazon, the world's largest rainforest, has been developed to cultivate food crops and make space for people's lives.

> 47. thus/therefore/consequently/as a result/hence; 그러므로/따라서
> 48. unless/if~not; 만약 ~이 아니라면
> 49. heedless/reckless/indiscreet; 무분별한
> 50. exploit/use/utilize/make use of; 이용하다

따라서 만약 그것이 열대 우림의 무분별한 파괴가 아니라면, 인간의 복지와 이익을 위해 그들은 이용될 수 있다.

Thus, unless it is the heedless destruction of the rainforests, they can be exploited for human welfare and interest.

> 51. to sum up/In conclusion/In short/In summary; 요약하자면
> 52. compromise/hurt/ruin/damage/undermine; 손상시키다
> 53. in exchange for; ~에 대한 대가로

요약하자면, 열대 우림이 보호되어야 하지만 그들은 개발의 대가로 어느 정도 손상되고 있다.

To sum up, rainforests should be protected, though. They have been somewhat compromised in exchange for development.

> 54. without regulation/without control; 규제 없이
> 55. pose a threat to/present a threat to/threaten; 위협을 가하다
> 56. significant amounts of/large amounts of/great deals of/good deals of; 많은 양
> 57. wipe out/die out/exterminate/cease to exist; 멸종시키다
> 58. in the end/in the long run/finally/eventually; 결국에

그러므로, 만약 열대 우림이 규제 없이 개발된다면, 동물과 식물에 위협을 가하고 결국에는 멸종시킬 수 있다.

Therefore, if rainforests are developed without restriction, it would pose a threat to significant amounts of plants and animals, which could wipe them out in the end.

1. Rainforest 217

> 59. should/had better/ought to/be supposed to; 해야만 한다
> 60. keep a balance; 균형을 맞추다
> 61. conservation/preservation/maintenance; 보존
> 62. wisely and properly/reasonably and appropriately; 현명하고 적절하게

그러므로, 개발자들과 정부들은 개발과 보존 사이에서 현명하고 적절하게 균형을 유지해야 한다.

In this context, developers and governments should keep a balance between exploitation and preservation wisely and appropriately.

구문연습

1. 일반적인 사실이다/많은 양의 열대 우림이/파괴되고 있다/공간을 만들기 위해서/인구의 팽창과 발전을 위한

---

2. 일부는 믿는다/열대 우림을 보존하는 것은/필수적이다/동식물들에게/인간뿐만 아니라

---

3. 반면에/다른 사람들은 주장한다/개발을 위해서/열대 우림의 파괴는/어느 정도/피할 수 없는 것이다

---

4. 이 에세이는/고려할 것이다/두 가지 의견을/다음과 같이

---

5. 우선/열대 우림은/보존되어야 한다/생태계를 위해서

---

6. 왜냐하면/생태계는 제공하기 때문이다/서식지들을/발견되지 않은 종/뿐만 아니라 현존하는 동식물

---

7. 만약 열대 우림의 파괴가/일어난다면/사람들은 기회를 잃을 수 있다/발견하는/새로운 식물과 동물군들을

8. 그러한 것은/해답을 가질 수 있다/불치병의 치료법에 대한

9. 이것에 덧붙여서/무모한 열대 우림의 파괴는/일으킨다/지구온난화를

10. 이것은 이유이다/엄청난 감소는/열대 우림에 있어서/돌이킬 수 없는 손상을 준다/환경에

11. 발생시킨다/심각한 문제들을/같은/기후의 변화 그리고 해수면 상승/~로 인한/녹는 빙하

12. 이러한 이유들로 인해/이것은 아주 바람직하다/열대 우림을 보호하는 것이/막기 위해서/지구온난화를

13. 다른 한편으로는/발전은 필요하다/열대 우림의 손실은/피할 수 없다/인간의 발전을 위해

14. 그것은 분명하다/많은 공간뿐만 아니라/인간을 위한 식량/필요해지다/때문에 계속 증가하는 인구수/세계적으로

_____
_____

15. 이러한 것을 위해/아마존/가장 큰 열대 우림/개발되고 있다/곡물을 경작하고 공간을 만들기 위해서/사람의 삶을 위해

_____
_____

16. 따라서/만약 아니라면/그것이/무분별한 파괴/열대 우림의/그들은 이용될 수 있다/인간의 복지와 이익을 위해

_____
_____

17. 요약하자면/열대 우림은/보호되어야 하지만/그들은/어느 정도/손상되고 있다/개발의 대가로

_____
_____

18. 그러므로/만약 열대 우림이/개발된다면/규제 없이/그것은 위협할 것이다/많은 양의 동물과 식물들을/이러한 것은 그들을 멸종시킬 수 있다/결국에는

_____
_____

19. 따라서/개발자들과 정부들은/균형을 유지해야 한다/개발과 보존 사이에/현명하게 그리고 적절하게

_____
_____

Answer

1. It is a common fact that large parts of rainforests are being flattened to make space for human population expansion and development.

2. Some believe that conserving rainforests is essential for fauna and flora as well as human beings.

3. In contrast, others argue that for the sake of advancement, the damage of rainforests to some extent is inevitable.

4. This essay will consider both opinions as follows.

5. First of all, rainforests should be preserved for the ecosystems

6. since it provides habitats for undiscovered species as well as existing fauna and flora.

7. If the destruction of rainforest occurs, people will lose opportunities to find out new plants and animal species

8. that could hold the answer to the treatment of incurable diseases.

9. In addition to that, the reckless destruction of rainforests contributes to global warming.

10. It is because the devastating decline of rainforests inflicts irreparable damage on the environment,

11. , giving rise to critical problems, including climate changes and rising generated by melting glaciers.

12. For these reasons, it is highly desirable to protect rainforests to curb global warming.

13. On the other hand, the loss of tropical rainforests is unavoidable for human progress.

14. It is clear-cut that not only more space but also food is needed for human beings, on account of the ever- increasing population worldwide.

15. For which the Amazon, the world's largest rainforest, has been developed to cultivate food crops and make space for people's lives.

16. Thus, unless it is the heedless destruction of the rainforests, they can be exploited for human welfare and interest.

17. To sum up, rainforests should be protected, though. They have been somewhat compromised in exchange for development.

18. Therefore, if rainforests are developed without restriction, it would pose a threat to significant amounts of plants and animals, which could wipe them out in the end.

19. In this context, developers and governments should keep a balance between exploitation and preservation wisely and appropriately.

You should spend about 40 minutes on this task.

Write about the following topic:

> **It is true that rainforests are threatened by human activities. Some people say that rainforests can be destroyed for human development. However, others are against this opinion. What is your view?**

Give reasons for your answer and include any relevant examples from your own knowledge or experience.

Write at least 250 words.

Answer

It is a common fact that large parts of rainforests are being flattened to make space for human population expansion and development. Some believe that conserving rainforests is essential for flora and fauna as well as human beings. In contrast, others argue that for the sake of advancement, the damage of rainforests to some extent is inevitable. This essay will consider both opinions as follows.

First of all, rainforests should be preserved for the ecosystem since it provides habitats for undiscovered species as well as existing fauna and flora. If the destruction of rainforest occurs, people will lose opportunities to find new plants and animal species that could hold the answer to the treatment of incurable diseases. **In addition to that, the reckless destruction of the rainforests contributes to global warming.** It is because the devastating decline of rainforests inflicts irreparable damage on the environment, giving rise to critical problems, including climate changes and rising sea generated by melting glaciers. For these reasons, it is highly desirable to protect rainforests to curb global warming.

On the other hand, the loss of tropical rainforests is unavoidable for human progress. It is clear-cut that not only space but also food is needed for human beings on account of the ever-increasing population worldwide, for which the Amazon, the world's largest rainforest, has been developed to cultivate food crops and make space for people's lives. Thus, unless it is the heedless destruction of the rainforests, they can be exploited for human welfare and interest.

To sum up, rainforests should be protected, though. They have been somewhat compromised in exchange for development. Therefore, if rainforests are developed without restriction, it would pose a threat to significant amounts of plants and animals, which could wipe them out in the end. In this context, developers and governments should keep a balance between exploitation and preservation wisely and appropriately.

2. Global warming

You should spend about 40 minutes on this task.

Write about the following topic:

> Global warming is one of the most serious issues the world faces today. What are the causes of global warming and what measures can governments and individuals take to tackle the issue?

Give reasons for your answer and include any relevant examples from your own knowledge or experience.

Write at least 250 words.

INTRODUCTION
　　지구 온난화는 긴급한 문제가 되고 있다. 몇 가지 원인을 분석하고 문제의 해결책들을 제시하겠다.

BODY1 원인
　　1. 인간활동
　　2. 나무의 벌채와 열대 우림의 파괴

BODY2 해결책
　　1. 개인적 측면
　　　　→ 대중교통이용
　　　　→ 일회용품 사용 자제
　　2. 정부측면
　　　　→ 교육과 캠페인을 통한 시민과 기업교육
　　　　→ 강력한 법규-법규위반 시 벌금

CONCLUSION
　　사람들과 정부들은 이 난제를 해결하기 위해 서로 협력해야 한다.

지구온난화는 오늘날 세계가 직면하는 가장 심각한 문제들 중 하나이다. 지구온난화의 원인은 무엇이고 정부와 개인들이 이 문제를 해결할 수 있는 조치는 무엇인가?

INTRODUCTION

지구온난화는 지난 십 년간에 걸쳐 중요하고 긴급한 환경적인 문제가 되고 있다. 지구온난화의 이면에는 몇 가지 원인들이 있고 이 문제를 해결하기 위한 몇 가지 해결책들이 있다. 이 에세이는 그들 원인들의 몇 가지를 분석하고 이 문제와 관련된 가능한 해결책들을 제안할 것이다.

BODY 1

지구온난화의 주요한 원인들 중의 하나는 광범위한 인간 활동이다. 특히, 과소비, 증가하는 차량들의 수는 이 현상에 대한 주요한 원인들이다. 이러한 상황들은 탄소가스, 매연 그리고 해로운 화학물질들을 발생시키고 이러한 것은 오존층파괴와 지구온난화를 야기한다. 오늘 날, 지구는 또한 인구 과잉 문제에 직면하고 있고 그리고 이러한 현상은 전보다 훨씬 더 심각하다. **이것에 덧붙여서, 개발을 위한 나무의 과다벌채와 열대 우림의 파괴는 지구온난화를 발생**시켜왔고, 극지방의 만년설의 해빙을 일으키고 홍수, 가뭄들 그리고 극심한 기후 조건들로 특징화된 기후변화를 가져오고 있다. 우리는 전 세계적으로 사람들이 기후변화로 인한 극심한 더위와 추위를 겪는 것을 볼 수 있다. 보여지는 것처럼, 몇 가지 원인들이 지구온난화에 상당한 영향을 준다

BODY 2

그럼에도 불구하고, 개인들과 정부가 지구 온난화를 둔화시킬 수 있는 해결책들이 또한 있다. 각 개인의 측면에서, 그들은 그들의 차 대신 대중교통을 이용해야 한다. 이러한 것은 가스 배출을 감소시킬 수 있고 지구 온난화를 지연시킬 수 있다. 다른 조치는 그들이 자연자원과 환경을 손상시키는 일회용상품 사용을 하지 말아야 한다. **정부 측면에서는**, 그들이 취해야 할 가장 주요한 조치는 시민들과 기업들이 지구온난화에 대해 인식하게 하기 위해서 환경 캠페인을 실행하는 것이다. 이와 함께, 정부는 그들의 역할을 그들 스스로 하게 할 수 있다. 두 번째는, 정부들은 이 문제를 예방하고 종결시키기 위해 강력한 법규를 만들고 시행해야 한다. 만약 시민들과 기업들이 그 법규를 어긴다면 그들은 과중한 벌금형을 받아야 한다. 이러한 방법들을 기반으로, 정부와 개개인들은 지구온난화를 줄이고 억제하기 위해 조치를 취해야만 한다.

CONCLUSION

위에서 언급한 것처럼, 인간의 활동들과 개발들은 지구온난화의 주요한 원인들이다. 그러나, 그것을 해결하기 위해 제시된 실행 가능한 해결 방법들이 있다. 그러므로, 개개인들과 정부들은 지구온난화를 막고 맞서기 위해서 서로 협력해야 한다.

문장에 필요한 어휘

> 1. global warming; 지구 온난화
> 2. critical/vital/important/significant/crucial; 중요한
> 3. pressing/urgent/burning; 긴급한
> 4. environmental concern(problem/challenge/difficulty); 환경적 문제
> 5. over the past decade; 지난 십 년에 걸쳐서

지구온난화는 지난 십 년간에 걸쳐 중요하고 긴급한 환경적인 문제가 되고 있다.

Global warming has been a critical and pressing environmental concern over the past decade.

> 6. culprit/reason/cause/ground; 원인/이유
> 7. solution/answer/key/remedy; 해결책
> 8. address/solve/resolve/tackle/sort out; 해결하다

지구온난화의 이면에는 몇 가지 원인들이 있고 이 문제를 해결하기 위한 몇 가지 해결책들이 있다.

There are several culprits behind global warming and a few solutions to address the problem.

> 9. analyse/examine; 분석하다/검토하다
> 10. associated with/related to/linked to; 관련된

이 에세이는 그들 원인들의 몇 가지를 분석하고 이 문제와 관련된 가능한 해결책들을 제안할 것이다.

This essay will analyse some of these reasons and propose possible remedies associated with the issue.

> 11. leading/primary/main/major; 주요한
> 12. far-reaching/extensive/broad/widespread/wide-ranging; 광범위한

지구 온난화의 주요한 원인들 중의 하나는 광범위한 인간 활동들이다.

One of the leading causes of global warming is far-reaching human activities.

> 13. in particular/particularly/especially; 특히
> 14. overconsumption/excessive spending; 과소비
> 15. the increasing number of vehicles(cars); 증가하는 차량의 수
> 16. phenomenon; 현상

특히, 과소비와 증가하는 차량들의 수는 이러한 현상에 대한 주요한 원인들이다.

In particular, overconsumption and the increasing number of vehicles are the key reasons for the phenomenon.

> 17. circumstances/conditions/surroundings; 상황
> 18. generate/produce/emit; 배출하다/발생시키다
> 19. carbon gases; 탄소 가스
> 20. hazardous/dangerous/perilous/risk; 위험한

이러한 상황들은 탄소 가스, 매연 그리고 해로운 화학물질들을 발생시킨다.

Those circumstances generate carbon gases, fumes and hazardous chemicals,

> 21. the depletion (destruction) of the ozone layer; 오존층 파괴
> 22. induce/incur/trigger/generate/provoke; 야기한다

이러한 것은 오존층 파괴와 지구온난화를 야기한다.

, which induce the depletion of the ozone layer and global warming.

> 23. today/nowadays/these days/recently/in recent years/in recent times; 오늘날/요즈음
> 24. face/confront; 직면하다
> 25. overpopulation/overflowing population; 인구과잉
> 26. the status quo/the current situation/the existent circumstances; 현재 상황
> 27. far/even/still/much(비교급강조); 훨씬

오늘날, 지구는 또한 인구과잉 문제에 직면하고 있고, 현재 상황은 전보다 훨씬 더 심각하다.

Today, the earth also faces the problem of overpopulation, and the status quo is far more serious than before.

> 28. furthermore/moreover/what is more/In addition; 더욱이
> 29. destruction/devastation/ruin/demolition; 파괴
> 30. rainforests/tropical rain forests; 열대 우림

2. Global warming

이것에 덧붙여서, 개발을 위한 나무의 과다벌채와 열대 우림의 파괴는 지구온난화를 발생시켜왔고,
Furthermore, the overcutting of trees and the destruction of rainforests for development have led to global warming,

---

31. melting/thawing; 해빙
32. polar ice-caps; 극지방의 만년설
33. characterized by/marked by; ~로 특징된/나타난
34. floods; 홍수
35. drought; 가뭄
36. extreme weather conditions; 극심한 기후 조건들

극지방의 만년설의 해빙을 일으키고 홍수들, 가뭄들과 극심한 기후 조건들로 특징화된 기후변화를 가져오고 있다.
, bringing about the melting of the polar ice-caps, and triggering climate changes characterized by floods, droughts and extreme weather conditions.

---

37. observe/watch/make observation; 관찰하다
38. globally/around the world/all over the world/worldwide; 전 세계적으로
39. cause A to B/lead A to B; A가 B에 이르게 하다
40. go through/undergo/experience/suffer; 겪다

우리는 전 세계적으로 사람들이 기후변화로 인한 극심한 더위와 추위를 겪는 것을 볼 수 있다.
We can observe globally that people go through severe hot and cold generated by climate change.

---

41. as can be seen; 보여지는 것처럼
42. a few/a couple of/several; 몇 가지
43. factor/aspect/reason/cause; 요인

보여지는 것처럼, 몇 가지 원인들이 지구온난화에 상당한 영향을 준다.
As can be seen, a few factors have significant influences on global warming.

---

44. nonetheless/nevertheless/for all that/still; 그럼에도 불구하고
45. slow down/curb/stop/prevent/block/deter; 둔화시키다/막다

그럼에도 불구하고, 개인들과 정부가 지구 온난화를 둔화시킬 수 있는 해결책들이 또한 있다.
Nonetheless, there are also a couple of solutions for individuals and governments to slow down global warming.

46. as for/in light of/when it comes to/in terms of/in the case of; ~ 측면에서/~에 대해 말하자면
47. instead of/in place of/in lieu of; ~대신에
48. the discharge of/the emission of; ~의 배출
49. delay/hold up on/postpone; 지연시키다

개인적인 측면에서, 그들은 그들의 차 대신 대중교통을 이용해야 한다. 이러한 것은 가스배출을 감소시킬 수 있고 지구 온난화를 지연시킬 수 있다.

As for people, they should use public transportation instead of their car, which can lessen the discharge of gasses and delay global warming.

50. disposable products(items); 일회용 상품들
51. undermine/damage/harm/hurt/mar; 손상시키다
52. natural resources; 자연자원

다른 조치는 그들이 자연자원과 환경을 손상시키는 일회용 상품사용을 하지 말아야 한다.

Another step is that they should not use disposable products that undermine natural resources and the environment.

53. measures/steps/action; 조치
54. carry out/organize/structure/conduct/implement; 시행하다
55. aware of; ~을 인식하는

정부측면에서는, 그들이 취해야 할 주요한 조치는 지구온난화에 대해 시민과 기업들이 인식하게 하기 위해서 환경캠페인을 실행하는 것이다.

In light of governments, the primary measures they should take are to carry out environmental campaigns to make citizens and companies aware of global warming.

56. play one's role/play a part; 역할을 하다
57. of one's own accord/personally/for themselves/on one's own; 스스로

이와 함께, 정부는 그들에게 그들의 역할을 스스로 하게 할 수 있다.

With this, governments can have them play their role of their own accord.

58. ought to/should/be supposed to/had better; 해야 한다
59. implement/carry out/practice A/put A into practice/put A into action; A를 실행하다
60. strong(powerful) regulations(rules); 강력한 법규
61. put an end to/finish/wind up with/bring an end to+N; 종결시키다/끝내다

두 번째는, 정치 지도자들은 이 문제를 예방하고 종결시키기 위해서 강력한 법규를 만들고 시행해야 한다.

Second, political leaders ought to make and implement strong regulations to prevent and put an end to this problem.

---

62. provided(that)/providing(that)/if; ~한다면
63. violate(break/infringe) the regulations; 법규를 어기다
64. incur(receive) a heavier(hefty) fine(penalty); 과중한 벌금형을 받다

만약 시민들과 기업들이 그 법규를 어긴다면 그들은 과중한 벌금형을 받아야 한다.

Provided that citizens and companies violate the regulations, they should incur a heavier fine.

---

65. take action(steps/measures); 조치를 취하다

이런 방법들을 기반으로, 국민들과 정부들은 지구온난화를 줄이고 억제하기 위해서 조치를 취해야만 한다.

Based on these ways, people and governments should take action to lessen and curb global warming.

---

66. as mentioned above/as stated above/as described above; 위에서 언급한 것처럼

위에서 언급한 것처럼, 인간의 활동들과 개발들은 지구 온난화의 주요한 원인들이다.

As mentioned above, human activities and developments are the major sources of global warming.

---

67. presented/shown/suggested/mentioned/proposed; 제시된

그러나, 그것을 해결하기 위해 제시된 실행 가능한 해결방법들이 있다.

However, there are feasible solutions presented to tackle it.

---

68. team up with/cooperate with/collaborate with/work together with; ~와 협력하다
69. fight against; 방지하다/맞서 싸우다

그러므로, 개개인들과 정부들은 지구온난화를 방지하고 맞서기 위해 서로 협력해야 한다.

Thus, individuals and governments should team up with each other to prevent and fight against global warming.

구문연습

1. 지구온난화는/되고 있다/중요하고 긴급한 환경문제가/지난 십 년에 걸쳐서

_____

_____

2. 몇 가지 원인들이 있다/지구온난화의 이면에는/그리고 몇 가지 해결책/해결하기 위한/이 문제들을

_____

_____

3. 이 에세이들은/분석할 것이다/그들 원인들 중 몇 가지를/그리고 제시할 것이다/가능한 해결책들을/이 문제와 관련된

_____

_____

4. 지구 온난화의/주요한 원인들 중의 하나는/광범위한 인간 활동이다.

_____

_____

5. 특히/과소비들과 증가하는 차량들의 수는/주요한 원인들이다/이 현상에 대한

_____

_____

6. 이러한 상황들은/발생시킨다/탄소 가스, 매연 그리고 해로운 화학물질들

_____

_____

7. 이러한 것은 일으킨다/오존층 파괴와 지구온난화를

_____
_____

8. 오늘날/지구는 또한 직면한다/과잉인구 문제에/그리고/현재 현상은/훨씬 더 심각하다/전보다

_____
_____

9. 이것에 덧붙여서/나무의 과다벌채와/열대 우림의 파괴/인간 발달을 위해서/발생시켜 왔다/지구온난화를

_____
_____

10. 그리고 일으킨다/극지방의 만년설의 해빙을/발생시킨다/기후 변화를/가뭄으로 특징된/그리고 극심한 기후 조건들

_____
_____

11. 우리는 볼 수 있다/세계적으로/사람들이/겪다/극심한 더위와 추위를/인한/기후변화로

_____
_____

12. 보여지는 것처럼/몇 가지의 요인들이/상당한 영향을 준다/지구 온난화에

_____
_____

13. 그럼에도 불구하고/또한 몇 가지 해결책들이 있다/사람들과 정부가/둔화시키기 위한/지구온난화를

_____
_____

14. 개인의 측면에서/그들은 이용해야만 한다/대중교통을/그들 자신의 차 대신에

---

15. 이러한 것은 감소시킬 수 있다/가스 배출을/그리고 지연시킬 수 있다/지구 온난화를

---

16. 다른 대책은/그들은 사용하지 말아야 한다/일회용 상품들을/그것은 손상시킨다/자연 자원과 환경을

---

17. 정부 측면에서는/가장 주요한 조치는/그들은 취할/시행하는 것이다/환경캠페인을/만들기 위해서/시민들과 회사들이/인식할 수 있도록/지구 온난화를

---

18. 이와 함께/정부는/이것은 하게 할 수 있다/그들이/그들의 역할을/스스로

---

19. 두 번째는/정치 지도자들은 해야만 한다/만들고 시행해야만 한다/강력한 규범들을/예방하고 종결시키기 위해서/그 문제를

---

20. 만약 시민들과 회사들이 어긴다면/그 법규들을/그들은/과중한 벌금형을 받아야 한다

_____
_____

21. 이러한 방법들을 기반으로/국민과 정부는/조치를 취해야만 한다/줄이고 억제하기 위해서/지구온난화

_____
_____

22. 위에서 언급한 것처럼/인간활동들과 개발들은/주요한 원인이다/지구온난화의

_____
_____

23. 그러나/해결책들이 있다/실행 가능한/제시된/그것을 해결하기 위해서

_____
_____

24. 그러므로/개개인들과 정부들은/해야 한다/서로 협력해야 한다/방지하고 맞서기 위해/지구온난화를

_____
_____

Answer

1. Global warming has been a critical and pressing environmental concern over the past decade.
2. There are several culprits behind global warming and a few solutions to address the problem.
3. This essay will analyse some of these reasons and propose possible remedies associated with the issue.
4. One of the leading causes is far-reaching human activities.
5. In particular, overconsumption and the increasing number of vehicles are the key reasons for the phenomenon.
6. Those circumstances generate carbon gasses, fumes and hazardous chemicals,
7. , which induce the depletion of the ozone layer and global warming.
8. Today, the earth also faces the problem of overpopulation, and the status quo is far more serious than before.
9. Furthermore, the overcutting of trees and the destruction of rainforests for development have led to global warming,
10. , bringing about the melting of the polar ice-caps triggering climate changes characterized by floods, droughts and extreme weather conditions.
11. We can observe globally that people go through severe hot and cold generated by climate change.
12. As can be seen, a few factors have significant influences on global warming.
13. Nonetheless, there are also a couple of solutions for individuals and governments to slow down global warming.
14. As for people, they should use public transportation instead of their car,
15. which can lessen the discharge of gases and delay global warming.
16. Another step is that they should not use disposable products that undermine natural resources and the environment.
17. In light of governments, the primary measures they should take are to carry out environmental campaigns to make citizens and companies aware of global warming.
18. With this, governments can have them play the role of their own accord.
19. Second, political leaders ought to make and implement strong regulations to prevent and put an end to this problem.
20. Provided that citizens and companies violate the regulations, they should incur a heavier fine.
21. Based on these ways, people and governments could take action to lessen and curb global warming.
22. As mentioned above, human activities and developments are the major sources of global warming.
23. However, there are feasible solutions presented to tackle it.
24. Thus, individuals and governments should team up with each other to prevent and fight against global warming.

You should spend about 40 minutes on this task.

Write about the following topic:

> **Global warming is one of the most serious issues the world faces today. What are the causes of global warming and what measures can governments and individuals take to tackle the issue?**

Give reasons for your answer and include any relevant examples from your own knowledge or experience.

Write at least 250 words.

Answer

    Global warming has been a critical and pressing environmental concern over the past decade. There are several culprits behind global warming and a few solutions to address the problem. This essay will analyse some of these reasons and propose possible remedies associated with the issue.

    One of the leading causes of global warming is far-reaching human activities. In particular, overconsumption and the increasing number of vehicles are the key reasons for the phenomenon. Those circumstances generate carbon gasses, fumes and hazardous chemicals, which induce the depletion of the ozone layer and global warming. Today, the earth also faces the problem of overpopulation, and the status quo is far more serious than before. **Furthermore, the overcutting of trees and the destruction of rainforests for development** have led to global warming, bringing about the melting of the polar ice-caps, and triggering climate changes characterized by floods, droughts, and extreme weather conditions. We can observe globally that people go through severe hot and cold generated by climate change. As can be seen, a few factors have significant influences on global warming.

    Nonetheless, **there are also a couple of solutions for individuals and governments to slow down global warming. As for people,** they should use public transportation instead of their car, which can lessen the discharge of gasses and delay global warming. Another step is that they should not use disposable products that undermine natural resources and the environment. **In light of governments,** the primary measures they should take are to carry out environmental campaigns to make citizens and companies aware of global warming. With this, governments can have them play the role of their own accord. Second, political leaders ought to make and implement strong regulations to prevent and put an end to this problem. Provided that citizens and companies violate the laws, they should incur a heavier fine. Based on these ways, people and government should take action to lessen and curb global warming.

    As mentioned above, human activities and development are the major sources of global warming. However, there are feasible solutions presented to tackle it. Thus, individuals and governments should team up with each other to prevent and fight against global warming.

3. Waste problem

You should spend about 40 minutes on this task.

Write about the following topic:

> A great amount of waste is becoming a social problem. What should individuals and the government do to lessen waste? Suggest feasible solutions.

Give reasons for your answer and include any relevant examples from your own knowledge or experience.

Write at least 250 words.

INTRODUCTION

쓰레기 문제가 사회적 문제가 되고 있다.

개개인들과 정부가 이 문제를 해결하기 위한 몇 가지 조치들이 있다.

BODY 1 개인의 역할

1. 분리수거와 재활용을 해야 한다.
   → 특히, 전자쓰레기를 적절히 처리해야 한다.

BODY 2 정부의 역할

1. 적절한 시설과 교육 제공
2. 강력한 법규와 처벌 필요

CONCLUSION

개개인들과 정부는 쓰레기 문제를 해결하기 위해 서로 협력해야 한다.

많은 양의 쓰레기들이 사회적인 우려가 되고 있다. 개인과 정부는 쓰레기를 줄이기 위해서 무엇을 할 것인가? 가능한 해결책을 제시하라.

INTRODUCTION

많은 사람들이 다양한 종류의 쓰레기에 노출되고 있다는 것은 확실하다. 대부분의 쓰레기는 무분별하게 버려지고 이런 것들은 오염과 다른 환경적 문제를 발생시킨다. 따라서 증가하는 쓰레기 양은 긴급한 사회적 문제가 되고 있다. 이 에세이에서 정부와 시민들은 쓰레기 문제를 해결하기 위해서 무엇을 해야 하는지에 대한 제안들이 제시될 것이다.

BODY 1

개인에 대해 말하자면, 그들은 많은 양의 쓰레기 문제를 해결하기 위해 무언가를 해야만 한다. 우선, 그들은 할 수 있는 한 쓰레기를 분리하고 재활용해야 한다. 쓰레기를 분리하고 물건들을 재활용하는 것은 에너지를 절약할 뿐만 아니라 제품들에 사용된 여러 종류의 원자재를 보존할 수 있다. 특히, 대량의 전자 쓰레기는 중대한 문제가 되고 있으므로, 쓸모 없는 전자제품은 더욱 주의 깊게 다뤄져야 한다. 알려진 것처럼, 건전지와 같은 독성 물질은 누출될 때 사람의 건강을 해친다. 한 가지 예는, 중국에서 분별없이 버려진 전자 쓰레기 때문에 강이 오염이 되어서 주변 주민들이 피부병에 걸린 사례들이 있다. 이러한 문제를 피하기 위해서 시민들은 전자 쓰레기를 분리하고 그것을 적절하게 폐기해야 한다.

BODY 2

반면에, 정부는 시민들이 재활용 그리고 쓰레기를 버릴 수 있는 적절한 시설과 교육을 제공해야 한다. 이러한 목적을 달성하기 위해서, 그들은 환경친화적인 시설을 만드는 데 예산을 투자해야 하고 공익광고 등과 같은 캠페인을 통해서 쓰레기의 버리는 방법과 재활용의 필요성에 대한 시민들의 인식을 높여야 한다. **쓰레기를 줄이는 다른 가능한 조치는 강력한 법규를 만들고 범법자에게 벌을 주는 것이다.** 만일 사람들이 쓰레기를 무분별하게 버리거나 재활용을 하지 않을 경우, 그들의 행동은 환경에 치명적인 영향을 준다. 그러므로, 법에 따라 벌금이나 처벌이 필요하다. 이러한 종류의 정책들은 시민들에게 이 문제에 대한 심각성을 제시하고 어느 정도 쓰레기를 줄일 것이다.

CONCLUSION

요약하면, 위에서 언급한 것처럼, 정부와 개개인들은 쓰레기 문제를 해결하기 위한 몇 가지 방법들이 있다. 결과적으로, 정부와 시민은 쓰레기 문제를 책임감 있게 다루기 위해서는 서로 협력하고 그들의 각자의 분담을 하는 것이 바람직하다.

문장에 필요한 어휘

> 1. it is certain that/it is clear that/it is true that/it is a fact that/it is sure that S+V; 확실하다/사실이다
> 2. a number of(plenty of/numbers of) people; 많은 사람들
> 3. be exposed to+N; ~에 노출되다
> 4. various kinds(sorts/types) of; 다양한 종류의

많은 사람들이 다양한 종류의 쓰레기에 노출되고 있다는 것은 확실하다.
It is certain that a number of people have been exposed to various kinds of waste.

> 5. trash/waste/rubbish/garbage/junk; 쓰레기
> 6. throw away/discard/dispose of/get rid of/dump; 버리다/처분하다
> 7. indiscreetly/thoughtlessly/irrationally; 무분별하게
> 8. give rise to/result in/bring about/lead to +N; 일으키다/야기하다/초래하다
> 9. environmental challenge(problem/concern/difficulty/trouble); 환경적 문제

대부분의 쓰레기는 무분별하게 버려지고 이런 것들은 오염과 다른 환경적 문제를 발생시킨다.
Most trash is thrown away indiscreetly, which gives rise to pollution and another environmental challenge.

> 10. an increasing(growing) amount of waste; 증가하는 쓰레기 양은
> 11. a pressing(an urgent) social issue; 긴급한 사회문제

따라서 증가하는 쓰레기 양은 긴급한 사회적 문제가 되고 있다.
Thus, an increasing amount of waste has become a pressing social issue.

> 12. suggestions/plans/proposals; 제안들
> 13. address/cope with/deal with/sort out/resolve/settle/tackle/battle/combat(문제/상황 등에 대해) 다루다, 해결하다
> 14. present/show/describe/explain/illustrate/discuss; 제시하다/설명하다

이 에세이에서, 정부와 시민들은 쓰레기 문제를 해결하기 위해서 무엇을 해야 하는지에 대한 제안들이 제시될 것이다.
In this essay, suggestions on what governments and citizens should do to address the waste problem will be presented.

> 15. when it comes to/with respect to/in terms of/in case of/in light of +N; ~에 대해 말하자면,
> 16. an enormous amount of (a great amount of/a large amount of/a large volume of) waste; 많은 양의 쓰레기

개인에 대해 말하자면, 그들은 많은 양의 쓰레기 문제를 해결하기 무언가를 해야만 한다.
When it comes to individuals, they should do something to resolve the issue of an enormous amount of waste.

> 17. segregate/sort out/assort/divide A into B; 분리하다/분류하다
> 18. as much as they can; 그들이 할 수 있는 한

우선, 그들은 할 수 있는 한 쓰레기를 분리하고 재활용해야 한다.
Above all, they have to segregate and recycle trash as much as they can.

> 19. preserve/conserve/keep; 보존하다
> 20. raw materials/resources/commodities; 원자재들
> 21. not only A but also B/B as well as A; A뿐만 아니라 B도 또한

쓰레기를 분리하고 물건들을 재활용하는 것은 에너지를 절약할 뿐만 아니라 제품들에 사용된 여러 종류의 원자재를 보존할 수 있다.
Sorting out waste and recycling items not only save on energy, but also preserve some of the raw materials used on the products.

> 22. in particular/particularly/especially/specifically; 특별히
> 23. e-waste/electronic waste; 전자쓰레기
> 24. useless/worthless/out of date; 쓸모 없는
> 25. electronic devices(products/items/goods); 전자기구/전자제품들
> 26. handle/treat/deal with/cope with; 다루다
> 27. grave/important/critical/vital/significant; 중요한/중대한

특히, 대량의 전자쓰레기는 중대한 문제가 되고 있으므로, 쓸모 없는 전자 제품은 더욱 주의해서 다뤄져야 한다.
In particular, useless electronic devices should be carefully handled as the large quantities of e-waste become a grave concern.

28. as it is known/admittedly/of course; 알려진 것처럼/물론
29. toxic components/poisonous substances; 독성 요소들
30. harm/hurt/be hazardous to/be harmful to; ~에게 해를 주다
31. leak; 누출하다

알려진 것처럼, 건전지 같은 독성물질들은 누출될 때 사람의 건강을 해칠 수 있다.
As it is known, toxic components like batteries harm people's health when they are leaked.

32. for one thing; 한 가지 예로
33. cases/examples; 사례들
34. residents/inhabitants; 거주민들
35. discreetly/thoughtlessly/imprudently/recklessly; 무분별하게
36. contract(develop/come down with) diseases; 질병에 걸리다

한 가지 예로, 중국에서 무분별하게 버려진 전자제품 쓰레기 때문에 강이 오염이 되어서 주변 주민들이 피부병에 걸린 사례들이 있다.
For one thing, there are some cases in China in which residents, living near a river polluted electronic waste discarded indiscreetly, contract skin diseases.

37. properly/adequately/suitably: 적절하게

이 문제를 피하기 위해서 시민들은 전자 쓰레기를 분리하고 그것을 적절하게 폐기해야 한다.
To avoid this problem, people should separate e-waste and dispose of them properly.

38. meanwhile/on the other hand/on the contrary/in contrast; 반면에/다른 한편으로는
39. provide B to(for) A/provide A with B; A에게 B를 제공하다
40. facilities and instructions; 시설과 교육
41. the public/citizens/the general public; 시민/일반대중

반면에, 정부는 시민들이 재활용 그리고 쓰레기를 버릴 수 있는 적절한 시설과 교육을 제공해야 한다.
Meanwhile, governments should provide adequate facilities and instructions for the public to recycle and get rid of junk.

42. to that end/to this end; 이러한 목적을 달성하기 위해
43. an environmentally friendly system/a eco-friendly system; 환경친화적인 시설

이러한 목적을 달성하기 위해서, 그들은 환경친화적인 시설을 만드는 데 예산을 투자해야 한다.
To that end, they should invest budget in building environmentally-friendly establishment.

44. raise awareness/increase awareness; 인식을 높이다
45. public service announcement; 공익광고

그들은 또한 공익광고와 같은 캠페인을 통해서 쓰레기의 버리는 방법과 재활용의 필요성에 대한 시민들의 인식을 높여야 한다.

They also raise the citizens' awareness of how to dump garbage and the necessity of recycling through campaigns like public service announcements.

46. possible(practical/viable/feasible) way; 가능성 있는 방법
47. build/establish/enact/legislate; 만들다/제정하다
48. inflict(impose) a penalty upon an offender(law-breaker); 범법자에게 벌을 주다

쓰레기를 줄이는 다른 가능한 조치는 강력한 법규를 만들고 범법자에게 벌을 주는 것이다.

Another possible way of reducing waste is to build strict regulations and inflict a penalty upon an offender.

49. have(has)pernicious(harmful/detrimental/adverse) influences(impacts/effects) on; 치명적인/유해한 영향을 준다.

만일 사람들이 쓰레기를 무분별하게 버리거나 재활용을 하지 않을 경우에, 그들의 행동은 환경에 치명적인 영향을 준다.

In case people throw waste away thoughtlessly and do not recycle it, their behaviors have pernicious influences on the environment.

50. fine(penalty) or punishment; 벌금 또는 처벌
51. according to law(regulation); 법에 따라

그러므로, 법에 따라 벌금 또는 처벌이 필요하다.

Thus, fine or punishment is necessary according to the law.

52. to some extent/to some degree/more or less/somewhat; 어느 정도
53. scale back/curtail/reduce/cut down on/cut back on; 줄이다

이러한 정책들은, 시민들에게 이 문제에 대한 심각성을 제시하고 어느 정도 쓰레기를 줄일 것이다.

Those kinds of policies would present the seriousness of this issue to citizens and, to some extent, scale back waste.

54. to sum up/In conclusion/to conclude; 요약하면/결론은

요약하면, 위에서 언급한 것처럼, 정부와 개개인들은 쓰레기 문제를 해결하기 위한 몇 가지 방법들이 있다.

To sum up, as stated above, there are several methods for governments and individuals to tackle the rubbish problem.

55. desirable/preferable/reasonable; 바람직한/권장할 만한
56. team up with/cooperate with/work together with; ~와 협력하다
57. respective share; 각자의 몫
58. responsibly; 책임감 있게

결과적으로, 정부와 시민은 쓰레기 문제를 책임감 있게 다루기 위해서는 서로 협력하고 그들의 각자의 분담을 하는 것이 바람직하다.

Consequently, it is desirable for governments and citizens to team up with each other and do their respective share in addressing the waste problem responsibly.

구문연습

1. 그것은 확실하다/많은 사람들이/노출되고 있다/다양한 종류의 쓰레기에

_____
_____

2. 대부분 쓰레기는 버려지고 있다/무분별하게/이것은 일으킨다/오염을 그리고 다른 환경적 문제들을

_____
_____

3. 따라서/증가하는 쓰레기 양은/되고 있다/긴급한 사회문제가

_____
_____

4. 이 에세이에서/제안들이/무엇을 정부들이나 개인들이 해야 하는지/해결하기 위해서/쓰레기 문제들을/제시될 것이다

_____
_____

5. 개인들에 대해 말하자면/그들은 해야만 한다/무엇인가를/문제들을 해결하기 위해/많은 쓰레기 양에 대한

_____
_____

6. 우선/그들은 해야만 한다/쓰레기를 분리시키고 재활용/그들이 할 수 있는 한

_____
_____

7. 쓰레기를 분리하고/물품을 재활용하는 것은/에너지를 절약할 뿐만 아니라/보존한다/몇몇의 원자재들을/생산에 사용된

_____

_____

8. 특히/~함에 따라서/대량의 전자쓰레기는/되고 있다/중대한 문제가/쓸모 없는 전자기기는/다뤄져야만 한다/주의 깊게

_____

_____

9. 알려진 것처럼/독성성분들이/건전지와 같은/해가 된다/사람들의 건강에/그들이 누출될 때

_____

_____

10. 한 가지 예로, 몇 가지 사례들이 있다/중국에서/지역 주민들/오염된 강 근처에 사는/버려진 전자쓰레기들이/분별없이/피부병 같은 질병에 걸리다

_____

_____

11. 이러한 문제들을 피하기 위해서/사람들은 분리해야 한다/전자 쓰레기를/그리고 그것을 처리해야 한다/적절하게

_____

_____

12. 반면에/정부는 제공해야 한다/적절한 시설과 교육을/지역주민이/재활용하고 쓰레기를 버리는

_____

_____

13. 이러한 목적을 달성하기 위해서/그들은 투자해야 한다/예산을/짓는 데/환경친화적인 시설을

_____

_____

14. 그들은 시민들의 인식을 높여야 한다/쓰레기를 처리하는 방법/그리고 재활용 필요성/캠페인을 통해서/공익광고와 같은

_____

_____

15. 다른 가능한 방법은/쓰레기를 줄이는/만드는 것이다/엄격한 법규/그리고/범법자에게 벌을 주는 것이다

_____

_____

16. 만일 경우에/사람이 쓰레기를 버린다/무분별하게/그리고 재활용하지 않다/그것을/그들의 행동은/치명적인 영향을 끼친다/환경에

_____

_____

17. 그러므로/벌금 또는 처벌이/필요하다/법에 따라

_____

_____

18. 이러한 종류의 정책들은/제시할 것이다/심각성을/이 문제에 대한/시민들에게/그리고 어느 정도/쓰레기를 줄일 것이다

_____

_____

19. 요약하면, 위에서 언급한 것처럼/몇 가지 방법들이 있다/정부와 개개인들이/해결하는 데/쓰레기 문제를

_____

_____

20. 결과적으로/그것은/바람직하다/정부들과 시민들이/서로 협력하는 것이/그들의 역할을 공유하는 것을/해결하는 데 있어서/쓰레기 문제를/책임감 있게

_____

_____

Answer

1. It is certain that a number of people have been exposed to various kinds of waste.
2. Most trash is thrown away indiscreetly, which gives rise to pollution and another environmental challenge.
3. Thus, an increasing amount of waste has become a pressing social issue.
4. In this essay, suggestions on what governments and citizens should do to address the waste problem will be presented.
5. When it comes to individuals, they should do something to resolve the issue of an enormous amount of waste.
6. Above all, they have to segregate and recycle trash as much as they can.
7. Sorting out waste and recycling items not only save on energy, but also preserve some of the raw materials used on the products.
8. In particular, useless electronic devices should be carefully handled as the large quantities of e-waste can become a grave concern.
9. As is known, toxic components like batteries harm people's health when they are leaked.
10. For one thing, there are some cases in China in which residents, living near a river polluted by electronic wastes discarded indiscreetly, contract skin diseases.
11. To avoid this problem, people should separate e-waste and dispose of it properly.
12. Meanwhile, governments should provide adequate facilities and instructions for the public to recycle and get rid of junk.
13. To that end, they should invest in building environmentally-friendly establishment.
14. They should raise the citizens' awareness of how to dump garbage and the necessity of recycling through campaigns like public service announcements.
15. Another possible way of reducing waste is to build strict regulations and inflict penalties upon an offender.
16. In case people throw waste away thoughtlessly and do not recycle it, their behaviors have pernicious influences on the environment.
17. Thus, a fine or punishment is necessary according to the law.
18. Those kinds of policies would present the seriousness of this issue to citizens and, to some extent, scale back waste.
19. To sum up, as stated above, there are several methods for governments and individuals to tackle the rubbish problem.
20. Consequently, it is desirable for governments and citizens to team up with each other and do their respective shares in addressing the waste issue responsibly.

You should spend about 40 minutes on this task.

Write about the following topic:

> A great amount of waste is becoming a social problem. What should individuals and the government do to lessen waste? Suggest feasible solutions.

Give reasons for your answer and include any relevant examples from your own knowledge or experience.

Write at least 250 words.

Answer

It is certain that a number of people have been exposed to various kinds of waste. Most trash is thrown away indiscreetly, which gives rise to pollution and another environmental challenge. Thus, an increasing amount of waste has become a pressing social issue. In this essay, suggestions on what governments and citizens should do to address the waste problem will be presented.

When it comes to individuals, they should do something to resolve the issue of an enormous amount of waste. Above all, they have to segregate and recycle trash as much as they can. Sorting out waste and recycling items not only save on energy but also preserve some of the raw materials used on the products. In particular, useless electronic devices should be carefully handled as the large quantities of e-waste can become a grave concern. As it is known, toxic components like batteries harm people's health when they are leaked. For one thing, there are some cases in China in which residents, living near a river polluted by electronic waste discarded indiscreetly, contract skin diseases. To avoid this problem, people should separate e-waste and dispose of it properly.

Meanwhile, governments should provide adequate facilities and instructions for the public to recycle and get rid of junk. To that end, they should invest in building environmentally-friendly establishment and also raise the citizens' awareness of how to dump garbage and the necessity of recycling through campaigns like public service announcements. **Another possible way of reducing waste is to build strict regulations and inflict a penalty upon an offender.** In case people throw waste away thoughtlessly and do not recycle it, their behaviors have pernicious influences on the environment. Thus, a fine or punishment is necessary according to the law. Those kinds of policies would present the seriousness of this issue to citizens and, to some extent, scale back waste.

To sum up, as stated above, there are several methods for governments and individuals to tackle the rubbish problem. Consequently, it is desirable for governments and citizens to team up with each other and do their respective shares in addressing waste issue responsibly.

4. Zoo

You should spend about 40 minutes on this task.

Write about the following topic:

> **Zoos have no longer purpose, so they should be closed. Do you agree or disagree?.**

Give reasons for your answer and include any relevant examples from your own knowledge or experience.

Write at least 250 words.

INTRODUCTION
동물원을 유지하는 데 많은 논란이 있어왔다. 나는 동물원의 필요성에 동의하지 않는다.

BODY 1
동물원은 더 이상 오락과 교육을 제공하지 않는다.

BODY 2
동물들이 신체적으로 동물원에서 제약을 받는다.

BODY 3
동물원에 있는 동물들은 인간의 이익에 이용된다.

CONCLUSION
동물원은 많은 부정적인 면을 가지고 있다. 그러므로 동물원 유지에 반대한다.

동물원들은 더 이상 명분을 가지고 있지 않다. 그래서 그들은 폐쇄되어야 한다. 동의하는지 아닌지?

INTRODUCTION

　동물원 유지에 대한 찬반이 오랫동안 논의가 되어 오고 있다. 어떤 사람들은 동물원은 동물들을 위해 여전히 필요하다고 주장한다. 그러나, 나는 전적으로 이 주제에 동의한다. 다음은 내 의견에 대한 이유들이다.

BODY 1

　우선, 동물원이 아이들과 성인들에게 오락과 교육을 제공한다는 것은 진부한 사고이다. 실제로 과거에는, 동물들을 보는 것을 즐기기 위해서, 동물원을 방문하는 것이 유일한 방법이었다. 그러나 요즈음, 현대 기술의 덕택으로, 동물들은 가정에서도 접근할 수 있는 온라인 비디오들이나 웹사이트들을 통해서 고화질로 보여질 수 있다. 그러므로, 사람들은 이러한 즐거운 경험과 교육을 위해 동물원에 갈 필요가 없다.

BODY 2

　덧붙여서, 사육상태에 있는 동물들은 제한된 공간에서 제약을 받는다. 동물들의 자연서식지들은 그들이 야생에서 자유롭게 뛰고 나무에 오를 수 있는 넓고 열린 공간이라는 것은 잘 알려진 사실이다. 동물들이 동물원에 머물 때, 그들은 그들의 야생성을 잃는 경향이 있고 어떤 동물들은 사육 상태에서 번식을 거의 할 수 없다. 한 가지 분명한 예는 판다이다. 그들은 갇혀 있을 때 번식이 느리다. 이것은 판다의 개체 수를 급격하게 줄였고, 이러한 것은 그들이 멸종위기 동물로서 분류가 되는 것으로 이어졌다.

BODY 3

　마지막으로, 동물원의 동물들은 단지 인간의 이익을 위해서 악용되는 많은 경우들이 있다. 몇 가지의 드문 경우에서, 동물들은 동물원에서 방치와 영양실조를 겪고 있고, 그리고 만일 더 이상 동물원에 이익이 생기지 않을 땐 일부는 다른 동물로 대체된다. 그 이외에도, 동물원에서 동물공연을 위해, 조련사들은 동물들을 훈련시키기 위해 고통을 준다. 이러한 것은 동물의 기본적인 권리를 침해한다.

CONCLUSION

　요약하자면, 위에서 언급한 것처럼 동물원이 동물들을 보호하는 데 있어 많은 부정적인 효과들이 있다. 따라서, 동물원은 존재할 가치가 없다. 이런 점에서 정부와 동물원과 관련된 기관들은 동물들을 위해 적절한 조치를 취하는 것이 바람직하다.

문장에 필요한 어휘

1. pros and cons; 찬반
2. maintain/keep/preserve; 유지하다
3. debate/discuss/argue; 논의하다/논쟁하다

동물원 유지에 대한 찬반이 오랫동안 논의가 되어 오고 있다.
The pros and cons of maintaining zoos have been debated for a long time.

4. claim/maintain/argue; 주장하다
5. necessary/essential; 필요한

어떤 사람들은 동물원은 동물들을 위해 여전히 필요하다고 주장한다.
Some people claim that zoos are still necessary for animals.

6. however/on the other hand/though; 그러나
7. strongly/truly/firmly/completely; 전적으로/확실하게
8. agree with/be in favor of/be for; 동의하다

그러나, 나는 전적으로 이 주제에 동의한다. 다음은 내 입장에 대한 이유들이다.
I, however, strongly agree with this idea. The following are the reasons for my position.

9. to begin with/first of all/first and foremost; 우선
10. provide A with B/provide B to(for) A; A에게 B를 제공하다
11. an out-dated(old-fashioned/antiquated/stereotyped) idea; 진부한 사고

우선, 동물원이 아이들과 성인들에게 오락과 교육을 제공한다는 것은 진부한 사고이다.
To begin with, the opinion that zoos provide children and adults with entertainment and education is an out-dated idea.

> 12. in fact/in reality/as an matter of fact; 사실은
> 13. in the past; 과거에는
> 14. look at/investigate/watch; 보다/관찰하다

실제로, 과거에는, 동물들을 보는 것을 즐기기 위한 유일한 방법은 동물원을 방문하는 것이었다.
In fact, in the past, the only way to enjoy looking at animals was to visit zoos.

> 15. nowadays/these days/recently/today; 요즈음
> 16. with the help of/thanks to; 덕택으로
> 17. high definition/high-quality; 고화질
> 18. be accessed; 접근되다

그러나 요즈음, 현대기술의 덕택으로, 동물들은 가정에서 접근할 수 있는 온라인 비디오들이나 웹사이트들을 통해서 고화질로 보여질 수 있다.
Nowadays, though, with the help of modern technology, animals can be viewed in high definition through online videos and websites that can be accessed even at home.

> 19. in this context/thus/hence/as a result/consequently/therefore; 그러므로/따라서

그러므로 사람들은 이러한 즐거운 경험과 교육을 위해 동물원에 갈 필요가 없다.
In this context, people do not need to go to zoos for enjoyable experience and education.

> 20. on top of that/in addition to that; 덧붙여서
> 21. in captivity; 사육상태에
> 22. restrict/restrain; 제한하다

덧붙여서, 사육상태에 있는 동물들은 제한된 공간에서 제약을 받는다.
On top of that, animals in captivity are restricted in limited spaces.

> 23. in the wild/in the state of nature; 야생에서

동물들의 자연서식지들은 그들이 야생에서 자유롭게 뛰고 나무에 오를 수 있는 넓고 열린 공간이라는 것은 잘 알려진 사실이다.
It is a well-known fact that the natural habitats are broad and open areas where they can run freely and climb trees in the wild.

> 24. tend to/have a tendency to/be inclined to/be liable to; ~하는 경향이 있다
> 25. wild nature; 야생성
> 26. hardly/rarely/scarcely/seldom; 거의 ~않다.
> 27. breed/propagate/reproduce; 번식하다

동물들이 동물원에 머물때, 그들은 그들의 야생성을 잃는 경향이 있고 어떤 동물들은 사육상태에서 번식을 거의 할 수 없다.

When animals stay in zoos, they tend to lose their wild nature, and some animals can hardly breed in captivity.

> 28. be classified/be sorted; 분류되다
> 29. endangered species/threatened species; 멸종 위기의 종
> 30. lead to/result in/bring about/give rise to+N; 이어지다/초래하다/야기하다

한 가지 분명한 예는 판다이다. 그들은 갇혀 있을 때 번식이 느리다. 이것은 판다의 개체 수를 급격하게 줄였고, 이러한 것이 그들이 멸종위기 동물로서 분류되는 것으로 이어졌다.

One obvious example is pandas. They are slow to reproduce when in captivity. It dramatically lowered the population of pandas, which led to them being classified as an endangered species.

> 31. finally/lastly/last but not least; 마지막으로
> 32. exploit/make ill use of/make bad use of/abuse; 악용하다/착취하다

마지막으로, 동물원의 동물들은 단지 인간의 이익을 위해서 악용되는 많은 경우들이 있다.

Finally, there are many cases in which animals kept in zoos are merely exploited for human's profits.

> 33. rare(unusual/uncommon) case; 드문 경우
> 34. undergo/go through/suffer; 고통 받다
> 35. neglect/inattention; 방치/소홀함
> 36. malnutrition/insufficient nutrition; 영양 부족

몇 가지의 드문 경우에서, 동물들은 동물원에서 영양실조와 방치로 고통을 겪는다.

In some rare cases, animals undergo malnutrition and neglect in zoos,

> 37. in case S+V; 만일 ~경우에
> 38. no longer A; 더 이상 A하지 않다
> 39. of value/valuable/of benefit/beneficial; 이익이 되는/가치가 있는

그리고, 만일 더 이상 동물원에 이익이 생기지 않을 땐 일부는 다른 동물로 대체된다.
, and in case they are no longer of any value, some are replaced by other animals.

---

40. aside from/other than/besides; 이외에
41. inflict pain on B; B에게 고통을 주다

그 이외에도, 동물원에서 동물공연을 위해, 조련사들은 그들을 훈련하기 위해서 동물들에게 고통을 준다
Aside from that, for animal performances in zoos, trainers inflict pain on animals to train them.

---

42. infringe/violate/disregard; 침해하다
43. fundamental/basic; 기본적인

이러한 것은 동물의 기본적인 권리를 침해한다.
Those things infringe fundamental animal rights.

---

44. to sum up/to conclude/In conclusion; 결론은
45. adverse(negative/unfavorable) effects; 부정적인 효과들

요약하자면, 위에서 언급한 것처럼 동물원에서 동물을 보호하는 데 있어 많은 부정적인 효과들이 있다.
To sum up, as mentioned above, there are many adverse effects of keeping animals in zoos.

---

46. deserve/merit; 가치가 있다
47. exist/remain/keep; 존재하다

따라서, 동물원은 존재할 가치가 없다.
Therefore, zoos do not deserve to exist.

---

48. given this/In this sense/in this respect/in this regard; 이런 점에서/이런 상황으로 볼 때
49. advisable/desirable/preferable/favorable/compelling/persuasive; 바람직한/설득력 있는
50. take action/take steps/carry out measures/take measures; 조치를 취하다
51. for the sake of/for the good of/for the benefit of; ~을 위해서

이런 점에서 정부와 동물원과 관련된 기관들은 동물들을 위해 적절한 조치를 취하는 것이 바람직하다.
Given this, it is advisable for governments and organizations involved in zoos to take action for the sake of the animals.

구문연습

1. 찬반이/동물원 유지에 대한/논의되고 있다/오랫동안

2. 어떤 사람들은/주장한다/동물원들은 여전히 필요하다/동물들을 위해

3. 나는/그러나/전적으로 동의하다/이 주제에

4. 다음은 이유들이다/나의 의견에 대한

5. 우선/의견은/동물원이 제공한다/아이들과 어른들에게/오락과 교육을/진부한 생각이다

6. 실제로/과거에는/유일한 방법은/동물들을 지켜보는 즐거움을 위한/방문하는 것이었다/동물원에

7. 요즈음/그러나/현대기술 덕택으로/동물들은/보여질 수 있다/고화질로/온라인 비디오나 웹사이트를 통해서/접근될 수 있는/가정에서도

8. 그러므로/사람들은 갈 필요가 없다/특정한 동물원에/즐거운 경험과 교육을 위해서

9. 덧붙여서/사육상태에 있는 동물들은/제약을 받는다/제한된 공간에 있어서

10. 그것은 잘 알려진 사실이다/동물들의 자연서식지는/넓고 열린 공간이다/거기서 그들은 자유롭게 달릴 수 있다/나무에 오른다/야생에서

11. 동물들이 동물원에 머물 때/그들은 경향이 있다/잃어버리다/그들의 야성을

12. 그리고/어떤 동물들은/거의 할 수 없다/번식을/사육상태에서

13. 한 가지 분명한 예는/판다이다/그들은/느리다/번식하는 데/갇혀 있을 때

14. 그것은/극적으로 줄였다/판다의 개체 수를/이러한 것은/이어졌다/그들이 분류되다/멸종위기의 종으로서

15. 마지막으로/많은 경우들이 있다/거기에서/동물원에 갇힌 동물들은/단지 악용된다/인간의 이익을 위해

16. 몇 가지 드문 경우에서/동물들은 겪다/영양실조와 방치/동물원에서/그리고/만일 그들이 더 이상 가치가 없다면/일부는 대체된다/다른 동물들로

17. 이외에도/동물공연을 위해/동물원에서/조련사들은/고통을 가한다/동물들에게/그들을 훈련시키기 위해

18. 이러한 것들은/침해한다/기본적인 동물의 권리를

19. 요약하자면/위에서 언급한 것처럼/많은 부정적인 효과들이 있다/동물을 보호하는 데/동물원들에서

20. 따라서/동물원은 존재할 가치가 없다

21. 이런 점에서/그것은 바람직하다/정부와 동물원과 관련된 단체들이/조치를 취해야 한다/동물들을 위해서

Answer

1. The pros and cons of maintaining zoos have been debated for a long time.
2. Some people claim that zoos are still necessary for animals.
3. I, however, strongly agree with this issue.
4. The following are the reasons for my position.
5. To begin with, the opinion that zoos provide children and adults with entertainment and education is an out-dated idea.
6. In fact, in the past, the only way to enjoy looking at animals was to visit zoos.
7. Nowadays, though, with the help of modern technology, animals can be viewed in high definition through online videos and websites that can be accessed even at home.
8. In this context, people do not need to go to zoos for enjoyable experience and education.
9. On top of that, animals in captivity are restricted in limited spaces.
10. It is a well-known fact that the natural habitats of animals are broad and open areas where they can run freely and climb trees in the wild.
11. When animals stay in zoos, they tend to lose their wild nature,
12. , and some animals even hardly breed in captivity.
13. One obvious example is pandas. They are slow to breed when in captivity.
14. It dramatically lowered the population of pandas, which led to them being classified as an endangered species.
15. Finally, there are many cases in which animals kept in zoos are merely exploited for human's profits.
16. In some rare cases, animals undergo malnutrition and neglect in zoos, and in case they are no longer of any value, some are replaced by other animals.
17. Aside from that, for animal performances in zoos, trainers inflict pain on animals to train them.
18. Those things infringe fundamental animal rights.
19. To sum up, as mentioned above, there are many adverse effects of keeping animals in zoos.
20. Therefore, zoos do not deserve to exist.
21. Given this, it is advisable for governments and organizations involved in zoos to take action for the sake of animals.

You should spend about 40 minutes on this task.

Write about the following topic:

> **Zoos have no longer purpose, so they should be closed. Do you agree or disagree?**

Give reasons for your answer and include any relevant examples from your own knowledge or experience.

Write at least 250 words.

Answer

The pros and cons of maintaining zoos have been debated for a long time. Some people claim that zoos are still necessary for animals I, however, strongly agree with this issue. The following are the reasons for my position.

To begin with, the opinion that zoos provide children and adults with entertainment and education is an out-dated idea. In fact, in the past, the only way to enjoy looking at animals was to visit zoos. Nowadays, though, with the help of modern technology, animals can be viewed in high definition through online videos and websites that can be accessed even at home. In this context, people do not need to go to zoos for enjoyable experience and education.

On top of that, animals in captivity are restricted in limited spaces. It is a well-known fact that the natural habitats of animals are broad and open areas where they can run freely and climb trees in the wild. When animals stay in zoos, they tend to lose their wild nature, and some animals can hardly breed in captivity. One obvious example is pandas. They are slow to reproduce when in captivity. It dramatically lowered the population of pandas, which led to them being classified as an endangered species.

Finally, there are many cases in which animals kept in zoos are merely exploited for human's profits. In some rare cases, animals undergo malnutrition and neglect in zoos, and in case they are no longer of any value, some are replaced by other animals. Aside from that, for animal performances in zoos, trainers inflict pain on animals to train them. Those things infringe fundamental animal rights.

To sum up, as mentioned above, there are many adverse effects of keeping animals in zoos. Therefore, zoos do not deserve to exist. Given this, it is advisable for governments and organizations involved in zoos to take action for the sake of the animals.

IELTS Easy Writing

Unit 5

Culture

1. Online shopping
2. Advertisement
3. Traveling
4. Traffic taxes

1. Online shopping

You should spend about 40 minutes on this task.

Write about the following topic:

> Most people believe that online shopping is better and more enjoyable than going to shopping centres. Do you agree or disagree?

Give reasons for your answer and include any relevant examples from your own knowledge or experience.

Write at least 250 words.

INTRODUCTION

인터넷의 발달로 online shopping 이용이 증가하고 있다.

online shopping은 많은 장점들이 있다.

BODY1 (agree)

편리함과 비용 절감

BODY2 (agree)

특히 취약계층에게 많은 이점

CONCLUSION

online shopping은 많은 장점들이 있고 계속 증가될 것이다.

대부분의 사람들은 온라인 쇼핑이 쇼핑 센터에 가는 것보다 더 좋고 더 즐겁다고 믿는다. 당신은 동의하는가? 또는 동의하지 않는가?

INTRODUCTION

인터넷의 도래로 세계 곳곳의 사람들은 온라인에서 쇼핑을 해오고 있다. 물건을 구입하는 이 방법은 사람들에게 많은 장점들을 제공한다. 그러나 많은 소비자들은 일반 상점은 여전히 더 많은 즐거운 경험을 준다고 믿는다. 나는 다음과 같은 이유들 때문에 전자에 동의한다.

BODY 1

우선, 인터넷을 통한 쇼핑은 편리함 그리고 비용 절감을 소비자들에게 제공한다. 온라인 쇼핑객들이 쇼핑몰까지 갈 필요가 없기 때문에, 온라인에서 쇼핑할 때 시간과 노력을 절약할 수 있다. 그것은 소비자들이 다른 활동들과 그들의 시간을 더 가치 있는 일에 보내는 것을 가능하게 한다. 상품의 가격적인 면에서, 온라인 쇼핑몰은 상품들을 합리적인 가격 또는 때때로 일반 상점의 상품과 비교될 때 훨씬 더 낮은 가격에 상품을 제공한다. 이것은 온라인 쇼핑몰 소매상들이 투자와 유지비를 덜 쓰기 때문이다. 그러한 가격들 때문에, 일부의 소비자들은 상점에서 상품을 확인한 다음 저렴한 가격으로 온라인으로 그 물건을 구매한다.

BODY 2

더욱이, 온라인 쇼핑은 노인들이나 장애인들 같은 취약한 사람들에게 몇 가지 장점들을 가지고 있다. 육체적 조건 때문에, 그들은 쇼핑몰에서는 편안하게 쇼핑할 수가 없다. 거기에는 차별과 신체적 제약과 같은 많은 장애들이 있다. 인터넷의 덕택으로, 그들은 그들이 구입을 원하는 물건을 선택하기 위해서 단지 마우스와 키보드만 필요하다. 이것은 즐겁고 편안한 쇼핑 경험을 가져온다. 이처럼, 온라인 쇼핑은 특히 노인들과 장애를 가진 사람들에게 유용하다.

CONCLUSION

이러한 모든 것을 고려할 때, 시간과 경비를 줄이는 것과 더불어, 온라인 쇼핑은 오프라인 쇼핑보다 구매자들을 포함한 모든 소비자들에게 훨씬 더 이롭다. 이러한 이유들로, 온라인 쇼핑몰은 그들의 성공과 인기가 계속될 것 같다.

문장에 필요한 어휘

> 1. with the advent of ~; ~가 도래하면서/출현하면서
> 2. method/way/manner; 방법
> 3. shop/buy/purchase/make a purchase; 구매하다
> 4. purchasing/buying; 구매
> 5. product/item/goods/merchandise/commodity; 상품
> 6. provide/offer/give; 제공하다/주다
> 7. advantage/benefit/merit/good point; 장점

인터넷의 도래로 세계 곳곳의 사람들은 온라인에서 쇼핑을 해오고 있다. 물건을 구입하는 이 방법은 사람들에게 많은 장점들을 제공한다.

With the advent of the Internet, people around the world have been shopping online. This method of purchasing products provides people with many advantages.

> 8. however/on the other hand/on the contrary; 그러나/그에 반하여
> 9. offline shopping mall/typical mall/general mall/brick-and-mortar shop(store); 일반상점
> 10. pleasant/delightful/entertaining/enjoyable; 즐거운

그러나 많은 소비자들은 일반상점은 여전히 더 많은 즐거움을 준다고 믿는다.

However, many consumers believe that offline shopping malls still offer more pleasant experiences.

> 11. be for/be in favor of/agree with/support; 동의하다
> 12. the former/the one; 전자
> 13. the latter/the other; 후자

나는 다음의 이유 때문에 전자에 동의한다.

I am for the former for the following reasons.

> 14. to begin with/first of all/above all/first and foremost/to start with; 우선/첫째로
> 15. via/through; 통해
> 16. convenience/handiness; 편리함
> 17. cost saving/cost cutting; 비용절감

우선, 인터넷을 통한 쇼핑은 편리함과 비용절감을 소비자들에게 제공한다.
To begin with, shopping via the Internet provides convenience and cost saving to customers.

> 18. travel(go) to a shopping mall; 쇼핑몰에 가다
> 19. time and effort/time and care; 시간과 노력

온라인 쇼핑객들이 쇼핑몰까지 갈 필요가 없기 때문에, 그들은 온라인에서 쇼핑할 때 많은 시간과 노력을 절약할 수 있다.
As online shoppers do not have to travel to shopping malls, they can save a lot of time and effort when shopping online.

> 20. enable A to B/make A B(동사원형)/allow A to B; A가 B하는 게 가능하다
> 21. consumer/shopper/buyer/client/user; 소비자
> 22. worthwhile/worth/valuable/of value; 가치 있는

그것은 소비자들이 다른 활동들과 그들의 시간을 더 가치 있는 일에 보내는 것을 가능하게 한다.
It enables consumers to do other activities and spend their time on more worthwhile work

> 23. when it comes to/in light of/with respect to/in terms of; ~측면에서
> 24. at a reasonable(affordable) cost(price); 적절한 가격에
> 25. compared to/in comparison with/as compared with; 비교하여
> 26. at times/sometimes/once in a while/now and then/on and off; 때때로

상품의 가격적인 면에서, 온라인 쇼핑몰은 상품들을 합리적인 가격 또는 때때로 일반 상점의 상품과 비교될 때 훨씬 더 낮은 가격에 상품을 제공한다.
When it comes to the price of products, online shopping malls supply items at a reasonable cost or at times, at an even lower price compared to products in brick-and-mortar shops.

> 27. retailer/retail dealer; 소매상인
> 28. the cost of investment and maintenance; 투자비와 유지비

이것은 온라인 쇼핑몰 소매상들이 투자비와 온라인 상점 유지비를 덜 쓰기 때문이다.
This is because online retailers spend less on the cost of their investment and online store maintenance.

> 29. on account of/due to/because of/owing to+N; ~때문에

그러한 가격들 때문에, 일부의 소비자들은 상점에서 물건을 조사한 후 온라인에서 그 물건을 저렴한 가격에 구입한다.

On account of those prices, some customers make a purchase of items online at low prices after examining them in real stores.

> 30. furthermore/moreover/in addition; 더욱이/덧붙여서
> 31. the vulnerable/vulnerable people; 취약한 사람들
> 32. the elderly/elderly people/senior citizens/the aged; 노인들
> 33. the disabled/disabled people/the handicapped/handicapped people; 장애인들

더욱이, 온라인 쇼핑은 노인들이나 장애인들과 같은 취약한 사람들에게 몇 가지 장점들을 준다.

Furthermore, online shopping has several advantages to the vulnerable like the elderly and the disabled.

> 34. obstacle/obstacle concern/obstacle factor; 장애요인
> 35. discrimination/prejudice; 차별/편견
> 36. physical limitations(restrictions/restraints); 신체적 제약들

육체적 조건 때문에, 그들은 쇼핑몰에서는 편안하게 쇼핑할 수가 없다. 거기에는 차별과 신체적 제약과 같은 많은 장애들이 있다.

Due to their physical condition, they are unable to shop comfortably in shopping malls where there are many obstacles, including discrimination and physical limitations.

> 37. with the help of ~/thanks to; ~의 도움으로

인터넷의 덕택으로, 그들은 그들이 구입을 원하는 물건을 선택하기 위해서 단지 마우스와 키보드만 필요하다.

With the help of the Internet, they need only their keyboard and mouse to choose items they wish to buy,

> 38. give rise to/lead to/result in/bring about+N; 야기하다
> 39. enjoyable and comfortable; 즐겁고 편안한

이것은 즐겁고 편안한 쇼핑 경험을 야기한다.

, which brings about an enjoyable and comfortable shopping experience.

> 40. useful/of use/beneficial/of benefit; 유용한/도움이 되는
> 41. disability; 장애

그러한 이유들로, 온라인 쇼핑은 특히 노인들과 장애를 가진 사람들에게 유용하다.
Like this, online shopping is useful especially for seniors and those with disabilities.

> 42. all things considered/taking all things into account(consideration); 모든 것을 고려할 때
> 43. coupled with/along with; ~와 더불어
> 44. curtail/cut down on/cut back on/lessen/diminish/reduce; 줄이다

모든 것을 고려할 때, 시간과 경비를 줄이는 것과 더불어,
All things considered, coupled with curtailing time and expense,

> 45. beneficial/helpful/advantageous; 이로운

온라인 쇼핑은 오프라인 쇼핑보다 민감한 고객들을 포함한 모든 소비자들에게 훨씬 더 이롭다.
online shopping is much more beneficial for all customers including sensitive shoppers than offline shopping.

> 46. be likely to; ~할 거 같다
> 47. popularity/public interest; 인기

그러한 이유들로, 온라인 쇼핑몰은 그들의 성공과 인기가 계속될 것 같다.
For those reasons, online shopping malls are more likely to continue their success and popularity.

구문연습

1. 인터넷의 도래로/세계 도처에 있는 사람들은/해오고 있다/쇼핑을/온라인에서

_____
_____

2. 이 방법은/상품을 구매하는/제공한다/사람들에게/많은 장점들을

_____
_____

3. 그러나/많은 소비자들은 믿는다/일반 상점은/여전히 제공한다/더 많은 즐거운 경험들을

_____
_____

4. 나는 동의한다/전자에/다음 이유들 때문에

_____
_____

5. 우선/인터넷을 통한 쇼핑은 준다/편리함 그리고 비용절감을/소비자들에게

_____
_____

6. 왜냐하면/온라인 고객들은/갈 필요가 없기 때문에/쇼핑몰에

_____
_____

7. 그들은 절약할 수 있다/시간과 노력을/온라인 쇼핑할 때

___

8. 그것은 가능하게 한다/소비자들이/다른 활동들을 하고/그들의 시간을 보내다/더 가치 있는 일에

___

9. 상품의 가격에 대해 말하자면/온라인 쇼핑몰은/상품들을 제공한다/적절한 가격에

___

10. 또는 때때로/훨씬 더 낮은 가격에/상품과 비교하여/일반 상점에

___

11. 이것은 때문이다/온라인 소매상인들이/덜 쓴다/투자비와 온라인 상점 유지비에

___

12. 그러한 가격들 때문에/일부 소비자들은/구매한다/그 물건들을/온라인에서/저렴한 가격으로/그들을 조사한 후/상점에서

___

13. 그외에도/온라인 쇼핑은/몇 가지 장점들을/취약한 사람들에게/노인들 그리고 장애인들과 같은

14. 그들의 신체적인 상황 때문에/그들은 쇼핑할 수 없다/편안하게/쇼핑몰에서/거기에는/있다/많은 장애물들이/차별과 신체적인 제약들과 같은

15. 인터넷의 덕택으로/그들은 필요하다/단지 그들의 키보드와 마우스/선택하기 위해서/그들 구입을 원하는 상품들을

16. 이것은 가져온다/즐거운 그리고 편안한 쇼핑경험을

17. 이처럼/온라인 쇼핑은 유용하다/특히 노인과 장애를 가진 사람들에게

18. 모든 것을 고려할 때/시간과 경비를 줄이는 것과 더불어

19. 온라인쇼핑은/훨씬 더 이롭다/모든 소비자들이/민감한 소비자들을 포함해서/오프라인 쇼핑보다

20. 그러한 이유들로/온라인 쇼핑몰은/계속될 거 같다/그들의 성공과 인기가

Answer

1. With the advent of the Internet, people around the world have been shopping online.
2. This method of purchasing products provides people with many advantages.
3. However, many consumers believe that offline shopping malls still offer more pleasant experiences.
4. I am for the former for the following reasons.
5. To begin with, shopping via the Internet provides convenience and cost saving to customers.
6. As online shoppers do not have to travel to shopping malls,
7. they can save a lot of time and effort when shopping online.
8. It enables consumers to do other activities and spend their time on more worthwhile work.
9. When it comes to the price of products, online shopping malls supply items at a reasonable cost,
10. or at times, at an even lower price compared to products in brick-and-mortar shops.
11. This is because online retailers spend less on the cost of their investment and online store maintenance.
12. On account of those prices, some customers make a purchase of items online at low prices after examining them in stores.
13. Furthermore, online shopping has several advantages to the vulnerable like the elderly and the disabled.
14. Due to their physical condition, they are unable to shop comfortably in shopping malls where there are many obstacles, including discrimination and physical limitations.
15. With the help of the Internet, they need only their keyboard and mouse to choose items they wish to buy,
16. , which brings about an enjoyable and comfortable shopping experience.
17. Like this, online shopping is useful especially for seniors and those with disabilities.
18. All things considered, coupled with curtailing time and expenses,
19. online shopping is much more beneficial for all customers including sensitive shoppers than offline shopping.
20. For those reasons, online shopping malls are more likely to continue their success and popularity.

You should spend about 40 minutes on this task.

Write about the following topic:

> **Most people believe that online shopping is better and more enjoyable than going to shopping centres. Do you agree or disagree?**

Give reasons for your answer and include any relevant examples from your own knowledge or experience.

Write at least 250 words.

Answer

With the advent of the Internet, people around the world have been shopping online. This method of purchasing products provides people with many advantages. However, many consumers believe that offline shopping malls still offer more pleasant experiences. I am for the former for the following reasons.

To begin with, shopping via the Internet provides convenience and cost saving to customers. As online shoppers do not have to travel to shopping malls, they can save a lot of time and effort when shopping online. It enables consumers to do other activities and spend their time on more worthwhile work. When it comes to the price of products, online shopping malls supply items at a reasonable cost or at times, at an even lower price compared to products in brick-and-mortar shops. This is because online retailers spend less on the cost of their investment and online store maintenance. On account of those prices, some customers make a purchase of items online at low prices after examining them in real stores.

Furthermore, **online shopping offers several advantages the vulnerable** like the elderly and the disabled. Due to their physical condition, they are unable to shop comfortably in shopping malls where there are many obstacles, including discrimination and physical limitations. With the help of the Internet, they need only their keyboard and mouse to choose items they wish to buy, which brings about an enjoyable and comfortable shopping experience. Like this, online shopping is useful especially for seniors and those with disabilities.

All things considered, coupled with curtailing time and expense, online shopping is much more beneficial for all customers including sensitive shoppers than offline shopping. For those reasons, online shopping malls are more likely to continue their success and popularity.

2. Advertisement

You should spend about 40 minutes on this task.

Write about the following topic:

> Some people say that advertising encourages us to buy things that we do not really need. Others say that advertisements tell us about new products that may improve our lives. What is your view?

Give reasons for your answer and include any relevant examples from your own knowledge or experience.

Write at least 250 words.

INTRODUCTION
광고는 소비자들에게 상품의 정보를 제공하고 또한 소비를 부추긴다.
이 에세이는 이러한 광고의 두 가지 측면에 대해 설명하겠다.

BODY1 (positive factors)
상품과 서비스에 대한 정보 제공

BODY2 (negative factors)
소비 권장

CONCLUSION
위에서 본 것처럼 광고는 부정적인 측면도 있지만 훨씬 더 긍정적인 영향을 소비자들에게 주고 있다.

일부 사람들은 우리가 필요하지 않은 것을 광고가 사도록 권한다고 주장한다. 다른 이들은 광고는 우리에게 우리의 삶을 개선시킬지도 모르는 새로운 상품에 대한 정보를 알려준다고 말한다. 당신의 의견은 무엇인가?

INTRODUCTION

현대사회에서 광고들은 사람들의 삶 속에 넘쳐나고 있고, 이것은 피할 수 없는 사실이다. 어떤 사람들은 광고들이 다양한 상품정보를 제공한다고 믿는다. 하지만, 다른 사람들은 광고들은 과도한 소비 습관을 키운다고 주장한다. 이 에세이에서, 나는 광고의 긍정적인 그리고 부정적인 두 측면을 설명하겠다.

BODY1

무엇보다 먼저, 광고의 목적은 기존의 것뿐만 아니라 새로운 상품들과 서비스들에 대한 정보를 주는 것이다. 이것은 소비자들에게 상품들을 사도록 자극한다. 예를 들어, 많은 사람들은 그들의 휴가 동안 해외여행을 계획한다. 그리고 그들은 여행회사의 광고를 통해서 다른 관광지를 알아 볼 수 있고 여행비용과 같은 정보를 얻는 것을 가능하게 한다. 광고가 없다면, 구매자들은 어떠한 새로운 상품들이 만들어졌는지 그리고 그들이 가지고 있는 특성이 무엇인지를 알아내는 데 많은 노력을 해야만 한다. 하지만, 그러한 정보를 알아내는 것은 쉬운 일이 아니다. 덧붙여서, 이 과정은 시간이 걸리고 비효율적이다. 그러므로, 광고들은 정보의 보급과 관련해서 긍정적인 면을 가지고 있다.

BODY 2

반면에, 광고들은 소비자에게 물건이 필요하지 않을 때에도 물건을 사도록 권장한다는 것은 부인할 수 없다. 그 이유는 광고들은 소비자들에게 필요 없는 상품을 구입하게 할 만큼 눈길을 끌기 때문이다. 휴대폰을 예를 들어보자. 새 모델은 전에 것에 비교하여 몇 가지의 부가적인 기능을 가지고 시장에 종종 출시된다. 그러나 시각적으로 매력적인 광고 때문에, 사람들은 그들의 폰이 잘 작동하는 사실에도 불구하고 새 것으로 바꾸고 싶어한다. 이러한 맥락에서, 구매자들은 광고 때문에 필요하지 않은 상품들을 사는 데 쉽게 유혹받는다.

CONCLUSION

요약하자면, 이러한 모든 것들을 고려할 때, 비록 부정적인 효과들을 가지고 있지만 광고는 훨씬 더 긍정적인 영향을 소비자들에게 주는 것 같다. 따라서, 소비자들이 광고를 현명하고 적절하게 이용하는 것이 이치에 맞다.

문장에 필요한 어휘

> 1. advertisement/ad/advertising/commercial; 광고
> 2. overflow; 넘쳐나다

현대사회에서 광고들은 사람들의 삶 속에 넘쳐나고 있다.
Advertisements in modern society are overflowing in people's lives,

> 3. inescapable/unavoidable; 피할 수 없는

그리고, 이것은 피할 수 없는 사실이다.
, and this is an inescapable fact.

> 4. a broad(whole/great/wide) range(variety/diversity) of; 다양한

어떤 사람들은 광고들이 다양한 상품정보를 제공한다고 믿는다.
Some people believe that ads offer a broad range of product information.

> 5. argue/state/maintain/claim/assert/voice; 주장하다
> 6. excessive spending(consumption)/immoderate spending; 과도한 소비

하지만, 다른 사람들은 광고들은 과도한 소비 습관을 키운다고 주장한다.
Others, however, argue that advertisements develop excessive spending habits.

> 7. elaborate on/spell out/account for/give an account of; ~에 대해 설명하다
> 8. positive/affirmative/bright/favorable/beneficial; 긍정적인
> 9. negative/minus/adverse/unfavorable; 부정적인
> 10. aspect/side/respect/factor; 측면

이 에세이에서, 나는 광고의 긍정적인 그리고 부정적인 두 측면을 자세히 설명하겠다.
In this essay, I will elaborate on both positive and negative aspects.

> 11. first and foremost/to begin with/first of all; 무엇보다 먼저
> 12. give information on; ~에 대한 정보를 주다
> 13. not only A but also B/B as well as A; A뿐만 아니라 B
> 14. product/goods/item/commodity; 상품

무엇보다 먼저, 광고의 목적은 기존의 것뿐만 아니라 새로운 상품과 서비스들에 대한 정보를 주는 것이다.
First and foremost, the purpose of advertisement is to give information not only on existing products or services but also on new ones.

> 15. stimulate/encourage/inspire/prompt; 자극하다/고무하다
> 16. make a purchase/buy/purchase; 사다/구입하다

이것은 소비자들에게 상품들을 사도록 자극한다.
It stimulates consumers to make a purchase.

> 17. for instance/for example/for one thing; 예를 들면
> 18. plan/make a plan/work out a plan; 계획하다

예를 들면, 많은 사람들은 그들의 휴가 동안 해외여행을 계획한다.
For instance, many people plan to travel abroad during their holiday,

> 19. find out/figure out/look into; 알아보다
> 20. travel destinations(attractions/spots); 여행지/관광지
> 21. travel agency/tourist agency; 여행회사
> 22. expense/cost/charge/expenditure; 비용

그들은 여행회사의 광고를 통해서 다른 관광지를 알아 볼 수 있고, 그것은 그들이 여행비용과 같은 정보를 얻는 것을 가능하게 한다.
, and they find out different travel destinations through a travel agency advertisement which enables them to obtain information, including traveling expenses.

> 23. make considerable efforts/make(exert) great efforts/put in a lot of work; 많은 노력을 하다
> 24. feature/character/distinction; 특징/특성

광고가 없다면, 구매자들은 어떠한 새로운 상품들이 만들어졌는지 그리고 그들이 가지고 있는 특성이 무엇인지를 알아내는 데 많은 노력을 해야 한다.
Without ads, buyers have to make considerable efforts to see what kinds of new items are produced and what features they have.

> 25. be aware of/know; 알다

하지만 다양한 상품의 종류를 안다는 것은 쉽지 않다.
, but it is not easy to be aware of various kinds of information about products.

> 26. additionally/in addition/besides/also/moreover; 덧붙여서
> 27. time-consuming; 시간이 걸리는
> 28. cost–ineffective; 비용 비효율적인

덧붙여서, 이 과정은 시간이 걸리고 비용 비효율적이다.
Additionally, this process could be time-consuming and cost–ineffective.

> 29. therefore/thus/hence/consequently/as a result/in this context; 따라서/그러므로
> 30. regarding/with regard to/concerning/with respect to/as regards; ~에 관련해서
> 31. dissemination/transmission; 전달/보급

그러므로, 광고들은 정보의 전달과 관련해서 긍정적인 면을 가지고 있다.
Therefore, advertisements have a positive side regarding the dissemination of information.

> 32. on the other hand/on the flip side/meanwhile/otherwise/whereas/while; 반면에
> 33. there is no denying that/it is certain that/it is undeniable that S+V; 부인할 수 없다
> 34. encourage A to B; A가 B하는 것을 권장하다

반면에, 광고들은 소비자에게 물건이 필요하지 않을 때에도 물건을 사도록 권장하는 것은 부인할 여지가 없다.
On the other hand, there is no denying that advertisements encourage consumers to purchase new items even when they do not need it.

> 35. eye-catching; 눈길을 끄는
> 36. unnecessary(needless/unneeded) products (items/goods); 필요 없는 상품들

이유는 광고들은 소비자들이 필요 없는 상품을 구입할 만큼 충분히 눈길을 끌기 때문이다.
The reason is that commercials are eye-catching enough for customers to buy unnecessary products.

> 37. release(launch/introduce) into the market; 시장에 출시하다
> 38. additional(extra/further) function; 부가적인 기능
> 39. compared to/as compared with/in comparison with; ~와 비교하여

휴대폰을 예를 들어보자. 새 모델들은 전에 것의 비교하여 몇 가지의 부가적인 기능을 가지고 시장에 종종 출시된다.
Take for example mobile phones. New models are often released into the market with just a few additional functions compared to the previous one.

> 40. on account of/due to/owing to/because of+N; ~때문에
> 41. attractive/appealing/charming/fascinating; 매력적인
> 42. be keen to/be eager to/be anxious to/be dying to; ~하고 싶어하다
> 43. despite the fact that S+V; ~라는 사실에도 불구하고

그러나 시각적으로 매력적인 광고 때문에, 사람들은 그들의 폰이 여전히 잘 작동한다는 사실에도 불구하고 새것으로 바꾸고 싶어한다.
However, on account of visually attractive advertisements, people are keen to change their phone to the new one despite the fact that their phone is still working well.

> 44. be lured into/be attracted to/be tempted to; ~하도록 유혹받다

이러한 맥락에서, 구매자들은 광고 때문에 필요하지 않은 상품들을 사는 데 쉽게 유혹받는다.
In this context, buyers are easily lured into buying unneeded items due to advertising.

> 45. to sum up/in conclusion/to conclude; 요약하자면/결론은
> 46. take A into consideration(account)/consider A; A를 고려하다
> 47. have(has) positive(affirmative/favourable) influences(effects/impacts) on A; A에게 긍정적인 영향을 끼치다

요약하자면, 이러한 모든 것들을 고려할 때, 비록 부정적인 효과들을 가지고 있지만 광고는 훨씬 더 긍정적인 영향을 소비자들에게 주는 것 같다.
To sum up, taking all these points into consideration, advertising, although having adverse effects, is far more likely to have favourable influences on consumers.

> 48. make sense/stand to reason/be logical; 이치에 맞는
> 49. adequately/properly/appropriately; 적절하게

따라서, 소비자들이 광고를 현명하고 적절하게 이용하는 것이 이치에 맞다.
Consequently, it makes sense for consumers to use advertisements wisely and adequately.

구문연습

1. 광고들은/현대 사회에서/넘쳐나고 있다/사람들의 삶 속에

2. 이것은/피할 수 없는 사실이다

3. 어떤 사람들은 믿는다/광고들은 제공한다/다양한 상품 정보를

4. 그러나/다른 사람들은 주장한다/광고들은 키운다/과도한 소비습관들을

5. 이 에세이에서/나는 자세히 설명하겠다/둘 다/긍정적인 그리고 부정적인 측면들

6. 무엇보다도 먼저/광고의 목적은/정보를 주는 것이다/기존의 상품들과 서비스뿐만 아니라/새로운 것에 대한

7. 이러한 것은 자극한다/소비자들은/구매하도록

8. 예를 들면/많은 사람들은 계획한다/외국여행을/그들의 휴가 동안

9. 그리고/그들은 알아낸다/다른 여행지들을/여행사의 광고를 통해서

10. 광고들은 가능하게 한다/사람들이/정보를 얻는 것을/여행경비들과 같은

11. 광고들 없이/구매자들은 해야 한다/많은 노력을 해야만 한다/알아내기 위해서/어떠한 종류의 새로운 물건들이/생산되는지/그리고/어떤 특성을/그들이 가지고 있는지

12. 그러나/그것은 쉽지 않다/아는 것은/다양한 종류의 정보/상품들에 대한

13. 덧붙여서/이 과정은 시간 소비일 수 있고/그리고/비용 비효율적이다.

14. 그러므로/광고들은/긍정적인 측면을 가지고 있다/정보의 보급과 관련하여

15. 반면에/부인할 수가 없다/광고들이 부추긴다/소비자들을/상품을 구매하도록/심지어/그들이 그것을 필요하지 않을 때도

_____
_____

16. 그 이유는 ~이다/광고들은/눈길을 끌다/충분히/소비자들이 /살 정도로/필요없는 물건들을

_____
_____

17. 휴대폰을 예를 들어보자/새로운 모델은 종종 출시된다/시장에/단지 몇 개의 부가적인 기능들과 함께/전의 것과 비교해서

_____
_____

18. 그러나/시각적으로 매력적인 광고 때문에/사람들은 하고 싶어한다/새것으로 바꾸고/사실에도 불구하고/그들의 폰이 여전히/잘 작동하다

_____
_____

19. 이러한 맥락에서/구매자들은/쉽게 유혹받는다/구매하도록/불필요한 상품들을/광고 때문에

_____
_____

20. 요약하자면/이러한 모든 것들을 고려할 때/광고/비록/부정적인 효과들을 가지고 있지만/훨씬 더인 것 같다/긍정적인 영향을/소비자들에게

_____
_____

21. 따라서/그것은 이치에 맞다/소비자들이/광고를 이용하는 것/현명하고 적절하게

_____
_____

Answer

1. Advertisements in modern society are overflowing in people's lives,

2. , and this is an inescapable fact.

3. Some people believe that ads offer a broad range of product information.

4. Others, however, argue that advertisements develop excessive spending habits.

5. In this essay, I will elaborate on both positive and negative aspects.

6. First and foremost, the purpose of advertising is to give information not only on existing products and services but also on new ones.

7. It stimulates consumers to make a purchase.

8. For instance, many people plan to travel abroad during their holiday.

9. They find out different travel destinations through a travel agency advertisement.

10. Advertisements enable them to obtain information, including travelling expenses.

11. Without ads, buyers have to make considerable efforts to see what kinds of new items are produced and what features they have,

12. , but it is not easy to be aware of various kinds of information of products.

13. Additionally, this process could be time-consuming and cost-effective.

14. Therefore, advertisements have a positive side regarding the dissemination of information.

15. On the other hand, there is no denying that advertisements encourage consumers to purchase new items even when these elements are not necessary.

16. The reason is that commercials are eye-catching enough for consumers to buy unnecessary products.

17. Take for example mobile phones. New models are often released into the market with just a few additional functions compared to the previous one.

18. However, on account of visually attractive advertisements, people are keen to change their phone to the new one despite the fact that phone is still working well.

19. In this context, buyers are easily lured into buying unneeded items due to advertising.

20. To sum up, taking all these points into consideration, advertising, although having adverse effects, is far more likely to have favourable influences on consumers.

21. Consequently, it makes sense for consumers to use advertisements wisely and adequately.

You should spend about 40 minutes on this task.

Write about the following topic:

> **Some people say that advertising encourages us to buy things that we do not really need. Others say that advertisements tell us about new products that may improve our lives. What is your view?**

Give reasons for your answer and include any relevant examples from your own knowledge or experience.

Write at least 250 words.

Answer

Advertisements in modern society are overflowing in people's lives, and this is an inescapable fact. Some people believe that ads offer a broad range of product information. Others, however, argue that advertisements develop excessive spending habits. In this essay, I will elaborate on both positive and negative aspects.

First and foremost, the purpose of advertisements is to give information not only on existing products or services but also on new ones. It stimulates consumers to make a purchase. For instance, many people plan to travel abroad during their holiday, and they find out different travel destinations through a travel agency advertisement which enables them to obtain information, including traveling expenses. Without ads, buyers have to make considerable efforts to see what kinds of new items are produced and what features they have, but it is not easy to be aware of various kinds of information about products. Additionally, this process could be time-consuming and cost- ineffective. Therefore, advertisements have a positive side regarding the dissemination of information.

On the other hand, there is no denying that advertisements encourage consumers to purchase new items even when they do not need it. The reason is that commercials are eye-catching enough for consumers to buy unnecessary products. Take for example mobile phones. New models are often released into the market with just a few additional functions compared to the previous one. However, on account of visually attractive advertisements, people are keen to change their phone to the new one despite the fact that their phone is still working well. In this context, buyers are easily lured into buying unneeded items due to advertising.

To sum up, taking all these points into consideration, advertising, although having adverse effects, is far more likely to have favorable influences on consumers. Consequently, it makes sense for consumers to use advertisements wisely and adequately.

3. Traveling

You should spend about 40 minutes on this task.

Write about the following topic:

> People are traveling to other countries more than before. What are the advantages and disadvantages of traveling abroad?

Give reasons for your answer and include any relevant examples from your own knowledge or experience.

Write at least 250 words.

INTRODUCTION
  최근에 해외여행이 증가하고 있다.
  해외여행의 장단점에 대해 제시하겠다.

BODY 1 (advantages)
  1. 다양한 경험
  2. 자립심 강화

BODY 2 (disadvantages)
  1. 고비용
  2. 위험에 직면

CONCLUSION
  여러 가지 사실을 고려할 때, 해외여행을 하는 것은 권장할 만하다.

사람들은 전보다 더 다른 나라를 여행하고 있다. 외국여행을 하는 것의 장점과 단점은 무엇인가?

INTRODUCTION

최근에 저렴한 교통의 발달과 높은 생활 수준으로 외국으로 여행가는 사례들이 늘고 있다. 외국으로 여행하는 것은 여행객들에게 다른 나라의 문화와 역사를 경험하는 것을 가능하게 하는 것은 사실이다. 그렇지만, 여행을 할 때, 그들은 많은 어려움들을 겪는다. 이 에세이에서, 여행을 위해 외국에 가는 것에 대한 장단점을 제시하겠다.

BODY 1

다른 나라로 여행하는 것은 장점들을 가지고 있다는 것은 부인할 수 없다. 첫 번째는 외국여행을 하는 것은 방문한 나라의 문화, 사회과학 그리고 역사에 관해 다양한 경험을 제공할 것이다. 여행객들은 많은 새로운 생각들과 많은 지식을 접할 수 있기 때문에 이러한 유익한 경험들은 그들의 시야를 넓힐 수 있다. **두 번째로, 특히 젊은 사람들은, 여행을 통해서 자립을 배울 수 있다.** 그들이 그들의 가족과 떨어져 있고 특히 혼자일 때, 그들은 때때로 예상하지 못한 상황이나 비상 상황에 직면할 것이다. 그러한 상황에서, 그들은 스스로 결정하고 문제들을 해결해야만 한다. 따라서, 해외여행은 세계에 대한 다양한 경험을 통해 시각을 넓히고 자립심을 길러준다.

BODY 2

다른 한편으로는 마찬가지로 해외여행에 대한 단점들이 있다. 우선, 다른 나라를 방문하는 데 교통비, 숙박비 같은 상당히 많은 돈을 지출해야만 한다. 그러므로, 사람들은 여행을 위해서 충분한 예산과 충분한 소득이 필요하다. **이것뿐만 아니라,** 여행하는 동안 등산, 스쿠버 다이빙 그리고 다른 위험한 활동들이 있고 이러한 것은 여행자들에게 위협을 가할 수 있다. 만약 그러한 활동들로 인해 상해를 당한다면, 여행자들은 언어장벽과 다른 의료 체계 때문에 치료하는 데 어려움을 겪을 수 있다. 실제로, 위험한 활동으로 인한 사고뿐만 아니라, 소매치기 그리고 최근 해외여행지에서의 테러 발생들과 같은 사건들이 일어나고 있다. 많은 사람들이 동유럽을 여행하는 동안 그들의 소지품을 절도당하는 경험을 했다고 보도된다. 이러한 문제들 때문에, 다른 나라를 여행하는 것은 처음 생각했던 것처럼 편안하지 않을지도 모른다.

CONCLUSION

결론은, 많은 요인들을 고려할 때, 비록 해외여행을 가는 것은 몇몇의 단점들이 있지만, 여행자들이 해외여행을 통해 가치 있는 경험들과 기회들을 가질 수 있는 것은 분명하다. 그러므로, 사람들이 다른 나라들을 여행하는 것은 권장할 만하다. 그러나 그들은 위협하는 활동을 피해야만 하고 항상 안전을 최우선적으로 둬야 한다.

문장에 필요한 어휘

> 1. in recent years/in recent times/lately/of late/recently; 최근에
> 2. instance/example/case; 사례
> 3. be on the rise/be on the increase; 증가하고 있다
> 4. transportation/traffic/transport; 교통
> 5. a standard of living/the living standard/the level of living; 생활 수준

최근에 저렴한 교통의 발달과 높은 생활 수준으로 외국으로 여행가는 사례들이 늘고 있다.
In recent years, the instances of traveling abroad have been on the rise with the development of cheaper transportation and a higher standard of living.

> 6. it is true that/it is a fact that S+V; 사실이다
> 7. enable A to B; A가 B하는 것을 가능하게 하다
> 8. nation/country/state; 나라

외국으로 여행하는 것은 여행객들에게 다른 나라의 문화와 역사를 경험하는 것을 가능하게 하는 것은 사실이다.
It is true that traveling overseas enables travelers to experience the culture and history of other nations.

> 9. nevertheless/though/however; 그렇지만
> 10. go though/suffer/experience/undergo; 겪다
> 11. difficulty/concern/trouble/problem ; 어려움

그러나 여행을 할 때, 그들은 많은 어려움들을 겪는다.
Nevertheless, they go through many difficulties when taking a trip.

> 11. present/explain/express/illustrate; 제시하다/설명하다
> 12. pro and con/advantage and disadvantage/merit and demerit/good and bad point/positive and negative thing; 장점과 단점
> 13. overseas/abroad; 외국의/해외의
>   Tip) travel overseas/abroad(전치사 안 붙음)

이 에세이에서, 나는 여행을 위해 외국에 가는 것에 대한 장단점들을 제시하겠다.
In this essay, I will present the pros and cons of going overseas for a trip.

> 14. it is undeniable that/there is no denying that S+V; 부인할 수 없다

다른 나라로 여행하는 것이 장점들을 가지고 있다는 것은 부인할 수 없다.
It is undeniable that traveling to other countries has advantages.

> 15. provide/give/serve/offer; 제공하다
> 16. a broad(whole/great/wide) range(variety) of; 다양한
> 17. regarding/with regard to/concerning/as regards+N/구; ~에 관해

첫 번째는 해외여행을 하는 것은 방문한 나라의 문화, 사회과학 그리고 역사에 관해 다양한 경험을 제공할 것이다.
Firstly, traveling abroad would provide a broad range of experiences regarding the culture, social sciences and history of the country people visit.

> 18. enlightening/instructive/beneficial/useful/helpful; 유익한
> 19. broaden(expand/widen) horizon(outlook); 시야를 넓히다
> 20. come across/learn/understand/experience; 접하다/이해하다/경험하다
> 21. novel(new/fresh) idea; 새로운/신선한 생각

여행객들은 많은 새로운 생각들과 많은 지식들과 접할 수 있기 때문에 이러한 유익한 경험들은 그들의 시야를 넓힐 수 있다.
These enlightening experiences could broaden their horizons as they come across many novel ideas and much knowledge.

> 22. independence/self-reliance; 자립

두 번째로, 특히 젊은 사람들은, 여행을 통해서 자립을 배울 수 있다.
Secondly, travelers, especially young people, could learn independence through traveling.

> 23. be away from/stay away from; ~로부터 떨어져 있다
> 24. particularly/specially/especially/in particular; 특히
> 25. at times/sometimes/now and then/on and off/once in a while; 때때로
> 26. face/encounter/confront; 직면하다
> 27. unforeseen(unexpected/unpredicted) circumstances(conditions/situations); 예상치 못한 상황

그들이 그들의 가족과 떨어져 있고 특히 혼자일 때, 그들은 때때로 예상하지 못한 상황이나 비상상황에 직면할 것이다.
When they are away from their family, particularly being alone, they will, at times, face unforeseen circumstances or emergencies.

> 28. make a decision/determine/decide; 결정하다
> 29. by oneself/alone/on one's own; 스스로

그러한 상황에서, 그들은 스스로 결정하고 문제들을 해결해야만 한다.
In those situations, they would have to make decisions and solve problems by themselves.

> 30. perspective/point of view/vision/outlook; 시각
> 31. cultivate/develop/form/keep/raise; 기르다/형성하다

따라서, 여행은 세계에 대한 다양한 경험을 통해 시각을 넓히고 자립심을 기른다.
Thus, traveling overseas widens the perspective of the world through a variety of experiences and cultivates self-reliance.

> 32. on the contrary/on the other hand/in contrast/by contrast/on the flip side; 다른 한편으로는
> 33. likewise/also/too/as well/in the same way; 마찬가지로/또한

다른 한편으로는 마찬가지로 해외여행에 대한 단점들이 있다.
On the contrary, there are likewise the disadvantages of foreign trips.

> 34. for one/most of all/first of all/above all; 우선
> 35. a considerable(enormous/great) amount of money/a great of money/a good deal of money; 많은 돈
> 36. expense/cost/charge/expenditure; 비용
> 37. accommodation/staying; 거처/숙소

우선, 다른 나라를 방문하는 데 교통비, 숙박비를 포함한 상당히 많은 돈을 지출해야만 한다.
For one, people have to spend a considerable amount of money on visiting other countries, including transportation, accommodation, and so on.

> 38. budget/finance/money; 예산
> 39. sufficient/enough/plentiful; 충분한

그러므로, 사람들은 여행을 위해서 충분한 예산과 충분한 소득이 필요하다.
Hence, people need to have a big enough budget or sufficient income to travel.

> 40. not only that/In addition; 이것뿐만 아니라/덧붙여서
> 41. activity/work/play; 활동

이것뿐만 아니라, 여행하는 동안 산행, 스쿠버 다이빙 그리고 다른 위험한 활동들이 있다.
Not only that, but there are also some activities such as mountain climbing, scuba diving, and other dangerous activities during traveling.

---

42. pose a risk to/pose a threat to/threaten/pose a danger to+N; ~에 위험을 가하다

이러한 것은 여행객들에게 위협을 가할 수 있다.
, which can pose some risks to tourists

---

43. due to/owing to/on account of/because of+N/구; ~때문에
44. language barriers; 언어 장벽

만약 그러한 종류의 활동들로 인해 상해를 당한다면, 여행자들은 언어장벽과 다른 의료 체계 때문에 치료하는 데 어려움에 직면할 수 있다.
If injured due to those kinds of activities, travelers could face difficulties in the treatment because of language barriers and different medical systems.

---

45. as well as accidents; 사고들뿐만 아니라
46. incident; 사건
47. pickpocket; 소매치기
48. tourist destinations/tourist resorts/tourist spots; 관광지들

실제로 위험한 활동으로 인한 사고뿐만 아니라, 소매치기 그리고 최근 해외여행지에서의 테러와 같은 많은 사건들이 발생하고 있다.
In fact, as well as accidents caused by risky activities, some incidents occur like pickpocketing and the recent terrorist incidences in foreign tourist destinations.

---

49. it is reported that S+V; ~로 보고된다/~로 보도된다

많은 사람들이 동유럽을 여행하는 동안 소지품들을 절도 당한 경험을 했다고 보도된다.
It is reported that many people experienced having their belongings stolen while traveling around Eastern Europe.

---

50. relaxing/easy/comfortable; 편안한

이러한 문제들 때문에, 다른 나라를 여행하는 것은 처음 생각했던 것처럼 편안하지 않을지도 모른다.
On account of these issue, traveling to other countries may not be relaxing as first thought.

> 51. in conclusion/to sum up/to conclude; 결론은
> 52. consider A/take A into consideration(account); A를 고려하다
> 53. drawback/disadvantage/demerit/bad point; 단점

결론은, 많은 요인들을 고려할 때, 비록 해외여행을 가는 것은 몇몇의 단점들이 있지만,

In conclusion, considering many factors, though there are several drawbacks of traveling abroad,

> 54. it is clear-cut that/it is certain that/it is obvious that S+V; 분명하다
> 55. valuable/of value/worthwhile/precious; 귀중한

여행자들이 해외여행을 통해 가치 있는 경험들과 기회들을 가질 수 있는 것은 분명하다.

It is clear-cut that tourists could have valuable experiences and opportunities through overseas traveling.

> 56. recommendable/reasonable/advisable/desirable/compelling/persuasive; 권장할 만한/바람직한
> 57. life-threatening; 생명을 위협하는
> 58. as a priority; 최우선적으로

그러므로, 사람들이 다른 나라들을 여행하는 것은 권장할 만하다. 그러나 그들은 생명을 위협하는 활동들을 피해야만 하고 항상 안전을 최우선적으로 둬야 한다.

Hence, it is recommendable for people to travel to other countries, but they should avoid life-threatening activities and always put safety as a priority.

구문연습

1. 최근에/해외여행의 사례들이/증가해 오고 있다/저렴한 교통의 발달과/높은 생활 수준

2. 그것은 사실이다/외국을 여행하는 것은/가능하게 하다/여행객들을/경험하게 하는/문화와 역사/다른 나라의

3. 그렇지만/그들은 겪는다/많은 어려움들을/여행할 때

4. 이 에세이에서/나는 제시하겠다/장점들과 단점들을/외국에 가는 것/여행하기 위해

5. 그것은 부인할 수 없다/다른 나라에 여행하는 것은/장점들을 가진다

6. 첫 번째는/외국여행하는 것은/제공한다/다양한 경험들을/관해/문화, 사회과학 그리고 역사/방문한 나라의

7. 이러한 유익한 경험들은/그들의 시야를 넓힐 수 있다/왜냐하면/그들은 접하기 때문이다/많은 새로운 생각들과 많은 지식을

_____

_____

8. 두 번째로/여행객들/특별히 젊은 사람들은/배울 수 있다/자립심을/여행을 통해서

_____

_____

9. 그들이 떨어져 있을 때/가족으로부터/특별히 혼자 있을 때/그들은/때때로/직면할 것이다/예상치 못한 상황들과 비상상황

_____

_____

10. 이러한 상황에서/그들은 해야만 할 것이다/결정하고 해결하다/문제점들을/스스로

_____

_____

11. 따라서/해외여행은/넓힌다/세계에 대한 시각과/다양한 경험을 통해서/기른다/자립심을

_____

_____

12. 다른 한편으로는/있다/마찬가지로/단점들이/해외여행의

_____

_____

13. 우선/사람들은 지출해야만한다/상당한 돈을/다른 나라들을 방문하는 데/포함하여/교통, 숙박비등과 같은

_____

_____

14. 따라서/사람들은 갖는 것이 필요하다/충분한 예산/또는 충분한 수입/여행하기 위해서

15. 이것뿐만 아니라/몇몇의 활동들이 있다/산행, 스쿠버 다이빙과 같은/그리고 다른 위험한 활동들/여행하는 동안

16. 이러한 것은/위협을 가할 수 있다/여행객들에게

17. 만약/상해를 당하면/그러한 종류의 활동들 때문에/여행객들은 직면할 수 있다/어려움들에/치료하는 데/언어장벽들 그리고 다른 의료 시스템 때문에

18. 실제로/위험한 활동으로 인한 사고뿐만 아니라/많은 사고 사건들이 발생한다/소매치기 같은/그리고 테러발생들/해외여행지에서

19. 그것은 보도된다/많은 사람들이 경험했다/그들의 소지품들이 절도당한 걸/동유럽을 여행하는 동안

20. 이러한 문제들 때문에/여행하는 것은/다른 나라들을/아닐지도 모른다/편안하지/처음 생각했던 것처럼

_____

_____

21. 결론은/이러한 요인들을 고려할 때/비록 있지만/몇 가지 단점들이 있지만/외국여행을 하는데

_____

_____

22. 이것은 분명하다/여행객들은/가질 수 있을 것이다/가치 있는 기회들과 경험들을/해외여행을 통해서

_____

_____

23. 그러므로/그것은 권장할 만하다/사람들이/여행하는 것은/다른 나라들을

_____

_____

24. 그러나 그들은 피해야만 한다/생명을 위협하는 행동들을/그리고 항상/안전을 놓아야 한다/우선적인 것으로서

_____

_____

Answer

1. In recent years, the instances of traveling abroad have been on the rise with the development of cheaper transportation and a higher standard of living.
2. It is true that traveling overseas enables travellers to experience the culture and history of other nations.
3. Nevertheless, they go through many difficulties when taking a trip.
4. In this essay, I will present the pros and cons of going overseas for a trip.
5. It is undeniable that traveling to other countries has advantages.
6. Firstly, traveling abroad would provide a broad range of experiences regarding the culture, social science and history of the country people visit.
7. These enlightening experiences could broaden their horizon as they come across many novel ideas and much knowledge.
8. Secondly, travelers, especially young people, could learn independence through travelling.
9. When they are away from their family, particularly being alone, they will, at times, face unforeseen circumstances or emergencies.
10. In those situations, they would have to make decisions and solve the problems by themselves.
11. Thus, traveling overseas widens the perspective of the world through a variety of experiences and cultivates self-reliance.
12. On the contrary, there are likewise the disadvantages of foreign trips.
13. For one, people have to spend a considerable amount of money on visiting other countries, including transportation, accommodation, and so on.
14. Hence, people need to have a big enough budget or sufficient income to travel.
15. Not only that, but there are also some activities such as mountain climbing, scuba diving, and other dangerous activities during traveling,
16. , which can pose some risks to tourists.
17. If injured due to those kinds of activities, travelers could face difficulties in the treatment because of language barriers and different medical systems.
18. In fact, as well as accidents caused by risky activities, some incidents occur like pickpocketing and the recent terrorist incidences in foreign tourist destinations.
19. It is reported that many people experienced having their belongings stolen while traveling around Eastern Europe.
20. On account of these issues, traveling to other countries may not be relaxing as first thought.
21. In conclusion, considering many factors, though there are several drawbacks of traveling abroad.
22. It is clear-cut that tourists could have valuable experiences and opportunities through overseas traveling.
23. Hence, it is recommendable for people to travel to other countries,
24. , but they should avoid life-threatening activities and always put safety as a priority.

You should spend about 40 minutes on this task.

Write about the following topic:

> **People are traveling to other countries more than before. What are the advantages and disadvantages of traveling abroad?**

Give reasons for your answer and include any relevant examples from your own knowledge or experience.

Write at least 250 words.

Answer

In recent years, the instances of traveling abroad have been on the rise with the development of cheaper transportation and a higher standard of living. It is true that traveling overseas enables travelers to experience the culture and history of other nations. Nevertheless, they go through many difficulties when taking a trip. In this essay, I will present the pros and cons of going overseas for a trip.

It is undeniable that traveling to other countries has advantages, Firstly, traveling abroad would provide a broad range of experiences regarding the culture, social science, and history of the country people visit. These enlightening experiences could broaden their horizons as they come across many novel ideas and much knowledge. **Secondly, travelers, especially young people, could learn independence through traveling.** When they are away from their family, particularly being alone, they will, at times, face unforeseen circumstances or emergencies. In those situations, they would have to make decisions and solve problems by themselves. Thus, traveling overseas widens the perspective of the world through a variety of experiences and cultivates self-reliance.

On the contrary, there are likewise the disadvantages of foreign trips. For one, people have to spend a considerable amount of money on visiting other countries, including transportation, accommodation and so on. Hence, people need to have a big enough budget or sufficient income to travel. **Not only that, but there are also some activities such as mountain climbing, scuba diving, and other dangerous activities during traveling, which can pose some risks to tourists.** If injured due to those kinds of activities, travelers could face difficulties in the treatment because of language barriers and different medical systems. In fact, as well as accidents caused by risky activities, some incidents occur like pickpocketing and the recent terrorist incidences in foreign tourist destinations. It is reported that many people experienced having their belongings stolen while traveling around Eastern Europe. On account of these issues, traveling to other countries may not be relaxing as first thought.

In conclusion, considering many factors, though there are several drawbacks of traveling abroad, it is clear-cut that tourists could have valuable experiences and opportunities through overseas traveling. Hence, it is recommendable for people to travel to other countries, but they should avoid life-threatening activities and always put safety as a priority.

4. Traffic taxes

You should spend about 40 minutes on this task.

Write about the following topic:

> To address traffic problems, governments should tax private car owners heavily and use the money to improve public transportation. To what extent do you agree?

Give reasons for your answer and include any relevant examples from your own knowledge or experience.

Write at least 250 words.

INTRODUCTION

　　교통혼잡이 심각한 문제가 되고 있다.

　　차 소유자들에게 세금을 부과해서 대중교통을 개선시키는 정책에 대해 토론하겠다.

BODY 1 (agree)

　　1. 차 소유를 주저 - 대중교통을 이용

　　2. 노후화된 대중교통 개선 - 더 많은 대중교통을 이용

BODY 2 (disagree)

　　1. 차 소유자들에게 재정적 부담(특히 차량을 소유할 수밖에 없는 사람들)

　　2. 대중교통을 이용하지는 않는다. (특히 세금 낼 여력이 있는 사람들)

CONCLUSION

　　이 정책에 대한 장단점들이 있다.

　　현재의 교통상황을 고려할 때, 세금부과 정책은 시도할 만하다.

교통문제를 해결하기 위해 정부는 개인 차 소유자들에게 세금을 부과해서 그 돈을 대중교통을 개선하는 데 사용해야 한다. 어느 정도 동의하는가?

INTRODUCTION

세계 전역의 도시들에서 교통혼잡은 더욱 심각해지고 있다. 이 문제에 대한 가능한 해결책은 개인 차량 운전자에게 무거운 세금을 부과하고 그 예산을 대중교통을 개선하는 데 사용하는 것이다. 이 에세이는 이러한 정책의 장단점에 대해 자세히 설명할 것이다.

BODY 1

우선, 더 나은 교통을 위해서 차 소유주에게 세금을 부과하는 것은 몇 가지 이점이 있다. 이점 중 하나는 과중한 세금은 잠재적인 차 구매자들이 차 구입하는 것을 주저하게 만들 것이다. 왜냐하면 세금은 차 소유자들에게 부담을 주기 때문이다. 개인용 차량을 이용하는 대신에, 그들은 대중교통을 이용할 것이고 이것은 교통문제를 줄일 것이다. **다른 이점은 세금은 대중교통을 더 편리하고 편안하게 만드는 데 사용될 수 있다.** 사실상 많은 도시들이 대중교통 상태가 좋지 않다. 노후화된 버스들과 기차들은 덜 편안하고, 그런 이유로 사람들은 대중교통을 이용하지 않는다. 만약 정부가 이러한 차량들을 개선하는 데 투자하면, 훨씬 더 많은 시민들이 그것을 이용할 것이고 교통문제는 해결될 것이다. 이것에 대한 한 가지 좋은 예로 싱가포르가 이 정책을 시행하는 첫 번째 나라들 중 하나이고 현재 그들은 잘 갖춰진 대중교통 시스템을 가지고 있다. 이러한 맥락에서, 차 소유주에게 세금 부과는 실제로 교통문제를 줄일 수 있다.

BODY 2

반면에, 이 해법에 대한 단점들이 있다. 무엇보다 먼저, **차에 대한 높은 세금은 현재의 차 소유주들이나 운전자들에게 실질적인 재정적 부담이 될 것이다.** 특히, 사업을 위해서 차량이 필요한 사업자들은 재정적으로 심한 경제압박 상태에 놓일 수 있다. **덧붙여서, 이러한 정책은 부자들에게 대중교통 이용을 유도하지 않기 때문에 효과적이지 않다.** 왜냐하면 그들은 부가적인 세금을 내고 그들의 차를 살 여력이 있기 때문이다. 그러므로, 운전자에게 세금을 부과하는 것은 교통문제를 해결하는 데 적절한 방법이 아니다.

CONCLUSION

결론은, 이러한 정책을 시행하는 데는 장점들과 단점들이 있다. 비록 몇 가지 단점들이 있지만, 현재의 교통상황을 고려해 볼때, 나는 차 소유자들에게 세금을 부과하는 것은 가치가 있다는 것에 동의한다.

문장에 필요한 어휘

> 1. traffic congestion/traffic jam; 교통 혼잡
> 2. severe/serious/grave; 심각한

세계 전역의 도시들에서의 교통혼잡은 더욱 심각해지고 있다.
Traffic congestion in cities around the world is becoming more severe.

> 3. feasible/workable/possible/actable/practicable/viable; 실행 가능한
> 4. solution/settlement/resolution/answer; 해법
> 5. impose(charge/levy/put/lay) heavy taxes on ~; ~에 무거운 세금을 부과하다
> 6. heavy (oppressive) taxes; 과중한 세금
> 7. improve/develop/better; 개선하다
> 8. public transport/public transportation; 대중교통

이 문제에 대한 가능한 해결책은 개인 차량 운전자에게 과중한 세금을 부과하고 그 예산을 대중교통을 개선하는 데 사용하는 것이다.
One feasible solution to this problem is to impose heavy taxes on private car owners and use the budget to improve public transport.

> 9. spell out/elaborate on/discuss in detail; 자세히 설명하다
> 10. positive and negative point/advantage and disadvantage/pro and con/merit and demerit; 장·단점
> 11. measure/policy/plan; 정책

이 에세이는 이러한 정책의 장단점에 대해 자세히 설명할 것이다.
This essay will spell out the positive and negative points of such a measure.

> 12. a couple of/several/a few; 몇 가지
> 13. benefit/good point/merit; 이점

우선, 더 나은 교통을 위해 차 소유주에게 세금을 부과하는 것은 몇 가지 이점이 있다.
First of all, taxing on car owners for better traffic has a couple of benefits.

> 14. first of all/to begin with/first and foremost; 우선/먼저
> 15. discourage A from B/deter(stop/prohibit) A from B; A가 B하는 것을 막다
> 16. prospective(potential) car buyers; 잠재적인 차 구매자들
> 17. purchase/buy/make a purchase; 구매하다
> 18. give a burden to(on); ~에게 부담을 주다

이점 중 하나는 과중한 세금은 잠재적인 차 구매자들이 차 구입하는 것을 주저하게 만들 것이다. 왜냐하면 세금은 차 소유주들에게 부담을 주기 때문이다.

One of the advantages is that the heavy taxes would discourage prospective car buyers from purchasing cars because taxes give a burden to car owners.

> 19. in place of/instead of/in lieu of; ~대신에
> 20. make use of/use/utilize/tap into; 이용하다
> 21. reduce/lessen/cut down on/alleviate; 줄이다
> 22. as well/also/likewise/too; 또한/마찬가지로

개인용 차량을 이용하는 대신에, 그들은 대중교통을 이용할 것이고 이것은 교통문제를 줄일 것이다.

In place of using private vehicles, they would begin to make use of public transport, which can also reduce traffic problems.

> 23. improve/develop/better; 개선하다
> 24. convenient and comfortable; 편리하고 편안한

다른 이점은 세금은 대중교통을 더 편리하고 편안하게 만드는 데 사용될 수 있다.

Another benefit is that the tax money could be used to make public transportation more convenient and comfortable.

> 25. in fact/in reality/actually/virtually; 사실상
> 26. be in an unfavorable condition; 상태가 좋지 않다

사실상, 많은 도시들이 대중교통 상태가 좋지 않다. 노후화된 버스들과 기차들은 덜 편안해서, 그런 이유로 사람들은 대중교통을 이용하지 않는다.

In reality, public transport in many cities is in an unfavorable condition, old buses and trains are less comfortable, and this is one reason why most people do not use them.

> 27. invest in/make an investment in; ~에 투자하다
> 28. vehicle/car; 차량
> 29. traffic concern(problem/difficulty); 교통 문제
> 30. unravel/solve/resolve/tackle/sort out/address/settle; 해결하다

만약 정부가 이러한 차량들을 개선하는 데 투자하면, 훨씬 더 많은 시민들이 그것을 이용할 것이고 교통문제도 해결될 것이다.

If the government invests in the improvement of these vehicles, more citizens will use them, and traffic concerns will be unraveled.

> 31. implement(carry out/practice/introduce/enforce) this policy; 정책을 시행하다

이것에 대한 한 가지 좋은 예로 싱가포르가 이 정책을 시행하는 첫 번째 나라들 중 하나이다.

An excellent example of this is Singapore which is one of the first countries to implement this policy.

> 32. at present/currently/today; 현재
> 33. a well-organized transport system; 잘 갖춰진 대중교통 시스템

그리고 현재 그들은 잘 갖춰진 대중교통 시스템을 가지고 있다.

And at present, they have a well-organized transport system.

> 34. in this context/therefore/as a result/thus/hence; 따라서
> 35. lessen/decrease/reduce/lower; 줄이다

이러한 맥락에서, 차 소유주에게 세금 부과는 실제로 교통문제를 줄일 수 있다.

In this context, putting taxes on car owners could indeed lessen traffic problems.

> 36. on the flip side/on the other hand/on the contrary/in contrast; 반면에
> 37. drawback/disadvantage/bad point/demerit/weakness; 단점

반면에, 이 해법에 대한 단점들이 있다.

On the flip side, there are drawbacks to this solution.

> 38. first and foremost/first of all/to begin with/above all; 무엇보다 먼저
> 39. a financial strain(burden/pressure); 재정적 부담

무엇보다 먼저, 차에 대한 높은 세금은 현재의 차 소유주들이나 운전자들에게 실질적인 재정적 부담이 될 것이다.

First and foremost, high taxes on cars would be put a real financial strain on current car owners and drivers.

> 40. in particular/particularly/especially; 특히

특히, 사업을 위해서 차량이 필요한 사업자들은 재정적으로 심한 압박상태에 놓일 수 있다.

In particular, business people who need vehicles for business could be under heavier financial pressure.

> 41. besides/aside from/other than; ~ 외에도
> 42. go nowhere/be ineffective/have no effect at all/be unsuccessful; 효과가 없다/아무 성과가 없다
> 43. lead(induce/drive) A to B; A가 B하도록 유도하다
> 44. the haves/the wealthy/the affluent/the privileged; 부자들
> 45. since/now that/because +S+V; ~때문에

덧붙여서, 이러한 정책은 부자들에게 대중교통이용을 유도하지 않기 때문에 효과적이지 않다.

Besides, this policy goes nowhere since this type of tax will not lead the haves to use public transportation,

> 46. can afford to; ~할 여력이 있다
> 47. additional(extra) tax; 부가적인 세금

왜냐하면 그들은 부가적인 세금을 내고 그들의 차를 살 여력이 있기 때문이다.

as they can afford to buy their cars and pay additional taxes.

> 48. proper/adequate/appropriate; 적절한

그러므로, 운전자에게 세금을 부과하는 것은 교통문제를 해결하는 데 적절한 방법이 아니다.

Therefore, levying taxes on car owners is not the proper way to tackle traffic concerns.

> 49. in conclusion/to sum up/in short; 결론은/요약하자면
> 50. policy/initiative/measures; 정책/조치

결론은, 이러한 정책을 시행하는 데는 장점들과 단점들이 있다.
In conclusion, there are the merits and demerits of introducing such a policy.

> 51. given; ~을 고려해 볼때
> 52. worthwhile/of value/valuable/meaningful; 가치가 있는/보람 있는

그러나, 현재의 교통 상황을 고려해 볼때, 비록 몇 가지 단점들이 있지만, 나는 차 소유자들에게 세금을 부과하는 것은 가치가 있다는 것에 동의한다.
However, given the current traffic situation, I agree that charging taxes on car owners, although having a few weaknesses, is worthwhile.

구문연습

1. 교통혼잡은/도시들에서/세계적으로/되고 있다/더욱 심각하게

2. 한 가지 가능한 해결책은/이 문제에 대한/무거운 세금을 부과하는 것이다/개인차량 운전자에게/그리고 사용하는 것이다/그 돈을/개선시키기 위해서/대중교통을

3. 이 에세이는/자세히 설명할 것이다/장단점들을/이러한 정책에 대한

4. 우선/세금 부과는/개인 차량 소유주에게/더 나은 교통을 위해/가지고 있다/몇 가지 이점들

5. 이점 중 하나는 ~이다/과중한 세금은/주저하게 하다/잠재적인 차 구매자들이/차를 사는 것을

6. 왜냐하면/세금은/부담을 주다/차 소유주들에게

7. 개인용 차량을 사용하는 대신에/그들은 이용하기 시작할 것이다/대중교통을/그리고 그것은/줄인다/교통문제들을

---

8. 다른 이점은/세금은 사용되고 있다/대중교통을 더 편리하고 편안하게 만들기 위해

---

9. 사실상/대중교통은/도시들에서/상태가 좋지 않다

---

10. 노후화된 버스들과 기차들은/덜 편안하다/그리고 한 가지 이유이다/왜 대부분 사람들이/그들을 이용하지 않은

---

11. 만약 정부가 투자하면/이런 차량들의 개선에/많은 시민들은/그들을 이용할 것이고/교통문제는 해결될 것이다.

---

12. 이것의 좋은 예로/싱가포르가 첫 번째 나라들 중 한 곳이다/시행하는/이 정책을

---

13. 그리고 현재/그들은 가지고 있다/잘 갖춰진 교통 시스템

---

14. 이러한 맥락에서/세금을 부과하는 것은/차 소유주에/실제로 줄일 수 있다/교통 문제들을

15. 반면에/단점들이 있다/이 해법에 대한/

16. 무엇보다도 먼저/높은 세금은/차량에 대한/일 것이다/실질적인 재정적 부담/현재의 차 소유주들과 운전자들에게

17. 특히/사업하는 사람들은/차량이 필요한/사업을 위해서/놓일 수 있다/심한 재정적 압박에

18. 덧붙여서/이 정책은/효과적이지 않다/왜냐하면/이러한 종류의 세금은/유도하지 않기 때문이다/부자들이/대중교통 이용을

19. 왜냐하면 그들이 여력이 있다/그들의 차를 살/지불할 수 있는/부가적인 세금들을

20. 그러므로/세금을 부과하는 것은/차 소유주들에게/적절한 방법이 아니다/교통문제를 해결할

21. 결론은/장점과 단점들이 있다/시행하는 데/그러한 정책을

_____

_____

22. 그러나/고려해 볼 때/현재의 교통 상황을/나는 동의한다/세금을 부과하는 것은/차 소유주들에게/비록 몇 가지 단점들을 가지고 있지만/가치가 있다

_____

_____

Answer

1. Traffic congestion in cities around the world is becoming more severe.
2. One feasible solution to this problem is to impose heavy taxes on private car owners and use the budget to improve public transport.
3. This essay will spell out the good and bad points of such a measure.
4. First of all, taxing on car owners for better traffic have a couple of benefits.
5. One of the advantages is that the heavy taxes would discourage prospective car buyers from purchasing cars
6. because taxes can give a burden to car owners.
7. In place of using private vehicles, they would begin to make use of public transport, which can also reduce traffic problems.
8. Another benefit is that the tax money could be used to make public transportation more convenient and comfortable.
9. In fact, public transport in cities is in an unfavorable condition.
10. Old buses and trains are less comfortable, and this is one reason why most people do not use them.
11. If the government invests in the improvement of these vehicles, more citizens will use them, and traffic concerns will be unravelled.
12. An excellent example of this is Singapore which is one of the first countries to implement this policy.
13. And at present, they have a well-organized transport system.
14. In this context, putting taxes on car owners could indeed lessen traffic problems.
15. On the flip side, there are drawbacks to this solution.
16. First and foremost, high taxes on cars would put a real financial strain on current car owners and drivers.
17. In particular, drivers who need vehicles for business could be under heavier financial pressure.
18. Besides, this policy goes nowhere since this type of tax will not lead the haves to use public transportation,
19. , as they can afford to buy their cars and pay additional taxes.
20. Therefore, levying taxes on car owners is not the proper way to tackle traffic concerns.
21. In conclusion, there are the merits and demerits of introducing such a policy.
22. However, given the current traffic situations, I agree that charging taxes on car owners, although having a few weaknesses, is worthwhile.

You should spend about 40 minutes on this task.

Write about the following topic:

> **To address traffic problems, governments should tax private car owners heavily and use the money to improve public transportation. To what extent do you agree?**

Give reasons for your answer and include any relevant examples from your own knowledge or experience.

Write at least 250 words.

Answer

Traffic congestion in cities around the world is becoming more severe. One feasible solution to this problem is to impose heavy taxes on private car owners and use the budget to improve public transport. This essay will spell out the positive and negative points of such a measure.

First of all, taxing on car owners for better traffic has a couple of benefits. One of the advantages is that the heavy taxes would discourage prospective car buyers from purchasing cars because taxes give a burden to car owners. In place of using private vehicles, they would begin to make use of public transport, which can also reduce traffic problems. **Another benefit is that the tax money could be used to make public transportation more convenient and comfortable.** In fact, public transport in many cities is in an unfavorable condition. Old buses and trains are less comfortable, and this is one reason why most people do not use them. If the government invests in the improvement of these vehicles, more citizens will use them, and traffic concerns will be unraveled. An excellent example of this is Singapore which is one of the first countries to implement this policy, and at present, they have a well-organized transport system. In this context, putting taxes on car owners could indeed lessen traffic problems.

On the flip side, there are drawbacks to this solution. First and foremost, high taxes on cars would put a real financial strain on current car owners and drivers. In particular, business people who need their vehicles for business could be under heavier financial pressure. **Besides, this policy goes nowhere** since this type of tax will not lead the haves to use public transportation, as they can afford to buy their cars and pay additional taxes. Therefore, levying taxes on car owners is not the proper way to tackle traffic concerns.

In conclusion, there are the merits and demerits of introducing such a policy. However, given the current traffic situation, I agree that charging taxes on car owners, although having a few weaknesses, is worthwhile.

IELTS Easy Writing

Unit 6

Health

1. Health and diet
2. Obesity
3. Smoking

1. Health and diet

You should spend about 40 minutes on this task.

Write about the following topic:

> Some people believe that it is the responsibility of individuals to take care of their own health and diet. Others, however, believe that governments should make sure that their citizens have a healthy diet. What is your opinion?

Give reasons for your answer and include any relevant examples from your own knowledge or experience.

Write at least 250 words.

INTRODUCTION

건강과 다이어트는 계속되어온 문제이다. 정부와 개인의 건강한 식단에 관한 책임을 설명하겠다.

BODY 1 개인 책임

1. 자유의지로 운동과 식사
   → 부모의 의지대로 어린아이들도 운동과 식사

BODY 2 정부 책임

1. 패스트푸드 그리고 미리 만들어진 음식 재료에 대한 규제 필요
2. 세금을 예방조치에 사용(캠페인 등)

CONCLUSION

개인과 정부는 서로 사람들의 건강과 다이어트를 위해 협력 필요

일부 사람들은 그들의 건강과 식단을 돌보는 것은 개인의 책임이라고 믿는다. 그러나 다른 사람들은 정부가 시민들이 건강한 식단을 가지도록 해야 한다고 믿는다. 당신의 의견은 무엇인가?

INNTRODUCTION

점점 더 많은 사람들이 건강문제들로 고통을 받고 있다. 그 결과, 건강과 식단은 많은 국가에서 계속되어 온 문제가 되고 있다. 어떤 사람들은 사람들의 건강을 개선시키는 데는 국가가 책임을 져야 한다고 주장한다, 반면에, 다른 사람들은 그것은 개인에 달려 있다고 말한다. 이 에세이는 이 논쟁의 두 가지 측면을 자세히 설명하겠다.

BODY 1

<u>우선, 개개인이 그들의 건강과 다이어트에 책임감을 가져야 한다.</u> 성인들은 자유의지를 가지고 있고 그들이 할 운동과 어떤 종류의 음식을 먹을 건지 스스로 선택을 한다. 이런 의미에서, 식단과 건강을 돌보는 것은 개인의 태도에 달려 있다. 덧붙여서. 어린이 건강에 대해 말하자면, 그것은 그 부모의 의무와 책임이다. 그것은 그들이 균형 잡힌 식단을 주어야 하고 햄버거, 프라이드 치킨 그리고 인스턴트 누들과 같은 정크 푸드를 먹지 않도록 지도해야 하기 때문이다. 그러므로, 건강과 식단은 정부가 아니라 개개인의 책임이다,

BODY 2

<u>그러나, 정부에 대해서 말하자면, 그들은 또한 사람들의 건강과 식단에 책임이 있다.</u> 현대 사회에서 사람들은 집에서나 직장에서의 바쁜 생활 때문에 설탕, 소금 그리고 지방이 높은 패스트푸드 또는 미리 준비된 음식에 의존하지 않을 수 없다. <u>정부가 건강 문제를 해결하기 위해서, 그들은 판매하는 음식에 사용되는 음식재료에 대한 일정한 규정을 만들어야 한다.</u> 법규에 대한 적절한 실행을 위해서 그 일을 위임받은 특별한 부서를 설립함과 함께 정부의 개입이 있어야 한다. <u>더욱이 정부는 건강과 건강한 식단에 대한 캠페인과 같은 예방조치에 많은 예산을 사용해야 한다.</u> 예를 들어, 우리나라가 시행해온 건강 캠페인들 중 하나로서, 보건 복지부에 의한 건강에 대한 TV 공익광고들이 있다. 그것은 일반대중들에게 건강을 유지하는 것에 대한 중요성을 알게 하는 데 도움이 되고 있다, 이러한 맥락에서, 정부가 사람들의 건강과 건강한 음식 장려에 책임을 가져야 하는 것은 분명하다.

CONCLUSION

요약하자면, 이 주제의 두 가지 측면을 고려할 때, 개인들이 그들의 건강과 식단을 돌봐야 한다. 정부는 시민들을 위한 건강과 식단에 훨씬 더 중요한 역할을 해야만 한다. 따라서, 핵심은 정부와 개개인들은 건강과 식단을 개선하기 위해 서로 협력해야만 한다.

문장에 필요한 어휘

> 1. an increasing number of/an growing number of; 점점 더 많은
> 2. suffer from/struggle with/go through; ~을 겪고 있다/~로부터 고통 받다

점점 더 많은 사람들이 건강문제들을 겪고 있다.
An increasing number of people are suffering from health problems.

> 3. health and diet; 건강과 식단
> 4. ongoing/constant/continual/lasting; 계속된
> 5. citizen/people/individuals; 시민들/사람들

그 결과, 건강과 식단은 많은 국가에서 계속되어온 문제가 되고 있다.
As a result, health and diet have become an ongoing issue in many countries.

> 6. A be responsible for/A have(take/shoulder) the responsibility for/A be to blame for/A be accountable for/be down to A; A가 책임이 있다
> 7. improve/better/enhance; 개선하다

어떤 사람들은 국민의 건강을 개선시키는 데는 국가가 책임을 져야 한다고 주장한다
Some people argue that governments should be responsible for improving people's health,

> 8. while/whilst/whereas; 반면에
> 9. be up to/depend on/rely on/have(has) a dependency on; 달려 있다

반면에, 다른 사람들은 그것은 개인에 달려 있다고 말한다.
, while others say that it is up to individuals.

> 10. elaborate on/explain in full detail/spell out; ~에 대해 자세히 설명하다
> 11. argument/issue/debate/controversy/discussion; 논쟁

이 에세이는 이 논쟁의 두 가지 측면을 자세히 설명하겠다.
This essay will elaborate on both sides of the argument.

> 12. to begin with/first of all/In the first place/first and foremost; 우선

우선, 개개인이 그들의 다이어트와 건강에 책임감을 가져야만 한다.
To begin with, individuals should have the responsibility for their diet and health.

> 13. free will/free volition; 자유 의지
> 14. make a choice/choose/select; 선택하다
> 15. what sorts(kinds/types) of food; 어떤 종류의 음식

성인들은 자유의지를 가지고 있고 그들이 할 운동과 어떤 종류의 음식을 먹을 건지 스스로 선택을 한다.
Adults have their free will and make their choices about what sorts of food they eat and the exercise they do.

> 16. in this sense/in this way/in this manner; 이런 의미에서
> 17. care for/take care of/look after; 돌보다
> 18. attitude/manner/behavior; 태도/행동

이런 의미에서, 다이어트와 건강을 돌보는 것은 개인의 태도에 달려 있다.
In this sense, caring for diet and health has a dependency on an individual's attitude.

> 19. on top of that/In addition to this/not only that; 덧붙여서
> 20. in the case of/when it comes to/in light of/In terms of; ~의 경우/말하자면
> 21. obligation/duty/liability; 의무
> 22. encourage A to B; A에게 B를 권장하다

덧붙여서, 어린이건강에 대해 말하자면, 그것은 부모의 의무와 책임이다.
On top of that, in the case of children's health, it is the parents' obligation and responsibility.

> 23. guide A not to B/encourage A not to B; A에게 B를 하지 않도록 지도하다(권장하다)

그것은 그들이 균형 잡힌 식단을 주어야 하고 햄버거, 프라이드 치킨 그리고 인스턴트 누들과 같은 정크 푸드를 먹지 않도록 지도해야 하기 때문이다.
It is because they should give a well-balanced diet and guide their children not to eat junk food such as hamburgers, fried chicken, and instant noodles.

> 24. therefore/thus/as a result/consequently/in this context; 따라서/그러므로

그러므로, 건강과 식단은 정부가 아니라 개개인의 책임이다.

Health and diet are, therefore, down to individuals, not governments.

> 25. as well/also/likewise/too; 또한

그러나, 정부에 대해서 말하자면, 그들은 또한 사람들의 건강과 다이어트에 책임이 있다.

However, when it comes to states, they are accountable for people's health and diet as well.

> 26. have little choice but to + 동사/cannot but +V/cannot help ~ing; ~하지 않을 수 없다
> 27. ready-made meals; 미리 만들어진 음식
> 28. be high in ~; ~이 많다
> 29. on account of/due to/because of/owing to+ N; ~ 때문에
> 30. a very hectic(busy) lifestyle; 바쁜 생활

현대 사회에서 사람들은 집에서나 직장에서의 바쁜 생활 때문에 설탕, 소금 그리고 지방이 높은 패스트푸드 또는 미리 준비된 음식에 의존하지 않을 수 없다.

People in modern society have little choice but to depend on fast food or ready-made meals, which are high in sugar, salt and fat on account of a very hectic lifestyle at home and in the workplace.

> 31. address/tackle/battle/settle/sort out/solve/resolve/unravel; 해결하다
> 32. health concern(problem); 건강문제
> 33. make regulations about; ~에 대한 규정을 만들다
> 34. ingredients/food sources; 음식재료/성분

정부가 건강 문제를 해결하기 위해서, 그들은 판매하는 음식에 사용되는 음식재료에 대한 일정한 규정을 만들어야 한다.

For governments to address health concern, they should make regulations about ingredients used in selling foods.

> 35. intervention/involvement; 개입
> 36. set up/establish/found; 설립하다
> 37. particular/special/peculiar; 특별한
> 38. entrusted with; 위임받은
> 39. implementation/practice/execute/enforcement; 실행

법규에 대한 적절한 실행을 위해서 그 일을 위임받은 특별한 부서를 설립함과 함께 정부의 개입이 있어야 한다.

There should be governmental intervention, with setting up a particular department entrusted with the job, for the proper implementation of rules.

> 40. furthermore/in addition/what is more/moreover; 더욱이
> 41. massive amounts of/a great deal of/a good deal of/loads of; 많은 양
> 42. preventative measure(action/step); 예방 조치
> 43. concerning/regarding/as regards/with respect to/with regard to; ~에 대한/~에 관련한

더욱이 정부는 건강과 건강한 다이어트에 대한 캠페인과 같은 예방 조치에 많은 예산을 사용해야 한다.

Furthermore, governments should spend massive amounts of tax funds on preventative measures such as campaigns concerning health and healthy diet.

> 44. public service announcement; 공익광고
> 45. the Ministry of Health and Welfare; 보건 복지부

예를 들어, 우리나라가 실행하는 건강 캠페인들 중 하나로서, 보건 복지부에 의한 건강에 대한 TV 공익광고 들이 있다.

For instance, as one health campaign our country has implemented, there are public service announcements on TV for good health by The Ministry of Health and Welfare.

> 46. of help/helpful/of benefit/beneficial; 도움이 되는
> 47. the general public/the public; 일반 대중
> 48. aware of; ~을 인식하는/~을 아는
> 49. keep fit/keep in shape/get in shape; 건강을 유지하다

그것은 일반 대중들에게 건강을 유지하는 것에 대한 중요성을 알게 하는 데 도움이 되고 있다.

This is of help to make the general public aware of keeping fit.

> 50. it is clear-cut(clear/obvious/apparent) that S+V; 분명하다

이러한 맥락에서, 정부가 사람들의 건강과 건강한 음식의 장려에 책임을 가져야 하는 것은 분명하다.

In this context, it is clear-cut that governments should shoulder the responsibility for people's health and encouragement of healthy food.

> 51. to sum up/In conclusion/In short; 요약하자면
> 52. take A into account(consideration)/consider A; A를 고려하면
> 53. ought to/should/had better; 해야만 한다

요약하자면, 이 주제의 두 가지 측면을 고려할 때, 개인들이 그들의 건강과 식단을 돌봐야 한다.

To sum up, taking both sides of the issue into account, individuals ought to look after their health and food.

> 54. play a crucial(important/vital/significant/essential)role in~; ~에 중요한 역할을 하다

정부는 시민들을 위한 건강과 식단에 있어 훨씬 더 중요한 역할을 해야만 한다.

Governments should play a much more crucial role in health and diet for citizens.

> 55. the bottom line is that S+V; 핵심은 ~이다
> 56. team up with/cooperate with/work together with; ~와 협력하다

따라서, 핵심은 정부와 개개인들은 건강과 식단을 개선하기 위해 서로 협력해야만 한다.

Thus, the bottom line is that governments and individuals should team up with each other to improve health and diet.

구문연습

1. 점점 더 많은 사람들이/겪고 있다/건강문제들을

2. 그 결과/건강과 식단은/되고 있다/계속되는 문제가/많은 나라들에서

3. 어떤 사람들은 주장한다/국가가 책임이 있다/개선하기 위해서/국민들의 건강을

4. 반면에/다른 사람들은 말한다/그것은 달려 있다/개개인의

5. 이 에세이는/자세히 설명하겠다/두 가지 측면을/이 논쟁의

6. 우선/개개인이 책임을 가져야 한다/그들의 건강과 식단에

7. 성인들은 가지고 있다/자유의지를/그리고 스스로 선택을 한다/어떤 종류의 음식을 먹을 건지/그리고 그들이 할 운동을

_____

_____

8. 이러한 의미에서/돌보는 것은/식단과 건강을/좌우한다/개인들의 태도

_____

_____

9. 덧붙여서/어린이 건강에 대해 말하자면/그것은/그 부모의 의무와 책임이다

_____

_____

10. 그것은 때문이다/그들은 주어야 한다/균형 잡힌 식단/그리고/지도한다/그들의 아이들이/먹지 않도록/정크푸드/같은/햄버거/프라이드 치킨/인스턴트 누들

_____

_____

11. 따라서/건강과 식단은/책임이다/사람들/정부가 아니라

_____

_____

12. 그러나/정부에 대해서 말하자면/그들은 책임이 있다/사람들의 건강과 식단에/또한

_____

_____

13. 현대 사회의 사람들은/하지 않을 수 없다/의지하다/패스트푸드나 미리 준비된 음식에

_____

_____

14. 이러한 것들은 많다/설탕, 소금 그리고 지방/바쁜 생활 때문에/집에서 그리고 직장에서

_____

_____

15. 정부는/건강문제를 해결하기 위해서/그들은 일정한 규정을 만들어야 한다/재료들에 대한/사용된/판매하는 음식에

_____

_____

16. 정부의 개입이 있어야 한다/설치함으로써/특별한 부서를/그 일에 위임을 받은/적절한 실행을 위해서

_____

_____

17. 더욱이 정부들은 사용해야 한다/많은 세금을/예방 조치들에/캠페인들과 같은/관련해서 건강과 건강한 다이어트

_____

_____

18. 예를 들어/건강 캠페인들 중 하나로써/우리나라가 실행해 오는/몇 가지 공익광고들이 있다/TV에서/건강을 위한/보건 복지부에 의한

_____

_____

19. 이것은/도움이 된다/일반대중이 인식하게 하는 데/건강을 유지하는 것에 대한

_____

_____

20. 이러한 맥락에서/그것은 분명하다/정부가 책임을 가져야 한다/사람들의 건강과 건강한 음식의 장려

_____

_____

21. 요약하자면/두 가지 측면을 고려해 볼 때/개인이/돌봐야 한다/그들의 건강과 식단을

_____
_____

22. 정부들은/훨씬 더/중요한 역할을 해야만 한다/건강과 식단에 있어/시민들의

_____
_____

23. 따라서/핵심은 이것이다/정부와 개개인들은 협력해야만 한다/서로/개선하기 위해서/사람들의 건강과 식단

_____
_____

Answer

1. An increasing number of people are suffering from health problems.
2. As a result, health and diet have become an ongoing issue in many countries.
3. Some people argue that governments should be responsible for improving people's health,
4. , while others say that it is up to the individuals.
5. This essay will elaborate on both sides of the argument.
6. To begin with, individuals should have the responsibility for their diet and health.
7. Adults have their free will and make their choices about what sorts of food they eat and the exercise they do.
8. In this sense, caring for diet and health has a dependency on an individual's attitude.
9. On top of that, in the case of children's health, it is the parents' obligation and responsibility.
10. It is because they should give a well-balanced diet and guide their children not to eat junk food such as hamburgers, fried chicken, and instant noodles.
11. Health and diet are, therefore, down to individuals, not governments.
12. However, when it comes to states, they are accountable for people's health and diet as well.
13. People in modern society have little choice but to depend on fast food or ready-made , meals,
14. , which are high in sugar, salt and fat, on account of a very hectic lifestyle at home and in the workplace.
15. For governments to address this health concern, they should make regulations about ingredients used in selling foods.
16. There should be governmental intervention, with setting up a particular department entrusted with the job, for the proper implementation of rules.
17. Furthermore, governments should spend massive amounts of tax funds on preventative measures such as campaigns concerning health and healthy diet.
18. For instance, as one health campaigns that our country has implemented, there are public service announcements on TV for good health by The Ministry of Health and Welfare.
19. This is of help to make the general public aware of keeping fit.
20. In this context, it is clear-cut that governments should shoulder the responsibility for people's health and the encouragement of healthy food.
21. To sum up, taking both sides of the issue into account, individuals ought to look after their health and food.
22. Governments should play a much more crucial role in the health and diet of the citizens.
23. Thus, the bottom line is that governments and individuals should team up with each other to improve health and diet.

You should spend about 40 minutes on this task.

Write about the following topic:

> **Some people believe that it is the responsibility of individuals to take care of their own health and diet. Others however believe that governments should make sure that their citizens have a healthy diet. What is your opinion?**

Give reasons for your answer and include any relevant examples from your own knowledge or experience.

Write at least 250 words.

Answer

An increasing number of people are suffering from health problems. As a result, health and diet have become an ongoing issue in many countries. Some people argue that governments should be responsible for improving people's health, while others say that it is up to the individuals. This essay will elaborate on both sides of the argument.

To begin with, individuals should have the responsibility for their diet and health. Adults have their free will and make their choices about what sorts of food they eat and the exercise they do. In this sense, caring for diet and health has a dependency on an individual's attitude. On top of that, in the case of children's health, it is the parents' obligation and responsibility. It is because they should give a well-balanced diet and guide their children not to eat junk food such as hamburgers, fried chicken, and instant noodles. Health and diet are, therefore, down to individuals, not governments.

However, when it comes to states, they are accountable for people's health and diet as well. People in modern society have little choice but to depend on fast food or ready-made meals, which are high in sugar, salt, and fat on account of their very hectic lifestyles at home and in the workplace. **For governments to address this health concern, they should make regulations about ingredients used in selling foods.** There should be governmental intervention, with setting up a particular department entrusted with the job, for the proper implementation of rules. **Furthermore, governments should spend massive amounts of tax funds on preventative measures such as campaigns concerning health and healthy diet.** For instance, as one health campaign that our country has implemented, there are public service announcements on TV for good health by The Ministry of Health and Welfare. This is of help to make the general public aware of the importance of keeping fit. In this context, it is clear-cut that governments should shoulder the responsibility for people's health and the encouragement of healthy food.

To sum up, taking both sides of the issue into account, individuals ought to look after their health and food. Governments should play a much more crucial role in the health and diet of the citizens. Thus, the bottom line is that governments and individuals should team up with each other to improve health and diet.

2. Obesity

You should spend about 40 minutes on this task.

Write about the following topic:

> The issue of obesity is a growing concern around the world. It affects children as well as adults. What are the reasons for this rise in obesity? How can it be tackled?

Give reasons for your answer and include any relevant examples from your own knowledge or experience.

Write at least 250 words.

INTRODUCTION
비만은 우리가 직면한 건강문제이다.
여기서 원인과 실행 가능한 방법을 논의하겠다.

BODY1 (causes)
1. 빈약한 식단
2. 좌식 생활양식

BODY2 (solutions)
1. 정부-패스트푸드나 포장음식에 세금부과
2. 지역 사회- 운동시설 설치
3. 개인-정기적 운동/건강음식

CONCLUSION
해결하기 위한 몇 가지 방법들이 있다. 실현하기 위해 서로 협력해야 한다.

비만의 문제는 전 세계적으로 커지는 고민거리이다. 그것은 성인들뿐만 아니라 아이들에게 영향을 끼친다. 비만증가 원인은 무엇이고 어떻게 그것을 해결해야 하는가?

INTRODUCTION

비만은 우리가 현재 직면한 계속 진행 중인 건강문제 중의 하나이다. 비만인 사람들이 훨씬 더 당뇨병, 심장병 그리고 뇌졸중과 같은 질병에 걸릴 수 있다는 것은 사실이다. 이외에도, 비만은 성인들뿐만 아니라 아이들 성장에도 상당한 영향을 준다. 이 에세이에서 원인들과 비만을 해결하기 위한 가능한 방법들을 제시하겠다.

BODY 1

<u>우선, 이 문제에 대한 주요한 원인은 빈약한 식단이다.</u> 오늘날, 사람들은 항상 바쁘고 제대로 된 식사를 준비할 시간이 거의 없다. 대부분의 사람들은 그들의 바쁜 생활방식 때문에 종종 칼로리가 높고, 중독성 그리고 보존력이 있는 포장음식들과 미리 만든 음식을 종종 선택한다. 사실상, 지난 10년에 걸쳐서, 패스트푸드 레스토랑의 수는 상당한 증가를 해왔고 패스트푸드는 삶의 방식이 되어 오고 있다. 이것은 사람들이 비만이 되게 한다. <u>비만을 상당히 일으키는 다른 요인은 대부분 사람들이 갖는 좌식 생활양식이다.</u> 일반적으로 많은 사람들은 요즘 직장에서 그리고 집에서 오랫동안 컴퓨터 앞에 앉는다. 따라서, 그들은 그들이 섭취하는 칼로리를 소모시키는 기회를 가질 수 없고 그것은 그들의 급격한 체중증가로 이어진다.

BODY 2

<u>그럼에도 불구하고, 비만문제를 해결하는 몇 가지 방법들이 있다.</u> 정부 측면에서는, 그들은 건강의 중요성을 소비자들에게 알림으로써 패스트푸드와 포장된 음식을 먹지 못하도록 할 수 있다. 덧붙여서, 정부는 그 상품들을 너무 저렴하게 만들지 않게 하기 위해서 그들에게 세금을 부과해야 한다. <u>지역 공동체에 대해 말하자면,</u> 그들은 지역 센터에 시민들이 쉽게 접근할 수 있는 체육관을 설치함으로써 시민들에게 운동하도록 권장해야 한다. 한 예로써, 일부의 지역 센터의 경우에, 당국은 시민들을 위한 다양한 운동 시설들을 갖춘 지역 체육관이나 공원들을 설치해 오고 있다. 그것은 효율적으로 운영되었고 지역시민들에 의해 환영받고 있다. <u>개인적인 측면</u>에서, 사람들은 정기적으로 운동하고 건강한 음식을 먹음으로써 그들의 건강을 돌보도록 노력해야만 한다. 이와 같이, 비만을 피하기 위한 실행 가능한 해결책들이 있다.

CONCLUSION

요약하자면, 몇몇의 상황들은 비만을 초래한다. 그러나, 또한 비만을 극복하기 위한 몇 가지 조치들이 있다. 이것과 관련해서, 정부와 공동체들은 비만 문제를 해결하기 위해서 시민들과 협력해야 한다.

문장에 필요한 어휘

---

1. obesity/overweight; 비만
2. ongoing/constant/continual/lasting; 진행 중인
3. concern/difficulty/problem/trouble; 문제
4. face/confront; 직면하다

비만은 우리가 현재 직면한 계속 진행 중인 건강문제 중의 하나이다.
Obesity is one of the ongoing health concerns we face today.

---

5. be far more likely to; 훨씬 ~할 것 같다
6. develop(contract/come down with) diseases; 질병에 걸리다
7. heart diseases; 심장 질환
8. diabetes; 당뇨
9. strokes; 뇌졸중

비만인 사람들이 훨씬 더 당뇨병, 심장질환 그리고 뇌졸중 같은 질병에 잘 걸릴 수 있다는 것은 사실이다.
It is a fact that obese people are far more likely to develop diseases such as diabetes, heart problems, and strokes.

---

10. besides/furthermore/in addition/additionally; 이외에도/덧붙여 말하면
11. have(has) great(considerable/significant) effects(impacts/influences) on; 상당한 영향을 주다
12. not only A but also B/B as well as A; A뿐만 아니라 B

이외에도, 비만은 성인 건강뿐만 아니라 아이들 성장에도 상당한 영향을 준다.
Besides, obesity has considerable impacts on not only adult health but also children's growth.

---

13. present/show/propose/suggest; 제시하다
14. cause/culprit/reason/factor/source; 원인
15. possible/workable/practicable/viable/actable/feasible; 실행 가능한
16. sort out/address/tackle/cope with/deal with/unravel; 해결하다

이 에세이에서, 나는 비만을 해결하기 위한 원인들과 가능한 방법들을 제시하겠다.
In this essay, I will present causes and possible ways to sort out overweight.

17. to begin with/first of all/for starters/first and foremost; 우선
18. primary/major/leading/main; 주요한
19. a poor(unhealthy) diet; 빈약한 식단

우선, 이 문제에 대한 주요한 원인은 빈약한 식단이다.
To begin with, the primary source of this problem is a poor diet.

20. be in a hurry; 바쁘다/서두르다
21. have little time to; ~할 시간이 거의 없다
22. decent (proper)meals; 제대로 된 식사

오늘날, 사람들은 항상 바쁘고 제대로 된 식사를 준비할 시간이 거의 없다.
Today, people are always in a great hurry and have little time to prepare decent meals.

23. hectic(busy) lifestyles; 바쁜 생활 방식
24. packed foods/take away foods; 포장음식
25. ready-made foods; 미리 만든 음식
26. be high in~; ~이 많은/높은
27. additives; 첨가물들
28. preservatives; 방부제들

대부분의 사람들은 그들의 바쁜 생활방식 때문에 종종 칼로리가 높고, 중독성 그리고 보존력이 있는 포장음식들과 미리 만든 음식을 종종 선택한다.
Most people, due to their hectic lifestyles, often choose packaged foods and ready-made meals which are high in calories, additives, and preservatives.

29. significant/considerable/huge/great; 상당한
30. increase/growth/rise; 증가
31. the number of+복수 명사; ~수
32. give rise to/result in/bring about/lead to +N; 일으키다/야기하다

사실상, 지난 10년에 걸쳐서, 패스트푸드 레스토랑의 수는 상당한 증가를 해왔고 패스트푸드는 삶의 방식이 되어 오고 있다. 이것은 사람들이 비만이 되게 한다.
In fact, over the last decade, there has been a significant increase in the number of fast food restaurants, and fast food has become a way of life, which gives rise to people being overweight.

> 33. contribute to +N/make a contribution to +N; 일으키다/기여하다
> 34. a great deal/considerably/significantly/highly; 매우/상당히
> 35. the sedentary lifestyle; 좌식 생활 방식

비만을 상당히 일으키는 다른 요인들은 대부분 사람들이 갖는 좌식 생활양식이다.
Another factor that contributes a great deal to obesity is the sedentary lifestyle most people have.

> 36. nowadays/these days/today/recently/of late; 요즘에는
> 37. in front of; ~앞에

일반적으로, 많은 사람들은 요즘 직장에서 그리고 집에서 오랫동안 컴퓨터 앞에 앉는다.
In general, plenty of people nowadays sit in front of the computer for a long time at their workplace and home.

> 38. as a result/consequently/therefore/thus/In this context; 따라서
> 39. have(has) opportunities(chances/occasions) to; ~할 기회를 갖다
> 40. consume(burn) calories; 칼로리를 소모시키다

따라서, 그들은 그들이 섭취하는 칼로리를 소모시키는 기회를 가질 수 없고, 그것은 그들의 급격한 체중증가로 이어진다.
As a result, they cannot have any opportunities to consume the calories they take, which lead to their rapid gaining of weight.

> 41. nevertheless/yet/in spite of that/for all that/nonetheless/still; 그럼에도 불구하고

그럼에도 불구하고, 비만문제를 해결하는 몇 가지 방법들이 있다.
Nevertheless, there are several methods to address the obesity problem.

> 42. in the case of/when it comes to/in light of/with respect to/In terms of; ~에 관해서는
> 43. discourage A from B; A가 B하는 것을 못하게 하다
> 44. let/have A(사람) + 동사원형; A에게 하게 하다
> 45. get A(사람) + to 동사원형; A에게 하게 하다
> 46. be aware of/know/have knowledge/learn; ~을 알다

정부에 관해서는, 그들은 좋은 건강의 중요성을 소비자들에게 알림으로써 패스트푸드와 포장된 음식을 먹지 못하도록 할 수 있다.
In the case of governments, they can discourage people from eating fast food and packaged foods by getting consumers to be aware of the importance of good health.

> 47. impose(levy/charge)taxes on; ~에 세금을 부과하다
> 48. in order not to/so as not to +동사; ~하지 않도록

덧붙여서, 정부는 그 상품들을 구매하기 쉬운 것으로 만들지 않게 하기 위해서 그들에게 세금을 부과해야 한다.

Moreover, governments should impose heavier taxes on them in order not to make the products so cheap.

> 49. work out/exercise/take exercise; 운동하다
> 50. encourage A to B; A가 B하도록 권장하다
> 51. have(get/gain) access to+명사/access; ~에 접근하다

지역 공동체에 관해서는 그들은 또한 시민들이 쉽게 접근할 수 있는 지역 사회 센터에 체육관을 지음으로써 운동하도록 권장해야 한다.

When it comes to communities, they should also encourage citizens to work out by building gyms in community centers that citizens can have easy access to.

> 52. concerning/regarding/as regards/with respect to/in relation to; 경우에/관하여
> 53. equip/place/install/build; 설치하다
> 54. health and fitness facilities; 운동 시설
> 55. hail; 환영하다

한 예로써, 일부의 지역 센터의 경우에, 당국은 시민들을 위해 다양한 운동 시설들을 갖춘 지역 체육관이나 공원들을 설치해 오고 있다. 그들은 효율적으로 운영되고 있고 지역시민들에 의해 환영받고 있다.

For one thing, concerning our community centre, the authorities have equipped local gyms and parks with various health and fitness facilities for its citizens. They have been operated efficiently and hailed by local citizens.

> 56. on a personal level/personally; 개인적 차원에서
> 57. look after/take care of/care for; 돌보다

개인적인 차원에서, 사람들은 정기적으로 운동하고 건강한 음식을 먹음으로써 그들의 건강을 돌보도록 노력해야만 한다.

On a personal level, individuals should try to look after their health by eating healthy foods and exercising regularly.

> 58. like this/in this way; 이와 같이
> 59. avoid/keep off/escape; 피하다

이와 같이, 비만을 피하기 위한 실행 가능한 해결책들이 있다.
Like this, there are viable solutions to avoid obesity.

> 60. to sum up/in conclusion/In short; 요약하자면
> 61. circumstances/situations/conditions; 상황들
> 62. measure/step/action; 조치
> 63. overcome/get over/cope with; 극복하다

요약하자면, 몇몇의 상황들은 비만을 일으킨다. 그러나, 또한 비만을 극복하기 위한 몇 가지 조치들이 있다.
To sum up, several circumstances result in obesity. However, there are also a few measures that be taken to overcome obesity.

> 64. in this context/therefore/thus/hence/consequently; 이것과 관련해서/따라서/그러므로
> 65. cooperate with/team up with/work together with; ~와 협력하다

이것과 관련해서, 정부와 공동체들은 비만문제를 해결하기 위해서 시민들과 협력해야 한다.
In this context, governments and communities should cooperate with citizens to unravel obesity concerns.

구문연습

1. 비만은 하나이다/계속 진행 중인 건강문제 중의/우리가 직면한/오늘날

_____
_____

2. 이것은 사실이다/비만인 사람들이/훨씬 더 가능성이 있다/질병을 발생시킬/당뇨,심장질환 그리고 뇌졸중 같은

_____
_____

3. 이외에도/비만은 상당한 영향을 준다/성인건강뿐만 아니라/아이들 성장에도

_____
_____

4. 이 에세이에서/나는 제시할 것이다/원인들과/가능한 방법들을/해결하기 위한/비만을

_____
_____

5. 우선/이 문제의 주요한 원인은/빈약한 식단이다

_____
_____

6. 오늘날/사람들은/항상 바쁘고/시간이 거의 없다/준비할/제대로 된 식사를

_____
_____

7. 대부분의 사람들은/그들의 바쁜 생활양식 때문에/종종/선택한다/포장된 음식들 그리고 미리 만들어진 식사를/칼로리가 높은, 중독성 그리고 보존력이 있는

_____

_____

8. 사실상/지난 10년에 걸쳐서/상당한 증가를 해 왔고/패스트푸드 레스토랑의 수가

_____

_____

9. 그리고 패스트푸드는 되어왔다/생활의 방식이/그러한 것은 야기한다/사람들이/비만이 되게

_____

_____

10. 또 다른 요인들은/비만을 상당히 일으키는/좌식 생활 방식이다/대부분의 사람들이 가지고 있는

_____

_____

11. 일반적으로/많은 사람들은/요즘/컴퓨터 앞에 앉는다/오랫동안/직장에서 그리고 집에서

_____

_____

12. 따라서/기회를 가질 수 없다/칼로리를 소모시키는/그들이 섭취하는/야기한다/그들의 급격한 체중증가를

_____

_____

13. 그럼에도 불구하고/몇 가지 방법들이 있다/비만문제를 해결하는

_____

_____

2. Obesity

14. 정부에 관해서는/그들은 먹지 못하도록 할 수 있다/패스트푸드음식과 포장된 음식을/소비자들에게 알림으로써/건강의 중요성을

_____
_____

15. 더욱이/정부는 세금을 부과해야 한다/그들에게/만들지 않게 하기 위해서/그 상품들이/너무 저렴한

_____
_____

16. 지역 사회에 대해 말하자면/그들은 또한 권장해야 한다/시민들이/운동할 수 있도록/설립함으로써/체육관들을/공동체 센터에서/시민들은 쉽게 접근할 수 있는

_____
_____

17. 한 예로써/일부의 지역 사회에 대해 말하자면/당국은 갖추고 있다/지역 체육관과 공원들/다양한 운동시설을 갖춘/시민들을 위한

_____
_____

18. 이것은 운영되고 있다/효율적으로/환영받고 있다/지역시민들에게

_____
_____

19. 개인적인 차원에서/사람들은 노력해야만 한다/그들의 건강을 돌보도록/운동하고 건강한 음식을 먹음으로써

_____
_____

20. 이와 같이/실행 가능한 해결책들이 있다/비만을 피해야 할

_____

_____

21. 요약하자면/몇몇의 상황들은/비만을 초래한다/그러나/또한 몇 가지 방법들이 있다/취해야 할/비만을 극복하기 위해

_____

_____

22. 이것과 관련해서/정부와 공동체들은/시민들과 협력해야 한다/비만 문제를 해결하기 위해서

_____

_____

Answer

1. Obesity is one of the ongoing health concerns we face today.
2. It is a fact that obese people are far more likely to develop diseases such as diabetes, heart problems, and strokes.
3. Besides, obesity has significant impacts on not only adult health but also children's growth.
4. In this essay, I will present causes and possible ways to sort out overweight.
5. To begin with, the primary source of this problem is a poor diet.
6. Today, people are always in a great hurry and have little time to prepare decent meals.
7. Most people, due to their hectic lifestyles, often choose packaged foods and ready-made meals which are high in calories, additives, and preservatives.
8. In fact, over the last decade, there has been a significant increase in the number of fast food restaurants,
9. , and fast food has become a way of life, which gives rise to people being overweight.
10. Another factor that contributes a great deal to obesity is the sedentary lifestyle most people have.
11. In general, plenty of people nowadays sit in front of the computer for a long time at their workplace and home.
12. As a result, they cannot have any opportunities to consume the calories they take, which lead to their rapid gaining of weight.
13. Nevertheless, there are several methods to address the obesity problem.
14. In the case of governments, they can discourage people from eating fast food and packaged foods by getting consumers to be aware of the importance of good health.
15. Moreover, governments should impose heavier taxes on them in order not to make the products so cheap.
16. When it comes to communities, they should also encourage citizens to work out by building gyms in community centers that citizens can have easy access to.
17. For one thing, concerning some community centre, the authorities have equipped local gyms and parks with various health and fitness facilities for its citizens.
18. They have been operated efficiently and hailed by local citizens.
19. On a personal side, individuals should try to look after their health by eating healthy foods and exercising regularly.
20. Like this, there are clearly solutions to avoid obesity.
21. To sum up, several circumstances result in obesity. However, there are also a few measures that be taken to overcome obesity.
22. In this context, governments and communities should cooperate with citizens to unravel obesity concerns.

You should spend about 40 minutes on this task.

Write about the following topic:

> **The issue of obesity is a growing concern. It affects children as well as adults. What are the reasons for this rise in obesity? How can it be tackled?**

Give reasons for your answer and include any relevant examples from your own knowledge or experience.

Write at least 250 words.

Answer

Obesity is one of the ongoing health concerns we face today. It is a fact that obese people are far more likely to develop diseases such as diabetes, heart problems, and strokes. Besides, obesity has considerable impacts on not only adult health but also children's growth. In this essay, I will present causes and possible ways to sort out overweight.

To begin with, the primary source of this problem is a poor diet. Today, people are always in a great hurry and have little time to prepare decent meals. Most people, due to their hectic lifestyles, often choose packaged foods and ready-made meals which are high in calories, additives, and preservatives. In fact, over the last decade, there has been a significant increase in the number of fast food restaurants, and fast food has become a way of life, which gives rise to people being overweight. **Another factor that contributes a great deal to obesity is the sedentary lifestyle most people have.** In general, plenty of people nowadays sit in front of the computer for a long time at their workplace and home. As a result, they cannot have any opportunities to consume the calories they take, which lead to their rapid gaining of weight.

Nevertheless, there are several methods to address the obesity problem. In the case of governments, they can discourage people from eating fast food and packaged foods by getting consumers to be aware of the importance of good health. Moreover, governments should impose heavier taxes on them in order not to make the products so cheap. **When it comes to communities,** they should also encourage citizens to work out by building gyms in community centres that citizens can have easy access to. For one thing, concerning our community centre, the authorities have equipped local gyms and parks with various health and fitness facilities for its citizen. They have been operated efficiently and hailed by local citizens. **On a personal level,** individuals should try to look after their health by eating healthy foods and exercising regularly. Like this, there are viable solutions to avoid obesity.

To sum up, several circumstances result in obesity. However, there are also a few measures that be taken to overcome obesity. In this context, governments and communities should cooperate with citizens to unravel obesity concerns.

3. Smoking

You should spend about 40 minutes on this task.

Write about the following topic:

> In some countries, people are no longer allowed to smoke in many public places and office buildings. Do you think this is a good rule or a bad rule?

Give reasons for your answer and include any relevant examples from your own knowledge or experience.

Write at least 250 words.

INTRODUCTION
많은 국가들은 공공장소와 사무실 건물에서 흡연하는 것을 허용하지 않고 있다.
이 의견에 전적으로 동의한다.

BODY 1 건강측면

BODY2 교육측면

BODY3 환경측면

CONCLUSION
정부나 당국자들은 공공장소에서 흡연을 금지시키기 위해 법규를 강화시켜야 한다.

일부 나라에서, 공공장소 그리고 사무실 건물에서 흡연하는 것을 허용하지 않는다. 이것은 좋은 규칙이라 생각하느냐 아니면 나쁜 규칙이라 생각하느냐?

INTRODUCTION

최근에 공공장소에서의 흡연에 대한 많은 논쟁들이 대중의 이목을 끌고 있다. 영국과 같은 몇몇 국가들은 지금 공공장소에서 엄격한 흡연금지정책을 시행하고 있다. 그럼에도 불구하고, 일부 사람들은 여전히 공공장소에서 담배를 피운다. 나는 흡연이 공공장소에서 금지되어야 한다는 의견을 가지고 있다. 다음은 그 이유들이다.

BODY 1

건강에 대해 말하자면, 공공장소에서의 흡연은 흡연자들이나 비흡연자들에게 해로운 영향을 끼친다. 담배가 암 발생, 천식 발작, 그리고 폐 질환에 상당히 원인이 되는 수많은 해로운 화학물질들을 포함하고 있다는 것은 사실이다. 특히, 임산부와 어린이 같은 취약한 건강문제를 가진 사람들은 더 심각하게 간접흡연자들로서 영향을 받을 수 있다. 연구에 따르면, 한 사람이 흡연자이고 다른 사람이 비흡연자인 결혼한 커플일 경우, 후자는 간접흡연 때문에 전자보다 30% 이상 심장질환의 높은 사망위험성을 가지고 있다고 보고되고 있다. 이러한 이유들 때문에, 공공장소에서의 흡연은 금지되어야 한다.

BODY 2

교육에 대해서, 흡연환경에 노출된 어린이들은 미래에 흡연자가 될 가능성이 크다. 그것은 그들은 흡연은 받아들일 수 있다고 생각하는 경향이 있기 때문이다. 만약에 공공장소에서 흡연이 허용되면, 어린이들은 흡연에 노출될 것이고 그것은 좋은 본보기가 되지 않는다. 따라서, 공공장소는 아이들의 교육과 발전을 위해서 금연장소로 지정되어야 한다.

BODY 3

환경적인 관점에서, 공공장소에서 흡연은 또한 환경적 문제를 발생시킨다. 한 가지 예로써, 담배꽁초나 재가 쌓이고 그것은 집중 폭우로 국지적인 범람을 일으킬 수 있다. 이것은 흡연자들이 흡연 후에 쓰레기를 아무데나 버리기 때문이다. 사실상, 우리는 지하철 역이나 버스 정류장들 주변에 흡연자들에 의해서 버려진 쓰레기를 쉽게 볼 수 있다. 이것은 주변환경을 해치고 있으며 청소하는 데 상당한 비용이 든다. 따라서, 공공장소에서의 흡연은 환경적인 이유들 때문에 허용되어서는 안 된다.

CONCLUSION

결론은, 모든 것을 고려할 때, 흡연이 공공장소에서 금지되어야 하는지에 대한 몇 가지 이유들이 있다. 따라서, 정부들과 관련된 당국들은 공공장소에서 흡연을 금지하기 위한 법규를 시행하는 것이 이치에 맞다.

문장에 필요한 어휘

---

1. in recent years/recently/lately/in recent times; 최근에
2. controversy/debate/argument/discussion; 논쟁
3. regarding/with regard to/concerning/respecting/as regards; ~에 관련하여
4. a high profile; 대중의 이목/높은 관심

최근에 공공장소에서의 흡연에 대한 많은 논쟁들이 대중의 이목을 끌고 있다.
In recent years, a lot of controversies regarding smoking in public places have been a high profile.

---

5. implement/enforce/put in force/practice/carry out/conduct; 시행하다/실시하다
6. an anti-smoking(smoke-free) policy; 금연정책

영국과 같은 몇몇 국가들은 지금 공공장소에서 엄격한 흡연금지정책을 시행하고 있다.
Several countries, like the UK, now implement a strict anti-smoking policy in public spaces.

---

7. nevertheless/for all that/nonetheless/still; 그럼에도 불구하고

그럼에도 불구하고, 일부 사람들은 여전히 공공장소에서 담배를 피운다.
Nevertheless, some people still smoke in public areas.

---

8. discourage/thwart/restrict/control/curb/stop/prohibit; 제한하다

나는 흡연이 공공장소에서 금지되어야 한다는 의견을 가지고 있다. 다음은 이유들이다.
I am of the view that smoking should be discouraged in public places. The following are the reasons.

---

9. when it comes to/in terms of/in the case of; ~의 경우에는/~에 대해 말하자면
10. has(have) harmful(detrimental/pernicious/adverse/negative) effects(impacts/influences) on; ~에 해로운 영향을 끼친다

건강에 대해 말하자면, 공공장소에서의 흡연은 흡연자들이나 비흡연자들에게 해로운 영향을 끼친다.
When it comes to health, smoking in public places has harmful effects on both smokers and non-smokers.

> 11. it is true that/it is a fact that/it is clear that/it is certain that S+V; 사실이다
> 12. detrimental(harmful/injurious) chemicals; 해로운/유해한 화학물질들
> 13. contribute to +N/make a contribution to+N; 기여하다
> 14. a great deal/considerably/significantly; 상당히
> 15. asthma; 천식
> 16. lung infection; 폐 감염

담배가 암의 발생, 천식 발작 그리고 폐 질환에 상당히 원인이 되는 수많은 해로운 화학물질들을 포함하고 있다는 것은 사실이다.

It is true that tobacco contains numerous detrimental chemicals which contribute a great deal to the development of cancers, asthma attacks, and lung infections.

> 17. in particular/particularly/in special/specially; 특별히
> 18. vulnerable/sensitive/susceptible; 취약한/민감한
> 19. concern/problem/trouble; 문제
> 20. second-hand smoker/passive smoker; 간접흡연자

특히, 임산부와 어린이 같은 취약한 건강문제를 가진 사람들은 간접흡연자들로서 더 심각하게 영향을 받을 수 있다.

In particular, people with vulnerable health care concerns like pregnant women and children could be more severely affected as second-hand smokers.

> 21. according to; ~에 따르면/~에 의하면

연구에 따르면, 한 사람이 흡연자이고 다른 사람이 비흡연자인 결혼한 커플일 경우,

According to research, in case of a married couple where one partner is a smoker and the other a non-smoker,

> 22. the former(the one)/the latter(the other); 전자/후자
> 23. be reported to/be said to/be believed to; ~라고 보고되고 있다.
> 24. a higher risk of death from; ~로 부터 높은 사망 위험성
> 25. heart disease; 심장 질환
> 26. because of/due to/on account of/owing to; 때문에

후자는 간접흡연 때문에 전자보다 30% 이상 심장질환의 높은 사망 위험성을 가지고 있다고 보고되고 있다.

the latter is reported to have a 30 percent higher risk of death from heart disease than the former because of passive smoking.

> 27. for these reasons; 이러한 이유들로 인해

이러한 이유들 때문에, 공공장소에서의 흡연은 금지되어야 한다.
For these reasons, smoking in public areas should be prohibited.

> 28. be exposed to+N/get exposure to+N; 노출되다
> 29. be more likely to+V; 더 ~일 거 같다

교육에 대해서, 흡연환경에 노출된 어린이들은 미래에 흡연자가 될 가능성이 크다.
As regards education, children exposed to a smoking environment are more likely to become smokers in the future,

> 30. tend to/have a tendency to/be inclined to; ~하는 경향이 있다
> 31. acceptable/possible; 받아들여질 수 있는

그것은 그들은 흡연은 받아들일 수 있다고 생각하는 경향이 있기 때문이다.
, which is why they tend to think smoking is acceptable.

> 32. a good example(model/pattern); 좋은 모범

만약에 공공장소에서의 흡연이 허용되면, 어린이들은 흡연에 자연스럽게 노출될 것이고, 그것은 좋은 본보기가 되지 않는다.
If smoking is allowed in public places, children will get exposure to smoking, and it does not set a good example.

> 33. thus/therefore/hence/as a result/consequently/in this context; 따라서/그러므로
> 34. be designated as smoke-free areas; 금연장소로 지정되다

따라서, 공공장소는 아이들의 교육과 발달을 위해서 금연장소로 지정되어야 한다.
Thus, public places should be designated as smoke-free areas for children education.

> 35. standpoint/viewpoint/perspective; 관점
> 36. cause/result in/lead to/bring about/give rise to; 야기하다/초래하다

환경적인 관점에서, 공공장소에서 흡연은 또한 환경적 문제를 발생시킨다.
From an environmental standpoint, smoking in public places also causes environmental problems.

> 37. cigarette butt; 담배 꽁초
> 38. accumulate; 쌓이다/누적하다
> 39. torrential(heavy) rains; 집중 폭우

한 가지 예로, 담배꽁초나 재가 쌓이고 그것은 집중 폭우로 국지적인 범람을 일으킬 수 있다.
For one thing, cigarette butts and ash are accumulated, which can result in localized overflowing after torrential rains.

> 40. throw away/discard/abandon/leave; 버리다

이것은 흡연자들이 흡연 후에 쓰레기를 아무데나 버리기 때문이다.
It is because smokers throw away their waste anywhere after smoking.

> 41. trash/waste/rubbish/garbage/litter; 쓰레기

사실상, 우리는 지하철 역이나 버스 정류장들 주변에 흡연자들에 의해서 버려진 쓰레기를 쉽게 볼 수 있다.
In fact, we can easily see trash thrown by smokers all over subway stations and bus stops.

> 42. in fact/in reality/actually/virtually/as a matter of fact; 사실상
> 43. undermine/damage/compromise/impair/hurt; 손상시키다
> 44. a lot of(a good deal of /a high amount of /a considerable amount of) money; 많은 돈
> 45. clean up/sweep; 청소하다

이것은 주변 환경을 해치고 있으며 청소하는 데 상당한 비용이 든다.
It undermines the surroundings and costs a lot of money to clean up.

> 46. permit/allow/approve/assent; 허락하다

따라서, 공공장소에서의 흡연은 환경적인 이유들 때문에 허용되어서는 안 된다.
Hence, smoking in public areas should not be permitted due to environmental reasons.

> 47. in conclusion/in short/to sum up; 결론은
> 48. consider A/take A into consideration(account); A를 고려하다

결론은, 모든 것을 고려할 때, 흡연이 공공장소에서 금지되어야 하는지에 대한 몇 가지 이유들이 있다.

In conclusion, considering all those things, there are several reasons why smoking should be banned in public places.

> 49. make sense/stand to reason/be logical; 이치에 맞다
> 50. organizations involved(related); 관련된 단체들
> 51. curb(stop/prohibit) smoking; 흡연을 금지하다/억제하다

따라서, 정부들과 관련된 당국들은 공공장소에서 흡연을 금지하기 위한 법규를 강화하는 것이 바람직하다.

Thus, it makes sense that governments and organizations involved should enforce the rules to curb smoking in public.

구문연습

1. 최근에/많은 논쟁들이 대중의 이목을 끌고 있다/흡연과 관련해서/공공장소에서

2. 몇몇 국가들은/영국과 같은/지금 시행한다/엄격한 금연정책을/공공장소에서

3. 그럼에도 불구하고/일부 사람들은/여전히 흡연한다/공공장소에서

4. 나는 의견이다/흡연이 금지되어야 한다/공공장소에서/다음이 이유들이다

5. 건강에 대해 말하자면/공공장소에서 흡연은/해로운 영향을 준다/흡연자들과 비흡연자들에게

6. 그것은 사실이다/담배는 포함한다/많은 해로운 화약약품들을/그것들은 상당히 원인이 된다/암 발생, 천식, 발작 그리고 폐 질환

7. 특히/취약한 건강문제를 가진/임산부들과 어린이들과 같은/심각하게 영향을 받고 있다/간접흡연자들로서

8. 연구에 따르면/결혼한 커플 경우에/한 파트너가 흡연자/그리고 다른 사람이 비흡연자인 경우

9. 후자는/가지고 있다고 보고되고 있다/30%의 높은 사망 위험성을/심장으로부터/전자보다/간접흡연 때문에

10. 이런 이유들 때문에/공공장소에서의 흡연은/금지되어야 한다

11. 교육측면에서는/흡연환경에 노출된 어린이들은/흡연자가 될 가능성이 크다/미래에

12. 그것은 때문이다/그들은 생각하는 경향이 있다/흡연이 받아들여질 수 있다

13. 만약에/흡연이/허용된다면/공공장소에서/아이들은/노출될 것이다/흡연에/자연스럽게

14. 그것은 형성하지 않는다/좋은 본보기를

15. 따라서/공공장소는/지정되어야 한다/금연구역으로서/어린이 교육을 위해

16. 환경의 관점에서/공공장소에서의 흡연은 또한/발생시킨다/환경적인 문제들을

17. 한 가지 예로/담배 꽁초들이나 재는/쌓인다/그것은/일으킬 수 있다/국지적인 범람을/집중호우 이후에

18. 그것은 때문이다/흡연자들은/버린다/그들의 쓰레기를/아무데나/흡연 후에

19. 사실상/우리는 쉽게 볼 수 있다/버려진 쓰레기를/흡연자들에 의해/지하철역 그리고 정류장 주변에

20. 그것은 해친다/주변환경을/그리고 많은 돈이 든다/그것을 청소하는 데

21. 따라서/공공장소에서의 흡연은 허락되면 안 된다/환경적 문제 때문에

_____

_____

22. 결론은/이러한 모든 것을 고려할 때/몇 가지 이유들이 있다/왜 흡연이 금지되어야 하는지/공공장소에서

_____

_____

23. 따라서/그것이 이치에 맞다/정부들과 관련된 기관들이/법칙들을 시행하다/흡연을 금지하기 위해/공공장소에서

_____

_____

Answer

1. In recent years, a lot of controversies regarding smoking in public places have been a high profile.
2. Several countries, like the UK, now implement a strict anti-smoking policy in public spaces.
3. Nevertheless, some people smoke in public areas.
4. I am of the view that smoking should be discouraged in public places. The following are the reasons.
5. When it comes to health, smoking in public places has harmful effects on both smokers and non-smokers.
6. It is true that tobacco contains numerous detrimental chemicals which contribute a great deal to the development of cancers, asthma attacks, and lung infections.
7. In particular, people with vulnerable health care concerns like pregnant women and children could be more severely affected as second-hand smokers.
8. According to research, in the case of a married couple where one partner is a smoker and the other a non-smoker,
9. , the latter is reported to have a 30 percent higher risk of death from heart disease than the former because of passive smoking.
10. For these reasons, smoking in public areas should be prohibited.
11. As regards education, children exposed to a smoking environment are more likely to become smokers in the future,
12. , which is why they tend to think smoking is acceptable.
13. If smoking is allowed in public places, children will get exposure to smoking naturally,
14. , and it does not set a good example.
15. Thus, public places should be designated as smoke-free areas for children education.
16. From an environmental standpoint, smoking in public places also causes environmental problems.
17. For one thing, cigarette butt and ash are accumulated, which can result in localized overflowing after torrential rains.
18. It is because smokers in public throw away their waste anywhere after smoking.
19. In fact, we can easily see trash thrown by smokers all over subway stations and bus stops.
20. It undermines the surroundings and costs a lot of money to clean up.
21. Hence, smoking in public areas should not be permitted due to environmental reasons.
22. In conclusion, considering all those things, there are several reasons why smoking should be banned in public places.
23. Thus, it makes sense that governments and organizations involved should enforce the rules to curb smoking in public.

You should spend about 40 minutes on this task.

Write about the following topic:

> **In some countries, people are no longer allowed to smoke in many public places and office buildings. Do you think this is a good rule or a bad rule?**

Give reasons for your answer and include any relevant examples from your own knowledge or experience.

Write at least 250 words.

Answer

In recent years, a lot of controversies regarding smoking in public places have been a high profile. Several countries, like the UK, now implement a strict anti-smoking policy in public spaces. Nevertheless, some people still smoke in public areas. I am of the view that smoking should be discouraged in public places. The following are the reasons.

When it comes to health, smoking in public places has harmful effects on both smokers and non-smokers. It is true that tobacco contains numerous detrimental chemicals which contribute a great deal to the development of cancers, asthma attacks, and lung infections. In particular, people with vulnerable health care concerns like pregnant women and children could be more severely affected as second-hand smokers. According to research, in the case of a married couple where one partner is a smoker and the other a non-smoker, the latter is reported to have a 30 percent higher risk of death from heart disease than the former because of passive smoking. For these reasons, smoking in public areas should be prohibited.

Regarding education, children exposed to a smoking environment are more likely to become smokers in the future, which is why they tend to think smoking is acceptable. If smoking is allowed in public places, children will get exposure to smoking, and it does not set a good example. Thus, public places should be designated as smoke-free areas for children's education.

From an environmental standpoint, smoking in public places also causes environmental problems as cigarette butts and ash are accumulated, which can result in localized overflowing after torrential rains. It is because smokers throw away their waste anywhere after smoking. In fact, we can easily see trash thrown by smokers all over subway stations and bus stops. It undermines the surroundings and costs a lot of money to clean up. Hence, smoking in public areas should not be permitted due to environmental reasons.

In conclusion, considering all those things, there are several reasons why smoking should be banned in public places. Thus, it makes sense that governments and organizations involved should enforce the rules to curb smoking in public.

IELTS Easy Writing

Task 1

Introduction

1. Line graph1
2. Line graph2
3. Pie chart1
4. Pie chart2
5. Bar graph1
6. Bar graph2

7. Table 1
8. Table2
9. Line+Pie
10. Bar+Table
11. Diagram
12. Flow chart

Writing Topics

Introduction

Graph 형태	Description 방법
Line graph	1. X 축 Y 축의 의미 파악 2. 전반적인 흐름을 묘사 3. 변화를 나타내는 다양한 동사/형용사/부사 적절히 사용
Bar graph	1. Data 비교/대조 2. 큰 수치부터 나열 3. 수치가 낮은 것은 같이 묶어서 표현 　(3% and 2% respectively)
Pie chart	1. data 비교/대조 2. 큰 수치부터 나열 3. 분수를 적절히 사용 a third/a quarter 4. 중요하지 않은 수치는 묶어서 나열하거나 생략해도 무관
Table 		2000	2005	2010
---	---	---	---
DVD	11%	23%	40%
FILM	23%	34%	43%		1. 주요 data를 select 해서 설명 2. Table은 변수가 많기 때문에 중요한 수치만 나열함 3. 수치가 크고 특징적인 것부터 나열
Complex type Figure1)　Figure2)	1. 서론에서 전체적으로 설명한 다음 　Figure1과 2에 대해 짧게 설명 2. Overall에서는 특징적인 변화를 선택해서 표현. 3. Body 1은 pie graph 설명. 　Body2는 pie graph와 비교하면서 table 설명.
Flow chart/diagram/map (출제빈도 낮음)	1. 과정을 표현하는 그래프 2. 적절한 순서를 나타내는 접속사 사용 　To begin with/first/second 3. Process 묘사할 때 수동태형

374　**IELTS Easy Writing**

Words for graph trends

word		Example sentence
(증가) 동사/increase/rise/ surge/soar 명사/an increase/a rise/a surge/a soar	예) 소비는 2005년에서 2010년 사이에 $100에서 $120으로 증가했다.	동사/Spending **increased** from $100 to $120 between 2005 and 2010. 동사/Spending **increased to** $120 over 5years 동사/Spending **increased by** $20 over 5years. 명사/There was **an increase in** spending of $20 over 5years. 명사/There was **an increase o**f $20 from 2005 to 2010. 명사/There was **a $20 increase** in spending over 5 years 명사/There was **an increase to** $120 by 2010
(감소) 동사/fall/drop/ decrease/decline 명사/a fall/a drop/a decrease/a decline	예) 소비는 2005년에서 2010년 사이에 $120에서 $100으로 줄었다.	동사/Spending **fell** from $120 to $ 100 between 2005 and 2010. 동사/Spending **fell to** $100 over 5years. 동사/Spending **fell by** $20 over 5years. 명사/There was **a fall in** spending of $20 from 2005 to 2010. 명사/There was **a $20 fall** in spending over 5years. 명사/There was **a fall of** $20 from 2005 to 2010.
분사구문	예) 소비는 3년 만에 상승했고 2005년과 2010년 사이 $120까지 감소했다. 그리고 다시 2012년까지 $140까지 증가했다.	Spending rose in three years, **decreasing to** $120 from 2005 to 2010, **and then rising again to** $140 by 2012.
문장연결	예1) 20%의 증가가 있었고 10년 뒤에 약간의 감소로 이어졌다. 예2) 그 이후에, 10년 뒤에 10%까지 약간의 감소가 있었다.	1. There was a 20% increase, **which was followed by(followed by/which led to)** a slight drop to 10% in a decade. 2. **After that (Following that),** there was a slight drop to 10% in a decade.

Adjective/adverb 사용

adjective	example	adverb	example
considerable	a considerable fall	considerably	fell considerably
rapid	a rapid rise	rapidly	rose rapidly
substantial	a substantial drop	substantially	rose substantially
sudden	a sudden increase	suddenly	increased suddenly
sharp	a sharp fall	sharply	fell sharply
dramatic	a dramatic decline	dramatically	declined dramatically

Fraction(분수)	Expression(표현)	Percent	Expression (표현)
1/2	a half	23%	roughly a quarter
1/3	a third	25%	a quarter
2/3	two thirds	27%	just over a quarter
1/4	a quarter	30%	slightly less than a third
3/4	three fourths	54%	a little more than a half
1/5	a fifth	60%	well over a half
2/5	two fifths	72%	just under three quarters

Use Synonyms

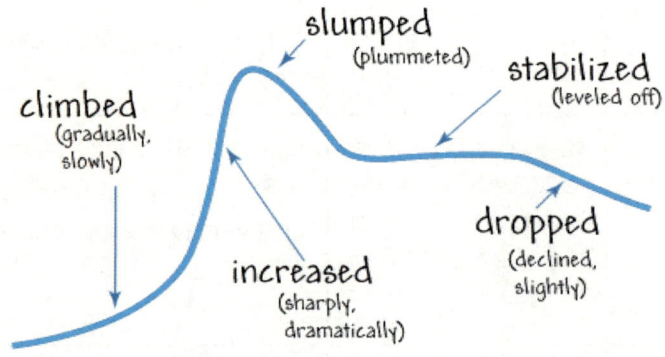

예) 이 그래프는 점차적으로 증가했고 가장 높은 수치까지 계속 증가했으며, 폭락으로 이어졌고 그러고 나서 약간의 감소 이전에 한동안 일정한 수치를 유지했다.

The given line graph climbed gradually and kept increasing to the highest figure, followed by a plummet, and then it leveled off for a while before a slight drop.

1. Line graph 1

You should spend about 20 minutes on this task.

> **The line graph shows the number of first-time visitors and returning visitors who visited Tasmania in Australia from 2002 to 2010.**
>
> Summarize the information by selecting and reporting the main features, and make comparisons where relevant.

Write at least 150 words.

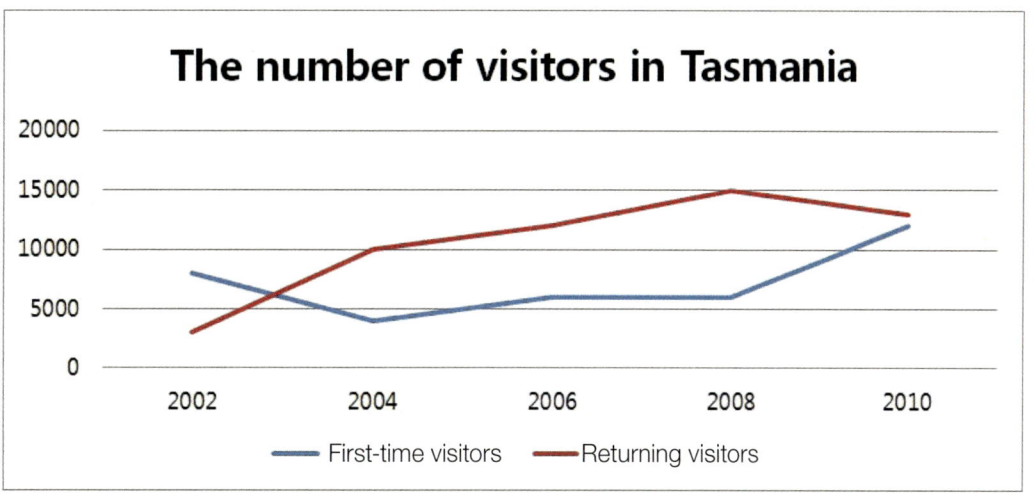

구조

Introduction: 문제 praphrase
Overall trend: 전반적으로 상승

Body 1 - from 2002 to 2004

Body 2 - from 2004 to 2010

INTRODUCTION

주어진 그래프는 2002년부터 8년 동안 2년 주기의 증가분의 데이터로 호주의 Tasmania에 방문하는 방문객 수를 설명하고 있다. 일반적으로, first-time visitors와 returning visitors 수는 주어진 기간에 걸쳐서 증가한 것이 분명하다.

BODY 1

2002년, 그 Tasmania에 처음 방문하는 사람의 수는, returning visitors 3,000명에 비교해서, 약 8,000명이다. 그러나, 2년 동안, 거의 10,000명의 returning visitors 수와 비교해서 4,000명이 조금 넘는 first-time visitors 수를 비교하면 이 경향은 완전히 역전되었다.

BODY 2

2004년부터, first-time visitor는 2년 동안 2,000명 증가했다. 뒤이어 6,000명으로 안정된 기간이 다음 2년에 걸쳐서 보여줬다. 그리고 그 수치는 2008년부터 2010년까지 다시 12,000명까지 상당히 상승했다. 다른 한편으로는, 2004년부터 다음 2년 동안 재방문자 수에 있어서 일반적인 증가가 있었다. 뒤이어 2008년까지 15,000명까지 급격한 상승이 이어졌다. 그 후에 재방문자 수치는 2년 안에 2,000명이 감소했다. 그럼에도 불구하고, 마지막 연도에 그 지역의 방문객의 전체수치는 약 25,000명에 달하고, 그것은 8년에 걸쳐 가장 큰 수치였다.

문장에 필요한 어휘

> 1. outline/depict/illustrate/give information about; 윤곽을 그리다/요점을 말하다
> 2. the total number of people; 전체 사람의 수
> 3. two-year increments; 2년 주기 증가

주어진 그래프는 2002년부터 8년 동안 2년 주기의 증가분의 데이터로 호주의 Tasmania에 방문하는 방문객 수를 설명하고 있다.

The given graph outlines the total number of people visiting Tasmania in Australia over an eight-year period from 2002, with data provided in two-year increments.

> 4. in general/generally/overall/as an overall trend; 일반적으로
> 5. it is evident that S+V/it can be seen that S+V; 분명하다/보여진다
> 6. increase/rise/climb/go up/soar/jump/rocket; 증가하다
> 7. over the specified(given/provided/presented) period; 주어진 기간 동안

일반적으로, first visitors와 returning visitors 수는 주어진 기간 동안 증가한 것이 분명하다.

In general, it is evident that the number of returning and first-time visitors increased over the specified period.

> 8. destination; 목적지
> 9. for the first time; 처음으로
> 10. compared to/in comparison with/as comparison with; ~와 비교해서

2002년, Tasmania에 처음 방문하는 사람의 수는 returning visitors 3,000명에 비교해서 약 8,000명이다.

In the year 2002, the number of people who visited Tasminia for the first time was about 8,000, compared to only 3,000 returning visitors.

> 11. however/on the contrary/in contrast/by contrast/on the other hand; 그와 반대로
> 12. trend/tendency; 경향
> 13. reverse/transfer/change; 바뀌었다

그러나, 거의 10,000명의 returning visitors 수와 비교해서 4,000명이 조금 넘는 first-time visitors visitors 수를 비교하면 이 경향은 2년 이내에 역전되었다.

However, this trend completely reversed within two years, with slightly more than 4,000 new visitors in comparison with almost 10,000 returning visitors.

> 14. , which led to B/, which was followed by B/, followed by B(명사); B로 이어지다
> 15. a steady period/a stable period; 안정된 기간

2004년부터, first-year visitors는 다음 2년 동안 2,000명 증가했다. 뒤이어 6,000명으로 안정된 기간이 다음 2년에 걸쳐서 보여줬다.

From 2004, first-time visitors showed an increase of around 2,000 for the following two years, which led to a stable period with 6,000 over the next two years,

> 16. the figure for/the data of; ~에 대한 수치는
> 17. significantly/considerably/fairly/a great deal; 상당히

그리고 그 수치는 2008년부터 2010년까지 다시 상당히 12,000명까지 증가했다.

, and again the figure soared significantly to 120,000 from 2008 to 2010.

> 18. a general rise/an overall rise(increase); 일반적인 상승
> 19. over the next 2-year period; 다음 2년 동안

다른 한편으로는, 2004년부터 2년 동안 재방문자 수에 있어서 일반적인 증가가 있었다.

On the other hand, there was a general rise in returning visitors for the next 2-year period from 2004,

> 20. rapid(dramatic/considerable/significant) growth; 급격한 증가
> 21. after that/following that/and then; 그 뒤로/그 다음

뒤이어 2008년까지 약 15,000명까지 급격한 증가를 했다. 그 후에 returning visitors 수치는 2년 안에 2,000명이 감소했다.

, followed by rapid growth to about 15,000 by 2008. After that, the number of returning visitors decreased by around 2000 in 2 years.

> 22. nevertheless/yet/unlike/however/still; 그럼에도 불구하고
> 23. in the final year/at the end of the period; 마지막 년도
> 24. the combined(total) number of people; 전체 사람의 수

그럼에도 불구하고, 마지막 연도에 그 지역의 방문객의 전체수치는 약 25,000명에 달하고 그것은 8년에 걸쳐 가장 큰 수치였다.

Nevertheless, in the final year, the combined number of people visiting this area amounted to around 25,000, which was the highest figure over 8 years.

구문연습

1. 주어진 그래프는/설명하고 있다/전체 방문한 사람의 수/호주의 Tasmania/8년에 걸쳐서/2002년부터/주어진 데이터와 함께/2년 주기의 증가에 있어

2. 일반적으로/그것은 분명하다/first-time visitors returning visitors 수는/증가했다/주어진 기간에 걸쳐서

3. 2002년에/사람의 수는/Tasmania를 방문한/처음으로/약 8,000명이다/비교해서/단지 3,000 returning visitors

4. 그러나/다음 2년 동안/이러한 경향은 완전히 바뀌었다/2년 이내에/약간 넘는 4,000명의 first-time visitors 함께/비교해서/거의 10,000 재방문객들과

5. 2004년부터/first-time visitors은 보여줬다/2,000명의 증가/다음 2년 동안/뒤이어 안정적인 기간이 이어졌다/6,000명과 함께/다음 2년에 걸쳐서

6. 그리고/다시/그 수치는/상당히 증가했다/12,000명까지/2006년부터 2008년까지

7. 다른 한편으로는/일반적인 증가가 있었다/재방문자 수에 있어서/다음 2년 동안/2004년부터

_____
_____

8. 이어지다/급격한 증가가/약 15,000명까지/2008년까지/그 이후/재방문객 수치는/감소했다/약 2,000명 차이/2년 안에

_____
_____

9. 그럼에도 불구하고/마지막 연도에/전체 사람의 수는/이 지역을 방문하는/약 25,000명에 달했다/그것은 가장 큰 수치이다/8년에 걸쳐

_____
_____

Answer

1. The given graph outlines the total number of people visiting Tasmania in Australia over an eight-year period from 2002, with data given in two-year increments.

2. In general, it is evident that the number of returning and first-time visitors increased over the specified period.

3. In the year 2002, the number of people who visited Tasmania for the first time was about 8,000, compared to only 3,000 returning visitors.

4. However, this trend completely reversed within two years, with slightly more than 4,000 new visitors in comparison with almost 10,000 returning visitors.

5. From 2004, first-time visitors showed an increase of around 2,000 for the following two years, which led to a stable period with 6,000 over the next two years,

6. , and again the figure soared significantly to 120,000 from 2008 to 2010.

7. On the other hand, there was a general rise in returning visitors for the next 2-year period from 2004,

8. , followed by rapid growth to about 15,000 by 2008. After that, the number of returning visitors decreased by around 2000 in 2 years.

9. Nevertheless, in the final year, the combined number of people visiting this area amounted to around 25,000, which was the highest figure over 8 years.

You should spend about 20 minutes on this task.

The line graph shows the number of first-time visitors and returning visitors who visited Tasmania in Australia from 2002 to 2010.

Summarize the information by selecting and reporting the main features, and make comparisons where relevant.

Write at least 150 words.

Answer

The given graph outlines the total number of people visiting Tasmania in Australia over an eight-year period from 2002, with data provided in two-year increments. In general, it is evident that the number of returning and first-time visitors increased over the specified period.

In the year 2002, the number of people who visited Tasmania for the first time was about 8,000 compared to only 3,000 returning visitors. However, this trend completely reversed within two years, with slightly more than 4,000 new visitors in comparison with almost 10,000 returning visitors.

From 2004, first-time visitors showed an increase of around 2,000 for the following two years, which led to a stable period with 6,000 over the next two years, and again the figure soared significantly to 12,000 from 2008 to 2010. On the other hand, there was a general rise in returning visitors for the next 2-year period from 2004, followed by rapid growth to about 15,000 by 2008. After that, the number of returning visitors decreased by around 2000 in 2 years. Nevertheless, in the final year, the combined number of people visiting this area amounted to around 25,000, which was the highest figure over 8 years.

2. Line graph 2

You should spend about 20 minutes on this task.

> The line graph shows the past and projected public transportation rates in three different countries between 2012 and 2020.
>
> Summarize the information by selecting and reporting the main features, and make comparisons where relevant.

Write at least 150 words.

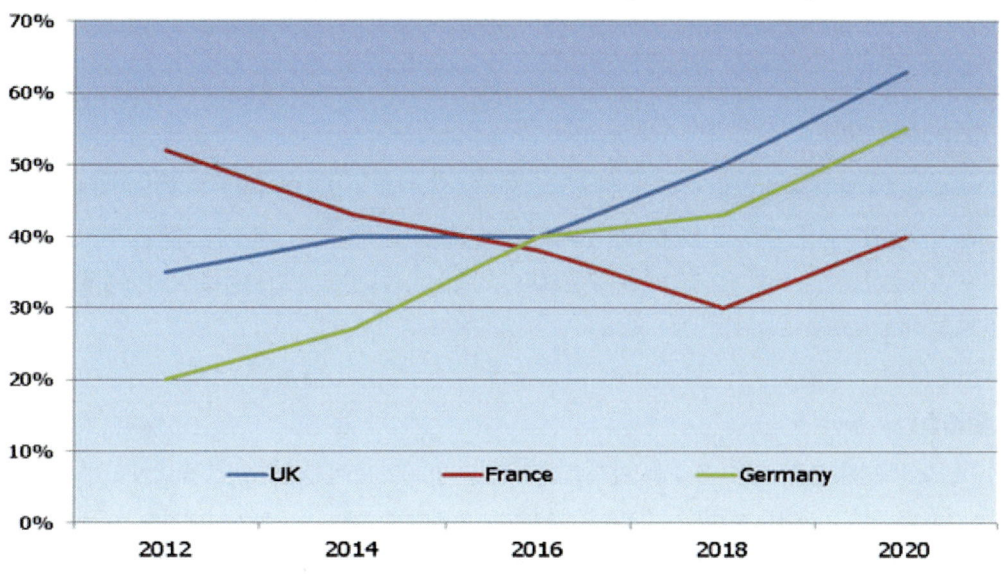

구조

> **Introduction:** 문제 paraphrase
> (문제를 다른 어휘와 문장으로 설명)
> **Overall trend:** 영국과 독일은 전반적 상승/반면에 프랑스는 하락 후 상승예상
> (no numbers)

> **Body 1** - 2012년 경향
> The UK와 Germany 동향

> **Body 2**- France 동향

INTRODUCTION

이 주어진 라인 그래프는 2012년부터 2020년까지 영국, 독일 그리고 프랑스의 과거와 미래의 대중교통 이용의 비율을 설명하고 있다. 일반적인 경향으로서, 영국과 독일에서 대중교통 비율은 주어진 기간 동안 꾸준한 증가를 경험하고 있다. 반면에 프랑스에서 감소추세가 있었으나 대중교통 비율을 상승시킬 것으로 기대된다.

BODY 1

2012년에, 영국 그리고 독일에서의 대중교통 비율은 각각 약 35%와 20%였다. 독일의 수치는 기간 동안 계속적으로 증가했고 프랑스의 비율을 2016년에 추월했고 그것은 마지막 연도에 55%에 도달할 것이다. 비슷하게도, 영국에서는 대중교통의 사용은 2014년에 40%까지 성장했고 2년 동안 일정하게 유지했다. 그 이후에, 2020년까지 60% 이상 사용할 것으로 예상되다.

BODY 2

영국, 독일과 비교해서, 프랑스는 2012년 출발연도부터 몇년간에 걸쳐 하향추세를 보이고 있다. 프랑스에서 2012년에 대중교통의 비율은 50% 이상이었고 세 국가 중 가장 높았다. 그러나, 그것은 2018년까지 30%까지 급격하게 감소가 예상된다. 그 이후 2020년까지 10%의 상당한 증가가 기대된다.

문장에 필요한 어휘

> 1. illustrate/show/give information about/give a breakdown of; 설명하다/분석하다
> 2. predicted/projected/expected; 예상된

이 주어진 라인 그래프는 2012년부터 2020년까지 영국, 독일 그리고 프랑스의 과거와 미래의 대중교통 이용의 비율을 설명하고 있다.

The given line graph illustrates the previous and predicted rates of public transportation usage in the UK, Germany, and France from 2012 to 2020.

> 3. as an overall trend/overall/in general/generally; 일반적인 경향으로
> 4. experience/present/represent/show; 보여주고 있다/경험하고 있다
> 5. a steady(consistent/continuous) rise(increase/growth); 꾸준한 증가
> 6. over the given period/over the period given/during the given period; 주어진 기간 동안

일반적인 경향으로서, 영국과 독일에서 대중교통 비율은 주어진 기간 동안 꾸준한 증가를 경험하고 있다.

As an overall trend, it can be seen that the proportions of public transit in the UK and Germany experienced a steady rise over the given period,

> 7. whereas/while/whilst; 반면에
> 8. a downward trend(tendency)/a declining tendency; 하향 추세
> 9. be expected to/be anticipated to/be projected to/be estimated to; 예상되다/~할 것이다

반면에 프랑스에서 감소추세가 있었으나 다시 대중교통 비율을 상승시킬 것으로 기대된다.

, whereas there was a downward trend in France where it is expected to raise the percentage of public transit.

> 10. the rate of/the percentage of/the proportion of; ~에 대한 비율
> 11. around/about/approximately/almost/roughly; 약/대략
> 12. respectively/each; 각각

2012년에, 영국과 독일에서의 대중교통 비율은 각각 약 35%와 20%였다.

In the year 2012, the rate of public transportation in the UK and Germany were around 35% and 20% respectively.

> 13. the figure for/the data of; ~에 대한 수치
> 14. increase/rise/climb/go up/grow/surge; 증가하다
> 15. exceed/surpass/outpace; 앞지르다/추월하다

독일의 수치는 기간 동안 계속적으로 증가했고 프랑스의 비율을 2016년에 추월했고 그것은 마지막 연도에 55%에 도달할 것이다.

The figure for Germany increased continuously through the given period, exceeding France's rate in 2016, and it is predicted to reach almost 55% in the final year.

> 16. similarly/nearly/likely; 비슷하게
> 17. remain(stay) stable/steady; 일정하게 유지하다

비슷하게도, 영국에서는 대중교통의 사용은 2014년에 40%까지 성장했고 2년 동안 일정하게 유지했다.

Similarly, the use of public transportation grew to 40% in the UK in 2014 and then remained steady for two years.

> 18. following that/after that/and then; 그 이후에
> 19. more than/over/above; 이상
> 20. rapidly/dramatically/significantly/considerably; 상당히/급격하게

그 이후에, 2020년까지 60% 이상까지 급격하게 증가할 것이다.

Following that, it is anticipated to surge rapidly to more than 60% in 2020.

> 21. as compared with/compared to/in comparison with; ~와 비교해서

영국 그리고 독일과 비교해서, 프랑스는 2012년 출발연도부터 몇년간에 걸쳐 하향추세를 보이고 있다.

As compared with the UK and Germany, France has shown a declining tendency over several years from the start of 2012.

> 22. be the highest; 가장 높다

프랑스에서 2012년에 대중교통의 비율은 50% 이상이었고 세 국가 중 가장 높았다.

The public transportation rate in France was over 50% in 2012, which was the highest rate among three countries.

> 23. decrease/decline/go down/fall; 감소하다

그러나, 그것은 2018년까지 30%까지 급격하게 감소가 예상되다. 그 이후 2020년까지 10%만큼 상당히 증가할 것으로 예상되다.

However, it is estimated to decrease dramatically to 30% until 2018. After which it is projected to rise considerably by 10 % until 2020.

구문 연습

1. 이 주어진 라인 그래프는 설명하고 있다/과거와 미래의 대중교통 이용의 비율/런던, 독일 그리고 프랑스/2012년부터 2020년까지

_____
_____
_____

2. 일반적인 경향으로써/보여질 수 있다/대중교통의 비율은/영국과 독일에서/경험했다/꾸준한 증가를/주어진 기간 동안

_____
_____
_____

3. 반면에/감소추세가 있었다/프랑스에서/거기에서 그것은 기대된다/상승시킬 것으로/대중교통의 비율

_____
_____
_____

4. 2012년에/대중 교통의 비율은/영국과 독일의/각각 약 35%와 20%였다

_____
_____
_____

5. 독일의 수치는 증가했다/계속적으로/그 기간을 통해/초과했다/2016년에 프랑스의 비율을/그리고 그것은 /도달할 것으로 기대된다/거의 55%/마지막 년도에

   _____
   _____

6. 비슷하게도/대중교통의 사용은/40%까지 증가했다/영국에서/2014년에/그런 다음/일정하게 유지했다/2년 동안

   _____
   _____

7. 그 이후에/그것은 증가할 것이다/급격하게/60% 이상/그리고 증가할 것이다/2020년에

   _____
   _____

8. 영국 그리고 독일과 비교해서/프랑스는 보이고 있다/감소추세를/몇년간에 걸쳐서/2012년 출발부터

   _____
   _____

9. 대중교통 비율은/프랑스에서/50% 이상이다/2012년에/그것은 가장 높은 비율/세 국가들 중에서

   _____
   _____

10. 그러나/그것은 감소가 예상되다/급격하게/30%까지/2018년까지/그 후에/증가가 상당히 예상되다/10% 차이/2020년까지

    _____
    _____

Answer

1. The given line graph illustrates the previous and predicted rates of public transportation usage in the UK, Germany, and France from 2012 to 2020.

2. As an overall trend, it can be seen that the proportions of public transit in the UK and Germany experienced a steady rise over the given period,

3. , whereas there was a downward trend in France where it is expected to raise the percentage of public transit.

4. In the year 2012, the rate of public transportation in the UK and Germany were around 35% and 20% respectively.

5. The figure for Germany increased continuously through the given period, exceeding France's rate in 2016, and it is predicted to reach almost 55% in the final year.

6. Similarly, the use of public transportation grew to 40% in the UK in 2014 and then remained steady for two years.

7. Following that, it is anticipated to surge rapidly to more than 60% in 2020.

8. As compared with the UK and Germany, France has shown a declining tendency over several years from the start of 2012.

9. The public transportation rate in France was over 50% in 2012, which was the highest rate among three countries.

10. However, it is estimated to decrease dramatically to 30% until 2018. After which it is projected to rise considerably by 10 % until 2020.

Task 1

You should spend about 20 minutes on this task.

The line graph shows the past and projected public transportation rates in three different countries between 2012 and 2020.

Summarize the information by selecting and reporting the main features, and make comparisons where relevant.

Write at least 150 words.

Answer

The given line graph illustrates the previous and predicted rates of public transportation usage in the UK, Germany, and France from 2012 to 2020. As an overall trend, it can be seen that the proportions of public transits in the UK and Germany experienced a steady rise over the given period, whereas there was a downward trend in France where it is expected to raise the percentage of public transit.

In the year 2012, the rate of public transportation in the UK and Germany were around 35% and 20% respectively. The figure for Germany increased continuously through the given period, exceeding France's rate in 2016, and it is predicted to reach almost 55% in the final year. Similarly, the use of public transportation grew to 40% in the UK in 2014 and then remained steady for two years. Following that, it is anticipated to surge rapidly to more than 60% in 2020.

As compared with the UK and Germany, France has shown a declining tendency over several years from the start of 2012. The public transportation rate in France was over 50% in 2012, which was the highest rate among three countries. However, it is estimated to decrease dramatically to 30% until 2018. After which it is projected to rise considerably by 10% until 2020.

3. Pie chart 1

You should spend about 20 minutes on this task.

> The pie chart shows the amount of leisure time enjoyed in a typical week by females and males in the UK in 2015.
>
> Summarize the information by selecting and reporting the main features, and make comparisons where relevant.

Write at least 150 words.

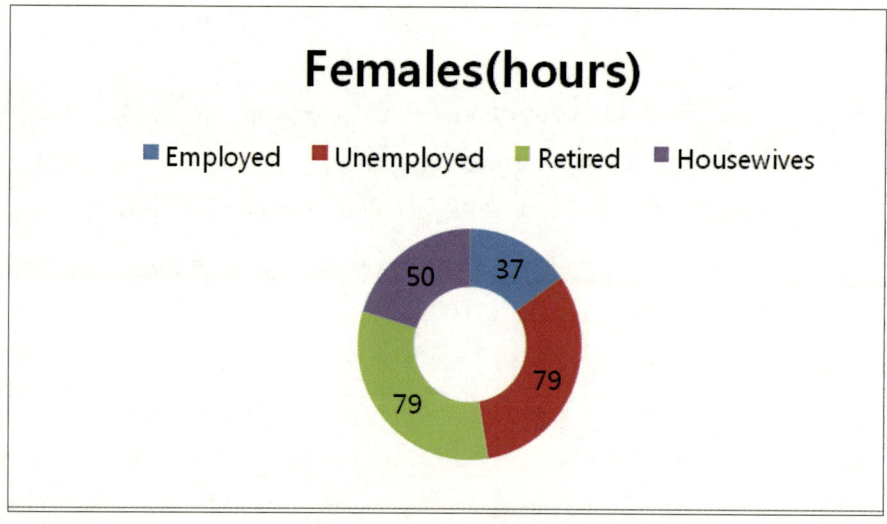

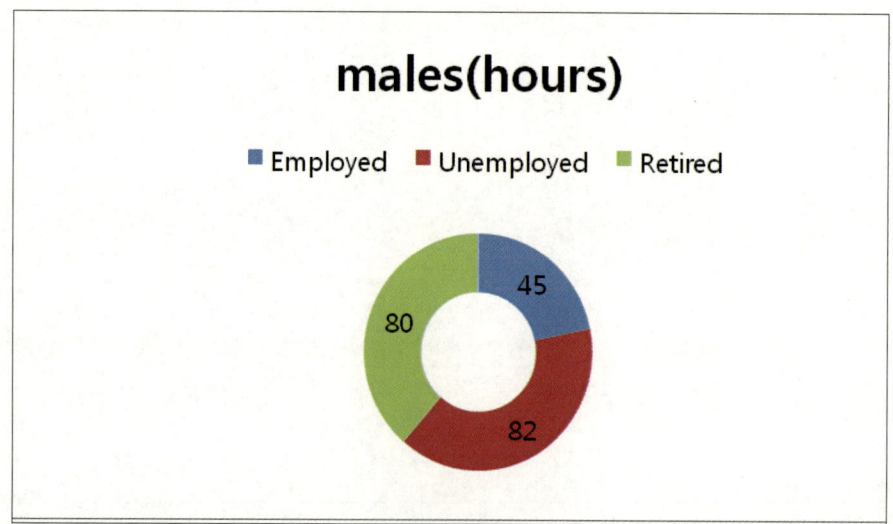

구조

> **Introduction:** 문제 paraphrase
> **Overall trend:** 여성이 남성보다 여가 시간을 덜 갖는다.

> **Body 1** - unemployed men and women/retired men and women

> **Body 2** - employed men and women/housewives

INTRODUCTION

주어진 파이 그래프는 2015년 영국에서 다른 직업 상황에 남자와 여자들의 일상적인 주중 여가시간에 대한 데이터를 비교한다. 단위는 시간으로 측정되었다. housewives에 대한 정보는 두 번째 차트에서 제공되지 않는다. 일반적으로 여자들은 주어진 분류에서 남자보다 여가 시간을 덜 갖는 걸로 보여질 수 있다.

BODY1

실업 상태에 있는 영국사람들에 대해서 말하자면, 그들은 남자, 여자 둘 다 가장 긴 시간을 여가활동에 보냈다. 남자는 평균적으로 일주일에 여자가 79시간을 보내는 것에 비해 82시간의 여가시간을 가졌다. 은퇴한 남자와 여자의 경우, 그들은 여유시간을 위해 80시간과 79시간씩 각각 시간을 소비한다. 흥미롭게도, 은퇴한 여자와 실업 상태의 여자들은 79시간으로 여가를 위해 똑같은 시간을 가졌다.

BODY2

반면에, 일하는 사람들 중에 여성 근로자들은 남성 근로자들의 45시간의 여가 시간에 비교해서 약 37시간을 차지한다. 이것은 주어진 항목에서 최저 수치다. 가정주부는 여가시간으로 대략 50시간을 즐긴다. 이것은 일하는 여성들에 의해 사용된 시간 이상이다.

문장에 필요한 어휘

> 1. compare/make a comparison; 비교하다
> 2. the data of/the figure for; ~에 대한 수치
> 3. general/typical/normal/ordinary; 일상적인/일반적인
> 4. in different status(circumstances); 다른 상황에서

주어진 파이 그래프는 2015년 영국에서 다른 직업 상황에 있는 남자와 여자들의 일상적인 주중 여가시간에 대한 데이터를 비교한다.

The given pie graphs compare the data of leisure time in a general week between females and males in the different work status in the UK in the year 2015.

> 5. measure/survey/research; 측정하다/조사하다

단위는 시간으로 측정되었다. housewives에 대한 항목은 두 번째 차트에서 제공되지 않는다.

Units are measured in hours. No information for the housewives is provided in the second chart.

> 6. in general/generally/as an overall trend/overall; 전반적으로
> 7. category/type/list/index; 목록

일반적으로 여자들은 주어진 분류에서 남자보다 여가 시간을 덜 갖는 걸로 보여질 수 있다.

In general, it can be seen that women had less leisure time than men in the presented categories.

> 8. when it comes to/in light of/in terms of; ~관한 한
> 9. recreational activities; 여가활동

실업상태에 있는 영국사람들에 대해서 말하자면, 그들은 남자 여자 둘 다 가장 긴 시간을 여가활동에 보냈다.

When it comes to British unemployed, they spent the longest time on recreational activities of both groups.

> 10. on average; 평균적으로
> 11. compared to/as compared with/in comparison with; 비교하여

남자는 평균적으로 일주일에 여자가 79시간을 보내는 것에 비해 82시간의 여가시간을 가졌다.
Men had about 82 hours of leisure time compared to women who spent 79 hours on average.

---
12. retired; 은퇴한
13. consume/spend/use/enjoy; 소비하다/사용하다
14. respectively/each; 각각

은퇴한 남자와 여자의 경우, 그들은 여유시간을 위해 80시간과 79시간씩 각각 시간을 소비한다.
For retired men and women, they consumed time for leisure with 80 and 79 hours respectively.

---
15. interestingly; 흥미롭게도

흥미롭게도, 은퇴한 여자와 실업 상태의 여자들은 79시간으로 여가를 위해 똑같은 시간을 가졌다.
Interestingly, retired women and unemployed women had the same hours of leisure with 79 hours.

---
16. meanwhile/on the other hand/then again/in the meantime; 반면에/한편
17. take up/account for/make up/make over/represent/occupy; 차지하다

반면에, 일하는 사람들 중에 여성 근로자들은 남자 근로자들의 45시간의 여가 시간에 비교해서 약 37시간을 차지한다.
Meanwhile, among working people, females took up about 37 hours in comparison with the 45 hours of leisure time for males,

---
18. figure/number/data; 수치

이것은 주어진 항목에서 최저 수치다.
, which was the lowest figure in the categories given.

---
19. approximately/about/almost/roughly; 약/대략

가정주부는 여가시간으로 대략 50시간을 즐긴다. 이것은 일하는 여성들에 의해 쓰여진 시간 이상이다.
Homemakers enjoyed approximately 50 hours of leisure time, which was more than that spent by working women.

구문연습

1. 주어진 파이 그래프는 비교한다/여가시간의 데이터를/일상적인 주중/여자와 남자 사이에/다른 상황에 있는/영국에서/2015년에

___

2. 그것은/측정되었다/시간으로

___

3. Housewives에 대한 정보는/제공되지 않았다/두 번째 차트에서

___

4. 전반적으로/보여질 수 있다/여성들은/여가시간을 덜 가진다/남자보다/주어진 분류에서

___

5. 영국사람에 대해 말하자면/실업 상태에 있는/그들은 보냈다/가장 긴 시간을/레저 활동 등에/남자와 여자 둘 다

___

6. 남자는 가졌다/약 82시간의 레저시간을/비교하여/여자들은 가졌다/**79**시간을/평균적으로

___

7. 은퇴한 남자와 여자에게 있어서/그들은 시간을 소비한다/여가를 위해서/**80**시간과 **79**시간 각각

_____
_____

8. 흥미롭게도/은퇴한 여성과 실업 상태의 여성은 갖는다/같은 시간을/여가를 위한/**79**시간으로

_____
_____

9. 반면에/일하는 사람 중에/여성근로자들은 차지한다/약 **37**시간을/비교하여/**45**시간의 여가시간과/남성근로자들의

_____
_____

10. 이것은 가장 최저 수치이다/주어진 항목에 있어서

_____
_____

11. 가정주부들은 즐긴다/약 **50**시간의 여가시간을/그것은/보낸 시간 이상이다/일하는 여성들에 의해

_____
_____

Answer

1. The given pie graphs compare the data of leisure time in a general week between females and males in the different status in the UK in the year 2015.

2. Units are measured in hours.

3. No information for the housewives is provided in the second chart.

4. In general, it can be seen that women had less leisure time than men in the presented categories.

5. When it comes to British unemployed, they spent the longest time on recreational activities of both groups.

6. Men had about 82 hours of leisure time compared to women who spent 79hours on average.

7. For retired men and women, they consumed time for leisure with 80 and 79 hours respectively.

8. Interestingly, retired women and unemployed women had the same hours of leisure with 79 hours.

9. Meanwhile, among working people, females took up about 37 hours in comparison with the 45 hours of leisure time for males,

10. , which was the lowest figure in the categories given.

11. Housewives enjoyed approximately 50 hours of leisure time, which was more than that spent by working women.

You should spend about 20 minutes on this task.

The pie chart shows the amount of leisure time enjoyed in a typical week by females and males in 2015

Summarize the information by selecting and reporting the main features, and make comparisons where relevant.

Write at least 150 words.

Answer

The given pie graphs compare the data of leisure time in a general week between females and males of different work status in the UK in the year 2015. Units are measured in hours. No information for the housewives is provided in the second chart. In general, it can be seen that women had less leisure time than men in the presented categories.

When it comes to British unemployed, they spent the longest time on recreational activities of both groups. Men had about 82 hours of leisure time on average per week compared to women who spent 79 hours on average. For retired men and women, they consumed time for leisure with 80 and 79 hours respectively. Interestingly, retired women and unemployed women had the same hours of leisure with 79 hours.

Meanwhile, among working people, females took up about 37 hours in comparison with the 45 hours of leisure time for males, which was the lowest figure in the categories given. Homemakers enjoyed approximately 50 hours of leisure time, which was more than that spent by working women.

4. Pie chart 2

You should spend about 20 minutes on this task.

> **The charts show the distribution of money spent on music in two different years in the UK.**
>
> Summarize the information by selecting and reporting the main features, and make comparisons where relevant.

Write at least 150 words.

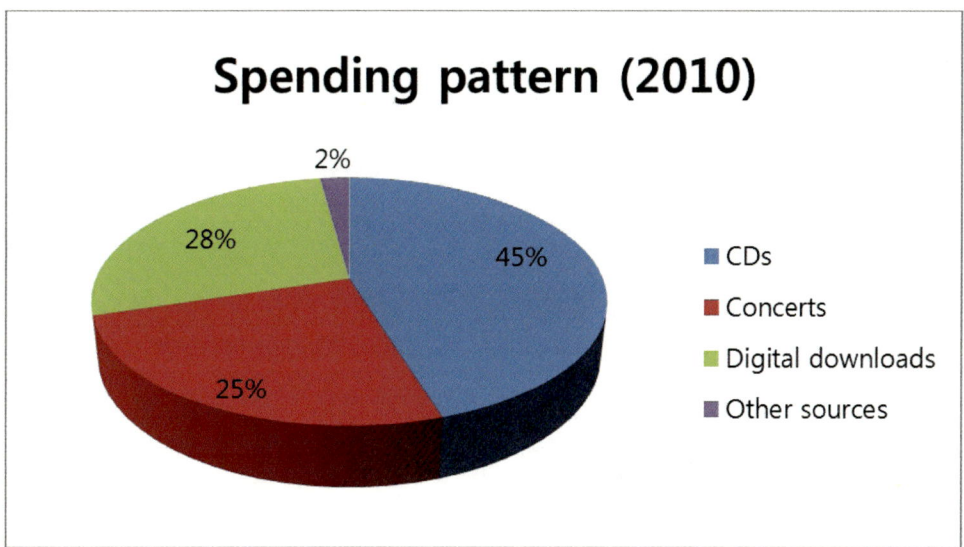

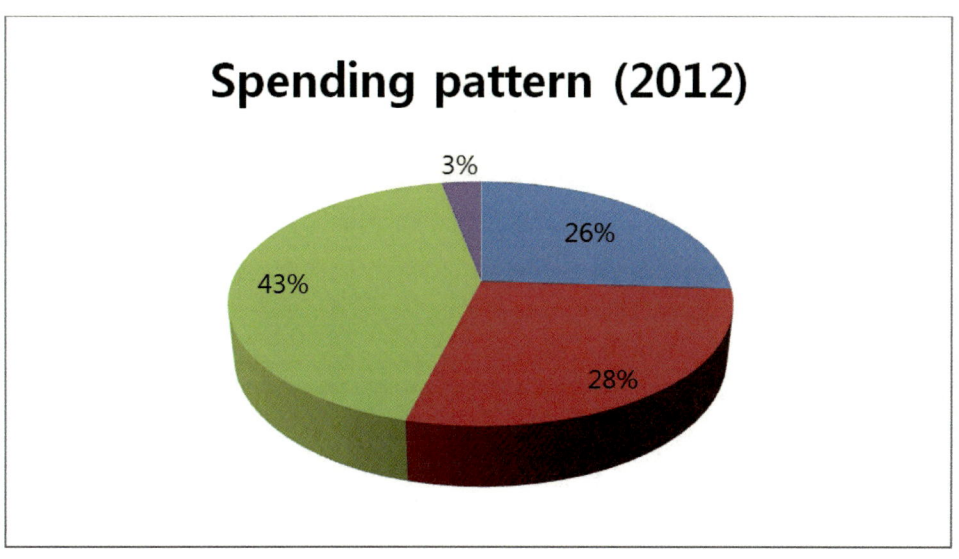

구조

> **Introduction:** 문제 paraphrase
> **Overall trend:** CD에 대한 비용을 제외한 모든 항목 증가

> **Body 1** - In 2010: 비율이 큰 항목부터 -CD/digital download/concerts/others

> **Body 2** - In 2012: 2010년과 비교/증감 분석

INTRODUCTION

파이 그래프는 음악(CD, 연주회 그리고 다운로드)과 관련해서 2010년과 2012년에 영국에서의 소비패턴에 대한 분석을 보여주고 있다. 이것은 퍼센트로 측정된다. 전반적인 경향으로서, 디지털 다운로드는 다른 항목들보다 더 일반적이 된 것은 분명하다. 반면에 CD 판매는 상대적인 하락을 보였다.

BODY 1

첫 번째 데이터는 2010년이다. 거기에서 대다수의 소비는 CD에 있었다. 45%를 차지하고 그 다음은 디지털 다운로드로써 25% 이상을 기록했다. 두 가지 영역(디지털 다운로드와 콘서트는)은 각각 28%와 25%로 비슷한 수치를 경험했다. 사용된 수치는 3%로 'other sources'로 표시된 항목이다.

BODY 2

2년 후에, 네 가지 영역의 순서는 바뀌었다. 디지털 구입이 CD를 추월했고 그들은 43%로 가장 큰 비용으로 증가했다. 반면에 CD비용에 있어 2년간에 걸쳐 46% 부터 19% 차이로 두드러진 감소가 있었다. 다른 Other sources는 2년 후에 거의 변화가 없었다.

문장에 필요한 어휘

> 1. compare/make(draw) a comparison: 비교하다
> 2. pattern/form/type; 구성
> 3. concerning/regarding/as regards/with respect to; ~에 관해서

파이 그래프는 음악(CD, 연주회 그리고 다운로드)과 관련해서 2010년과 2012년에 영국에서의 소비패턴을 비교한다.

The pie charts compare spending patterns in the UK concerning music: CDs, concerts, digital downloads and other sources, in 2010 and 2012.

> 4. measure/gauge/survey; 측정하다

이것은 퍼센트로 측정된다.
It is measured as a percentage.

> 5. as an overall trend/overall/in general/generally; 전반적으로
> 6. it is clear that/it is certain that S+V; 분명하다
> 7. relative/comparative; 상대적인
> 8. a drop/a fall/a decrease/a decline; 감소

전반적인 경향으로서, 디지털 다운로드는 다른 항목들보다 더 일반적인 것이 된 것은 분명하다. 반면에 CD 판매는 상대적인 하락을 보였다.

As an overall trend, it is clear that digital download became more common than the other items, while CDs sales presented a relative drop.

> 9. the majority of/most; 대부분
> 10. expenditure/expense/spending/outlay; 지출/비용
> 11. account for/take up/make up/make over/have/represent/occupy/stand at; 차지하다
> 12. which was followed by/which led to/followed by +N; 이어진다
> 13. category/item/provision; 항목/조항

첫 번째 데이터는 2010년이다. 거기에서 대다수의 소비는 CD에 있었다. 45%를 차지하고 그 다음은 디지털 다운로드로서 25% 이상을 기록했다.

The first data is for 2010, where it can be seen that the majority of expenditure was on CDs, accounting for 45%, which was followed by digital downloads, standing at just over a quarter.

---
14. figure/number/percent/data; 수치
15. respectively/each; 각각

두 가지 영역(디지털 다운로드와 콘서트)은 각각 28%와 25%로 비슷한 수치를 경험했다.
Two categories, digital downloads and concerts, experienced almost similar figures at 28% and 25% respectively.

---
16. label/mark/indicate; 표시하다

사용된 가장 적은 양은 3%로 'other sources'로 표시된 항목이다.
The least amount spent was labeled as 'other sources' at just 3%.

---
17. order/sequence; 차례/순서

2년 후에, 네 가지 영역의 순서는 바뀌었다.
Two years later, the order of the four categories changed.

---
18. while/whereas/whilst; 반면에
19 marked/striking/prominent/remarkable; 두드러진

디지털 구입이 CD구매를 추월했고 그들은 43%로 가장 큰 비용으로 증가했다. 반면에 CD 비용에 있어 2년간에 걸쳐 19% 두드러진 감소가 있었다.
Digital purchase overtook buying CDs, and it increased to the most significant spending at 43%, whereas there was a marked decrease in CDs expenditure by 19% from 45% over 2 years.

---
20. few changes; 거의 변화가 없는

다른 Other sources는 2년 후에 거의 변화가 없었다.
The other sources spending had few changes after two years.

구문연습

1. 파이 그래프는/비교하다/소비패턴을/영국에서/음악과 관련해서/CDs, Concerts, Digital downloads 그리고 다른 자료들/2010년과 2012년의

2. 이것은/측정된다/퍼센트로써

3. 전반적인 경향으로서/그것은 분명하다/Digital downloads는 더 일반적이 되다/다른 항목들보다/반면에 CDs 판매는 보였다/상대적인 하락을

4. 첫 번째 데이터는 2010년이다/그것은 보여질 수 있다/대다수의 소비는/CDs에 있었다/45% 차지한다/그것은 이어진다/디지털 다운로드로/기록했다/25% 이상을

5. 두 가지 영역/디지털 다운로드와 콘서트/경험했다/거의 비슷한 수치/28%와 25% 각각

6. 사용된 가장 적은 양은/표시된 항목이다/others sources로/단지 3%

7. 2년 후에/네 가지 영역의 순서는/바뀌었다

8. 디지털 구입이/추월했다/CD 구매를

9. 그리고/그것은 증가했다/가장 큰 비용 43%까지

10. 반면에/있었다/두드러진 감소가/CDs 비용에 있어/19% 차이로 45%부터/2년에 걸쳐서

11. Other sources 비용은/거의 변화가 없었다/2년 후

Answer

1. The pie charts compare spending patterns in the UK concerning music: CDs, concerts, digital downloads and other sources, in 2010 and 2012.

2. It is measured as a percentage.

3. As an overall trend, it is clear that digital downloads became more common than the other items, while CDs sales presented a relative drop.

4. The first data is for 2010, where it can be seen that the majority of expenditure was on CDs, accounting for 45%, which was followed by digital downloads, standing at just over a quarter.

5. Two categories, digital downloads and concerts, experienced almost similar figures at 28% and 25% respectively.

6. The least amount spent was labeled as 'others sources' at just 3%.

7. Two years later, the order of the four categories changed.

8. Digital purchase overtook buying CDs,

9. , and it increased to the most significant spending at 43%,

10. , whereas there was a marked decrease in CDs expenditure by 19% from 45% over 2 years.

11. The other sources spending had few changes after two years.

Task 1

You should spend about 20 minutes on this task.

The charts show the distribution of money spent on music in two different years in the UK.

Summarize the information by selecting and reporting the main features, and make comparisons where relevant.

Write at least 150 words.

Answer

The pie charts compare spending patterns in the UK concerning music: CDs, concerts, digital downloads and other sources, in 2010 and 2012. It is measured as a percentage. As an overall trend, it is clear that digital downloads became more common than the other items, while CD sales showed a relative drop.

The first data is for 2010, where it can be seen that the majority of expenditure was on CDs, accounting for 45%, which was followed by digital downloads, standing at just over a quarter. Two categories, digital downloads categories and concerts, experienced almost similar figures at 28% and 25% respectively. The least amount spent was labeled as 'other sources' at just 3%.

Two years later, the order of the four categories changed. Digital purchase overtook buying CDs, and it increased to the most significant spending at 43%, whereas there was a marked decrease in CDs expenditure by 19% from 45% over 2 years. The other sources spending had few changes after two years.

5. Bar graph 1

You should spend about 20 minutes on this task.

The bar chart shows the typical weekday of students in three different countries.

Summarize the information by selecting and reporting the main features, and make comparisons where relevant.

Write at least 150 words.

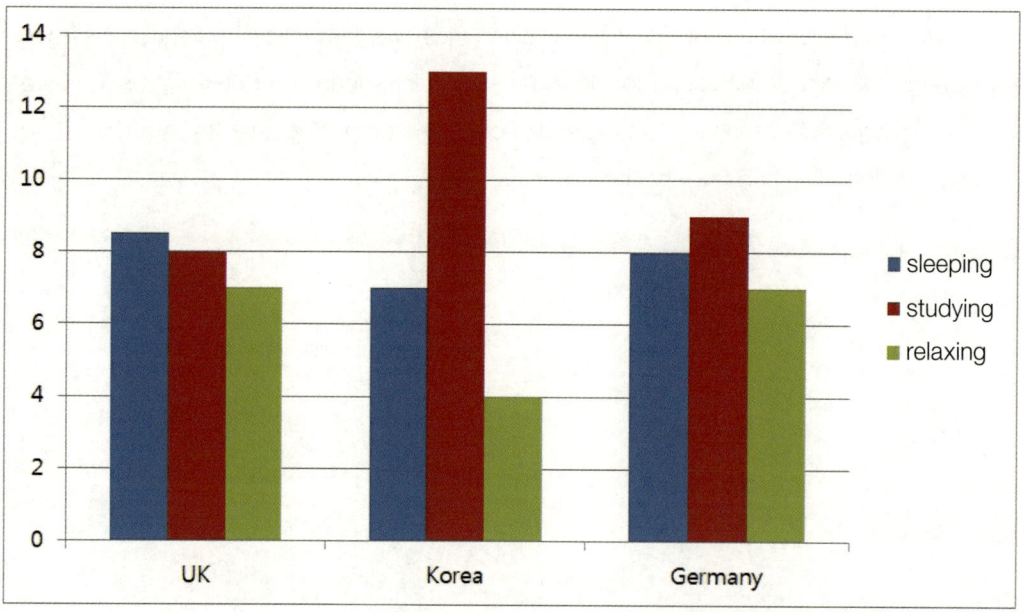

구조

> **Introduction:** 문제 paraphrase
> **Overall trend:** 독일과 영국은 비슷한 통계/반면에 한국학생은 공부에 더 집중한다.

> **Body 1. In detail**
>   1. 공부에 관하여
>   2. 수면에 관하여
>   3. 휴식에 관하여

INTRODUCTION

주어진 바 차트는 영국, 한국 그리고 독일 세 나라 학생들의 주중 일상적인 24시간에 대한 분석을 보여준다. 일반적으로, 독일과 영국의 학생들은 비슷한 통계를 가지고 있고, 반면에 한국 학생들은, 학습에 훨씬 더 집중한다.

BODY 1

가장 두드러진 특징은 한국의 학생이 공부에 사용하는 하루에 약 13시간이라는 시간의 양이다. 이것은 영국과 독일보다 각각 약 5시간, 그리고 4시간 더 길다. 수면과 관련해서, 영국과 독일 학생들 사이에 작은 차이가 있다. 영국의 학생들은 하루에 약 8.5시간의 가장 많은 시간을 잠자는 데 보낸다. 다음은 독일 학생이 8시간, 그러나 한국의 학생들은 7시간으로 잠을 덜 잔다. 휴식에 대해 말하자면, 영국과 독일 학생은 하루에 7시간을 쉬고 반면에 한국 학생들은 4시간 휴식을 갖고 이것은 주어진 항목 중에서 가장 적은 시간이다

문장에 필요한 어휘

---

1. the given(provided/supplied/presented/shown); 주어진
2. illustrate/show/give an overview of/outlines; 보여주다/설명하다
3. breakdown; 분석
4. a weekday/a workday/a business day; 평일
5. typical/ordinary/usual; 일상적인
6. namely/that is; 즉

주어진 바 차트는 영국, 한국 그리고 독일 세 나라 학생들의 주중 일상적인 24시간에 대한 분석을 보여준다.
The given bar chart illustrates the breakdown of students' regular 24 hours during weekdays in 3 different countries, namely the UK, Korea, and Germany.

---

7. in general/generally/as an overall trend/taken as a whole; 일반적으로/전체적으로 볼 때
8. it can be seen that S+V; 보여진다/볼 수 있다
9. while/whereas/whilst; 반면에
10. focus on/concentrate on/pay attention to; 집중하다

일반적으로, 독일과 영국의 학생들은 비슷한 통계를 가지고 있고, 반면에 한국 학생들은 학습에 훨씬 더 집중한다.
In general, it can be seen that students from Germany and the UK have similar statistics, while Korean students focus much more on studying.

---

11. notable/marked/striking; 두드러진
12. feature/trait/distinction; 특징
13. the amount of time; 시간의 양
14. around/about/approximately/roughly/almost; 약/대략

가장 두드러진 특징은 한국의 학생이 공부에 사용하는 하루에 약 13시간이라는 시간의 양이다.
The most notable feature is the amount of time spent studying by Korean children, with around 13 hours a day,

---

15. respectively/each; 각각

---

414 **IELTS Easy Writing**

, 이것은 영국과 독일보다 각각 약 5시간 그리고 4시간 더 길다.
, which is almost 5 hours and 4 hours longer than the UK and Germany respectively.

> **16. concerning/with regard to/regarding/with respect to; ~에 대해서**

수면과 관련해서, 영국과 독일 학생들 사이에 작은 차이가 있다.
Concerning sleeping, there is a minor difference between students in the UK and Germany.

> **17. , which is followed by/, followed by/, which leads to +N; 뒤이어/잇달아**

영국의 학생들은 하루에 약 8.5시간의 가장 많은 시간을 잠자는 데 보낸다. 다음은 독일 학생이 8시간, 그러나 한국의 학생들은 7시간으로 잠을 덜 잔다.
The UK schoolchildren spend the most time in bed, with around 8.5 hours a day, which is followed by those from Germany with 8 hours, but students in Korea have less sleeping time with only 7 hours a day.

> **18. when it comes to/in terms of/in the case of/in light of/in view of; ~에 대해 말하자면**
> **19. share/have/spend/consume; 가지다/보내다**

휴식에 대해 말하자면, 영국과 독일은 똑같이 하루에 7시간을 쉰다.
When it comes to relaxation, students from the UK and Germany take a rest for 7 hours per day,

> **20. given categories(items); 주어진 항목들**

반면에 한국에 학생들은 4시간 휴식을 갖고 이것은 주어진 항목 중에서 가장 적은 시간이다.
, whereas students in Korea have 4 hours for relaxation that is the least amount of time among provided categories.

구문연습

1. 주어진 바 차트는/분석을 보여준다/학생들의 일상적인 24시간/주중/세 개 다른 나라들에/즉 영국, 한국 그리고 독일

_____
_____

2. 일반적으로/그것은 보여진다/독일과 영국 학생은 가지고 있다/비슷한 통계를/반면에 한국 학생들은/집중한다/더 많이/공부하는 데

_____
_____

3. 가장 두드러진 특징은/공부에 보낸 시간의 양이다/한국 학생이/하루에 약 13시간

_____
_____

4. 이것은 거의 5시간 그리고 4시간이다/보다 더 긴/영국 그리고 독일/각각

_____
_____

5. 수면과 관련해서/작은 차이가 있다/영국과 독일 학생들 사이에

_____
_____

6. 영국 학생들은 보낸다/가장 많은 시간을/잠자는 데/약 8.5 시간을 하루에

_____
_____

7. 뒤이어 독일 학생들/8시간으로

_____
_____

8. 그러나 한국에 있는 학생들은/덜 수면을 가진다/7시간으로

_____
_____

9. 휴식에 대해 말하자면/학생들/영국과 독일로부터/휴식을 갖다/7시간 하루에

_____
_____

10. 반면에/한국 학생들은 갖는다/4시간을/휴식을 위해서/그것은 가장 적은 시간의 양이다/주어진 항목들 중에서

_____
_____

Answer

1. The given bar chart illustrates the breakdown of students' regular 24 hours during weekdays in 3 different countries, namely the UK, Korea, and Germany.

2. In general, it can be seen that students from Germany and the UK have similar statistics, while Korean students focus much more on studying.

3. The most notable feature is the amount of time spent studying by Korean children, with around 13hours a day,

4. , which is almost 5 hours and 4 hours longer than the UK and Germany respectively.

5. Concerning sleeping, there is a minor difference between students in the UK and Germany.

6. The UK schoolchildren spend the most time in bed, with around 8.5 hours a day,

7. , which is followed by those from Germany with 8 hours,

8. , but students in Korea have less sleeping time with only 7 hours a day.

9. When it comes to relaxation, students from the UK and Germany take a rest for 7 hours per day,

10. , whereas students in Korea have 4 hours for relaxation that is the least amount of time among provided categories.

You should spend about 20 minutes on this task.

The bar chart shows the typical weekday for students in three different countries.

Summarize the information by selecting and reporting the main features, and make comparisons where relevant.

Write at least 150 words.

Answer

The given bar chart illustrates the breakdown of students' regular 24 hours during weekdays in 3 different countries, namely the UK, Korea, and Germany. In general, it can be seen that students from Germany and the UK have similar statistics, while Korean students focus much more on studying.

The most notable feature is the amount of time spent studying by Korean children, with around 13 hours a day, which is almost 5 hours and 4hours longer than the UK and Germany respectively. Concerning sleeping, there is a minor difference between students in the UK and Germany. The UK schoolchildren spend the most time in bed, with around 8.5 hours a day, which is followed by those from Germany with 8 hours, but students in Korea have less sleeping time with only 7 hours. When it comes to relaxation, students from the UK and Germany take a rest for 7 hours per day, whereas students in Korea have 4 hours for relaxation that is the least amount of time among provided categories.

6. Bar graph 2

You should spend about 20 minutes on this task.

The bar chart shows the yearly expenditure in pounds of family in the UK on three goods from 2000 to 2003

Summarize the information by selecting and reporting the main features, and make comparisons where relevant.

Write at least 150 words.

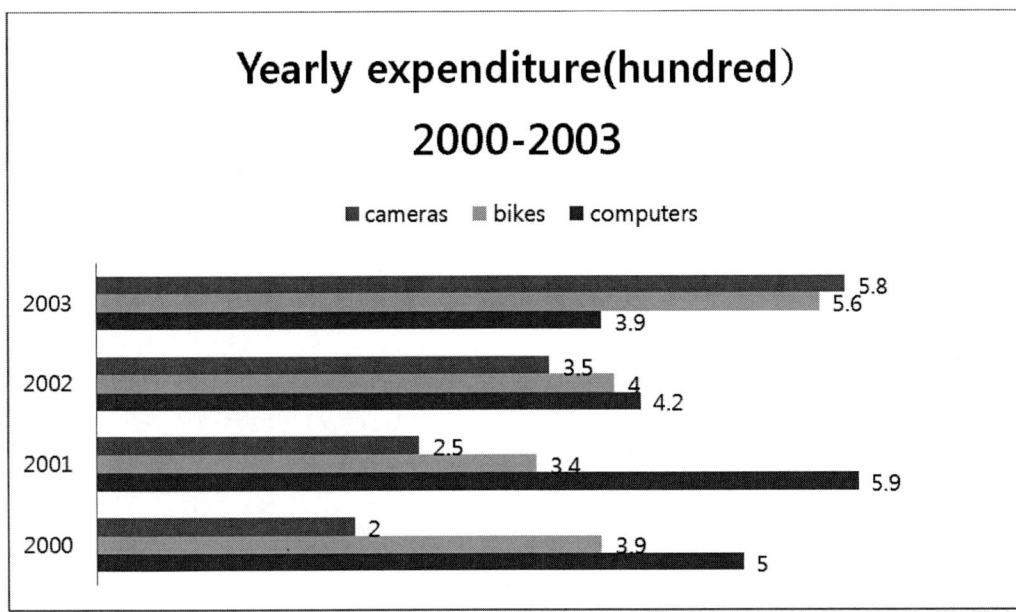

구조

Introduction: 문제 paraphrase
overall trend: 카메라 구입에 대한 비용이 꾸준히 증가

Body 1 - computers - 2001년 최고 지출 후 계속 감소

Body 2 - bikes - 2001년 이후 증가추세(2001년 약간 하락)

Body 3 - cameras - 2000년 최저 지출 - 계속 증가 추세

INTRODUCTION

주어진 막대 그래프는 2000년부터 2003년까지 컴퓨터, 자전거 그리고 카메라에 사용된 영국 가족의 일년간의 금액에 대한 정보를 제공하고 있다. 전반적인 경향으로서, 카메라에 쓰는 비용이 주어진 기간 동안 꾸준히 증가하고 있는 것으로 보여진다.

BODY 1

세부적으로, 2000년에 컴퓨터에 대한 비용은 500파운드였다. 비록 그것은 다음 해에 주어진 기간 동안 가장 많은 비용으로서 다음 해에 590파운드로 증가했지만, 2003년에 390파운드로 컴퓨터 비용 중에서 가장 적은 비용을 차지했다.

BODY 2

자전거에 대해 말하자면, 그것은 컴퓨터 비용과 다른 구성을 보였다. 그것은 기간 초반에 390파운드로 시작했고 전년대비 340파운드까지 약간의 하락과 함께 마지막 연도에 560파운드 증가로 이어졌다.

BODY 3

카메라는 2000년에 200파운드로 가장 적은 양의 지출을 차지했으나, 그것은 매년 증가했고 마지막 연도에는 580파운드로 많이 상승했다. 그것은 4년 동안에 3가지 상품 중에서 두 번째로 많은 지출이다.

문장에 필요한 어휘

1. give information about/illustrate/explain/present/show; 정보를 주다/보여주다
2. the amount of money; 금액/액수

주어진 막대 그래프는 2000년부터 2003년까지 컴퓨터, 자전거 그리고 카메라에 사용된 영국 가족의 일년간의 금액에 대한 정보를 제공하고 있다.

The given bar graph provides information about the amount of money spent on computers, bikes, and cameras by an English family per year between 2000 and 2003.

3. as an overall trend/in general/generally; 전반적으로
4. it can be seen that V+S; 보여진다
5. spending/expenditure/expense/budget; 비용/예산
6. steady/constant; 꾸준한
7. increase/rise/jump/growth/upsurge/increment; 증가
8. over the given period/during the given period; 주어진 기간 동안

전반적인 경향으로써, 카메라에 쓰는 비용이 주어진 기간 동안 꾸준히 증가하고 있는 것으로 보여진다.

As an overall trend, it can be seen that spending on cameras revealed a steady increase over the given period.

9. in detail/in particular; 자세히

세부적으로, 2000년에 컴퓨터에 대한 비용은 500파운드였다.

In detail, expenditure on computers was at £500 per year in 2000.

10. the following month/next month; 다음달
11. item/product/goods; 상품/물건

비록 그것은 다음 해에 주어진 기간 동안 가장 많은 비용으로서 다음 해에 590파운드로 증가했지만,

Although it presented an increment to £590 in the following year as the most significant spending among the given items over the period,

> 12. account for/make up/make over/have/take up/represent/occupy; 차지하다

2003년에 390파운드로 컴퓨터 비용 중에서 가장 적은 비용을 차지했다.
it then accounted for the lowest expenditure of computers at £390 in the year 2003.

> 13. when it comes to/in terms of/in the case of/in light of; ~에 대해 말하자면
> 14. appear to; 보인다

자전거에 대해 말하자면, 그것은 컴퓨터 비용과 다른 구성을 보였다.
When it comes to bikes, it appeared to follow a different pattern from computer spending.

> 15. at the beginning of the period; 초기에
> 16. at the end of the period; 마지막 기간에
> 17. which led to/which was followed by/followed by; 이어지다
> 18. slight/small/gradual; 약간의
> 19. year-on-year/over last year; 전년대비

그것은 초기에 390파운드로 시작했고 전년대비 340파운드까지 약간의 하락과 함께 마지막 연도에 560파운드 증가로 이어졌다.
It started at £390 at the beginning of the period, which led to an increase to £560 at the end of the period with a slight fall to £340 year-on-year.

> 20. jump to/soar to/rocket to/increase to/rise to; ~로 증가하다
> 21. every year/each year/annually; 매년
> 22. in the final year/in the last year; 마지막 연도에

반면에, 2001년에 200파운드로 가장 적은 비용을 차지했으나 그것은 매년 증가했고 마지막 연도에는 580파운드로 많이 상승했다.
Meanwhile, cameras made up the least amount of expenses at £200 in 2000, but this rose every year and jumped to £580 in the final year,

> 23. the second largest spending; 두 번째로 많은 지출

그것은 4년 동안에 3가지 상품 중에서 두 번째로 많은 지출이다.
, which was the second largest spending amongst three items for four years.

구문연습

1. 주어진 막대 그래프는/정보를 제공하고 있다/사용된 금액에 대한/컴퓨터, 자전거 그리고 카메라에/영국가정에서 의해/일년간/2000년부터 2003년까지

_____
_____

2. 전반적인 경향으로/그것은 보여진다/카메라에 쓴 비용이/꾸준한 증가했다/주어진 기간 동안

_____
_____

3. 세부적으로/컴퓨터에 대한 비용은/500파운드였다/2000년에

_____
_____

4. 비록 그것은 제시했지만/590파운드까지 증가를/다음달에/가장 많은 비용으로써/주어진 상품들 중에/기간에 걸쳐

_____
_____

5. 그것은 차지했다/가장 적은 비용/컴퓨터의/390파운드로/2003년에

_____
_____

6. 자전거에 대해 말하자면/그것은 따르는 것을 보였다/다른 구성을/컴퓨터 비용과

_____
_____

7. 그것은 시작했다/390파운드로/초기에/그것은 이어졌다/560파운드의 증가로/마지막 연도에/약간의 하락과 함께/340파운드까지/전년 대비/

8. 반면에, 카메라는 차지했다/가장 적은 양의 지출/200파운드/2001년에/그러나 이것은 증가했다/매년 그리고 580파운드로 상승했다/마지막 연도에

9. 이것은 두 번째로 많은 지출이다/3가지 상품 중에서/4년동안

> **Answer**
>
> 1. The given bar graph provides information about the amount of money spent on computers, bikes, and cameras by English family per year between 2000 and 2003.
> 2. As an overall trend, it can be seen that spending on cameras revealed a steady increase over the given period.
> 3. In detail, expenditure on computers was at £500 per year in 2000.
> 4. Although it presented an increase to £590 in the following year as the most significant spending among the given items over the period,
> 5. it then accounted for the lowest expenditure at £390 in the year 2003.
> 6. When it comes to bikes, it appeared to follow a different pattern from computer spending.
> 7. It started at £390 at the beginning of the period, which led to an increment to £560 at the end of the period with a slight fall to £340 year-on-year.
> 8. Meanwhile, cameras made up the least amount of expenses at £200 in 2000, but this rose every year and jumped to £580 in the final year.
> 9. , which was the second largest spending amongst three items for four years.

You should spend about 20 minutes on this task.

The bar chart shows the yearly expenditure in pounds of family in the UK on three goods from 2000 and 2004

Summarize the information by selecting and reporting the main features, and make comparisons where relevant.

Write at least 150 words.

Answer

The given bar graph provides information about the amount of money spent on computers, bikes, and cameras by an English family per year between 2000 and 2003. As an overall trend, it can be seen that spending on cameras revealed a steady increase over the given period.

In detail, expenditure on computers was at £500 per year in 2000. Although it presented an increase to £590 in the following year as the most significant spending figure among the given items over the period, it then accounted for the lowest expenditure at £390 in the year 2003.

When it comes to bikes, it appeared to follow a different pattern from computer spending. It started at £390 at the beginning of the period, which led to an increment to £560 at the end of the period with a slight fall to £340 year-on-year.

Meanwhile, cameras made up the least amount of expenses at £200 in 2000, but this rose every year and jumped to £580 in the final year, which was the second largest spending amongst three items for four years.

7. Table 1

You should spend about 20 minutes on this task.

> **The table gives information about the average hours spent on the Internet by Australians of different age groups in 2012.**
>
> Summarize the information by selecting and reporting the main features, and make comparisons where relevant.

Write at least 150 words.

Age(years)	Male	Female
11-15	8	6
16-20	19	18
21-25	7	5
26-30	4	4
31-50	3	4
51+	2	3

구조

Introduction: 문제 paraphrase
Overall trend: 16~20 연령대에서 인터넷 사용시간이 가장 많다.

Body 1 - 가장 긴 인터넷 사용 그룹 16~20
 11~15 그룹과 비교

Body 2 - 20살 이상 여성 남성그룹- 인터넷 시간이 줄어 든다.

NTRODUCTION

주어진 테이블은 2012년 호주에서 다양한 연령그룹이 인터넷에서 보내는 주 평균시간을 분석한다. 전반적으로 16세에서 20세의 연령대는 두 성별 모두에서 가장 많은 인터넷 사용시간을 보이고 있다.

BODY 1

주어진 데이터의 가장 두드러진 특징으로 인터넷 사용은 16세에서 20세 사이 연령대가 가장 길었다. 남성은 19시간, 그리고, 여성은 한 시간 적은 수치를 보이고 있다. 이러한 수치는 11세와 15세인 이전 연령대의 분류와 비교할 때, 여성은 세 배의 증가를 보여줬고 남자인 경우 거의 두 배였다.

BODY 2

21세 이상부터, 호주인들이 인터넷상에서 사용하는 평균시간이 급격하게 줄었다. 26-30 사이의 연령대는 남성과 여성이 4시간으로 같은 시간의 양을 온라인에서 보냈다. 그 이후, 여성은 남성보다 온라인상에서 조금 길게 보냈다. 남은 두 항목은 남성은 3시간에서 2시간으로 감소했고 여성은 4시간에서 3시간으로 각각 감소했다.

문장에 필요한 어휘

> 1. the provided(given/shown/presented) table; 주어진 테이블은
> 2. give a breakdown of/give information about/outline; 분석한다
> 3. the median number of weekly hours/the average number of hours per week; 주 평균시간 수

주어진 테이블은 2012년 호주에서 다양한 연령 그룹이 인터넷에서 보내는 주 평균시간을 분석한다.

The provided table gives a breakdown of the median number of weekly hours for various age groups spending time on the Internet in Australia in the year 2012.

> 4. overall/in general/generally/as an overall trend/taken as a whole; 전반적으로
> 5. it can be seen that S+V; 보여진다/볼 수 있다.

전반적으로 16세에서 20세의 연령대는 두 성별 모두에서 가장 긴 인터넷 사용시간을 보이고 있다.

Overall, it can be seen that the age range from 16 to 20 showed the most considerable amount of time on the Internet for both genders.

> 6. the most marked(striking/remarkable) feature; 가장 두드러진 특징
> 7. the figure for/the data of; ~에 대한 수치

주어진 데이터의 가장 두드러진 특징으로 인터넷 사용은 16세에서 20세 사이 사람들이 가장 길었다. 남성은 19시간, 여성은 한 시간 적은 수치를 보이고 있다.

The most marked feature of the given data was that the Internet usage was the highest for those aged between 16 and 20, with the figure for men being 19 hours and women being just one hour less.

> 8. represent/indicate/present/show/reveal/uncover; 보여주다
> 9. three-fold/triple; 세 배의
> 10. as compared with/compared to/in comparison with; ~와 비교하여

이러한 수치는 11세와 15세인 이전 연령대의 분류와 비교할 때, 여성은 세 배의 증가 그리고 남성은 거의 두 배였다.

These numbers represented a three-fold increase for women and nearly doubled for men as compared with the previous age category, which was the group aged between 11 and 15 years old.

> 11. reduce/diminish/cut back on/cut down on/down; 줄이다

21세 이상부터, 호주인들이 인터넷상에서 사용하는 평균 시간이 급격하게 줄었다.
From 21 years old onwards, the average time that Australians spent on the Internet dramatically declined.

> 12. the amount of time; 시간의 양

26세에서 30세 사이의 연령대 남성과 여성은 온라인상에서 4시간으로 똑같은 시간의 양을 사용했다.
By the ages of 26 to 30 years, males and females spent the same amount of time online with 4 hours each,

> 13. after which/following which; 그 이후
> 14. slightly/marginally/moderately/simply; 조금/약간

그 이후, 여성은 남성보다 온라인상에서 조금 길게 보냈다.
after which females spent slightly longer online than males.

> 15. category/type/item; 항목/분류

남은 두 항목은 남성은 3시간에서 2시간으로 감소했고 여성들은 4시간에서 3시간으로 각각 감소했다.
The remaining two categories fall to only 3 and 2 hours for men and 4 and 3 hours for women respectively.

구문연습

1. 주어진 테이블은 분석한다/주 평균시간을/다양한 연령그룹이/시간을 보내는/인터넷상에서/호주에서/2012년에

2. 전반적으로/보여진다/16세에서 20세의 연령대는/가장 많은 시간/인터넷상에서/두 성별

3. 가장 두드러진 특징은/주어진 데이터 중에서/인터넷 사용은 가장 길다/사람들/연령대인 16세에서 20세/19시간의 남성수치와 1시간 적은 여성

4. 이 수치들은 보여줬다/세 배의 증가를/여성에 있어/거의 두 배였다/남성에 있어서/그전 연령의 분류와 비교하여/이러한 것은 /연령대 그룹/11세와 15세 사이의

5. 21세 이상부터/평균시간/호주인들은 보냈다/시간을/인터넷상에서/급격하게/줄었다

6. 26세에서 30세 사이/남성들과 여성들은 사용했다/같은 시간의 양을/온라인에서/4시간으로 각각

7. 그 이후/여성은 보냈다/조금 더 긴/온라인에서/남성보다

8. 남은 두 항목은 감소했다/단지 3시간에서 2시간으로/남자들에게 있어/그리고 4시간에서 3시간으로/여성들에게 각각

> **Answer**
>
> 1. The provided table gives a breakdown of the median number of weekly hours for various age groups spending time on the Internet in Australia in the year 2012.
> 2. Overall, it can be seen that the age range from 16 to 20 showed the most considerable amount of time on the Internet for both genders.
> 3. The most marked feature of the given data was that the Internet usage was at the highest for those aged between 16 and 20, with the figure for men being 19 hours and women being just one hour less.
> 4. These numbers represented a three-fold increase for women nearly doubled for males as compared with the previous age category, which was the group aged between 11 and 15 years old.
> 5. From 21 years old onwards, the average time that Australians spent on the Internet dramatically declined.
> 6. By the ages of 26 to 30 years, males and females spent the same amount of time online with 4 hours each,
> 7. after which females spent slightly longer online than males.
> 8. The remaining two categories fall to only 3 and 2 hours for men and 4 and 3 hours for women respectively.

You should spend about 20 minutes on this task.

The table gives information about the average hours spent on the Internet by Australians of different age groups in 2012.

Summarize the information by selecting and reporting the main features, and make comparisons where relevant.

Write at least 150 words.

Answer

The provided table gives a breakdown of the median number of weekly hours for various age groups spending time on the Internet in Australia in the year 2012. Overall, it can be seen that the age range from 16 to 20 showed the most considerable amount of time on the Internet for both genders.

The most marked feature of the given data was that the Internet usage was the highest for those aged between 16 and 20, with the figure for men being 19 hours and women being just one hour less. These numbers represented a three-fold increase for women and nearly doubled for men as compared with the previous age category, which was the group aged between 11 and 15 years old.

From 21 years old onwards, the average time that Australians spent on the Internet dramatically declined. By the ages of 26 to 30 years, males and females spent the same amount of time online with 4 hours each, after which females spent slightly longer online than males. The remaining two categories fall to only 3 and 2 hours for men and 4 and 3 hours for women respectively.

8. Table 2

You should spend about 20 minutes on this task.

> **The table shows the figures for imprisonment in five countries from 1960 to 2010**
>
> Summarize the information by selecting and reporting the main features, and make comparisons where relevant.

Write at least 150 words.

(The data of the number of prisoners)

	1960	1970	1980	1990	2000	2010
Great Britain	35,000	35,000	40,000	50,000	65,000	82,000
Australia	70,000	50,000	43,000	60,000	65,000	50,000
New Zealand	100,000	54,000	52,000	62,000	65,000	83,000
United states	100,000	130,000	120,000	118,000	95,000	137,000
Canada	120,000	110,000	115,000	100,000	82,000	85,000

구조

> Introduction: 문제 paraphrase
> Overall trend: 1960년 캐나다가 가장 많은 수감자를 가졌음/2010년은 그 수치가 줄어들고 반면에 미국이 가장 많은 수감자들을 보유하고 있음.

> Body 1 - 1960년 분석
>   영국/호주 수감자 분석

> Body 2 - 뉴질랜드/미국/캐나다 분석

INTRODUCTION

주어진 테이블은 영국, 호주, 뉴질랜드, 미국 그리고 캐나다의 5개 국가의 수감자들의 수에 대한 데이터를 1960년에 시작해서 50년에 걸쳐서 분석하고 있다. 전반적인 경향으로서, 캐나다는 1960년에 가장 높은 수치를 가졌다. 반면에 캐나다에서 2010년에 전체 수감자의 수가 떨어졌고 미국이 가장 상당한 수감자들을 가지고 있었다.

BODY 1

상세하게, 1960년에 캐나다는 120,000명의 수감자가 있는데 그것은 주어진 국가들 중에서 가장 많은 수치이다. 미국과 뉴질랜드는 100,000으로서 같은 수치를 가지고 있다. 반면에 영국은 35,000을 가지고 있고 그것은 가장 낮은 수치이다. 10년 이내에 영국에서의 수감자의 수는 같은 수치를 가지고 있고 2010년에 82,000까지 꾸준히 증가하고 있다. 호주에 대해 말하자면 1980년에 데이터는 43,000으로 주어진 기간 동안 가장 낮은 수치를 보이고 있고 2010년에 50,000 수감자들이 기록되고 있다. 이것은 다섯 국가 중에서 가장 적은 수치를 나타냈다.

BODY 2

뉴질랜드에 대해 말하자면, 수감자의 수치는 1960년부터 20년에 걸쳐 48,000이 감소했다. 그러나 다음의 30년 동안 상향경향을 보였고 2010년에는 83,000에 이르렀다. 가장 흥미로운 것은, 미국은 1970년과 2010년 130,000과 137,000으로 각각 1980년에서 2000년 사이의 약간의 하락과 함께 가장 높은 수치를 가지고 있었다. 캐나다는 약간의 변동의 특징을 가지고 있으나 수감의 수치는 마지막 연도에 85,000으로 떨어졌다.

문장에 필요한 어휘

> 1. give a breakdown of/give information about/illustrate; 분석하다/설명하다
> 2. the number of 복수명사+단수동사; ~의 수
> 3. prisoner/prison inmate; 수감자

주어진 테이블은 영국, 호주, 뉴질랜드, 미국 그리고 캐나다의 5개 국가의 수감자들의 수에 대한 데이터를 1960년에 시작해서 50년에 걸쳐 분석하고 있다.

The provided table gives a breakdown of the data on the number of prisoners in five countries, Great Britain, Australia, New Zealand, the US and Canada, over a 50 year period starting in 1960.

> 4. as an overall trend/overall trend/in general/generally; 전반적 경향으로서/전반적으로
> 5. it can be seen that S+V; 보여진다

전반적인 경향으로서, 캐나다는 1960년에 가장 높은 수치를 가졌다.

As an overall trend, it can be seen that Canada had the largest number of prisoners initially in 1960,

> 6. while/whereas/whilst; 반면에
> 7. the largest number of; 가장 큰 수치

반면에 캐나다에서 2010년에 전체 수감자의 수가 떨어졌고 미국이 가장 상당한 수감자들을 가지고 있었다.

, while in 2010 the number of total prisoners fell in Canada and the United States had the most significant number of inmates.

> 8. in detail/in particular; 상세히

상세하게, 1960년에 캐나다는 120,000명의 수감자가 있는데 그것은 주어진 국가들 중에서 가장 많은 수치이다.

In detail, in the year 1960, there were 120,000 inmates in Canada, which was the greatest number of the given countries.

> 9. figure/data/numbers; 수치

미국과 뉴질랜드는 100,000으로서 같은 수치를 가지고 있다. 반면에 영국은 35,000을 가지고 있고 그것은 가장 낮은 수치이다.

The United States and New Zealand had the same figure with 100,000, whereas Great Britain had only 35,000 and that was the lowest number.

> 10. which was followed by/followed by/which led to+N; 이어지다
> 11. a constant(steady) increase(rise/growth); 꾸준한 증가

10년 이내에 영국에서의 수감자의 수는 같은 수치를 가지고 있고, 2010년에 82,000명까지 꾸준히 증가하고 있다.

In a decade, the number of prisoners in Britain showed the same figure, which was followed by a constant increase to 82,000 in 2010.

> 12. concerning/in terms of/in light of/when it comes to/~에 관한 한/말하자면

호주에 대해 말하자면 1980년에 데이터는 43,000으로 주어진 기간 동안 가장 낮은 수치를 보이고 있다.

Concerning Australia, in 1980, the data presented the lowest number of prisoners with 43,000 during the given period.

> 13. record/show/indicate/present; 기록되다/나타내다

2010년에 50,000 수감자들이 기록되고 있다. 이것은 다섯 국가 중에서 가장 적은 수치를 나타냈다.

In 2010, 50,000 prisoners were recorded, which showed the smallest figure among five countries.

> 14. the figure for/the data of; ~에 대한 수치
> 15. decrease/decline/fall/go down/drop/lessen; 감소하다

뉴질랜드에 대해 말하자면, 수감자의 수치는 1960년부터 20년에 걸쳐 48,000이 감소했다.

When it comes to New Zealand, the figure for prisoners decreased by 48,000 over 20 years from 1960,

> 16. an upward trend/an upward tendency/a tendency to rise; 상향 경향
> 17. result in/come to/account for/make up/make over/take up; 이르다/차지하다

그러나 다음 30년 동안 상향경향을 보였고 2010년에는 83,000에 이르렀다.
, but there was an upward trend for the following 30 years, resulting in 83,000 in 2010.

> 18. most interestingly; 가장 흥미로운 것은
> 19. respectively/each; 각각

가장 흥미로운 것은, 미국은 1970년과 2010년에 130,000과 137,000으로 각각 1980년에서 2000년 사이의 약간의 하락과 함께 가장 높은 수치를 가지고 있었다.
Most interestingly, the United States had the largest number of prisoners in 1970 and 2010 with 130,000 and 137,000 respectively, with a slight fall from 1980 to 2000.

> 20. feature; 특징을 가지다
> 21. imprisonment/confinement; 수감/감금
> 22. in the final year; 마지막 연도

캐나다는 약간의 변동의 특징을 가지고 있으나 수감의 수치는 마지막 연도에 85,000으로 떨어졌다.
Canada featured a small fluctuation, but its data of imprisonment dropped to 85,000 in the final year.

구문연습

1. 주어진 테이블은/분석하고 있다/데이터를/수감자들의 수에 대한/5개국/영국, 호주, 뉴질랜드, 미국 그리고 캐나다/지난 50년에 걸쳐서/시작으로 1960년에

2. 전반적인 경향으로서/그것은 보여진다/캐나다는 가지고 있었다/가장 많은 수감자들의 수를/처음에 1960년/

3. 반면에 2010년에/전체 수감자들의 수는/떨어졌다/캐나다에서/그리고 미국은 가졌다/가장 상당한 수감자들의 수를

4. 상세하게/1960년에/120,000명 있었다/캐나다에/그것은 가장 많은 수치이다/주어진 국가들 중에

5. 미국과 뉴질랜드는/100,000의 똑같은 수를 가지고 있었다/반면에 영국은 가지고 있다/단지 35,000 그리고 그것은 가장 적은 수이다

6. 10년 내에/수감자의 수는/영국에서/보여주고 있다/같은 수치를/이어서 꾸준한 증가가 있다/82,000명까지/2010년에

7. 호주에 대해 말하자면/1980년에/데이터는 보여줬다/43,000의 가장 낮은 수감자들의 수치를/주어진 기간 동안

_____
_____

8. 그리고 2010년에/50,000의 수감자들이 기록되었고/이것은 가장 적은 수치를 나타냈다/5개국 중에서

_____
_____

9. 뉴질랜드에 대해 언급하자면/수감자의 수치는/48,000 차이로 감소했다/20년에 걸쳐서/1960년부터

_____
_____

10. 그러나/상승추세가 있었다/다음의 30년 동안/2010년에 83,000으로 되었다

_____
_____

11. 가장 흥미로운 것은/미국은 가장 큰 수를 가졌다/1970년과 2010년에 130,000과 137,000으로 각각/약간의 감소와 함께 1980년부터 2000년까지

_____
_____

12. 캐나다는 특징을 가지고 있다/약간의 변동을/그러나 그 수감에 대한 수치는 떨어졌다/85,000까지/마지막 연도에

_____
_____

Answer

1. The provided table gives a breakdown of the data on the number of prisoners in five countries, Great Britain, Australia, New Zealand, the US, and Canada, for over a 50 year period starting in 1960.

2. As an overall trend, it can be seen that Canada had the highest number of prisoners initially in 1960,

3. , while in 2010, the number of total prisoners fell in Canada, and the United States had the most significant number of inmates.

4. In detail, in the year 1960, there were 120,000 inmates in Canada, which was the highest number of the given countries.

5. The United States and New Zealand had the same figure with 100,000, whereas Great Britain had only 35,000 and that was the lowest number.

6. In a decade, the number of prisoners in Britain showed the same figure, which was followed by a constant increase to 82000 in 2010.

7. Concerning Australia, in 1980, the data presented the lowest number of prisoners with 43,000 during the given period,

8. , and in 2010, 50,000 prisoners were recorded, which showed the smallest data among five countries.

9. When it comes to New Zealand, the figure for prisoners decreased by 48,000 over 20 years from 1960,

10. , but there was an upward trend for the following 30 years, resulting in 83,000 in 2010.

11. Most interestingly, the United States had the largest number of prisoners in 1970 and 2010 with 130,000 and 137,000 respectively, with a slight fall from 1980 to 2000.

12. Canada featured a small fluctuation, but its data of imprisonment dropped to 85,000 in the final year.

You should spend about 20 minutes on this task.

The table shows the figures for imprisonment in five countries from 1960 to 2010

Summarize the information by selecting and reporting the main features, and make comparisons where relevant.

Write at least 150 words.

Answer

The provided table gives a breakdown of the data on the number of prisoners in five countries, Great Britain, Australia, New Zealand, the US, and Canada, over a 50 year period starting in 1960. As an overall trend, it can be seen that Canada had the highest number of prisoners initially in 1960, while in 2010, the number of total prisoners fell in Canada, and the United States had the most significant number of inmates.

In detail, in the year 1960, there were 120,000 inmates in Canada, which was the highest number of the given countries. The United States and New Zealand had the same figure with 100,000, whereas Great Britain had only 35,000 and that was the lowest number. In a decade, the number of prisoners in Britain showed the same figure, which was followed by a constant increase to 82000 in 2010. Concerning Australia, in 1980, the data presented the lowest number of prisoners with 43,000 during the given period, and in 2010, 50,000 prisoners were recorded, which showed the smallest data among five countries.

When it comes to New Zealand, the figure for inmates decreased by 48,000 over 20 years from 1960, but there was an upward trend for the following 30 years, resulting in 83,000 in 2010. Most interestingly, the United States had the largest number of prisoners in 1970 and 2010 with 130,000 and 137,000 respectively, with a slight fall from 1980 to 2000. Canada featured a small fluctuation, but its data of imprisonment dropped to 85,000 in the final year.

9. Line+Pie

You should spend about 20 minutes on this task.

> The line graph and pie charts show the cost of watching movies and the change of market share in three forms each in Australia from 2008 to 2014.
>
> Summarize the information by selecting and reporting the main features, and make comparisons where relevant.

Write at least 150 words.

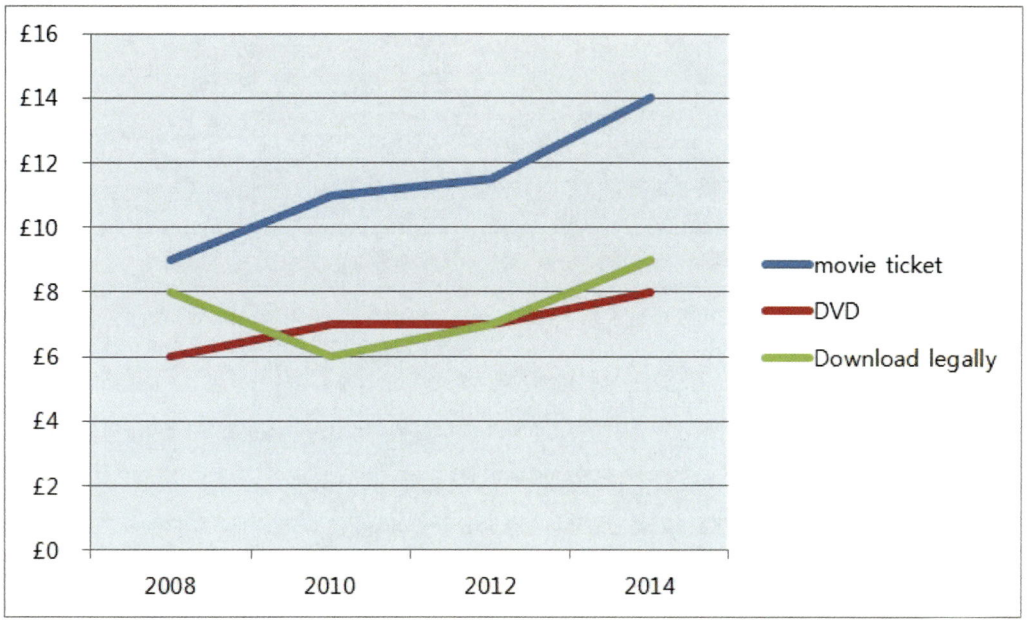

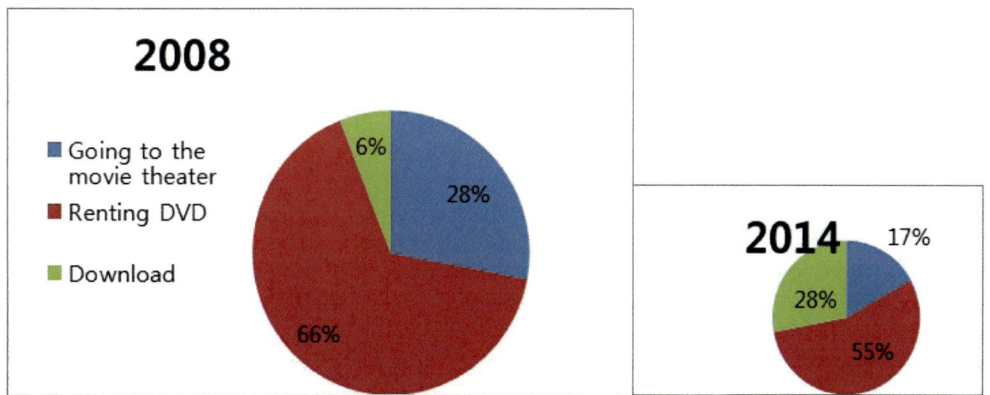

구조

> **Introduction:** 문제 paraphrase
> **Overall trend:** 영화에 대한 비용이 증가/대부분 사람들이 DVD를 선호

> **Body 1** - Line graph에 대한 설명: 모든 항목이 상승 추세
> 　　　　　세 가지 항목 자세히 설명

> **Body 2** - Pie chart에 대한 설명
> 　　　　　2008년 기준으로 해서 증감을 표시

INTRODUCTION

주어진 그래프와 파이차트는 2008년부터 6년에 걸쳐 호주 사람들이 선택하는 세 가지 다른 형태의 시장변화뿐만 아니라 영화를 보는 비용에 대해 알려주고 있다. 일반적으로, 세 가지 형태에서 영화의 비용은 증가했고, 대부분의 사람들은 주어진 기간 동안 DVD를 선택한 것으로 보여진다.

BODY 1

비용측면에서 가장 두드러지는 경향은 영화 티켓에 대한 비용이 6년간에 걸쳐서 가장 큰 수치를 보여주고 있는 것이고 2008년 £9에서 2014년에 £14까지 증가했다. DVD에 대한 가격은 £6로 시작했고 2008년에 가장 낮은 수치이다. 그러나 2년 이내에 다운로드의 가격을 앞질렀다. 그리고 그것은 거의 2년 동안 £7를 유지했고 2014년 £8까지 다시 상승했다. 다운로드 측면에서, 시작 연도의 비용은 £8였다. 그러나, 2년 후 비록 DVD 가격보다 거의 3년 동안 이하였지만, 그것은 지속적으로 상승했다. 마침내 2014년에 인터넷상에서 영화를 다운로드 하는 것은 DVD보다 더 높은 가격의 품목이 되었다.

BODY 2

2008년에, 대다수의 사람들은 DVD를 선택했는데 전체 조사된 인구의 반 이상을 훨씬 더 차지했다. 영화관을 가는 사람들은 1/3보다 낮은 수치이다. 단지 6% 만이 온라인상에서 영화를 다운로드 하는 것을 선택했다. 2014년까지 DVD, 그리고 영화관에 가는 것은 11%, 9%로 각각 감소했다. 그러나 DVD는 영화를 보는 가장 선호하는 방법이었다. 다른 한편으로, 영화를 다운로드 하는 것은 약 20%의 상당한 증가를 보였다.

문장에 필요한 어휘

> 1. the given(provided/shown/presented) graph; 주어진 그래프
> 2. give information about/give a breakdown of; 정보를 주다
> 3. B as well as A/not only A but also B; A뿐만 아니라 B도

주어진 그래프와 파이차트는 2008년부터 6년에 걸쳐 호주 사람들이 선택하는 세 가지 다른 형태의 시장 변화뿐만 아니라 영화를 보는 비용에 대해 알려주고 있다.

The given line graph and pie chart inform us about the cost of watching films as well as the change in market shares of three different forms that people prefer in Australia over 6 years from 2008.

> 4. in general/generally/overall/as an overall trend; 일반적으로
> 5. during the given period/over the given period; 주어진 기간 동안

일반적으로, 세 가지 형태에서 영화의 비용은 증가했고, 대부분의 사람들은 주어진 기간 동안 DVD를 선택한 것으로 보여진다.

In general, the movie fees increased in all three forms, but it can be seen that most people chose to rent DVDs during the given period.

> 6. the most striking(marked/remarkable) trend; 가장 두드러진 경향은
> 7. regarding/concerning/as to/as regards/with respect to; ~에 대한/관련해서
> 8. account for/make up/make over/take up/represent/occupy; ~을 차지하다
> 9. significantly/considerably/greatly/a great deal; 상당히

비용측면에서 가장 두드러지는 경향은 영화 티켓에 대한 비용이 6년간에 걸쳐서 가장 큰 수치를 보여주고 있는 것이고 2008년 £9에서 2014년에 £14까지 증가했다.

The most striking feature regarding the costs was that the expenses for cinema tickets accounted for the largest figure over 6 years, increasing significantly from about £9 in 2008 to £14 in 2014.

> 10. outpace/surpass/exceed; 앞지르다/추월하다

DVD의 £6로 시작했고 2008년에 가장 낮은 수치이다. 그러나 2년 이내에 다운로드의 가격을 앞질렀다.

The prices of DVDs started at £6, the lowest in 2008, but outpacing that of the download within two years,

> 11. remain/keep/maintain; 유지하다

그리고 그것은 거의 2년 동안 £7를 유지했고 2014년 £8까지 다시 상승했다.
, and it remained at £7 for almost 2 years, increasing again to £8 in 2014.

> 12. in light of/in terms of/when it comes to; ~측면에서
> 13. increase/rise/soar/climb/go up; 증가하다

다운로드 측면에서, 시작 연도에 비용은 £8였다. 이것은 DVD의 가격보다 높았다. 그러나 2년 후 비록 거의 3년 동안 DVD 가격 이하였지만, 그것은 지속적으로 상승했다.
In light of downloads, the cost was £8 in the starting year, which was higher than that of DVDs. However, 2 years later, it was under the price of DVDs for almost 3 years. It was rising consistently.

> 14. higher-priced; 높은 가격의

마침내 2014년도에 인터넷상에서 영화를 다운로드 하는 것은 DVD보다 더 높은 가격의 품목이 되었다.
Finally, downloading films on the Internet became a higher-priced item than DVDs in the year 2014.

> 15. the majority of people/most people/a great number of people; 대다수의 사람들
> 16. expensive/costly/pricey; 비싼

2008년에, 대다수의 사람들은 DVD를 선택했는데 전체 조사된 인구의 반 이상을 훨씬 더 차지했다. 영화관을 가는 사람들은 1/3보다 낮은 수치이다.
In 2008, the majority of people chose DVDs, accounting for well over a half of the total surveyed population, while those going to the movie theaters made up less than a third.

> 17. slide/fall/decrease/decline/go down/shrink; 감소하다/하락하다
> →slide/slid(과거)/slid(과거분사)

단지 6%만이 온라인상에서 영화를 다운로드 하는 것을 선택했다. 2014년까지 DVD 그리고 영화관에 가는 것은 11%, 9%로 각각 감소했다.
Only 6% preferred to download movies online. By 2014, DVDs and cinema sales slid by 11% and 9%, respectively.

> 18. on the other hand/but/however/on the contrary; 다른 한편으로는/그러나
> 19. considerable/significant/good/dramatic/great; 상당한

그러나 DVD가 영화를 보는 가장 선호하는 방법이었다. 다른 한편으로, 영화를 다운로드 하는 것은 약 20%의 상당한 증가를 보였다.

, but DVDs were the most preferred way of watching a movie. On the other hand, downloading movies showed a considerable rise of around 20%.

구문연습

1. 주어진 그래프와 파이차트는/알려주고 있다/우리에게/영화를 보는 비용에 대해서/뿐만 아니라/시장에서 점유율 변화/세 가지 다른 형태/사람들이 선호하다/호주에서/6년에 걸쳐/2008년부터

---

2. 일반적으로/영화비용은 증가했다/세 가지 형태 모두에서/그러나 그것은 보여질 수 있다/대부분의 사람들은 선택했다/빌리는 것을 DVD를/주어진 기간 동안

---

3. 가장 놀라운 경향은/비용과 관련해서/영화티켓에 대한 비용은/차지했다/가장 높은 수치를/6년에 걸쳐서/증가했다/상당하게/2008년부터 £9, 2014년까지 £14

---

4. DVD 가격은 £6로 시작했다/가장 낮은 2008년에/그러나 추월했다/다운로드 비용을/그리고 그것은 £7를 유지했다/거의 2년 동안/다시 £8까지 증가했다/2014년에

_____
_____

5. 다운로드 측면에서/비용은 £8였다/시작하는 연도에/더 높았다/DVD 비용보다

_____
_____

6. 그러나 2년 후/비록 그것은 DVD 가격 이하였다/거의 3년 동안/그것은 증가했다/지속적으로

_____
_____

7. 마침내/영화를 다운로드 하는 것은/인터넷상에서/되었다/높은 가격 품목이/2014년에

_____
_____

8. 2008년에/대다수의 사람들은 선호했다/DVD를/반 이상을 훨씬 더 차지했다/전체 조사된 인구의

_____
_____

9. 반면에/영화관에 간 사람은/차지했다/3분의 1이하를

_____
_____

10. 단지 6%/선호했다/영화를 다운로드를/온라인상에서

_____
_____

11. 2014년까지/DVD와 영화판매는/감소했다/11% 그리고 9% 각각/그러나/DVD는 가장 선호된 방법이었다/영화를 보는

12. 다른 한편으로는/영화를 다운로드 한 것을/보여줬다/상당한 증가를/약 20%의

Answer

1. The given line graph and pie chart inform us about the cost of watching films as well as the change in market shares of three different forms that people prefer in Australia over 6 years from 2008.
2. In general, the movie fees increased in all three forms, but it can be seen that most people chose to rent DVDs during the given period.
3. The most striking feature regarding the costs was that the expenses for cinema tickets accounted for the largest figure over 6 years, increasing significantly from about £9 in 2008 to £14 in 2014.
4. The prices of DVDs started at £6, the lowest in 2008, but outpacing that of the download within two years, and it remained at £7 for almost 2 years, increasing again to £8 in 2014.
5. In light of downloads, the cost was £8 in the starting year, which was higher than that of DVDs.
6. However, two years later, although it was under the price of DVDs for almost 3years, it was rising consistently.
7. Finally, downloading films on the Internet became a higher-priced item than DVDs in the year 2014.
8. In 2008, the majority of people chose DVDs, accounting for well over a half of the total surveyed population,
9. ,while those going to the movie theaters made up less than a third.
10. Only 6% preferred to download movies online.
11. By 2014, DVDs and cinema sales slid by 11% and 9% respectively, but DVDs were the most preferred way of watching a movie.
12. On the other hand, downloading movies showed a considerable rise of around 20%.

You should spend about 20 minutes on this task.

The line graph and pie charts show the cost of watching movies and the change of market share in three forms each in Australia from 2008 to 2014.

Summarize the information by selecting and reporting the main features, and make comparisons where relevant.

Write at least 150 words.

Answer

The given line graph and pie chart inform us about the cost of watching films as well as the change in market shares of three different forms that people prefer in Australia over 6 years from 2008. In general, the movie fees increased in all three forms, but it can be seen that most people chose to rent DVDs during the given period.

The most striking feature regarding the costs was that the expenses for cinema tickets accounted for the largest figure over six years, increasing significantly from about £9 in 2008 to £14 in 2014. The prices of DVDs started at £6, the lowest in 2008, but outpacing that of the download within two years, and it remained at £7 for almost 2 years, increasing again to £8 in 2014. In light of downloads, the cost was £8 in the starting year, which was higher than that of DVDs. However, two years later, although it was under the price of DVDs for almost 3 years, it was rising consistently. Finally, downloading films on the Internet became a higher-priced item than DVDs in the year 2014.

In 2008, the majority of people chose DVDs, accounting for well over a half of the total surveyed population, while those going to the movie theaters made up less than a third. Only 6% preferred to download movies online. By 2014, DVDs and cinema sales slid by 11% and 9% respectively, but DVDs were the most preferred way of watching a movie. On the other hand, downloading movies showed a considerable rise of around 20%.

Task 1

10. Bar+Table

You should spend about 20 minutes on this task.

> The two charts show the spending the percentage of GDP on Health & Education and indicate infant mortality and life expectancy in Brazil from 1995 to 2005.
>
> Summarize the information by selecting and reporting the main features, and make comparisons where relevant.

Write at least 150 words.

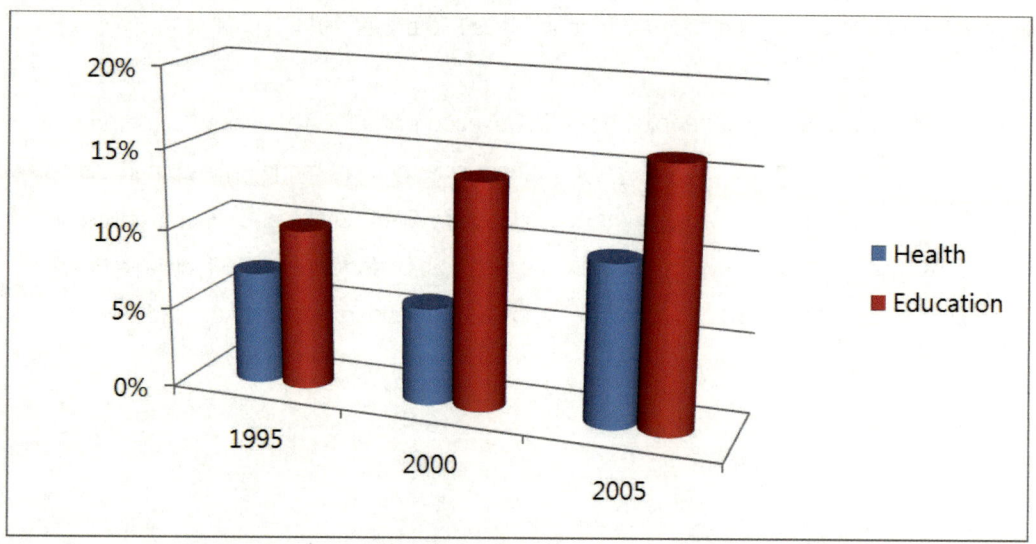

	Life expectancy(years)	Infant Mortality (per 1000 births)
1995	64	70
2005	72	20

구조

> **Introduction:** 문제 paraphrase
> **Overall trend:** 브라질의 예산은 증가했고/영아 사망률 감소/기대수명 증가

> **Body 1** - 막대 그래프: 건강과 교육분야에 지출증가

> **Body 2** - 기대수명 증가/영아 사망률 감소

INTRODUCTION

주어진 바 그래프는 1995년과 2005년 사이의 브라질에서의 건강과 교육분야에 쓰여진 GDP의 퍼센트를 분석한 것이다. 반면에 테이블은 같은 기간 동안 그 나라의 기대수명과 영아 사망률을 나타낸 것이다. 전반적인 경향으로서, 건강과 교육을 위한 예산은 증가했고 그 결과로 영아 사망률은 감소했고 기대수명은 개선된 것이 분명하다.

BODY 1

막대그래프에 관해서, 브라질이 1995년에 GDP 중에 약 6% 그리고 교육에 9%을 사용했다는 것을 볼 수 있다. 5년 후에, 건강에 대한 예산은 5%까지 조금 감소했고 반면에 교육에 대한 비용은 거의 13%까지 증가했다. 이것은 마지막 연도에 15%까지의 계속적인 증가로 이어진다. 같은 연도에 브라질 정부는 건강에 대한 지출을 GDP의 9%까지 늘렸다.

BODY 2

테이블에서 보여지는 것처럼, 증가된 건강과 교육에 대한 예산과 함께 두 가지 항목인 기대수명과 영아 사망률은 개선되었다. 브라질의 기대수명은 1995년에 64세였다. 10년 후에, 그것은 71세로 증가했다. 반면에 영아 사망률은 1,000명의 출생당 70명이었다. 그것은 10년 후에 1,000명 출생당 20명으로 상당한 감소로 이어졌다.

문장에 필요한 어휘

> 1. the provided(supplied/presented/ shown/given) graph; 주어진 그래프
> 2. give a breakdown of/give information about/illustrate/compare; 분석하다/비교하다
> 3. field/area/sector/department; 분야

주어진 바 그래프는 1995년과 2005년 사이의 브라질에서의 건강과 교육분야에 쓰여진 GDP의 퍼센트를 분석한 것이다.

The provided graph gives a breakdown of the percentage of GDP spent on health and education fields in Brazil between 1995 and 2005,

> 4. while/whereas/whilst; 반면에

반면에 테이블은 같은 기간 동안 그 나라의 기대수명과 영아 사망률을 나타낸 것이다.

, while the table illustrates the death rate of infants and the lifespan of this country over the same period.

> 5. as an overall trend/as is presented/as is observed/as a general trend/as can be seen/overall; 전반적인 경향으로서
> 6. it is clear that/it is certain that/it can be seen that/we can see that S+V; 확실하다/보여진다
> 7. budget/spending/money/finance; 예산
> 8. rise/increase/go up/soar/climb; 증가하다
> 9. decrease/fall/decline/plummet/plunge/drop/reduce; 감소하다
> 10. as a result/thus/therefore; 따라서/그래서
> 11. infant mortality rate; 영아 사망률
> 12. longevity/lifespan/life expectancy; 수명
> 13. improve/better/prolong/extend; 개선하다/연장하다

전반적인 경향으로서, 건강과 교육을 위한 예산은 증가했고 그 결과로 영아 사망률은 감소했고 기대수명은 개선되었다.

As an overall trend, it is clear that Brazil's budget for the health and education sector rose and as a result, the infant mortality rate decreased and longevity improved.

> 14. when it comes to/in terms of/in the case of/in light of; ~에 관해서는
> 15. around/about/approximately/roughly/almost; 약/대략
> 16. spend/use/put to use; 사용하다

막대그래프에 관해서, 브라질이 1995년의 GDP 중에 건강에 약 6% 그리고 교육에 9%을 사용했다는 것을 볼 수 있다.

When it comes to the bar graph, we can see that Brazil spent around 6% of its GDP on health and 9% on education in 1995.

> 17. show/present/illustrate/experience/display/represent; 나타내다
> 18. a slight (slow/mild/tedious)/fall(decrease/reduction/decline/drop); 약간의 감소
> 19. expenditure/money/expense/cost; 비용

5년 후에, 건강에 대한 예산은 5%까지 조금 감소했고 반면에 교육에 대한 비용은 거의 13%까지 증가했다.

After 5 years, the heath budget showed a slight fall to 5%, whereas the expenditure on education went up to almost 13%,

> 20. , which led to/, which was followed by/, followed by; 이어졌다
> 21. a constant(steady) increase/rise; 계속적인 증가

이것은 마지막 연도에 15%까지의 계속적인 증가로 이어진다. 같은 연도에 브라질 정부는 건강에 대한 지출을 GDP의 9%까지 늘렸다.

, which led to constant growth to around 15% in the final year. In the same year, the Brazilian government increased its spending on health to 9% of the GDP.

> 22. as is observed/as can be seen/as is presented; 보여지는 것처럼
> 23. improve/better; 개선되다/개선하다/나아지다

테이블에서 보여지는 것처럼, 증가된 건강과 교육에 대한 예산과 함께 두 가지 항목인 수명과 영아 사망률은 개선되었다. 브라질의 기대수명은 1995년에 64세였다.

As is observed from the table, with increased finances on health and education, two categories, life expectancy and infant mortality, improved. Lifespan in Brazil was 64 years in 1995.

> 24. decade; 10년
> 25. birth/childbirth; 출생/탄생

10년 후에 그것은 71세로 증가했다. 반면에 영아 사망률은 1,000명의 출생당 70명이었다.
In a decade, it soared to 71 years, whilst infant mortality rate was 70 per thousand births,

> 26. a considerable(dramatic/rapid/sharp)/drop(decrease/decline/fall); 상당한 하락/감소

그것은 10년 후에 1,000명 출생당 20명으로 상당한 감소로 이어졌다.
, which was followed by a considerable drop to 20 per thousand births after 10 years.

구문연습

1. 주어진 바 그래프는/분석한 것이다/사용된 GDP의 퍼센트를/건강과 교육에/브라질에서/1995년과 2005년에

___

2. 반면에/테이블은 설명한다/영아 사망률과 기대수명을/이 나라의/같은 기간에 걸쳐

___

3. 전반적인 경향으로서/그것은 분명하다/브라질의 예산은/건강과 교육분야를 위한/증가했다

___

4. 그리고 그 결과/영아 사망률이 감소했다/그리고 기대수명은 개선되었다

___

5. 막대 그래프에 대해서 말하자면/우리는 볼 수 있다/브라질은 사용했다/GDP의 약 6%를 건강에/그리고 9%를 교육에/1995년에

_____
_____

6. 5년 후에/건강예산은/보여줬다/5%까지의 약간의 감소를

_____
_____

7. 반면에/교육에 대한 지출은/약 13%까지 증가했다/그것은 이어졌다/계속적인 증가로/약 15%까지/마지막 연도에

_____
_____

8. 같은 연도에/브라질 정부는 증가했다/그들의 건강에 대한 지출/GDP의 9%까지

_____
_____

9. 테이블에서 보여지는 것처럼/증가된 예산과 함께/건강과 교육에 대한/두 가지 항목인/기대수명과 영아 사망률은/개선되었다

_____
_____

10. 기대수명은/브라질에서/64세였다/1995년에

_____
_____

11. 10년 후에/그것은 증가했다/71세까지

12. 반면에/영아 사망률은/70명이다/1,000명 출생당

13. 이것은 이어졌다/상당한 감소로/1,000명 출생당 20명까지/10년 후에

> **Answer**
>
> 1. The provided graph gives a breakdown of the percentage of GDP spent on health and education fields in Brazil between 1995 and 2005,
> 2. , while the table illustrates the death rate of infants and the lifespan of this country over the same period.
> 3. As an overall trend, it is clear that Brazil's budget for the health and education sector rose
> 4. and as a result, the infant mortality rate decreased and longevity improved.
> 5. When it comes to the bar graph, we can see that Brazil spent around 6% of its GDP on health and 9% on education in 1995.
> 6. After 5 years, the health budget showed a slight fall to 5%,
> 7. , whereas the expenditure on education went up to almost 13%, which led to constant growth to around 15% in the final year.
> 8. In the same year, the Brazilian government increased its spending on health to 9% of the GDP.
> 9. As is observed from the table, with increased finances on health and education, two categories, life expectancy and infant mortality, improved.
> 10. Lifespan in Brazil was 64 years in 1995.
> 11. In a decade, it soared to 71 years,
> 12. , whilst infant mortality rate was 70 per thousand births,
> 13. , which was followed by a considerable drop to 20 per thousand births after 10 years.

You should spend about 20 minutes on this task.

The two charts show the spending the percentage of GDP on Health & Education and indicate Infant mortality and life expectancy In Brazil from 1995 to 2005.

Summarize the information by selecting and reporting the main features, and make comparisons where relevant.

Write at least 150 words.

Answer

The provided graph gives a breakdown of the percentage of GDP spent on health and education fields in Brazil in 1995 and 2005, while the table illustrates the death rate of infants and the lifespan of this country over the same period. As an overall trend, it is clear that Brazil's budget for the health and education sector rose and as a result, the infant mortality rate decreased and longevity improved

When it comes to the bar graphs, we can see that Brazil spent around 6% of its GDP on health and 9% on education in 1995. After five years, the health budget showed a slight fall to 5%, whereas the expenditure on education went up to almost 13%, which led to consistent growth to around 15% in the final year. In the same year, the Brazilian government increased its spending on health to 9% of the GDP.

As is observed from the table, with increased finances on health and education, two categories, life expectancy and infant mortality, improved. Lifespan in Brazil was 64 years in 1995. In a decade, it soared to 71 years, whilst infant mortality rate was 70 per thousand births, which was followed by a considerable drop to 20 per thousand births after 10 years.

11. Diagram

You should spend about 20 minutes on this task.

> **The diagram below shows the environmental issues raised by a product over its life cycle.**
>
> Summarize the information by selecting and reporting the main features, and make comparisons where relevant.

Write at least 150 words.

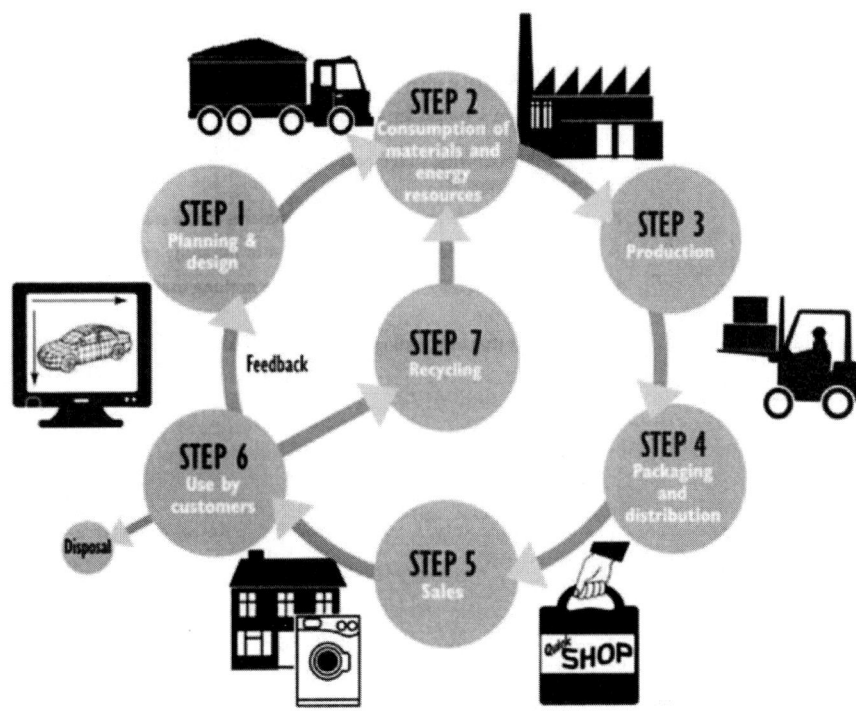

구조

Instruction: 문제 paraphrase
Overall trend: 계획과 디자인으로부터 재활용 과정까지 있다.

Body 1 - Step1 ~ step7 단계 분석

INTRODUCTION
　　주어진 다이어그램은 라이프 사이클 동안 상품의 사용과 제조에 의해 야기된 환경에 관한 문제에 대한 정보를 주고 있다. 다이어그램에서 주어진 데이터에 따르면, 이 과정에 있어서 7단계들이 있는 것이 관찰되고 있고, 그것은 계획과 디자인으로부터 재활용까지이다.

BODY 1
　　세부적으로, 초기의 과정은 계획과 디자인으로 시작한다. 제조업자들은 재료들과 에너지 자원의 소비를 가지고 다양한 상품을 공장에서 생산한다. 이러한 것은 상품들이 포장되기 위해 운반되고 다음단계에서 소매판매점에 분배된다. 곧이어, 소비자에게 제품들은 팔리고 이용된다. 그들은 계획과 디자인에 피드백을 준다. 그 제품들을 이용한 후에 소비자들은 처분되고 재활용돼야 할 쓸모없는 제품들을 어떻게 다루는지를 선택한다. 일단 상품들을 재활용하면, 그들은 에너지자원을 위해 사용된다. 그것은 다양한 상품 생산에 의해 발생된 환경적 문제들을 줄이는 데 중요하다.

문장에 필요한 어휘

> 1. the provided(given) diagram; 주어진 다이어그램
> 2. give information on/give a breakdown of; 정보를 주다/분석하다
> 3. regarding/concerning/as regards; ~와 관련된/~에 대한
> 4. caused by/generated by/resulting from; ~에 의해 야기된
> 5. manufacture/production/making; 제조

주어진 다이어그램은 라이프 사이클 동안 상품의 사용과 제조에 의해 야기된 환경에 관한 문제에 대한 정보를 주고 있다.

The provided diagram gives information on the concerns regarding the environment caused by the manufacture and the use of products during its life cycle.

> 6. according to; ~에 따르면
> 7. it can be observed that S+V; 관찰될 수 있다
> 8. stage/step/process/phase; 단계/과정

다이어그램에서 주어진 데이터에 따르면, 이 과정에 있어서 7단계들이 있는 것이 분명히 관찰되고 있고, 그것은 계획과 디자인으로부터 재활용까지이다.

According to the data given in the diagram, it can be observed that there are seven stages in the process, which progress from planning and design to recycling.

> 9. in detail; 세부적으로/상세하게
> 10. initial/early; 초기의/초반의

세부적으로, 초기의 과정은 계획과 디자인으로 시작한다.

In detail, the initial process begins with planning and design.

> 11. manufacturer/producer; 생산자/제조업자
> 12. consumption; 소비
> 13. material/stuff/source; 재료

제조업자들은 재료들과 에너지 자원의 소비를 가지고 다양한 상품을 공장에서 생산한다.

Manufacturers produce various products in factories with the consumption of materials and energy resources,

Task 1

11. Diagram 467

14. , which is followed by/, followed by/, which leads to+N; 이어지다
15. convey/carry/transport; 운반하다
16. pack/wrap; 포장하다
17. distribute/divide; 분배하다
18. retail outlet; 소매판매점

이러한 것은 상품들이 포장되기 위해 운반되고 다음단계에서 소매판매점들에 분배된다.
, which is followed by the conveying of products to be packed and distributed to retail outlets in the next step.

19. Afterward/and then; 곧이어/후에
20. give feedback to; ~에게 의견을 주다
21. improve/better/develop; 개선하다/발전하다

곧이어, 소비자에게 제품들은 팔리고 이용된다. 그들은 계획과 디자인에 피드백을 준다
Afterward, the products are sold and used by consumers, who give feedback to planning and design.

22. deal with/handle/dispose of; 처분하다/다루다

그 제품을 이용한 후에, 소비자들은 처분되고 재활용되어야 할 쓸모없는 제품들을 어떻게 다루는지를 선택한다
Following the utilization of the goods, consumers choose how to deal with useless products which are disposed of or recycled.

23. once S+V; 일단 ~하면

일단 상품들을 재활용하면, 그들은 에너지자원을 위해 사용된다.
Once items are recycled, they are used for energy resources,

24. vital/important/essential/significant/crucial/critical; 중요한
25. environmental problem(concern/issue/difficulty); 환경적 문제

그것은 다양한 상품 생산에 의해 발생된 환경적 문제들을 줄이는 데 중요하다.
, which are vital in decreasing environmental problems generated by the production of various products.

구문연습

1. 주어진 다이어그램은/정보를 주고 있다/문제에 대한/환경에 관한/야기된/상품의 제조와 상품의 사용/그것의 라이프 사이클 동안

_____
_____

2.. 다이어그램에서 주어진 데이터에 따르면/이것은 관찰될 수 있다/7개의 단계가 있다/이 과정에 있어서/이것은 진행한다/계획과 디자인으로부터 재활용까지

_____
_____

3. 세부적으로/초반의 과정은/시작한다/계획과 디자인으로

_____
_____

4. 제조업자들은/생산한다/다양한 제품들을/공장들에서/제품과 에너지 자원의 소비와 함께

_____
_____

5. 이러한 것은/제품이 전달되고/포장되기 위해/그리고 분배된다/소매판매점들에게/다음단계에서

_____
_____

6. 곧이어/제품들은 팔리고 이용된다/소비자들에 의해/그들은 피드백을 준다/계획과 디자인에

_____
_____

7. 제품을 이용한 후에/소비자들은 선택한다/어떻게 다룰 것인지/쓸모없는 제품을/버려지거나 또는 재활용되는

8. 일단 상품들이 재활용되면/그들은 사용된다/에너지 자원을 위해

9. 그것은 중요하다/줄이는 데/환경문제들을/발생된/다양한 상품의 생산에 의해

Answer

1. The provided diagram gives information on the concerns regarding the environment caused by the manufacture and the use of products during its life cycle.
2. According to the data given in the diagram, it can be observed that there are seven stages in the process, which progress from planning and design to recycling.
3. In detail, the initial process begins with planning and design.
4. Manufacturers produce various products in factories with the consumption of materials and energy resources,
5. , which is followed by the conveying of products to be packed and distributed to retail outlets in the next step.
6. Afterward, the products are sold and used by consumers, who give feedback to planning and design.
7. Following the utilization of the goods, consumers choose how to deal with useless products which are disposed of or recycled.
8. Once items are recycled, they are used for energy resources,
9. , which are vital in decreasing environmental problems generated by the production of various products.

You should spend about 20 minutes on this task.

The diagram below shows the environmental issues raised by a product over its life cycle.

Summarize the information by selecting and reporting the main features, and make comparisons where relevant.

Write at least 150 words.

Answer

The provided diagram gives information on the concerns regarding the environment caused by the manufacture and the use of products during its life cycle. According to the data given in the diagram, it can be observed that there are seven stages in the process, which progress from planning and design to recycling.

In detail, the initial process begins with planning and design. Manufacturers produce various products in factories with the consumption of materials and energy resources, which is followed by the conveying of products to be packed and distributed to retail outlets in the next step. Afterward, the products are sold and used by consumers, who give feedback to planning and design. Following the utilization of the goods, consumers choose how to deal with useless products which are disposed of or recycled. Once items are recycled, they are used for energy resources, which are vital in decreasing environmental problems generated by the production of various products.

12. Flow chart

You should spend about 20 minutes on this task.

The process explains diamonds moving from the mine to the retailer.

Summarize the information by selecting and reporting the main features, and make comparisons where relevant.

Write at least 150 words.

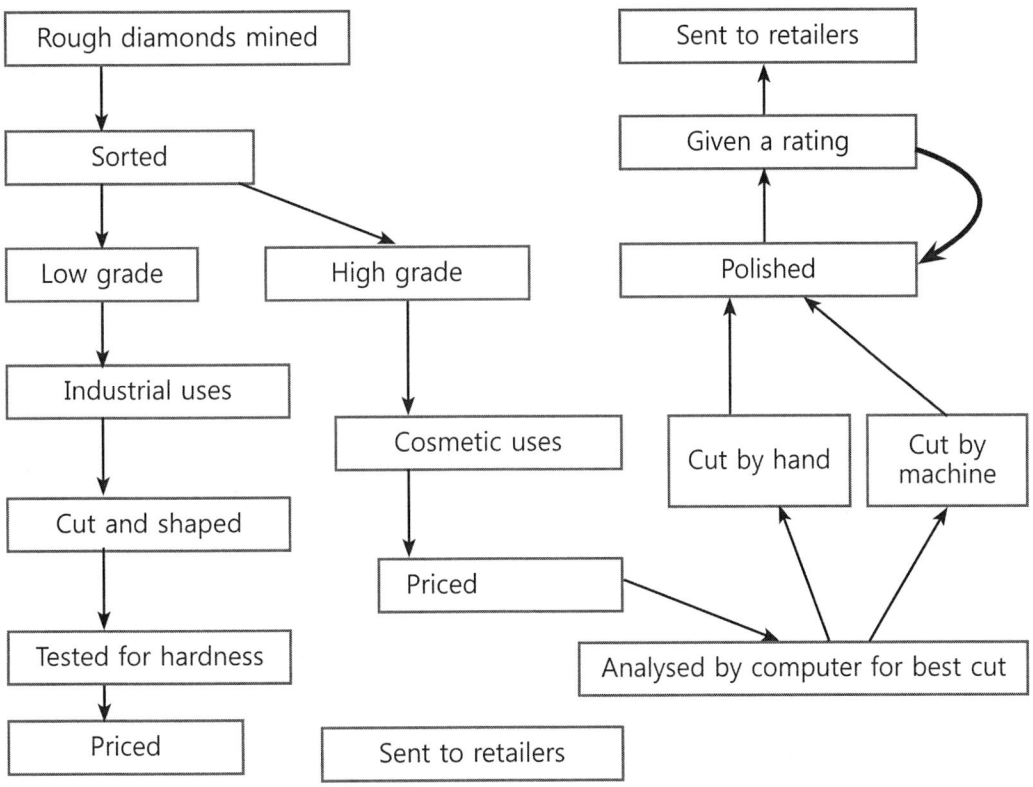

구조

> **Instruction:** 문제 paraphrase
> **Overall trend:** 두 가지 방법

> **Body 1** - Rough diamonds mined(채광된 거친 다이아몬드)

> **Body 2** - High - grades diamonds(높은 등급의 다이아몬드)

INTRODUCTION

Flow 차트는 광산에서 판매자들까지 다이아몬드 판매 과정에 대한 정보를 주고 있다. 두 가지 기본적인 방법은 다이아몬드 등급에 따라 다르다.

BODY 1

과정은 그들의 다이아몬드를 포함한 돌을 거친 형태로 채광하는 것으로 시작한다, 그 이후에 그들은 두 가지 등급 즉 높은 등급과 낮은 등급으로 나눠진다. 낮은 등급의 다이아몬드 경우에, 그들은 산업적인 목적으로 사용된다. 그리고 이것들은 잘려지고 형태가 만들어진다. 그 이후에 그들은 경도의 수준에 맞게 평가된다. 소매업자들에게 보내지기 전에, 마지막 단계로서 그들은 가격이 책정된다.

BODY 2

반면에, 높은 등급의 다이아몬드들은 화장품을 만드는 데 사용된다. 이 다이아몬드는 또한 몇 가지 과정을 진행한다. 그들은 가격 책정이 되고 그리고 가장 효율적인 마름질을 위해 컴퓨터에 의해 분석된다. 그리고 그 후에 그들은 손이나 기계로 광택이 나기 전에 마름질된다. 그 단계에서, 그들은 등급화되고 만약 그들이 잘되지 않았다면 그들은 더 광택을 위해 다시 돌려 보내진다. 그 이후에 그들은 판매를 위해 소매상인들에게 보내진다. 높은 등급의 다이아몬드들을 위한 공정은 비슷하다. 그러나 그들은 그들의 품질에 따라 더 단계를 진행할지도 모른다.

문장에 필요한 어휘

> 1. give information on/give an overview/outline; ~에 대한 정보를 주고 있다/보여주다
> 2. process/stage/course/method; 과정/방법

Flow 차트는 광산에서 판매자들까지 판매 과정에 대한 정보를 주고 있다.
The flowchart gives information on the process of diamond selling, from mine to sellers.

> 3. primary/main/major; 기본적인
> 4. depend on; ~에 따라 다르다/의존하다
> 5. grade/rating/level; 등급

두 기본적인 방법은 다이아몬드 등급에 의해 결정된다.
Two primary methods depend on the grade of the diamond.

> 6. contain/include; 포함하다

그 과정이 그들의 다이아몬드를 포함한 돌을 거친 형태로 채광하는 것으로 시작한다.
The stage begins with the mining of stones containing diamonds in their rough form.

> 7. after that/following that; 그 이후에
> 8. be sorted into/be divided into; ~로 나눠진다
> 9. namely/that is; 즉

그 이후에 그들은 두 가지 등급 즉 높은 등급과 낮은 등급으로 나눠진다.
After that, they are sorted into two different grades, namely high grade and low grade.

> 10. in the case of/in terms of/in light of/when it comes to; ~경우에/~에 말하자면

낮은 등급의 다이아몬드 경우에, 그들은 산업적인 목적으로 사용된다. 그것은 잘려지고 형태가 만들어진다.
In the case of low-grade diamonds, they are used for industrial purposes, and these are cut and shaped.

Task 1

11. afterward/and then; 그 이후에/그런 다음에
12. assess/value/evaluate; 평가하다

그 이후에 그들은 경도의 수준에 맞게 평가된다.
Afterward, they are assessed for their level of hardness.

13. retailer; 소매업자
14. price/put a price/set a price; 가격을 매기다/가격을 정하다

소매업자들에게 보내지기 전에, 그들은 마지막 단계로서 가격이 책정된다.
Before sending to retailers, as the final stage, they are priced.

15. meanwhile/in contrast/by contrast/on the contrary; 반면에
16. undergo/go through/process; 진행하다

반면에, 높은 등급의 다이아몬드들은 화장품을 만드는 데 사용된다. 이 다이아몬드는 또한 몇 가지 과정을 진행한다.
　Meanwhile, high-grade diamonds are utilized to make cosmetic products. These diamonds undergo a couple of processes as well.

17. efficient/effective; 효율적인

그들은 가격책정이 되고 그리고 가장 효율적인 마름질을 위해 컴퓨터에 의해 분석된다.
They are priced and then analyzed by a computer for the most efficient cut.

18. polish/put a polish; 광택을 내다

그 후에 그들은 손이나 기계로 광택이 나기 전에 마름질된다.
Following that, they are cut by hand or by machine before they are polished.

19. rate/evaluate/assess; 등급화하다/평가되다
20. send back; 돌려 보내다

그 단계에서 그들은 등급화되고 만약 그들이 잘되지 않았다면 그들은 더 광택을 위해 다시 돌려 보내진다. 그 이후에 그들은 판매를 위해 소매상인들에게 보내진다.
　At this point, they are rated. If they are not done well, they are sent back for further polishing, following which they are sent to retailers for sale.

21. similar/alike; 비슷한
22. according to; ~에 따라서

높은 등급의 다이아몬드들을 위한 공정은 비슷하다. 그러나 그들은 그들의 품질에 따라 더 단계를 진행할지도 모른다.

The process for high-grade diamonds is similar, but they may go through more stages, depending on their quality.

구문연습

1. Flow 차트는 정보를 주고 있다/과정에 대한/다이아몬드 판매/광산에서 판매자들까지

2. 두 가지 기본적인 방법은/~에 따라 다르다/다이아몬드 등급

3. 그 과정은 시작한다/돌을 채광하는 것으로/다이아몬드를 포함한/그들의 거친 형태로

4. 그 이후에/그들은 나눠진다/두 가지 등급/즉 높은 등급과 낮은 등급으로

5. 낮은 등급의 다이아몬드 경우에/그들은 사용된다/산업적인 목적으로/그리고/이것들은/잘려지고 형체가 만들어진다

6. 그 이후에/그들은 평가된다/그들의 경도의 수준에 맞게

7. 보내기 전에/소매업자들에게/그들은 책정된다/마지막 단계로서/가격이 책정된다

8. 반면에/높은 등급의 다이아몬드는/사용된다/화장품제품을 만드는 데/이러한 다이아몬드들은/진행한다/몇 가지 과정을 또한

9. 그들은 가격책정이 되고/그리고 나서/컴퓨터에 의해 분석된다/가장 효율적인 마름질을 위해

10. 그리고 그 후에/그들은 잘려진다/손이나 기계로/그들이 광택되기 전에

11. 그 단계에서/그들은 등급화된다/만약 그들이 잘되지 않았다면/그들은 돌려보내진다/더 광택을 위해

12. 그 이후에/그들은 보내진다/소매상인들에게/판매를 위해

13. 공정은/높은 등급의 다이아몬드를 위한/비슷하다/그러나/그들은/더 진행할지도 모른다/품질에 따라서

Answer

1. The flowchart gives information on the process of diamond selling from mine to sellers.
2. Two primary methods depend on the grade of the diamond.
3. The stage begins with the mining of stones containing diamonds in their rough form.
4. After that, they are sorted into two different grades, namely high grade and low grade.
5. In the case of low-grade diamonds, they are used for industrial purposes, and these are cut and shaped.
6. Afterward, they are assessed for their level of hardness.
7. Before sending to retailers, as the final stage, they are priced.
8. Meanwhile, high-grade diamonds are utilized to make cosmetic products. These diamonds undergo a couple of processes as well.
9. They are priced and then analyzed by a computer for the most efficient cut.
10. Following that, they are cut by hand or by machine before they are polished.
11. At this point, they are rated. If they are not done well, they are sent back for further polishing,
12. , following which they are sent to retailers for sale.
13. The process for high-grade diamonds is similar, but they may go through more stages, depending on their quality.

You should spend about 20 minutes on this task.

The process explains diamonds moving from the mine to the retailer.

Summarize the information by selecting and reporting the main features, and make comparisons where relevant.

Write at least 150 words.

Answer

The flowchart gives information on the process of diamond selling from a mine to sellers. Two primary methods depend on the grade of the diamond.

The stage begins with the mining of stones containing diamonds in their rough form. After that, they are sorted into two different grades, namely high grade and low grade. **In the case of low-grade diamonds,** they are used for industrial purposes, and these are cut and shaped. Afterward, they are assessed for their level of hardness. Before sending to retailers, as a final stage, they are priced.

Meanwhile, **high-grade diamonds** are utilized to make cosmetic products. These diamonds undergo a couple of processes as well. They are priced and then analyzed by a computer for the most efficient cut. Following that, they are cut by hand or by machine before they are polished. At this point, they are rated. If they are not done well, they are sent back for further polishing, following which they are sent to retailers for sale. The process for high-grade diamonds is similar, but they may go through more stages, depending on their quality.

Writing Topics

Technology

1. Advanced technology has been beneficial to human life. However, there are also disadvantages of modern technologies. Describe the merits and demerits. Support your answer with appropriate examples.
2. Computers have been made use of the way people study. Do the advantages of using computers as a study tool outweigh the disadvantages?
3. It is true that the use of Mobile phone has been on the rise and it has also great influences on people's lives. What is your opinion of using mobile phone?
4. Nuclear technology provided clean, efficient energy, while it also poses a threat to world peace. What are its advantages and disadvantages?

Education

1. Some parents say corporal punishment is at times necessary to educate children. They state that the benefits of this punishment far outweigh the demerits. What is your opinion? Give reasons for your answer and include any relevant examples from your own experience or knowledge.
2. Some people believe that universities should offer theoretical knowledge rather than give vocational training to students. Do you agree or disagree?
3. Some people believe that studying English in an English-speaking country is the best way to learn the language. What is your opinion? Justify your ideas with appropriate explanations.
4. Recently, teenagers have a job while they are still students. Do the advantages of this trend outweigh the disadvantages?
5. Some people think that it is better to educate boys and girls in separate schools. Others, however, believe that boys and girls benefit more from attending mixed schools. Discuss both views and give your own opinion
6. It is true that watching TV has become a part of daily life for many people around the world. However, movies and TV programs have negative effects on people's lives and society. Discuss their negative effects.

Social issues

1. The crime rate has increased rapidly around the world. Discuss some causes for this rise and suggest workable solutions to this problem.
2. A few countries punish the criminal with death penalty. However, others think life imprisonment is a better punishment for What is your view? What is your view?
3. In most developed countries, average life expectancy is increasing. What problems will this cause for individuals and society? Suggest some measures that could be taken to reduce the impact of ageing populations
4. Many advanced countries are giving financial aid to underdeveloped countries. However, this has not solved the problem of poverty in these nations and so other types of help are provided. To what extent do you agree or disagree with this statement?
5. Overpopulation of urban areas has led to numerous problems. Identify one or two serious ones and suggest ways that governments and individuals can tackle these problems.
6. In recent years, there has been a considerable rise in crimes committed by young people in cities. What are the reasons for this rise in youth crimes? How can it be tackled?

The environment

1. Global warming is one of the most serious issues the world is facing today. What are the causes of global warming and what measures can governments and individuals take to tackle the issue?
2. It is true that rainforests are threatened by human activities. Some people say that rainforests can be destroyed for human development. However, there are people who are against this issue. What is your opinion?
3. A great amount of waste is becoming a social problem. What should individuals and the government do to lessen waste? Suggest feasible solutions.
4. Zoos have no longer purpose, so they should be closed. Do you agree or disagree? Give reasons for your answer and include any relevant examples from your own knowledge or experience.

Culture

1. Some people say that advertising encourages us to buy things that we really do not need. Others say that advertisements tell us about new products that may improve our lives. What is your view?
2. Most people believe that online shopping is better and more enjoyable than going to shopping centres. Do you agree or disagree? Sustain your opinion with appropriate explanations or examples.
3. Traffic has been a big concern in many countries. Discuss what individuals and government can do to prevent traffic problems
4. To address traffic problems, governments should tax private car owners heavily and use the money to better public transportation. To what extent do you agree?
5. People are traveling to other countries more than before. What are the advantages and disadvantages of traveling other countries?

Health

1. Some people believe that it is the responsibility of individuals to take care of their own health and diet. Other, however, believe that governments should make sure that their citizens have a healthy diet. What is your opinion?
2. All over the world societies are facing a growing problem with obesity. Obesity affects children as well as adults. What are the reasons for this rise in obesity? How can it be tackled?
3. In some countries, people are no longer allowed to smoke in many public places and office buildings. Do you think this is a good rule or a bad rule? Use specific reasons and details to support your position.